The IT Professional's Guide

to Managing Systems, Vendors & End Users

DATE DUE

The IT Professional's Guide

to Managing Systems, Vendors & End Users

NEIL **PLOTNICK**

Osborne/**McGraw-Hill**

Berkeley   New York   St. Louis   San Francisco
Auckland   Bogotá   Hamburg   London   Madrid
Mexico City   Milan   Montreal   New Delhi   Panama City
Paris   São Paulo   Singapore   Sydney
Tokyo   Toronto

Osborne/**McGraw-Hill**
2600 Tenth Street
Berkeley, California 94710
U.S.A.

For information on translations or book distributors outside the U.S.A., or to arrange bulk purchase discounts for sales promotions, premiums, or fund-raisers, please contact Osborne/**McGraw-Hill** at the above address.

**The IT Professional's Guide
to Managing Systems, Vendors & End Users**

1234567890 DOC DOC 019876543210

ISBN 0-07-212051-7

Publisher	**Copy Editor**
Brandon A. Nordin	Vivian Jaquette
Associate Publisher and	**Proofreader**
Editor-in-Chief	Stefany Otis
Scott Rogers	**Indexer**
Acquisitions Editor	Valerie Robbins
Gareth Hancock	**Computer Designer**
Project Editor	Gary Corrigan
Patty Mon	Elizabeth Jang
Acquisitions Coordinator	Dick Schwartz
Tara Davis	**Illustrator**
Technical Editor	Rhys Elliott
Maggie Biggs	**Series Design**
	Peter F. Hancik

This book was composed with Corel VENTURA™ Publisher.

With love to Lisa and Marty for making my life complete.

ABOUT THE AUTHOR

Neil Plotnick is a veteran IS department manager and *PC Week* columnist. In his biweekly columns, he provides valuable insights into systems and policies that readers can implement to better manage their daily IT/IS department functions. Many of his columns deal with the systems issues of his readers, providing steps to rectify the problem. He considers himself a consummate generalist in regards to computer systems, but he specializes in the construction of stable, reliable servers, and troubleshooting systems.

Neil is a graduate of the State University of New York at Binghamton with a BA in Geography. Born in the Bronx, New York, he is a lifelong Yankee fan and currently lives in the heart of Downtown Boston with his wife Lisa, son Marty, and cats Morgan and Melanie.

AT A GLANCE

CONTENTS

ACKNOWLEDGMENTS

'∙ve discovered that writing a book can be both a deeply personal endeavor and a team effort. While I spent many late nights alone at my keyboard, struggling to create the contents of this book, many others were deeply involved in the process as well. My heartfelt thanks go out to many people.

First I need to acknowledge the opportunity that Gareth Hancock of Osborne/McGraw-Hill presented. His initial inquiries and numerous follow-up phone calls and emails helped me define what this book was to become. He has provided hand-holding, feedback, and encouragement, for which I am truly grateful. Tara Davis helped shuttle me through the many steps involved in putting a book together, answering all my questions with grace and humor.

I owe a tremendous debt to my technical editor, Maggie Biggs. Her insightful comments and careful editing have undoubtedly made my work better. She kept my focus clear and helped me direct my attention where it was needed most.

All of the support crew at Osborne did their best to make my words shine. Vivian Jaquette demonstrated the skills that all copy editors should exhibit. My thanks to project editors Patty Mon and Nancy McLaughlin for staying on top of all the chapters and artwork throughout the various stages of production.

Many of my associates at *PC Week* have been supportive of my efforts as a writer. Eric Lundquist and Linda Bridges gave me the initial opportunity to create the *Net Adviser* column; my life as the "Dear Abby" of *PC Week* has always been fun and interesting. My readers have been an inspiration for me, and their constant stream of questions has validated the need for a book of this scope.

Lorna Garey, Lisa Vaas, and others at the *PC Week* copy desk kindly reviewed and commented on my initial outlines, encouraging me to write at every stage. My friend Andy Extract read all my chapter drafts, providing invaluable input.

Thanks must also go to my parents, not only for buying me my first computer in 1982, but also for instilling in me a respect for language and learning. My wonderful son Marty has already demonstrated a love for computers, and he did his best to leave me alone when I needed to work. Last, but certainly not least, I want to thank my wife Lisa, not only for reading much of what I wrote, but also for supporting my efforts every step of the way.

INTRODUCTION

I wrote this book to cover all the subjects that are never taught in network management classes. It is intended to provide the IT specialist with the tools and techniques to maximize the impact of technology at their firms. The constant building of skills and the importance of professional growth are other subjects that I see a tremendous need to cover. I want to dedicate this book to all the people everywhere challenged with making computers work. Our contributions to companies are often unappreciated yet our efforts go to the core of every vital business function.

Being a successful IT specialist requires a mix of many talents and personality traits. Virtually all of the computer books being sold today are concerned strictly with the minutiae of operating systems, applications, and programming languages. Certainly a mastery of numerous technical subjects is critical to success as an IT specialist. However, the depth and breadth of the books—and training classes, trade shows, and magazines—targeted at those of us working in the IT field do little to address the areas outside of software and hardware operations.

Many of us who are charged with supporting computer networks spend a majority of our time dealing with the people who use the technology and not with the systems themselves. Helping readers to better understand users' problems and to maximize their ability to use the machines we put in front of them is a key aim of this book.

Having spent nearly 15 years as essentially a computer support generalist, I have learned the hard way all the things you need to know to succeed in this career. While there may be different ways to address the particular challenges at your own workplace, I offer the ones that have best served me over the years.

A keen sense of humor is sometimes more important than a deep understanding of TCP/IP protocol operations. You can always use a reference manual to get details on a particular program's configuration options, but few books teach you the most important concepts you need to master.

Purchasing products and services can consume a great deal of your time. You will discover the techniques to deal with various types of vendors and to maximize your purchasing power. Your suppliers can often be the best place to get service and technical support, and I cover these methods in-depth.

Obtaining technical support is easily one of the most critical aspects of being an IT specialist. In this book you will explore both the obvious and not so obvious ways to get help when something goes wrong. I have detailed many "classic" tips and unique approaches for diagnosing problems.

Building your own skills and raising your level of professional achievement is also covered in this book. So much job satisfaction is drawn from the opportunity to learn new things and gain additional responsibility. Read this book and you will also learn how to ensure that your employees are constantly challenged to grow professionally.

If you have been working in IT for a long time, I hope this book will inspire you to become the best IT specialist you can be. If you are new to the field, Welcome! This is one of the greatest jobs in the world. With the constant march of technology, you will never get bored. If you manage other IT people, this book will tell you all the things you can do to make them work smarter and to reward them appropriately.

CHAPTER 1

The Many Faces of IT

Information technology is evolving from just another division within a company into the driving force shaping the modern corporation. Business and society as a whole have embraced computer systems as an integral and indispensable part of life. These days, the ready availability of electronic communications and database access is just as critical as electrical power for any company to function.

Computers have penetrated to every level and size of businesses. The explosion of the Internet and the popularity of the World Wide Web have enabled new industries to form almost overnight. Companies now have radical new ways to communicate directly with customers and suppliers as well as internally. The rush toward "dot com" signals that electronic commerce has arrived and will result in fundamental changes to the ways corporations function.

Lying at the heart of all the technologies that enable companies to do business are the people who design, build, and maintain the networks that link computers and users together. Because it supports the most critical asset of any company—information—and its access, the IT department is perhaps the most important element in a modern company. Being able to provide and manage solutions that support business needs takes a wide range of skills. IT managers must also cope with the pressure that this responsibility carries.

Survival in the demanding world of constantly emerging and evolving technologies requires a complete understanding of all the various components of hardware and software. Even more critical is an appreciation for all the human elements involved. The IT department must support both its company's machines and those that use them.

In this book, I will introduce you to the tremendous breadth of abilities you'll need to succeed in IT. More importantly, you will learn many techniques and timesaving tips to maximize your effectiveness. Finally, you will be shown how to leverage your systems capabilities to your company's advantage.

THE MYRIAD RESPONSIBILITIES OF IT SPECIALISTS

Ensuring that computer systems function reliably is just one of the many responsibilities for those in IT. One must be able to demonstrate the mastery of a smorgasbord of products and technologies. Network operating systems, workstations, computer hardware, printers, hubs, digital telephone links, protocols, and other components must be melded together expertly to provide the function that companies require.

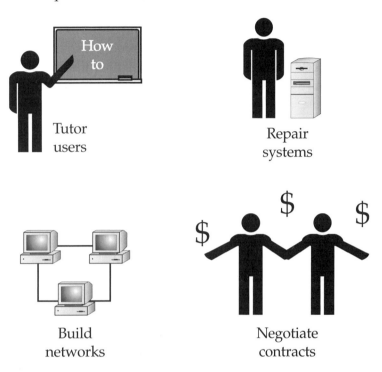

Tutor users

Repair systems

Build networks

Negotiate contracts

While the first and most prominent characteristic of an IT specialist is technical competence, there are many others that are equally important. You must be familiar with accounting procedures in order to produce and manage budgets for the purchase or lease of computing goods and services. Space planning and construction details are sure to occupy the mind of anyone building or expanding a computer room. (Electrical codes and HVAC considerations may consume more of your time than deciding on the amount of memory to configure for your new AS/400!)

There are also many Human Resources department issues that IT managers must be familiar with. Hiring, promoting, and disciplining IT staff members are increasingly difficult in an era of rapidly escalating salaries and widespread technical labor shortages. Ensuring that your existing staff is adequately trained and able to meet the constantly evolving products they support requires constant effort.

Research and development may typically be construed to apply only to your company's core products, but devoting research and development money to IT provides the opportunity to find alternative methods for using computers that can provide a competitive edge. New technologies such as Voice Over IP (VoIP) or Linux may provide a compelling opportunity to reduce costs and boost productivity. Being able to reach new customers and better service existing ones often requires an investment in IT services.

Software development is important no matter how small a company is. While your employer may rely solely on off-the-shelf applications, constructing spreadsheets and writing word processing macros are common activities. Of course, some companies develop complex systems in-house or in consort with vendors. Possessing at least rudimentary programming skills should be part of your core competencies.

In the following section, I will detail the major responsibilities that IT typically bears. I have had to handle every one of them at different times in my career. Later chapters will examine these important skills in depth. Learn to appreciate the incredibly broad range of expertise you must possess to meet the challenges of your job.

Keeping the Servers Up

Maintaining system availability is one of the easier tasks that IT performs. Ensuring that workstations can be booted up and that they have ready access to servers is a core requirement for IT. The people who use the computers you support should be able to count on having any resource they require be fully functional and available with a minimum of fuss. Printers, databases, applications, and Internet access are common to virtually any networked workstation today. Supporting each of these elements requires a different set of skills.

Infrastructure

IT is responsible for the design and maintenance of the physical connections that allow all the network devices to function. The various cabling systems must meet exacting specifications and be properly installed. Reliability can be enhanced with the installation of redundant cable runs and fault-tolerant hubs.

The topology must be logical and easy to administer for any moves, additions, or changes. Flexibility of design eases the adoption of new technology. For example, your network may evolve from 10 Mbps Ethernet to 100 Mbps Fast Ethernet nodes. Sound cabling design requires an understanding of various industry standards bodies such as IEEE and EIA/TIA and their numerous specifications.

Cabling installation is frequently handled by contractors or by licensed union electricians when building codes or other laws require it. However, IT managers must be familiar with the various standards and cabling options so they can requisition the appropriate type for their networks.

At a bare minimum, you should be aware of what types of cabling are needed for the predominant topology your network has. For example, Category 5 (unshielded twisted pair) is the accepted standard for running 100 Mbps Ethernet. Fiber optic cables are another popular choice for high-speed networks. There are several competing standards for the types of connectors used with fiber hubs and NICs. With any cabling system, be aware of the variety and types of connector support to ensure that all of your components can function together.

Server Hardware and Software

Fault tolerance necessitates the use of redundant components such as power supplies and hard drive arrays. Clustering and automatic fail-over technologies can be exploited to maximize system availability. Archival storage with tape and other media should be installed to guard against data loss.

IT managers must be equally familiar and skilled with the software controlling their servers. Tools for configuring network operating systems and monitoring their behavior are key to enhancing stability and performance. Administrators should hold disaster recovery drills to practice the steps necessary to recover from downed or damaged servers.

User Account Administration

Companies are always going through changes in personnel. When people are hired or transferred to new departments, IT must create network accounts to accommodate them. Granting a password and generating a system account is only one small part of the entire process. User rights to access specific resources, such as server volumes and printers or to run certain applications, must be correctly defined for each account.

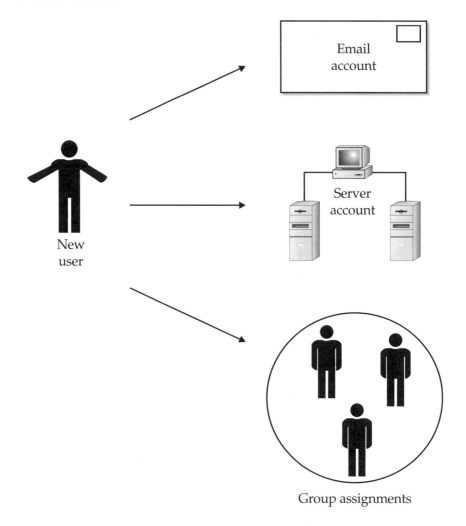

Group assignments

Email is a vital tool for most networks. Controlling the distribution of email necessitates the management of users into groups. In many corporations, electronic messaging is the primary way for information and job assignments to be distributed. In order for new workers to become effective quickly, you must ensure that they receive all the information they require in order to use their email accounts. New users can often be members of multiple groups, so email address book management is another major area of concern for IT.

Transfers and Promotions

While a new account may not be needed, changes to a user's job status will often require changes to email distribution lists and network access rights. Whenever the need to view particular information changes, IT must be diligent in matching the user access to the appropriate level. Remember that granting additional rights, such as the ability to modify data rather than just viewing it, must sometimes be countered by enforcing restrictions on user accounts.

Fires, Retires, and Other Transitions

A corollary to the rules for introducing new users to a system is the need to close accounts when people retire or their employment is otherwise terminated. When a user quits or is given a "pink slip" from Human Resources, this should normally trigger IT to halt network access. Be sure to communicate actively with your HR department to keep informed of all employee status changes.

NAME CHANGES   When staff members change their name upon marriage, this can create a special problem for IT. Most network operating systems cannot easily accommodate a change in username. Of course, name changes don't just occur when someone gets married. People may change their name for religious or business reasons. Lew Alcindor became Kareem Adbul Jabar, for example, and Archibald Leach became Cary Grant.

IT REALLY HAPPENED: One of my IT staffers became an American citizen. He was a Chinese national who had been born and raised in Vietnam. Like many others living in a foreign land, he had to render his last name differently to avoid persecution. When he was sworn in as a citizen, he changed his last name back to his family's original Chinese surname. While I was very proud for him, I had to make sure that all of the email directed to his old name would flow to his new account.

LEAVES OF ABSENCE   Sometimes a user leaves a company for a predetermined period. Maternity leave, illness, sabbaticals, or study programs may see an account go unused for several months. Temporarily suspending email access for users on hiatus will keep hundreds of email messages that will never be read from clogging up mailboxes on your network.

TIP: It is usually easier to re-enable an existing account than to set up a new one from scratch. It's preferable to preserve access rights and group assignments than to enter all the information again.

Login Scripts and Desktop Configuration

Network operating systems each have different tools to control the user environment. IT may want to restrict the use of specific network resources or limit the ability of users to change their displays or menus. Enforcing limits and controlling desktop appearance benefits everyone, since a consistent setup is easier to support and train users on.

Absorbing new users requires a significant amount of time and effort. IT must identify all the tasks required in order for users to become productive. Software and network client licenses may require adjustment to accommodate additional logins. Cumulative increases in email and other data storage can often necessitate the purchase of extra server drives.

Troubleshooting Master

Everyone that works in IT—network administrators, desktop application support specialists, programmers, and other professionals—will spend time tracking down bugs, error messages, and aberrant behavior. Problems that are reported by end users need to be assigned to specific response systems like help desks or intranet-based support Web servers.

Many issues are confined to your server room and the various components involved with supporting modern, technology-dependent corporations. Supporting your hardware and software means drawing on a range of resources, including resellers, manufacturers, Internet newsgroups, training classes, publications, and consultants.

Tuning and Optimization

Closely related to problem solving are efforts to maximize the performance of your computing environment. Ensuring that data packets are moving swiftly and efficiently can require the purchase of new equipment or subtle tweaking of configuration parameters. Armed with system performance monitoring equipment and a keen eye for network behavior, IT specialists can spot bottlenecks and plan appropriate responses to boost throughput.

Attention to end user workstations deserves just as much devotion as work on central system resources. Enabling users to get their work done faster and more efficiently is certainly a valuable contribution that IT can make. In addition, there are often benefits to all users if individual workstations can be optimized. Networked systems must each vie for available bandwidth; you can reduce the burden on your routers and hubs by tuning an excessively busy node, reducing the need to purchase new equipment.

Doing Detective Work

Need to find a driver for old equipment? Looking for documentation for some obsolete yet still functioning software? Searching out technical support Web sites for products from companies that have changed ownership or names three times in the past five years? Uncovering the information you desire can take some clever and determined sleuthing.

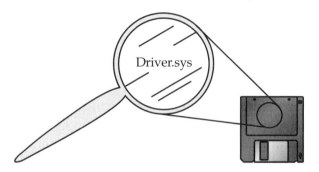

Looking for drivers or documentation for older equipment can be a time-consuming adventure including searches through piles of old diskettes and FTP sites. Savvy IT professionals will create well indexed libraries where they can easily locate manuals and software for future reference. Extensive documentation on how hardware and software are deployed is key to the efficient support of networks and users.

However, there are often cases in which IT encounters poorly documented systems that must be "reverse engineered" to determine the configuration used. Checking for BIOS revisions, network card settings, software driver versions, and numerous other interrelated components is best done while systems are being deployed, but this practice is too rare. You must become familiar with utilities that can scour your network for configuration information and learn how to interpret the results.

Repairing Systems

Computers are generally quite reliable. Because their only moving parts are fans or disk drives, failures of running electronic equipment are thankfully fairly rare. However, power surges and the statistics that lie behind calculating MTBF (Mean Time Between Failure) both conspire to cause system failures. Manufacturers use statistical methods and lab tests to calculate an expected life cycle for their products. Monitors' CRTs, mouse buttons, CD-ROM drives, and laser printer fuser toner assemblies are all subject to wear and breakage. The "Pepsi Syndrome" has also doomed many a keyboard and laptop.

Provisions may be made at your company to maintain facilities to fix broken systems. Typically various external resources will augment any depot that you establish for repairs. For some equipment, you should establish service contracts with vendors that can supply highly skilled and trained technicians. Access to specific parts or services can often be accomplished only through authorized dealers. Many systems purchased for corporate use will automatically include on-site service contracts that cover parts and labor charges for extended periods.

Loaners and Spares

Whenever downtime in system availability is an issue, IT must seek to provide standby solutions. You may wish to establish a ready pool of computers that can be distributed and set up quickly. Mobile workers will be well served by service contracts that promise advanced exchange of broken laptops. Centralized backup of workstation data can also aid in the speedy reestablishment of user files lost when a hard drive crashes.

Setting Up Desktop Hardware

Establishing network accounts for users is meaningless if they do not have a computer to use. A common task for IT is preparing systems for new hires, which may entail setting up a brand-new computer and installing all the operating system and application software.

Deploying new computers can be a very time-consuming process. IT should be familiar with the various hard drive cloning products that simplify the repetitive chore of installing operating systems and applications. In addition, network-based file distribution and upgrade utilities permit centralized management of user desktops.

Transfers, promotions, and other personnel moves are constantly happening. Another common practice for IT is reallocating existing equipment to new users. While this may require little more than granting new system passwords, IT must carefully examine equipment to ensure that any sensitive data left by previous users is cleared from hard disks. In addition, configuration settings should be checked to verify compliance with corporate standards.

Asset Management

When distributing equipment, IT should also make an effort to track which products are installed in each location. Corporate management should be able to determine easily which department has been assigned machines so that they can calculate expenses and track other information. Computers are expensive products, and their allocation and depreciation must be monitored carefully.

Another good reason to track such things is that you may need to update hardware BIOS to fix bugs or add features. Being able to locate all the equipment requiring attention is much easier when you've stored the information in a database. I will explore this important subject in greater depth in Chapter 11.

Programming

Many IT professionals live and breathe high-level programming languages. UNIX administrators have a special affinity for C and C++. Fortran still has a formidable presence in engineering and the sciences. COBOL code written many years ago is constantly being updated. Even if you don't write many programs yourself, you still should be familiar with the process.

Network login scripts and batch files rely on the same techniques that govern programming languages. Administration of Apache Web servers and UNIX systems requires an understanding of configuration file structure. Even the smallest macro should be written with an eye toward modularity and reuse. The following is an example of a network login script:

```
IF "DAY OF WEEK" = MONDAY THEN
    PRINT "Please Update Inventory Database"
    END
IF "USERGROUP" = SALES THEN
    DIRECT LPT1 TO PRINTER_1
    END
```

The Y2K problem and new Internet-driven languages like Java have focused more attention on programming languages than ever before. Microsoft application specialists have solved many problems with Visual Basic and its derivatives. Clearly the ability to understand and appreciate the importance of programming cannot be understated.

Unfortunately, many IT specialists downplay the importance of having at least a fundamental background in programming. Knowing how to construct logical, functional programs in any language pays big benefits when you are struggling with spreadsheet macros or configuring a router. The same type of logic and techniques that are required to program a Perl script could be called upon to create a network login script or to perform specific tasks triggered by certain events.

Custom Applications

Many corporations need to develop software to address unique corporate needs. Even small firms may hire or contract programming expertise to create small utilities or complex suites of tools. I've occasionally struggled with Windows batch processing and Apple script applications that promise easy coding and fast execution. It is often more effective to use a compiler and write a program specifically geared to the task at hand.

Commercial Software Programming

Even some off-the-shelf applications are highly customizable, but this capability can only be exploited through programming. Databases often require SQL instructions to present the required data to a user. HTML and the explosion of the World Wide Web has certainly made programming skills a hot commodity even with the availability of numerous Web page editors and word processing translators.

Virtually every major database, word processor, spreadsheet, and other applications have macro and scripting capabilities. While many people can be quite productive and never create a single macro, these tiny programs can be instrumental in expediting repetitive tasks and reducing errors by forcing a specific sequence of events to be followed to solve a task.

Providing Technical Support

Here is another broad area in which IT is expected to provide exceptional service. Throughout my career, I have always been expected to handle problems with every single piece of hardware and software my users relied on. Even a small number of people will rely on several different programs to perform a variety of tasks. Further complicating matters is the varied methods that people employ to exploit the applications they use.

Those who are working on newspaper stories use a word processor very differently from those writing annual reports. Spreadsheets can be exploited to handle the payroll for thousands or by day traders charting stock prices. Expertise in one particular aspect of application use may not be applicable to other uses. IT managers must be aware of the depth and breadth of system usage in their company and tailor their staff's expertise to cover the necessary areas.

Answer All Questions

Providing technical support usually involves dealing with the myriad questions that users generate. IT must establish systems of support staff and automated support servers to answer this challenge. Users—*and even your boss*—sometimes think that if you cannot solve a quandary immediately, then either you are incompetent or the problem will simply have to be lived with.

It is critical that you set appropriate expectations and communicate them to users. Not every problem can be instantly checked off in the "successfully completed" column of your "to do" list. You must build response systems to collect and then resolve technical issues raised in your company. Relationships with your vendors and consulting firms often provide the information that you must later apply for your users.

The primary objective is to create an environment in which users are confident that the people dedicated to fixing problems with their machines are competent and determined. You may be expected to establish an in-house help desk or to create troubleshooting guides. At the very least, you will need to document procedures that capture problems and direct them to IT for resolution.

WARNING: Remember to remind yourself and your company that no application or operating system is ever bug-free. Some problems require the introduction of service packs that are still in beta testing. Others may be so obscure that simply being aware of a bug and avoiding any references to it will be the only work-around available. New bugs are uncovered constantly, so you should frequently consult news sources on the products you most rely on.

Documentation Librarian

IT professionals should be familiar with every type of binder, folder, and labeling system available. Every piece of hardware and software packaging includes reams of data sheets outlining dip-switch settings and dialog box choices. Managing all of the paper and related errata consumes a significant amount of time.

Virtually every piece of hardware ships with floppy disks or CD-ROMs that include setup utilities, numerous README files, or other documentation. These must be cataloged for easy access when required. Since software is continuously being updated and various patches released, you must make an ongoing effort to augment your library with the newest versions.

Relocations and "spring cleaning" are often fatal to your carefully organized efforts to maintain instruction manuals. The older the products you have, the more difficulty you are likely to have acquiring lost manuals or programs. License disks can be costly and expensive to replace, so guard yours carefully.

TIP: Not every driver or OS upgrade is successful; keeping numerous versions will allow you to return to an older and more stable release if necessary.

Documentation Creator

Developing instructional information for your users can be another valuable service that IT provides. Creating helpful user guides that illustrate program operations and highlight typical problems are a boost to worker efficiency and reduce dependence on support services. Technical writing is a special discipline, and the clear elucidation of specific procedures can be difficult to accomplish.

Not only do you need to provide this information for end users, but all of the equipment in your server room deserves equal attention. Labeling cables and recording IP address information should be a routine and continuous effort. Spotting network problems and repairing them are always faster if you don't first have to uncover how a router that has suddenly gone offline was initially configured.

TIP: Use this as a guiding principle: What information would you need most if you were suddenly placed in charge of your own network and a problem had occurred?

In-House Consultant

Perhaps the most exciting aspect of my job is when I have the opportunity to work as a technical consultant for my firm. Here is where my abilities and experience as an IT professional are most important to solving a business problem. Technology is so vital to how corporations function that having IT integrally involved in the decision-making process, from the boardroom to the shop floor, is critical.

Therefore, your understanding of how your company conducts business and works with its suppliers and customers should be as deep as your appreciation for how its technology is utilized. This requires that you can speak and understand the same language as the various company units speak. You will never be effective if you cannot understand the jobs of the people you support.

Learn to Listen

If you cannot satisfy the needs of your users, then you have failed at your primary responsibility. There must be a continuous effort to seek out feedback and gauge how well the systems you install meet needs. Simply plopping down a new computer with the latest software on someone's desktop is useless unless there was a specific plan to address a particular demand.

You must also go beyond the requirement of just providing standard tools like spreadsheets and instead look for areas that are begging for automation or a new way of tackling a problem. The unique skills of IT specialists allow us to approach challenges with specific technologies that ordinary users are either unaware of or lack the expertise to manage.

Provide New Functions

Networks should be flexible and open to the addition of new capabilities. For example, you may want to add a fax server someday. The ability for users to send and receive a fax from within their email client can be a powerful tool, saving the time needed to print and then manually feed a document into a conventional fax machine.

IT must always be on the lookout for new products that can boost productivity or open up new markets for their company. A steady and controlled evolution of your network is vital if you want to increase the value of the investment in all the equipment you manage.

Purchasing

Computer hardware and software are always being improved and upgraded versions are continually being introduced. In order to exploit the new features and retire obsolescent systems, it is important that careful attention be paid to the acquisition of new products. IT is often called upon to manage budgets for the purchase or leasing of all the technical equipment needed for their company.

The constantly evolving products and price erosion complicates preparing annual budgets. Manufacturers introduce newer and faster processors and phase out older models constantly. While this usually means getting more computing power for each dollar spent, it makes standardization difficult to achieve.

Each new computer model may have different video cards or interface busses that require unique software drivers. Providing support in an environment where homogeneity is seldom found is certainly more challenging because of the constantly changing equipment used. Software is also undergoing constant updating. Even programs that sound similar can have significant differences. For example, the Microsoft Office series is found in standard, small business, developer's, and other editions. Windows 95 was also released in various forms as new features and support for additional hardware was added.

Security Guard

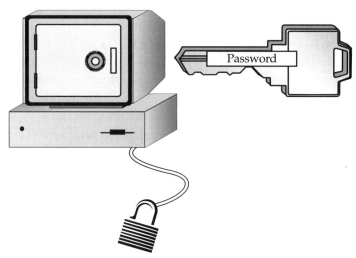

Safeguarding company resources requires protection of both data and the computers themselves. IT must be aware of a whole range of threats to corporate information infrastructures. Viruses, hackers, espionage, and outright theft of equipment are all areas where you need to focus your attention.

There needs to be both physical and logical barriers to stop unauthorized access to your networks. With the increasing degree of connectivity fueled by Internet technologies, many business systems can be attacked by a single user located virtually anywhere.

Theft

Laptop computers are the core technology products of a traveling executive. High performance and portability create hefty price tags. Even alert travelers have had their laptops stolen in busy airports or from their hotel rooms. Portable alarms provide some protection, but investing in a rapid replacement strategy may be a prudent expenditure.

Companies may also contend with losses of larger desktop systems. Expensive memory chips or processors are often targeted, since they are easy to conceal and their loss may be unnoticed. Judicious use of system locks to secure computer covers and cable locks can prevent this quick and easy crime.

Viruses

The presence of rogue and destructive files is a constant threat to any server or workstation. Hard-to-detect changes to core system files can render some machines unbootable. Destruction of data can be limited to just a single system or can spread insidiously throughout an entire network.

The infamous Melissa virus of March 1999 earned a great deal of publicity by attacking corporate email systems that relied on Microsoft Exchange and Outlook. By grabbing email account information and exploiting Microsoft Word macros, Melissa was able to rapidly propagate throughout widely dispersed systems. Millions of dollars can be lost every hour if a company is unable to rely on its email servers. New operating systems and applications are constantly introducing new holes that viruses can exploit.

While installing and monitoring virus detection and eradication software is an important aspect of IT responsibility, attention should also be paid to preventing behaviors or lazy system administration practices that allow viruses to spread more easily. Denying user access to certain network drives or denying unnecessary permissions can help guard your network. Alert everyone of scanning procedures and make sure that a clear protocol exists so users can contact support staff in the event a virus is suspected.

Hackers

While a virus can strike indiscriminately, groups or individuals may intentionally target your corporate network for a variety of reasons. They may simply be looking for a challenge and want to see if they can find weaknesses in your security and gain unauthorized access to your systems. More nefarious hackers may look to destroy data or deface your Web servers.

Mention the name Mitnick and images of horror synonymous with the hacker threat will leap to the mind of many IT specialists. Even supposedly highly secure systems are not immune to the attack of hackers. In early 1999, Great Britain had their spy satellite controls taken over. While the ramifications of such a hack are chilling, IT must be aware of such threats and enact precautions to guard their own systems.

Retiring Old Systems

All computer hardware and software goes through an evolutionary cycle. First, new products are tested and introduced to a company. Then there is a period in which the systems are used daily and provide a useful function. Eventually, faster hardware and more feature-rich software items are introduced that render the older products obsolete. IT must provide a path for the graceful retirement and replacement of existing systems.

Older hardware can still provide valuable services to many. Donations to local schools, daycare centers, churches, and other community groups are all good choices. Many firms offer employees a chance to purchase old systems at substantial savings, and those who do gain the ability to work from home as a bonus. Old computers can be scavenged for replacement parts such as drives, power supplies, memory, and other components.

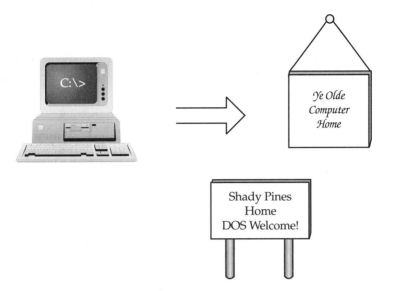

Keep a Back Door

I've always made it a policy to preserve as much of the retired infrastructure as possible when moving to a new system. It often takes several weeks or months for certain activities to be performed. Quarterly sales reports or data archiving may not be adequately tested on your new solutions. Problems that don't show up initially may later surface on new equipment.

Long-term preservation of legacy products is an ideal way to provide emergency services in the event of a system crash. Even if older, slower products are rarely used, their mere presence can be great insurance. The greatest fault-tolerance solution is one that replicates entire systems.

IT REALLY HAPPENED: An entire department's network was moved from older Chipcom hubs to new 3Com Etherstack Switched Ethernet hubs to boost performance. After two weeks of stellar operation, all the clients suddenly lost their network connection. No amount of rebooting could get the servers and workstations to communicate. I reactivated the old hub and got the network going again. With the important services restored, I was able to diagnose the trouble on the 3Com equipment offline. Upgrading the switch firmware rectified the dropped connection problem, and I was able to methodically return nodes to the faster switch.

Coordinating Moves and Relocations

One of the most dreaded activities that IT can perform is the large-scale movement of users and their networks from one location to another. A tremendous amount of coordination and planning must be completed prior to moving so that every facet of computer use can be preserved. Work must typically be done during nights and weekends to minimize the impact on corporate functions.

All network connections, servers, printers, and other devices must be made ready for the relocated equipment while still preserving the existing infrastructure until the last workstation is disconnected. Once the new location is brought to life, there are inevitable problems that must be addressed. A big part of IT's relocation function is chasing down loose ends that were not anticipated prior to the move and attending to equipment that fails to work in its new home.

Combining Forces after Mergers and Acquisitions

Institutions both large and small are subject to changes when management acquires new businesses or the company is bought by another competitor. Banks, newspapers, department stores, hospitals, and other organizations seek strength and cost efficiencies through mergers with similar institutions. While melding business philosophies and sales teams can be accomplished with some effort, bridging IT infrastructures can be maddening.

The problems with data file compatibility with different word processors on the same operating system are trivial when compared to joining inventory data from an Oracle database on UNIX together with a DB2 database on the AS/400. Merging mailing lists, user account information, and other schema can be a daunting proposition.

IT should be closely consulted whenever a corporation is pondering a major change of this type. The time and effort associated with merging disparate systems can be enormous and must be considered when trying to determine the cost savings that a corporate takeover can bring.

Working with Customers

Every corporation has suppliers, subcontractors, clients, and numerous other partners. Making sure that communications between a company and its customers are easy and productive is a major concern for IT. Information must be shared between all these groups and reliable systems must be in place.

You must investigate how your company or department works with other companies and divisions. Even if the internal networks are quick and efficient, there may be major headaches sharing data externally. Being able to handle your sales force data needs may require that you look for better ways for your shipping company to be apprised of outstanding orders, for example, or there may be better ways for your manufacturing systems to be tied into your vendors' requisition systems.

E-Commerce

E-commerce is a popular buzzword used to describe the phenomenon of commerce conducted via the Internet. New companies such as Amazon.com and eBay have come from nowhere to demonstrate how sales can be handled directly between a seller and a consumer with a Web browser. Online trading with brokers such as E*TRADE and Charles Schwab have also revolutionized how stocks and funds are bought and sold.

The power of the Internet has allowed entirely new forms of businesses to grow. Existing corporations have scrambled to exploit the many opportunities that Internet technology provides. While the ramifications for traditional retailing are obvious, many other industries have also made the Internet a key component of their plans. The Internet is simply one of the best ways yet invented for information to be shared easily.

Training Users

Providing all the latest technologies to users is only one of IT's responsibilities. Making sure that users receive instruction in the use of the computers and software is one way to make sure that everything is being utilized to its full potential. Just as a new driver must take driving lessons, a user new to a computer system must be taught the complex steps to follow in order to perform their tasks successfully.

In many companies, the IT department is responsible for overseeing all technical training courses. You may need to produce all of the educational materials utilized, but the most likely scenario entails a combination of off-the-shelf computer-based training modules (CBTs), outsourced instruction, and Web and video classes. Having an outstanding set of options in this area yields a much more effective workforce.

Being able to conduct effective training requires a great deal of outreach and communication with your users. Classes must be tailored to meet the myriad levels of abilities and skill requirements of those in your organization. New technologies demand that there be a constant updating of coursework to reflect the latest hardware and software.

Looking Out for New Opportunities

One of the most pleasurable aspects of working in IT is the opportunity to investigate new tools. Playing with new servers and operating systems may not be the average person's idea of fun, but a true IT specialist relishes the chance to put the latest and fastest machines or applications through their paces.

Manufacturers are always introducing new technologies or improving their products to meet specific customer needs. You must constantly be on the watch for significant new products that can permit your company to perform more efficiently and economically. Many firms also actively recruit current or prospective customers to become beta testers.

Testing new equipment can give your company a competitive advantage, since you can be the first to adopt better technology. Having prior experience with a product will also make wide implementation easier. Of course, the vendors benefit by having real-world customers bang on their solutions and propose improvements before the product is widely released.

Testing Labs

Maintaining facilities to evaluate new products should be part of any modern IT effort. There should be a place where you can delve deeply into the management and use of any new products you are contemplating for later introduction into your infrastructure. It is important that your testing efforts be kept separate from your actual production networks. There are always risks associated with using unproven products, since their behavior may be unpredictable and result in negative repercussions.

Managing IT Departments

Some of those reading this book are responsible for managing large IT departments or groups of IT specialists. People in those positions must master a broad range of skills necessary for directing a varied staff of individuals to complement their own technical competence. In many cases, it is more important that the IT director possess exceptional personnel management capabilities than be versed in the latest advances in Visual Basic techniques.

The Many Kinds of IT Specialists

All IT departments are made up of people with various ability levels and different areas of expertise. The people who work for you cover all aspects of network operations. There may be service technicians who are responsible for workstation installations, programmers who create and maintain custom applications, and still others who manage servers and tape backup chores.

Those that work in IT often come from a wide variety of backgrounds. While there are certainly a fair share of people with Computer Science degrees, it is just as likely to discover excellent IT professionals with backgrounds in business and the arts. As an example, my college degree is in Geography. While it may sound only distantly related to a computing background, I spent a great deal of time learning and using Fortran for statistical analysis and satellite image manipulation. I've also met programmers with degrees in Philosophy and Political Science.

Attitude and Communication

I've worked for a wide range of managers over the years. Some were strictly business people charged with financial responsibility who possessed little technical prowess aside from spreadsheet design. Some enjoyed hollering and micromanaging every aspect of my work. Others were strictly hands-off in their approach and only demanded that those I support be satisfied with the job I was performing.

Many IT specialists that I've worked with in teams or supervised have also displayed a wide range of personalities. Some were highly reserved people who desired only to be able to code in privacy. Their engaging personalities and sense of humor have distinguished most of the people who work as support specialists. The greatest attribute that anyone in this field can possess is an ability to communicate well with others.

You must be able to listen carefully to users with problems so you can determine exactly what is wrong. When a department head describes a situation that begs for an innovative technology solution, being able to ask the right questions enables you to identify critical business operations and the most appropriate solution. Being able to express yourself clearly, both verbally and in written form, is essential when developing documentation or conducting a training seminar.

Staffing Issues

Managing IT professionals requires a constant effort to obtain a quality workforce. You may be charged with interviewing prospective job candidates and placing Help Wanted ads or even visiting college campuses to meet eager young recruits.

The flip side of hiring new staff is the responsibility for terminating those who have failed to contribute to your department. You need to learn how to correctly discipline and motivate people before you get rid of anybody.

Maintain a Positive Environment

To many people, the opportunity to learn new products and to be challenged professionally is more important than absolute salary figures. Providing a fun and interesting environment can go a long way in ensuring that your staff members enjoy their work and do an effective job. Cross-training and team-building help foster an esprit de corps and make your IT department stronger.

Motivated employees are always looking for new opportunities. Providing a growth path and clear career directions will make your employees strive for greater responsibility and clamor for additional training. An environment that promotes from within is attractive and allows IT staff members to set goals and achieve them.

WHAT COMES NEXT

Throughout this book you will be instructed in many techniques and learn about the common problems and pitfalls that IT faces every single day. All of the following chapters draw from my nearly two decades of experience with computers and the people that use them. Many of the issues I raise will be examined with examples drawn directly from my work supporting computing systems used in a variety of ways.

While it is impossible to cover every particular contingency or operating system, all the methods I cover can be applied to virtually any environment. While network operating systems can be radically different in the way they are managed, each has common tools, such as those to add users, assign printers, or modify access rights. Users on any platform will require support and documentation. Recording and responding to problems can be handled with a similar approach no matter what type of systems you have.

Feel free to skip around and approach each chapter as a separate unit. I have attempted to construct each section of this book to address a particular set of skills or tightly related issues. Since every reader will have different needs, certain chapters may be more applicable to your particular job.

I won't proclaim that any solution is the best for a particular application. IT must be able to meld many different components together and adopt existing systems to meet new demands. I hope that my real-world examples clearly reinforce the concepts I describe.

Finally, I want to emphasize that the single most important factor in making anyone a consummate IT professional is appreciating how much users depend on your efforts. For many people, computers are terrifying and difficult-to-understand machines. Making sure that people see them as manageable tools and not as cryptic adversaries is a continuing challenge.

I've always been known as someone who possesses a keen sense of humor and a somewhat painful addiction to puns. Never underestimate how much your own personality defines what type of job you do. Unless you are sitting in an office all day coding away, your ability to work with and communicate with others is perhaps your most important attribute.

CHAPTER 2

Maximizing Your Infrastructure

IT has always been responsible for creating dependable and speedy networks. This requires attention to a wide variety of concerns. Software, hardware, and various configuration settings must be juggled to create unique platforms that allow users to get their jobs done.

MAXIMIZING YOUR ENTIRE NETWORK

As an IT manager, the key to making your daily life easier and more productive is to build a stable, yet flexible, foundation. You must ensure that all of your hardware including the servers, routers, hubs, and cabling, is designed for maximum reliability. Network operating systems and applications only work correctly if you first ensure that the hardware they run on is functioning optimally.

Whenever you prepare to deploy any solutions on your network, there are three factors to consider before building or buying them. The first is to make sure that the computers and other systems are built as dependably as possible. Your second concern should be making components in your network flexible and expandable. Only after you've given attention to issues of reliability and versatility can you safely optimize for speed.

This chapter examines what every IT specialist should know to successfully address all the challenges of constructing and maintaining the modern high-tech workplace. The first part discusses ways to acquire detailed knowledge about how computer systems are configured. Next, the fundamentals of building stability and dependability will be explored. Only after ensuring reliability can we progress to issues of flexibility. While I don't mean to downplay the importance of performance, fine-tuning for greater speed is only a bonus earned by paying attention to the other factors first.

What Your Users Demand from their Network

People utilizing your networks expect solutions that support them without fail. Network resources must be available at all times. Users count on using the network to log in, access data, print, and browse the World Wide Web, and they demand the same dependability as they would expect from their telephone. This requires systems that are robust, exceedingly predictable, and reliable.

Equally important, the network of hardware systems and software must be easily adaptable, capable of taking on new jobs as well as extending its existing functions. While typically constructed to satisfy a particular set of business needs, networks always evolve to provide support for additional tasks. For example, accounts payable software applications may be extended to handle payroll as well. Point-of-sale terminals in retail stores may get closely aligned with inventory control systems at distribution centers.

It costs a great deal of money to construct and maintain a company IT infrastructure. Business and common sense dictate that this investment reap as many benefits as possible. It is IT's responsibility to harvest the capabilities inherent in all the servers, hubs, and software and to use them as leverage in meeting the company's goals. I doubt that any other department of a corporation in any industry is confronted by a more complex task.

This book is not intended to examine any particular application or topology in detail nor to tout one particular solution over another. Rather, I will present the many techniques for understanding, supporting, and exploiting whatever technology you employ to serve the users at your job. Whether you are responsible for a single Novell NetWare server, a Microsoft Windows NT environment spread across the country, or a cluster of Linux servers, these tactics will help make your job easier and more productive.

Understand Your Hardware

The first significant skill to acquire as an IT specialist is a solid foundation in computer hardware. In the same manner that every soldier in boot camp learns to take apart and put together a rifle blindfolded, the successful IT specialist should have the same degree of comfort and familiarity with hard drives, NICs, hubs, and computers.

Many of the themes presented here are not just relevant to the deployment of network systems. Chapter 12 will describe additional issues to consider when dealing with individual users' computers or the nodes you support. Troubleshooting techniques and strategies for system setup are often the same whether you are approaching a complex network or a single workstation.

While the range of information you need to master is quite broad, there is really one subject that is central to making everything work correctly: configuration. You must learn how individual hardware components are configured so that they interact correctly with each other and with the software that controls them. Essentially, you need to make sure that each device has the correct "address" so the proper signals can be sent and received. Your equipment documentation will describe the necessary steps for ensuring proper configuration, either using software or jumper settings.

Interrupts, Jumpers, and Termination... Oh My!

While some hardware components are configured solely by software settings, many still rely on the correct positioning of lilliputian jumpers and switches. Whatever method your equipment uses to modify its setup, you must be able to configure these parts for correct operation. It is essential that conflicts over system resources are avoided and that you understand how to achieve this goal.

For example, while Windows 98 supports plug-and-play, you still must be familiar with how Intel PC architecture uses interrupts and DMA channels to allocate resources for expansion cards and ports. Plug-and-play technology is not foolproof, nor are all hardware products compliant with its usage. A failure to comprehend the basics of computer architecture can lead to problems such as technicians installing legacy hardware that attempts to use interrupt number 3 (IRQ3). Knowledgeable IT specialists know that the typically standard second serial port already uses IRQ3. Table 2-1 is a typical interrupt table used by millions of Intel-compatible systems. Any IT specialist should learn these numbers with the same familiarity that a child learns the alphabet.

When the early Macintosh models began shipping, one of the biggest complaints about them was their lack of expandability. While

IRQ Number	Function
0	System Timer
1	Standard 101/102-Key Keyboard
2	Programmable Interrupt Controller
3	Communications Port 2 (COM2)
4	Communications Port 1 (COM1)
5	Creative AWE64 16-Bit Audio
6	Standard Floppy Disk Controller
7	ECP Printer Port (LPT1)
8	System CMOS/real time clock
9	OPEN
10	IRQ Holder for PCI Steering
10	Adaptec AHA-2940U/AHA-2940UW PCI SCSI Controller
11	Intel 82371AB/EB PCI to USB Universal Host Controller
11	IRQ Holder for PCI Steering
12	PS/2 Mouse Port
13	Numeric data processor
14	Intel 82371AB/EB PCI Bus Master IDE Controller
14	Primary IDE Controller (dual fifo)
15	Secondary IDE Controller (dual fifo)
15	Intel 82371AB/BE PCI Bus Master IDE Controller

Table 2-1.   A Sample Interrupt Table for Intel-Compatible Systems

the IBM PC had several expansion slots for optional hardware, the Macintosh lacked them. However, Apple aficionados were quick to point out that the included SCSI, or small computer system interface, was a simple and effective way to externally connect peripherals to their beloved Macintosh computers. Indeed, SCSI became the way to connect hard disk drives, scanners, removable cartridge drives, and other hardware to the Macintosh.

Macintosh system administrators were the first to become familiar with how to set SCSI identification numbers. While the Macintosh was an early adapter of SCSI technology, file servers and WinTel computers are likely to use them today. Each device on a SCSI chain must have a unique address or SCSI ID to work correctly. Installing two hard drives with identical ID numbers is bound to cause problems; either the system will recognize only one drive or it will simply fail to boot. It is equally important to remember that SCSI chains must be correctly terminated at both ends. While you may encounter additional jumpers on drives that you utilize, you can select the SCSI ID for virtually any SCSI device, including CD-ROM and tape drives. Consult Figure 2-1 for ID information.

While WinTel computers are often equipped with SCSI drives, especially high-end workstations and servers, most rely on various

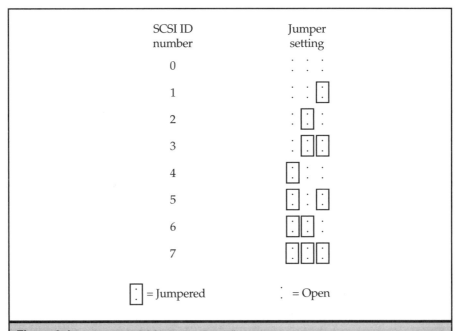

Figure 2-1. Common SCSI device ID configuration

flavors of integrated drive electronic disk storage, or IDE. IDE units were introduced as an inexpensive hard drive interface in 1989. While not as versatile as SCSI, the IDE interface has continuously been improved and today very fast and prodigious storage options are available.

IDE drives use a slave/master relationship that requires diligence in setting correct configuration jumpers. The simple rule is that any IDE bus must have only a single device set as a master. When you have two drives on a single bus, the second drive must be configured as a slave in order to operate.

I cannot over-emphasize the importance of having this type of information available and making sure you understand it. Always keep documentation for your drives handy so you can verify the correct jumper settings. Drive manufacturers' Web sites also contain this information. Check out www.seagate.com, www.quantum.com and www.westerndigital.com for the majority of drives being installed in computers.

Properly configuring systems is the only way you can guarantee that the solutions you deliver will not be crippled by misbehaving hardware. Virtually every troubleshooting situation demands that you first make an exhaustive assessment of the underlying hardware before you apply software fixes.

TIP: Make it a habit to run exhaustive diagnostics on all systems you acquire before deploying them to your users. I typically run vendor-supplied software to qualify the functioning of components like hard drives, memory, and network cards.

Some may argue that having a strong expertise first in software applications or NOS administration is the most important and consequential ability to possess. While indeed it is meaningful to develop such skills, I believe that understanding the underlying hardware components is never given the attention that it deserves. Consider that no matter how advanced and capable an operating system is, it can never function properly without well-designed and properly configured computer hardware to run on.

Virtually all problems are easier to troubleshoot if you first ensure that your hardware is running correctly. Make it a practice to thoroughly test your systems before loading any application software on them. It makes little sense to build anything if the foundation is faulty.

You must never forget that the goal of building stable systems is to ensure that your users have uninterrupted access to data. All of your effort in building bulletproof network servers and infrastructure must be matched by an equal dedication to protecting the data from inadvertent deletion or corruption. The accidental loss of a single small file can be extremely costly for any corporation, so treat each byte of company data as a precious commodity.

Start with Reliable Hardware

Users expect that all the systems you provide will be available every minute they are at work. Computers are generally very reliable products. Actual hardware failures are rarer than they were several years ago, as manufacturing and designs have continually been improved. Comparing motherboards or expansion cards from a few years ago to today shows that many fewer chips are required now to perform the same function. Simply reducing the number of parts increases reliability, because there are fewer items to break.

Even with new designs, it is still important to take precautions and to make an effort to maximize system uptime. Guarding against individual component failure—the loss of a hard drive, for example—is the first and easiest step to take. Technologies that allow computers to function even with a failed hard disk are well established and supported in a variety of ways.

A much more complex feat is designing and implementing solutions that allow a network to function despite the loss of an entire computer or hub. Environments that demand such a high level of system availability, such as banks and financial institutions, are required to invest a great deal of money and time to build an infrastructure robust enough to handle this requirement. It is no small step to improve a system's uptime from 98 percent to nearly 100 percent. The level of sophistication and intelligence of the related hardware and software to provide continuous service is indeed daunting.

File Servers

Computers intended to be used as file servers are usually quite different and often much more expensive than ones typically found on a user's desktop. One would be wrong to assume that servers are always equipped with the fastest processors and greatest amount of memory of all the computers in a company, though this is usually the case. Rather, servers are differentiated from desktop computers by features that promote reliability, fault tolerance, and expansion.

The most noticeable difference you'll see when examining a system expressly designed as a file server is that it is larger and heftier than the typical chassis. There are several reasons for the increased size. Housing sufficient disk capacity to handle the needs of many connected users requires at least one high-capacity disk drive, and likely several. Greater memory capability and the many expansion card slots require a larger system. Rack mounting of servers is facilitated by slide rails and specially designed cases. Finally, running all of the extra hardware necessitates that a beefy power supply be included. Certain types of network hardware may require current other than the ubiquitous 115 volts found in most power outlets. Make sure your electrical supply is sized correctly for the equipment you intend to install.

Numerous expansion card slots are provided to allow installation of option hardware for a variety of purposes. Multiple network cards can be used to provide routing capability or to establish dedicated connections to high-speed backbones. Multiport serial communication cards can be used to provide dial-in connections for remote users. Sophisticated disk drive controllers that support higher-speed drive interfaces and fault tolerance are also common features of file servers.

RAID An important and popular addition to many file servers is a fault-tolerant disk system. Various schemes can be used to permit a server to function despite the loss of a disk. RAID, or a redundant array of inexpensive disks, is a method proven to guard your hard disk data. There are several ways to implement a RAID system, each with associated features and costs.

Mirrored, or RAID 1, systems use a pair of hard drives, and each one records identical data. As data is written to a primary drive, the second drive mirrors the data and contains an exact copy. In the event that a single drive fails, the second working drive allows the server to continue to function. The major drawback to a RAID 1 solution is the amount of storage that is "wasted." For every byte of data that is stored, two complete copies are created. This means that you are only getting 50 percent of the total capacity of the disks you install.

RAID 1

While the amount of disk space used appears wasteful, the RAID 1 system is very easy to set up. Another great advantage is that most popular network operating systems contain software that allows the server administrator to build a mirrored array. There is no requirement for specialized disk controllers, so cost can be very reasonable. Also, since you are creating identical copies of your data, this can be a very reliable method to utilize.

A more elaborate variation of RAID technology that is quite popular is RAID 5. Rather than sacrificing half of the disk capacity, this parity-checking design may use only 20 to 33 percent of the total disk space to ensure fault tolerance. For example, you can use two data drives and need only one parity drive to ensure data integrity. Drive arrays that use four data drives and a single parity drive are also very common.

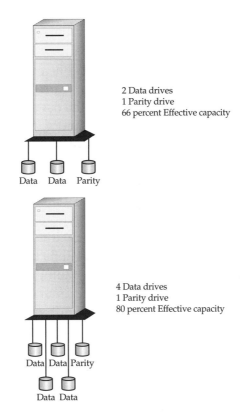

2 Data drives
1 Parity drive
66 percent Effective capacity

Data   Data   Parity

4 Data drives
1 Parity drive
80 percent Effective capacity

Data Data Parity

Data Data

Most often, a RAID 5 storage system requires dedicated hardware to manage the disks. You need to do a good deal of calculation and error-checking to get all the drives working in unison. Simpler mirrored arrays typified with RAID 1 can usually be governed by software alone. An added benefit with the use of dedicated hardware is greater speed. RAID disk controllers can be equipped with high-speed processors and dedicated cache memory. File servers place a premium on file access performance, so the added cost of hardware RAID is a sound investment.

SERVER CLUSTERING   While you may construct a server with all manner of redundant features, the server itself may still fail, blocking access to data. Perhaps the motherboard or memory chips will break. By melding two or more servers together, IT managers can build a cluster that provides great reliability. In the event that a single server fails, other servers in the cluster can seamlessly take over the processing of client requests from the broken system.

Microsoft Cluster Server in its current iteration supports a two-server configuration. In the event that a member of the cluster fails, the remaining server takes control of the failed server's disks, processes, and IP addresses. The entire procedure should take only one minute to complete. While the current Microsoft product only supports a two-node configuration of Windows NT Enterprise Server, vendors such as IBM have been developing software for Netfinity servers that will support much larger clusters.

Not only does clustering provide greater fault tolerance, but there can be considerable performance gains when using software that is cluster-aware. Each separate system in a cluster can be used to share the load in a piecemeal fashion. By intelligently parsing requests among the cluster nodes, applications like SQL can really benefit from the shared horsepower. Installing additional cluster nodes can be a great way to scale your performance as demand grows. It often proves to be a more economical and powerful choice than replacing a single computer with another that boasts a speedier processor and more memory.

Clustering solutions are available for a wide range of architectures and platforms. The Compaq (formerly Digital) line of VAX systems has been synonymous with clustering for many years. Sun network administrators can use Sun Cluster 2.2 for support of up to four nodes, which can be located several miles apart. Linux clustering is being pursued by PHT with its TurboLinux product line. S.u.S.E. and Red Hat also are targeting large, enterprise-level needs with clustering products.

POWER SUPPLY REDUNDANCY   Once you have protected your hard disk data with RAID technology, the next component to address is the server power supply. Computers that are designed specifically as file servers often allow the installation of a second power supply. While only one power supply is required to run the system and all its components, a power supply can be prone to failure. The high temperature generated by electronics will age them over time. Fans, like any other moving part, are also subject to wear.

DATA ARCHIVING

Only fools will ignore the importance of making consistent efforts to archive data. Data that is lost due to user error or hardware failure can be costly and time consuming. There are many proven methods that can be employed to create backup copies of files.

Software products such as Retrospect from Dantz or ArcServe from Computer Associates makes the task of doing backups fast and easy. Once properly configured all that is usually necessary is manually swapping tapes and checking log files for errors. There is simply no excuse for ignoring this important task.

Tape Drives

Once you have installed products that guard against the loss of disk drives or a power supply, you still must have some form of backup device. The single most popular type of backup hardware is a tape drive. Speed, capacity, and convenience will determine the price and technology of the drive. Digital audio tape (DAT) and digital linear tape (DLT) are good choices.

As I stated earlier, you must treat every shred of data as precious. Tapes allow you to make daily copies of every file stored on your network. Recovering a file lost to accidental deletion, program error, virus, or any other cause may be a rare event, but retrieval is easily one of the most highly valued activities that an IT specialist can perform.

One of the nice attributes of a more advanced tape drive is the greater convenience of automatic tape handling. This feature allows the rotation of tapes—using a different tape for each day of the week, for example—to be done by robotics in the tape drive. While the most disciplined IT specialist may check daily that the correct tape is in the drive prior to a scheduled backup, you can be sure a computer-driven tape drive will not forget. The extra expense is well worth the insurance it brings. Missing a day's backup may never become a factor where you work, but a good tape backup can sometimes be a lifesaver.

Off-Site Storage of Tapes

The single worst place to keep your precious tape archives is on the same shelf as your server. Imagine the problems you'd have if your server room were damaged by fire and your only backup went up in smoke with the rest of your equipment. A much safer strategy is to keep your tape archives in a location away from the servers.

There are several simple ways to do this. Modest storage demands can be met by placing your tapes in a fireproof safe. I've used these refrigerator-sized vaults to store NOS serialized license disks and other critical materials. Some network administrators rent a safe deposit box in a local bank to serve the same purpose.

Those who maintain more extensive networks that generate large volumes of data can contract with companies that specialize in off-site archival storage. Perhaps the best-known firm in this industry is Iron Mountain. You can contract with them to pick up your data on a regular basis and store it in centers with elaborate fire and theft protection.

Understand that there will be occasions that require you to retrieve data from your off-site archives. Banks won't be available outside of normal business hours or on weekends. If you rely on outside resources for archival storage, make sure that you can retrieve your data in a timely fashion.

Other Types of Archival Storage

While tapes boast a prodigious capacity and a very low cost per megabyte, they may not be the ideal media for archives at your site. Tapes are not speed champs when it comes to data recovery. If your network requires faster access or simply ready online access to data archives, then you may need to consider optical or CD-ROM storage.

I strongly advocate the use of tape for all of your active data. Data that is not subject to updates—for example, last year's final sales figures—should be migrated off expensive magnetic hard disks and onto optical or similar media. These technologies complement each other and you should match them carefully to your specific needs.

Any backup solution should be reexamined periodically to determine whether all your network needs are being met. Capacity issues are always crucial, because data seems to grow exponentially whenever a new server is purchased. Be sure you can restore time-sensitive information quickly and efficiently.

Optical systems are similar to magnetic disk drives but offer far greater capacity. Rather than relying on magnetism to record data, optical drives use lasers to etch all the ones and zeros. They offer read-write capability and are very stable media. Companies often deploy huge multiple-platter jukebox devices when vast quantities of data need to be available. With this alternative, hundreds of optical disks are paired with several readers, and robotics swap the disks as needed.

CD-ROMs are another good choice for archives. The medium is stable and the disks can be read by any computer with a CD-ROM drive; you don't need to buy an exotic and expensive device. CD-ROMs are written to once and the data is fixed or read-only. Jukebox devices that can handle hundreds of disks are also available.

Secure Your Data

In addition to investing in fault tolerance and redundancy of your various network components, you should do a vigorous appraisal of your data center's security. Natural disasters such as floods, tornadoes, earthquakes, and hurricanes can all disrupt your company's ability to access its data. Obvious threats also include fire and vandalism. A converted warehouse of brick and beam construction is at greater risk of fire than a more modern steel and cement tower. However, there is a range of issues that may place your computers at risk.

Consider how close your building is to major highways or railways. Toxic or explosive cargoes are transported daily on our nation's roads. Thankfully this is a rare event, but there have been instances in which an overturned tractor-trailer or boxcar has forced the evacuation of nearby buildings.

Perhaps there are other companies in your building or nearby that handle volatile substances. Even cleaning crews can force the evacuation of a facility when there is a spill of powerful solvents. Your proximity to a military base or airport can also raise the potential of problems. You should also consider whether nearby embassies or government installations raise the likelihood of protestors blocking access to your offices.

For all of these reasons, companies that demand absolute guaranteed access to their data should invest in solutions that promote maximum uptime. While banks and financial institutions have typically required this level of data availability, the rise in e-commerce and just-in-time manufacturing has broadened the demand for technologies that maximize uptime.

Redundant and Remote Data Storage

There are several solutions available that provide redundant storage of corporate data at an alternate location. Using high-speed data links, these products mirror all of your files and allow the switch to a backup site if the primary systems fail.

Data General's Clarion line of storage products is a good example of this technology. The current version of their Remote Mirroring solution supports Sun Solaris and Windows NT, and it promises to support IBM AIX and HP UX in a future version.

One technology that has been gaining increased support is the deployment of storage area networks, or SANs. By employing very high-speed fiber channel hardware, network administrators can merge a variety of disk, tape, and other storage resources to servers. The SAN can operate independently of the corporate network infrastructure, freeing up valuable bandwidth and making operations such as backups run faster.

Emergency Recovery Services

In many industries, a core duty of IT is to maintain an almost fanatical obsession with system availability. Financial institutions, e-commerce sites, and manufacturing are all highly sensitive to a transitory loss of computer access to data. For these types of companies, it makes sense to partner with vendors that can help design and maintain procedures to restore your operations as quickly as possible.

Comdisco is one of several companies that tailor recovery plans for demanding IT customers. They can deliver an entire self-contained trailer with diesel generator, raised floor, and workstations with telephones. Iron Mountain's Arcus subsidiary, Databridge Services, can even provide armed couriers to escort your data to a recovery center.

Solutions of this magnitude are not something that I feel comfortable designing and relying on in-house. There are too many variables to consider without the benefit of experience, and learning these techniques during an actual disaster is not the way to go. Any IT department considering this level of support should consult with vendors that have a demonstrated ability to handle such a critical need. As always, practice the procedures to familiarize all your staff for actual emergencies.

Hubs, Switches, and Routers

These critical devices, which allow all the nodes on the network to communicate, also have features that promote reliability. As with servers, redundant power supplies are a wise investment. Power supplies are the most likely component to fail.

More sophisticated hubs such as 3Com CoreBuilder, HP Procurve, Cisco Catalyst, and other vendor's offerings allow the administrator to create redundant links between devices. These extra links typically provide two functions. The first way they are used is to aggregate the total bandwidth of all the links so that total throughput is greater than what would be available with a single connection. The second alternative is to construct resilient links. In this configuration, the loss of a single network link is automatically compensated for by fail-over to a secondary line.

Links can be lost due to a variety of causes. A cable can simply be cut or unplugged. Ports on a hub can fail and stop transmitting. Inadvertent configuration changes can also render a port dead. If my past experience is any indicator of future behavior, your hubs should be extremely reliable and actual hardware failures a rare occurrence.

Install Quality Cabling

Even the best hubs and servers won't work reliably without quality data cabling. Every networking class that I ever took always emphasized that 70 percent of all network problems are due to cabling issues. As transmission speeds increase, it becomes even more critical that all the cable runs, punch-down blocks, and station cables meet exacting standards for the protocol and transmission speed in use.

Remember that you will install new servers, workstations, and other nodes on a continual basis, but your wiring infrastructure is virtually impossible to upgrade without a wholesale (and costly) rewiring. The best way to prevent headaches in the future is to be certain that your network is built by professional cable installers who thoroughly test and guarantee their work.

There are a dizzying variety of cabling standards in general use today. Coaxial cables that were typical of many ArcNet and Ethernet networks have been supplanted by twisted pair cabling. Fiber optic, which was once an exotic choice for extreme-speed networking, has become easier to handle and increasingly popular.

Providing the highest-speed connections to every node on a LAN can be both expensive and wasteful. Fiber optic lines are typically reserved for network backbones and server rooms. There are indeed certain workgroups or specific situations that will benefit from special high-bandwidth connections. For example, developers of multimedia files utilizing full-motion video require sustained network throughput to edit and play their presentations. Providing these users with the throughput they need benefits the entire organization, since it will prevent their usage from saturating the network and using up all the available bandwidth. Servers are often equipped with network connections to a dedicated backbone to speed backups or data replication.

Adhere to Cabling Standards

There are domestic and international bodies that publish certain standards for cable performance and infrastructure design. For example, 100 Mbps, or Fast Ethernet, requires Category 5 components for dependable operation. Your components should be certified to meet the demands of your network.

The ANSI/TIA/EIA-606 specification calls for detailed documentation and color-coding of your cabling. Too often, network cabling resembles spaghetti, and it is difficult if not impossible to determine where each connection is made. Careful installation should include not only exhaustive testing but also meticulous labeling of every port and cable used. Time invested on proper cable identification will reap enormous time savings when you need to trace a problem later on.

TIP: When installing important links for backbones or dedicated links for Internet or other communication, make it a point to use different routes for your cable runs. Redundant links will not be effective if all the cables in a single bundle are damaged. I've often had installations done at separate times by different people to ensure that independent solutions result. Each installer takes a unique route to establish the desired links.

Get Components That Permit a Hot-Swap

Many network servers support hot-swapping of failed parts. Power supplies, hard disk drives, and even network interface cards can be removed and installed without having to turn the system unit off. This allows the network administrator to replace faulty hardware without disrupting the operations of attached users. Environments that cannot tolerate a loss of connectivity should make sure to invest in equipment with these advanced capabilities.

Sophisticated RAID controllers, when paired with compatible hard disks, allow the administrator to remove a failed drive and the server to continue functioning, with users totally unaware that a problem has occurred. Alerts can be sent to the administrator automatically via email or beeper when the server operating system detects the failed disk drive. This process often requires the use of a third-party product such as Intel's LANDesk Server Monitor. Additional alerts can be set to go off when predetermined thresholds are exceeded, letting IT know when there is a problem with disk space availability or CPU utilization, or if a potential intruder has been detected.

When the broken hard drive is replaced with a new one, the data is automatically reconstructed from the parity information on the remaining hard disks. This process is perhaps the most satisfying one that a nervous network administrator will ever witness.

Larger network hubs are highly modular, permitting the use of many types of network cabling and communication standards. Ports on numerous independent cards support nodes on the network. In a similar manner to swapping a failed drive in a RAID, you can often remove and replace a network card module without harming nodes on other unaffected cards.

Install Adequate Power Protection

You should never trust the quality of power that comes from a generic wall outlet. Servers, hubs, and critical communications equipment should only be plugged into circuits that have adequate voltage regulation and backup power. Electronic circuitry can be very sensitive to mild fluctuations in current. While your lights only flicker slightly when an air conditioner compressor kicks in, computers can suffer from corrupted memory chips and lock up. Clearly, if you want your networks to run reliably, you must invest in power-conditioning products to smooth out any impurities in the delivery of electricity.

An uninterruptible power supply, or UPS, is common equipment for all types of networks. These vary from shoebox-sized units designed to support a single computer to room-filling products that can support a large company data center. Only the most foolhardy of network administrators would not employ them.

Power backups usually include a battery system to allow computers to run until power is restored or they can be safely shut down. Most backup power supplies have the capability to communicate with software on the servers they protect and can initiate an automatic shutdown. Units are sold with two major specifications. One is the amount of load they can sustain, and the other is the length of time that power is supplied. Better systems will be able to detect and correct a greater range of power problems and switch over to the backup source quickly and smoothly.

Many environments will demand that power be maintained for long periods of time, which may exceed the limits of what even the heaviest batteries can provide. Hospitals, jails, police stations, and many other operations invest in independent power generators that can take over if commercial power is down for extended periods. While the investment can be very costly, a diesel generator should be seriously considered if your network demands continuous power.

Use HVAC for Comfortable Computers

Even if your hardware employs fault-tolerant components and draws its power from a high-quality regulated circuit, there is still another step you must take to ensure smooth operations. HVAC (heating/ventilation/air conditioning) units are used to provide a stable temperature and humid environment. Anyone who has ever been shocked by touching a doorknob will remember that it almost never happens on a hot, sticky day.

Keeping the level of humidity at a certain level helps prevent static discharge, which can harm the integrity of electronics. Excessive heat can seriously damage electronics and cause random errors to occur. Keeping a computer room cool will extend the life of your systems and make them more reliable.

IT REALLY HAPPENED: One of my departments was using a heavily loaded server. Every expansion slot in the Dell EISA system was filled with disk controllers and other cards, and the server was generating a great deal of heat. Intermittent errors and crashes could not be traced to any installation problem or software configuration error. I removed the system case and pointed a standard 12-inch fan directly at the motherboard. With the constant breeze flowing over the chips, the server ran perfectly. My next step was to purchase a bigger server with more slots, a bigger power supply, and extra internal cooling fans.

Some HVAC installations can also filter the air in the computer room. Keeping dust out of your disk drives and system ventilation holes will make your expensive server equipment last longer.

Make Your Systems Flexible

One of the ways to increase reliability is to limit flexibility. Operating a closed system in which nothing can be added or modified allows you to concentrate only on factors that promote stability. Flexibility demands that changes be allowed. Many who support computer systems fear change, because it can introduce factors that impact system operation. However, planning your network carefully will permit these divergent needs to be satisfied.

Buy More than You Need

While this idea may make the fiscally prudent cringe, it is always cheaper to get more capacity than you need now, rather than adding more later. In the same way that gas disperses to fill a vacuum, users' data needs grow to use available disk space. This is not simply caused by lazy system users who never delete unwanted data, although this is an important factor. Networks simply take on new functions over time that are never accounted for when they are first constructed.

GET EXTRA DISK SPACE   It makes sense to purchase additional disk space when you first acquire your servers. The extra cost of some spare gigabytes is well worth the investment. I guarantee that, even if your users don't clamor for extra storage, any systems manager will find a use for it. Disk images files, old application files, or server room for testing are all valid candidates.

If you want to avoid the high cost of extra disk drives up front, seek to purchase servers and storage systems that are designed for easy additions. Servers that are equipped with RAID controllers can already manage multiple drives (specify systems that allow for easy installation of new disks). The more sophisticated RAID products are, the easier the addition of a drive is to a running system especially those that do not require a complete restart to recognize the added storage.

Sometimes an external expansion unit is supported that can house a significant number of additional drives. This can be a model made by the server vendor in a matching case or a third-party solution that attaches via SCSI or another interface.

INSTALL ADDITIONAL NETWORK PORTS   Extra network ports in the computer room allow much more flexible configuration of the servers and hubs. It's much easier to set up test networks or isolate groups of users if independent connections can be utilized. There are also occasions when you need to deploy extra systems in user work areas. Having additional port capacity where your users sit often comes in handy.

PURCHASE EXTRA CLIENT LICENSES   Many network operating systems require that each connected user possess an individual license to access a server. While it may seem easy to simply tally all the users and arrive at the adequate number of licenses, this overlooks several important points. Unless extra client access permits are purchased, you may be caught when you need to add several users. Some servers will reject logins once a limit is reached. Often, power users and others may need several concurrent sessions.

Find out whether your company has a busy season when extra workers are added in bunches. Consider what retailers do during the pre-Christmas period. The tax season prior to April 15 fuels a similar hiring frenzy in some firms. Power plants are constructed to handle peak capacity, and network systems are no different. Make sure that you can deal with the acme of users and that you won't get caught short.

Licenses are usually priced on a per-server or per-seat basis. A per-server license sets an absolute limit on the number of active logins that a server will accept. Novell NetWare has typically followed this model. Windows NT Server can be set up with licensing for each user; in this arrangement, it does not count the number of users attached and deny service when a limit is reached. The Open Source model from Linux does not require any client (or server) licenses at all. The various flavors of UNIX and other operating systems can have fairly complex licensing structures. Pricing can vary not just by the total number of total clients, but also by the number of processors in a server. This makes it difficult to determine and compare the total cost of ownership for competitive solutions. Carefully review your vendor's licensing policies; these should always include provisions for upgrades and support.

Remember that desktop applications can also carry license restrictions. Products from Adobe, Quark, and other vendors can actually inhibit programs from launching at the user's desktop if too many copies are detected to be running on the network. Server-hosted applications such as fax gateways may be configured with usage restrictions. Be sure to check the restrictions for all your software.

Buy Easily Expandable Systems

Look for products that are constructed for simple expansion. As stated earlier, RAID storage systems can often accommodate additional drives. Make sure that your tape backup solution is sized to handle any additional storage capacity you purchase.

File servers can often be equipped with additional processors and memory to boost capacity and performance. Make sure that your NOS will actually make use of the additional processors and memory. There is often a "sweet spot" of RAM and a number of processors with which the server will operate optimally. Adding more capacity will not automatically guarantee increased performance. Check carefully with the vendors of your hardware and software to match them correctly. It doesn't make sense to spend a lot of money for a little benefit.

Hubs and switches can also be designed for easy growth. Adding new users may simply require the purchase of additional network cards. Increasing the port density of a hub is not the only benefit of an easily expandable hub. New technology can often be melded easily into your network by the installation of a single card. For example, you may want to introduce Gigabyte Ethernet to a portion of your nodes, yet retain the existing 10 Mbps clients.

3Com, for example, sells a line of networking equipment called the SuperStack series. These tools are specifically designed to permit easy scaling of capacity to meet new demands. It is much simpler to administer a single growing group of products rather than an environment that can only be enlarged by adding separately controlled components. Always seek solutions that won't create more work if you later decide to increase their capabilities.

For your workstations, purchase network interface cards that support multiple topologies. Many Ethernet NICs can run at either 10 or 100 Mbps. Token Ring cards may be capable of 4 or 16 Mbps operation. Even if your network operates at the lower speeds, the upgrade path carries a fairly nominal price. It may even make sense to purchase cards that support different types of wiring if various types are in use or a change to a new corporate standard is being debated. Remember that a fast card will usually be backwardly compatible with its slower brethren, but a slow operating card will always be stuck at its limit.

MAKING THE WHOLE NETWORK EASIER TO SUPPORT

Even with a bunch of reliable servers connected over quality wiring to expandable hubs, there is still plenty of work to keep the IT specialist busy. Making your life easier is one of the main goals of this book. With all the types of hardware and software you use, there are several things you can do to limit the number of skills you need to keep them all running.

Every piece of hardware you use will probably have its own software to configure and test its operation. Servers require utilities for setup and drivers to enable certain features. Various competing methods for network management require that you adopt more than one application for systems that are not compliant with a single standard. Technical support can be a nightmare if various vendors' wares are not operating correctly with each other, and each vendor blames the others.

Limit the Variety of Equipment Installed

Henry Ford revolutionized industry with mass production. Limiting options and maintaining incredible consistency were the keys to cranking out the Model T in record numbers. While it is impractical to take such a rigid approach to your network, there are certainly great benefits to be had with standardization.

Purchase Similar Servers from the Same Manufacturer

Being solidly familiar with your equipment makes installation, maintenance, and troubleshooting much easier. Various products in a single vendor's line share many common features. It certainly saves you money if you can use spare parts for many different systems.

Software drivers for video cards and network and hard disk controllers are something that I loathe hunting for in anonymous piles of disks. Utilizing a single brand reduces clutter since you can limit which disks you need to keep. Also, utilities that permit you to partition a hard drive or change a system's configuration can often be complex and confusing. Having to learn only one application will make your use of these utilities faster and less daunting.

When you are very comfortable with a particular piece of hardware or software, you can approach operational errors with confidence. Problems are easier to identify and fix. Aberrant system behavior can be more readily detected when there are several peers to compare performance to.

There is a corollary to the general rule of using a single manufacturer. Try to make purchases from a limited number of sources even if multiple sellers carry the same equipment. Running around in search of the best price is not always the best way to conduct the acquisition of hardware and software. A strong relationship with your vendors is important for support and many other issues. The entire purchasing process will be covered in great detail in Chapter 10.

SIMILAR, NOT THE SAME   The pace of technology makes it impossible for any vendor to offer the exact same system for any length of time. New motherboard chipsets, processors, and other technologies continually push the envelope of system design. Vendors periodically offer new models that supplant the ones they sold only a few months before. Product lines are continually refreshed with higher-speed processors, denser RAM, and more copious disk storage.

Even in systems that carry identical model numbers, there may be variations. System manufacturers have several suppliers for hard disks and other components. Depending on the date the unit was assembled, you can expect to see different items in the products you buy. Even when storage capacity is similar, drive geometry will vary. While reputable vendors and dealers should stand behind the products they sell, you may want to specify a particular sub-assembly or revision number to maintain as homogenous an environment as possible.

Standardize on a Brand of Hub

All of your internetworking equipment—hubs, routers, and switches—should be treated in the same fashion as your servers. Concentrating your attention on a few vendors will limit the number of software packages you need to master in order to configure your network hardware. While the ability of products from a wide range of vendors to communicate together is admirably high, you don't want to become an unwitting tester of an unusual configuration.

Vendors will always be more comfortable and forthcoming when dealing with networks limited to their line of solutions.

There are many methods available to administrators who wish to closely monitor and manage their networks. RMON and SNMP compliance are often touted on product data sheets. These protocols allow hardware to communicate with management software such as HP Openview, CA UniCenter TNG, or SUN Solstice. Make sure that your hardware's implementation of these protocols is appropriate for the management suite your company uses. This is certainly one of the most complex applications that any IT specialist will ever grapple with. It will only be more difficult if some of your devices cannot be centrally controlled or generate information that cannot be interpreted at a management console.

Avoid Using Too Many NOS Products

In the good old days of computing, it was common to encounter companies that could be characterized as strictly IBM or DEC shops. Virtually all of the installed hardware, software, and services were purchased from a single vendor. This was a good way to ensure compatibility across all systems, but it limited innovation and choice. In addition, confining yourself to only one supplier is not the way to spur competition and lower prices.

Today, many network administrators rely on several different NOS products. Novell, Microsoft, UNIX, and others are woven together to satisfy business needs. Some firms rely on Novell NetWare for file and print services and use Windows NT Server to handle the corporate email. The same firms might turn to a UNIX solution for running their intranet sites.

The major problem with this type of scenario is the still-emerging state of the tools and standards for administration of user accounts and access privileges across the many platforms. It is often aggravating for users to have to remember specific login account names and passwords for different resources. In addition to frustrating users, this type of setup increases the amount of work for the system administrator with every extra account that is created.

SEARCH FOR COMMON DENOMINATORS   Facing the challenge of disparate systems requires that IT specialists look for standards that can be used to reduce the difficulty of managing different platforms or uniting them. Directory services are a prime area in which to concentrate your efforts. By merging user accounts and email systems, you simplify network administration and use. Novell, for example, has developed NDS (Novell Directory Services) to answer this need. This allows a centralized database of user accounts and access privileges to be used for all access to servers, databases, and other resources.

Directory services are critical to the efficient management of complex networks. Competition by various vendors has led to the introduction of many different standards. NDS is available for Microsoft Windows NT, SUN Solaris, and other network operating systems. Cisco and other router manufacturers support NDS to enable the use of a single directory for managing security and access rights.

Lightweight Directory Access Protocol, or LDAP, is a standards-based method for systems to utilize various network, email, and database directory structures. Based on the X.500 directory standard, LDAP is considered an easier approach to program. LDAP allows the use of TCP/IP protocols for client browsing of directory systems on a wide range of platforms.

There have always been and will continue to be both unique and incompatible methods for controlling networked systems. Each approach has its benefits and limitations, and each has legions of administrators that swear by or swear at them. While you might expect that any product you select will eventually be replaced or supplanted by a newer technology, seek products that support broad industry standards and you will ease future upgrade woes. Upgrades are much simpler when you can adopt existing directory information rather than translate proprietary data into a new format.

While it may be impossible to adopt a "one size fits all" network operating system or management suite, it makes sense to try to concentrate as much of your infrastructure as possible on a single solution. It is difficult enough to develop a significant expertise with a product as complex as a NOS without being distracted by competing systems. I suggest that most companies adopt a core platform and only stray from it when truly compelling reasons exist.

Even with the many strong and weak points inherent with every NOS, virtually all can be counted on to provide most of the solutions you require. You can find Web servers that run on NT, NetWare, or Linux. Each platform has tools for managing gateways, remote client access, printing, and other tasks. You need to find a balance between ease of support and administration and the optimal solution for a specific need, such as hosting large SQL databases.

BUILDING UP SPEED

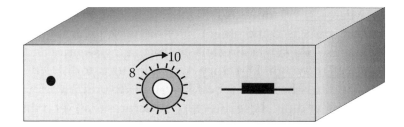

Once you have made sure that everything is stable, reliable, expandable, and relatively easy to support, you can turn your attention to optimization for performance. Remember that performance is pointless if systems crash frequently. There are sometimes issues of stability that are only addressed when an effort is made to throttle back performance.

Adding performance to your network is made much easier when you follow the earlier rules of building expandable systems. With computers, versatility means that a clear and easy upgrade path can be followed. Bargain systems are much more expensive in the long run if they reach their limits and must be replaced rather than upgraded.

Elegant Tweaking

Increasing the speed of your networks is exceedingly more difficult than flooring the accelerator on your car. The two competing approaches that one can take are elegant tweaking or brute force. Each operating system will have its own way of tuning various settings for modifying behavior.

NetWare has literally dozens of settings that one can tune to affect memory usage, network communications buffering, disk writing behavior, and many other features. Windows NT is intended to be more self-regulating by comparison, but one can still use programs like Registry Editor to adjust performance parameters. Administrators of Microsoft Internet Information Server may wish to tweak cache settings to improve download times of the FTP service.

CAUTION: I have *never* seen instructions that mention the use of Windows NT Registry Editor that don't issue strong warnings about the danger in using it. Any powerful tool that directly modifies the core behavior of an operating system should be used with a great deal of caution. Make sure that any modifications are done to specific areas that are known to address the exact settings you need to adjust. Also, be certain to retain a backup in case you need to restore a previous setting.

Reduce the Number of Protocols Used

Networks rely on a variety of communication protocols to send signals between all the servers and nodes. TCP/IP, NetBIOS, IPX/SPX, and others can all be used to transmit information. Traffic on your cabling has a finite limit, and reducing the number of protocols and various frame types reduces the total overhead on the wires. This not only can boost speed but also answers the need for easier administration and management.

The predominant protocol in use today is TCP/IP. Running a pure IP network is the goal of many network administrators as they look away from supporting several competing standards.

Highly skilled and experienced network diagnosticians can use analysis tools to determine where your bottlenecks exist. It makes sense to consult with these experts and ask them to perform a system-wide diagnosis.

IT REALLY HAPPENED: I was investigating a Novell NetWare network that used several Ethernet frame types to support various types of clients. Ethernet Snap frames were used for Mac clients. Ethernet_802.3 was in use by Windows IPX/SPX workstations. Ethernet II frames were carrying TCP/IP traffic for UNIX terminal access to a database application hosted at another site. Finally, NetBIOS transmissions were being used for Lotus Notes Server access. Every time a NetBIOS broadcast occurred, it was propagated across every Ethernet frame type. With three different frames in use, each broadcast was being done three times. Using a Network Associates Sniffer (www.nai.com), it was easy to see the tremendous amount of unnecessary traffic that was being generated. Migrating every client to a single frame type dramatically reduced overhead, boosted performance, and increased reliability.

Check Your Cabling Paths

A simple yet often overlooked factor in networks is how your clients and servers are wired together. It is easy to create a massive network with numerous hops between cabling segments. Each packet that has to transverse a hop—for example, a router that connects two Ethernet LANs together—will take more time than a packet that travels within a single Ethernet segment.

A common problem occurs when clients using a specific printer or server are forced to send packets across several routers to reach the printer. Placing the printer and the clients on the same LAN segment reduces network overhead and boosts performance for everyone. Unnecessary routing of packets is one of the primary ways that network bandwidth is wasted.

Intelligent cable use requires that you understand where your clients and other nodes connect. Making the best use of your higher-speed links to connect the busiest systems will benefit everyone. Make every effort to utilize the simplest topology possible with the fewest disparate segments.

NETWORK DESIGN TOOLS There are several tools IT can use to chart existing networks or plan new ones. Software such as Micrografx NetworkCharter Pro or Visio Professional will help you gain a visual appreciation and understanding of your topology. Extensive graphic libraries can identify your hubs and routers with appropriate pictures rather than generic labels.

Automated discovery agents or Wizards can be used to gather information about your infrastructure. This key feature makes what can be an enormously arduous task much more palatable. Remember that most networks are somewhat amorphous, so make it a habit to periodically check yours for changes.

Brute Force Enhancements

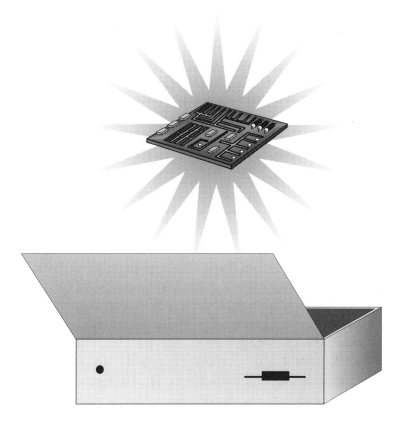

No matter which type of system you purchased as a file server, the maker is undoubtedly bringing to market products that utilize faster processors than those that were available when you made your initial investment. Certain motherboard chipsets allow the installation of faster CPU chips. Designs that use Intel BX control chips allow the use of Pentium II processors from 233Mhz to the latest 500Mhz models. The slot 1 architecture permits a rapid upgrade via the simple installation of a faster CPU.

As I mentioned earlier, you can purchase expandable systems that allow installation of additional processors and memory. Sometimes these are precisely the fix necessary to boost performance. It is important to first use operating system tools to determine whether the system is indeed being taxed and where the biggest bottlenecks are. It makes little sense to upgrade CPU speed if the network card is overwhelmed by the amount of packets being sent to it.

Monitor Server Performance

The NetWare Monitor program and the NT Performance Monitor application are both ideal ways to gauge system operation. Always make sure to get a baseline reading and compare measurements at different parts of the day. You need to look for sustained high readings or peaks in activity.

It should be a habit of every IT specialist to gather and review performance information on a regular basis. You should also seek feedback from users, since their anecdotal experience with your network may point out problems that your monitoring efforts miss. Don't forget that you may not be looking at the type of information that would indicate whether certain problems exist. Your users should be able to tell you if certain periods of the day show a dramatic drop-off in system responsiveness.

Hubs and routers also have the capability of reporting performance parameters. Products that work well under low loads may suddenly stop transmitting packets of data if their buffers fill up with requests that cannot be handled before additional requests are made. This again illustrates that buying a more capable, albeit more expensive, hub may be a better investment since it has a much greater capacity. Unfortunately, you must always plan for peak load conditions when sizing all your solutions to prevent loss of services.

Upgrade Your OS

Sometimes it is necessary to upgrade or even replace your core network operating system to address performance issues. Manufacturers often release service packs and kernel updates that contain more efficient code. Device drivers that allow the NOS to communicate with network cards and disk drives are often updated with an eye toward better throughput.

Replacing any driver or installing any upgrade must first be balanced against the risk of harming stability. Windows NT Server service packs have been notorious for introducing new problems that require additional fixes. I always advocate taking a very slow and measured approach to any update program. It pays to wait a long time and allow others to try out and discover any problems with the new programs first.

Run a Test Network

With the inexorable advances in technology, IT needs to find ways to balance the need for stability with investigation of new software and hardware solutions. Installing service packs or similar updates on any of your live network components without first testing their behavior is a sure way to court disaster.

Network operating systems, servers, telecommunications links, workstation clients, and every other component of your network will evolve over time. Ten years ago, the default corporate desktop was an IBM PC AT compatible with a 20-megabyte hard drive and 6Mhz processor. Today 500Mhz Pentium III speed demons with gigabytes of storage and video card memory, many times larger than the total system memory of typical file servers in 1990, are available for an ever-lower cost.

Exploring new technology that promises greater throughput and reliability is an important consideration in planning for performance upgrades. IT needs to develop test centers and methodologies that will help identify which trends in the industry can make a significant impact.

This subject is so critical that it will be given special coverage in Chapter 12, which is dedicated to managing IT projects. You should pursue new and advanced products and services vigorously. However, maintaining a stable and predictable environment requires the utmost care and planning.

CHAPTER 3

Understanding the Users You Support

In the many technical training classes I have taken, there has been little, if any, attention paid to the needs of computer users. The emphasis has always been on NOS administration, with subjects such as printer queue and server directory management given detailed coverage, while customer relationship skills were largely ignored. Certainly IT managers need a profound proficiency with all the intricacies of running a network, but technical ability is only one part of the total formula for support. Disgruntled and angry users will care little about whether a server has an efficient directory structure if they feel that dealing with IT personnel is a frustrating and degrading process.

There are dozens of books available that examine in minute detail the nuances of every popular network operating system. This book is not intended to address the need for that type of information. Rather, I want readers of this book to better understand the entire range of skills that are just as important as technical acumen.

Information technology specialists will always be judged by how productive and confident users are with the systems that they design, deploy, and support. Providing the most powerful servers, quickest backbones, and most advanced custom software solutions will be meaningless if those who depend on the network to get their jobs done find these features buggy and unreliable. Systems with interfaces that are impossible to decipher or that hinder the performance of what should be the most basic tasks will cause users to complain loudly. Ultimately, the single guiding force in directing how you do your job should be how happy you make those you support.

Always remember that every task you undertake should be directed at a single goal: *Enable the people in your company who use technology to do so with confidence that every effort has been made to maximize their ability to successfully fulfill their jobs.* It is not trivial to realize that IT services play among the most critical functions of almost any company. Like no other department or division, IT supports every person and all the data that they produce. The ability to create, manage, and share information is a matter of pure survival in most industries today. Providing easy and continuous access to that information so that it can be acted on will be sure to earn IT respect and kudos for a job well done.

There are several key areas to study that will allow you to better understand computer system users and how they interact. This chapter covers three broad subjects. The first will be an exploration of the individual types of users and their habits and relative abilities. Next will be an introduction to the relationships that exist between groups of users. The chapter concludes with the "User's Bill of Rights." Consider this to be a minimum guarantee of service that everyone you support should expect.

WHAT TYPES OF USERS ARE THERE?

Perhaps the best first step in approaching the challenges of providing user support is doing a detailed examination of the types of users one encounters in all companies. Think of it as an itemized taxonomy of the various user types and personalities. It is important to appreciate the wide spectrum of abilities, expectations, and habits that users exhibit. Tailoring support strategies means approaching people with more than just a cookie-cutter set of solutions to be forced on them. Rather, you should understand that different types of people work and respond differently to the systems you provide. Like the coach who understands that some players need a quiet word of encouragement while others require a swift kick in the pants, you should learn to work in ways that garner the most positive relationships with your users.

While you may be thrilled to have the fastest Alpha server humming away in your server room, that means nothing to someone who can't locate a report he just had on his screen that needed to be faxed out 30 minutes ago. Screaming computer users will always get your attention faster than any faulty computer will. A computer probably prints your paycheck, but only the humans you support will enter into the equation when you are in line for your next raise.

Don't assume that the following list of computer users is exhaustive and absolute. I have found that everyone at one time or another exhibits some of the traits listed for each of these personality types. However, I have found the quirks and temperament of those I have supported to be of particular importance when I determine the best ways to maintain their efforts to use the equipment and applications that I set up. Having an appreciation for the approach that your users take toward technology will make it easier to design solutions to maximize their efficiency.

The Click-a-Holic

Perhaps the most frustrating, yet occasionally rewarding, type of user to work with is the one I refer to as the Click-a-Holic. This is the type of person who attacks every application and operating system with a vengeance. Every button, pull-down menu, option dialog box, and preference setting is selected and probed with a staccato click of a mouse. Not satisfied with merely adjusting configurations, this keyboard beast will not be satisfied until every folder is opened to the deepest level, any application discovered is executed, and the desktop pattern is adjusted to use gaudy colors and bizarre icon placement. Remember that many IT specialists are straight from this school of computer use, so you shouldn't feel too much disdain for those who exhibit this behavior.

Click-a-Holics rarely have a specific purpose behind their tinkering. They would rather explore blindly than rely on a manual to tell them where to go. Their greatest problem is the trouble they bring on themselves. These are the types of users most likely to render their computers dead simply by "playing with it" too much. It is for these users that I look to develop support strategies that can most quickly return their systems to a basic setup once more. This includes old-fashioned batch programs that overwrite critical configuration files back to their default settings as well as more elaborate rescue techniques. It is important to emphasize that changing bad habits, once discovered, is much more efficient than constantly restoring programs.

Once you realize that you have such users in your group, plan to showcase some steps that they can use to avoid anguished calls for help in the future. Demonstrate the operating system's methods for restoring default settings. Explain how much they are affecting their own and others' productivity by rendering their machines unusable. Point out the most common settings they will need to be aware of and adjust. Make sure that they are educated so that they may approach applications and operating systems with a calculated and measured approach, rather than a haphazard one. For those who defy all of these efforts, learn ways that you can progressively lock down and limit the degree of damage that they can incur by fixing settings in place with passwords and read-only configuration files.

A typical problem that calls for such stringent management control is incorrect configuration of displays. Selecting the wrong resolution or color depth can cause incomplete data to be displayed onscreen. Some applications are optimized for a particular pixel width and height. Administrators of Windows NT networks can utilize the System Policy Editor to prevent users from modifying their screens.

Not only can you prohibit users from mangling their workstation configuration, but you can also design a controlled desktop appearance. You can control precisely which programs appear on the Start menu or specify which shortcuts are available. Imagine how much easier support would be if all systems were consistent throughout a company. Consider all the extra time you'd save if you didn't have to search for specific application programs that have been relocated to different menu positions.

You are doing your job right if you can teach Click-a-Holics to respect and better understand the systems they are using. Showing them how to fix problems independently is a great step. The ultimate hope is to have users grow so that they can deftly exploit all the capabilities and functions of their software and hardware. Locking out features and settings is a somewhat more drastic step and should be instituted only after a user has demonstrated a chronic disregard for your time. After all, it is typically the IT specialist who is called upon to rescue these individuals from their self-inflicted problems.

Some environments demand that the more drastic approach be taken proactively, *before* Click-a-Holics get themselves in trouble. Limiting choices to begin with will help to prevent inadvertent destructive mouse clicks later on. It's much easier to support large groups of users who all use the same applications if consistency is maintained from desktop to desktop. Personally, I want to allow the users who rely on me to have the greatest degree of flexibility in use of their computers. On the other hand, I don't want my job to be any more difficult than it already is. Most of the time, the users I support exercise the good judgment of asking before making changes and noting what the original setup was in case they need to revert to it. There are those, however, that make me wish they had to rely on pencil and paper to get their jobs done.

Accidental Discoveries

As I mentioned earlier, the Click-a-Holic is sometimes privy to a discovery that makes all the frustration inherent with them tolerable. There are certainly occasions that mad mouse clicks uncover hidden menus and options that directly address a question I have been unable to answer. Documentation is rarely exhaustive and often incomprehensible, so there is often no other choice than to explore every option screen and attempt various settings to fix problems. While not an elegant way of using a computer, this brute-force approach is sometimes a valid and necessary way to exploit a system to its fullest.

When one of your users discovers a real gem of a setting or feature, make sure to give him or her credit and record exactly what steps were taken to chance upon it. These procedures should all be added to FAQ files that can be distributed to your users. Later chapters will describe other methods for the gathering and dissemination of instructional and reference materials for users and IT staffers.

The Click-a-Phobe

At the opposite end of the user spectrum is the person I describe as the Click-a-Phobe. These are the people who are terrified that the computer itself will consider them idiots for not knowing which key to press. Convinced that every move will somehow erase their data and crash their computers, they seldom stray from procedures that they know work even when infinitely simpler methods exist. Even when shown how to accomplish tasks in a different manner, they are reluctant to try anything new. I've dealt with users who were literally in tears as I attempted to help them with problems. You must accept that some people are very intimidated by computers. The sheer mystery of how computers work and the seemingly endless cryptic commands and messages seem to conspire to frustrate their efforts and desire to learn more.

You can sometimes discover these people in your company by the huge number of sticky notes taped to their monitors and keyboards. Each note seems to convey a particular set of commands with a specific sequence geared toward certain tasks they need to perform.

I've seen disk drives labeled A and CD drives with letter designations on them. These users write themselves instructions on how to print, copy files, and login, and even their passwords are noted in plain view.

A savvy support specialist will understand that this creates a wealth of information that she should use to her advantage. Right before your eyes, the users most afraid of using their machines have distilled the most essential hints and directions they need to get their work accomplished. When looking to develop training, user interfaces, FAQs, or any kind of material intended to support users, remember that you need to emphasize the most commonly used commands and tasks.

Look for users that scribble reminders like "Every Tuesday, email completed sales tracking data to David G., Sue T., and Paul C.!" pasted on their monitors. See if specific names are grouped, and inquire how and why these people are important. Showing users how to construct a personal email distribution list can be a great time saver for them. Often this information prompts you to create an email group for an entire department.

Drawing from the information you gather, you can more easily determine which users need help with what processes. Always remember that instructions you consider clear and complete may be indecipherable to others.

When dealing with Click-a-Phobes, it is of utmost importance to always build on what they know well before presenting more complex tasks. Ensuring that there is confidence and understanding with the technical demands of their job is the single greatest gift you can give them. Over time and as their experience grows, Click-a-Phobes may even begin to explore areas that push the envelope of their understanding. Making sure that there is proper schooling in the fundamentals of computer use will ensure that they apply sound techniques and don't get themselves into trouble. You need to accept that this type of user may never want to try anything new. If they can get their job done confidently, then you have accomplished yours!

The Daredevil

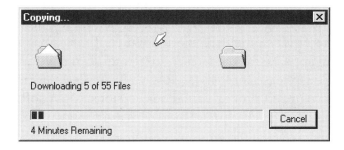

Daredevils are the ones most anxious to try new programs and settings. They are explorers like Click-a-Holics, but instead of randomly selecting every option, they have a specific intent behind their mouse clicks. They are sure to volunteer to try out new application programs or operating system upgrades. In that role they are an invaluable resource to any IT person. While IT specialists will and should always test products before deploying them to the general company user community, no test is valid and complete until a representative from the intended audience is asked to participate. This personality is the perfect type for this role.

There are several other characteristics common to Daredevil users. They often download updates and patches themselves for the applications they use. Anyone who deals with program upgrades knows how bug fixes can introduce new problems when applied. While you can appreciate Daredevils' interest in pressing ahead with the newest release, make sure they understand that this may not always be in their best interest.

You must admit that it is impossible to keep on top of all your applications and drivers when updates are released so frequently. There is nothing wrong with relying on some users to scan various magazines and Web sites for information about software that they are using. I know that I am nowhere near as expert on certain applications used by the people I support as they are, since they are the ones who work with it every day. It is important to keep the lines of communication open so that you are at least aware of their activity and can provide some guidance.

The adventuresome spirit of the Daredevil is their greatest danger. It is wonderful to support people who are not shy in attempting to use new things. Implementing new solutions is easier when they are greeted with enthusiasm. However, sometimes an appetite for the latest and greatest can have a negative impact. New releases of software often create files in formats that are not recognized properly by older versions. Microsoft Office word processing and spreadsheet files are prime examples of the failure of new versions to maintain full backward compatibility.

It is important to temper the enthusiasm some users have and outline the problems that a headlong approach to upgrades and other downloads can cause. Communication, as always, is the key. Impress upon all your users that none of them operates in a vacuum. The data that is created at one desk often has to be used by others. Emphasize that ensuring compatibility of data is a critical requirement for the health of companies' information systems. Encourage your users to adopt a careful and measured approach to all upgrades.

While some administrators use an iron-fisted style, insisting that every scrap of code go through a rigorous approval and installation regimen, I believe that allowing some degree of freedom enables workers to do their jobs more efficiently and happily. Look for ways for the Daredevil to utilize specific methods for communicating with IT staff so you can approach the problems inherent in new releases together and not as adversaries. Putting your foot down will often be perceived as confrontational and a hindrance to innovation. While there are times when central IT departments must have control and demand strict adherence to policy, no user appreciates an inflexible reaction if they don't understand why you must be so stoic. Being seen as a partner to their efforts is a great way to build trust and respect. Steps like these will have the greatest benefit to your own workday. Think of how much time you save if you don't have to respond to support calls generated by an over-anxious computer user.

IT REALLY HAPPENED: Someone I supported was having stability problems with his Macintosh computer. He decided to upgrade to the newest operating system by himself. While the upgrade to Mac OS 8.5 went well, it did not make his system behave any better. The upgrade did not address the underlying problem, which was a buggy driver. After using the Macintosh Extension Manager to identify the problem program, I had to patch and upgrade many application programs that were not compliant with the new OS. Remind Daredevils that simply loading updates is not an automatic panacea.

The Demander

No other type of user frustrates me more than the Demander. Simply put, these are the people who want things *now*. Not only do they demand that everything they want take priority over any other task you have, but they seem unable to determine what exactly constitutes an emergency and what should be done only when time permits. Whether their request involves a simple software installation on a single workstation or an entire new computer, they always request that the work be done as quickly as possible.

What makes these people particularly troublesome is that they typically have the habit of contacting your boss and having them force you to drop everything to tend to their needs. Sometimes your boss determines that this is the easiest way to quiet the Demander. With this approach, you give them what they want and hope that they leave you alone for a while. My guess is that Demanders handle every aspect of their lives in the same way. Learning at an early age that "the squeaky wheel gets the grease," they badger everyone and anyone who has something they want. Yelling and stamping their feet may have proven an effective tool for them, but the drain they can put on resources is a danger to everyone in your company.

There are often times when the Demander seems like nothing more than "the boy who cried wolf." I've supported people who brought me a supposedly critical problem that needed to be handled right away. After devoting time and energy to their problem at the detriment of other projects, it annoyed me to discover that the systems I deployed to address their urgent need went sitting unused. While it is tempting to simply ignore Demanders' requests, it makes much more sense to create a structure that forces them to understand and appreciate the position they force you in with their egocentric habits.

After a particularly galling session with an individual who placed wildly unrealistic expectations on what he thought my work schedule should be, I told him that I did not work just for him. Rather, I continued, we all worked together for the same company and it was critical for me to satisfy the needs of many people throughout the organization. Placing his demands for help within the context of others' need for my time seemed to give him a perspective that he had lacked. It must be made clear that helping one particular individual must be balanced with the various other calls for attention.

Anyone who has visited a busy deli or similar service counter has experienced the "take a number" strategy for requesting help. While the first-in, first-out scenario may be appropriate in some settings, this approach does not allow the setting of priorities, nor does it consider the relative amount of time that each request will require. IT professionals must develop systems that can balance the demands of everyone in a company yet not sacrifice the flexibility to handle issues that are indeed emergencies. Hospital emergency rooms have elaborate triage procedures so they can adequately serve the needs of everyone without ignoring the most critical patients. Chapter 4 will explore methods for building support organizations and policies for your company.

If you can demonstrate to your users that your support systems are robust enough to handle emergencies and still allow timely resolution of more mundane problems, you have indeed solved one of the most difficult aspects of user support. Of all the user types I have encountered, it is the Demander who is most resistant to change and to accepting standardized treatment. While you will undoubtedly quickly learn who fits this description in your company, you should be thankful that it is normally a fairly rare personality.

The Power User

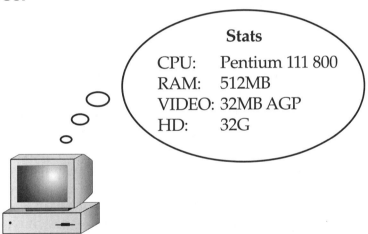

Power Users are the most technically skilled workers you support. They possess significant abilities with their computers and are often experts in particular programs. What makes them special is not the level of support that they require, which is often minimal, but the contribution they can make to the rest of the organization. When IT staff is concerned with installation of applications, managing user server accounts, and troubleshooting email, the Power User is learning how to fully exploit the capabilities of their machines. It is precisely this expertise that should be leveraged to make others more productive and to remove the burden on IT staff to be an expert in everything.

While you should expect that every IT specialist can at least execute the basic functions of every application and manipulate the standard data files that the company produces, it is virtually impossible for each IT staffer to obtain the same level of competence that day-to-day users of specific programs have. Someone who works all day with spreadsheets, for example, will have a better understanding of the various commands and functions in the program than someone who uses it only occasionally or only when called upon to fix a particular problem.

When someone in your company demonstrates a particular competency with an application, I see nothing wrong in using that ability to help when another user is faltering. Informal technical support structures will always develop when someone is recognized as having skills within an organization. Questions will fly back and forth between cubicles, and confounded users usually seek answers from a neighbor first. This makes sense, since others in their department are probably using the same tools to perform the same functions. It is also easier to get a quick answer from the next office than have to deal with the Help Desk, no matter how efficient it is.

In the same manner that you cultivate support ideas from the sticky notes of the Click-a-Phobe, it is sound policy to rely on the experience of the Power User. They often are the ones who have already figured out all the menus and "gotchas" of programs. Invite them to contribute to the support of other users by compiling hints and answers to typical questions. In some organizations, these users naturally become the first line of contact for all support problems. A local resource person is quicker and more attuned to the needs of his or her peers than a centralized IT. In later chapters I will discuss the type of relationship you may want to develop with the Power User, but for now you can see the possibilities for this level of user to make your job easier.

Problems with the Sophisticated User

Not everything about the Power User is so great, however. While they may indeed have significant skills in particular fields, they sometimes assume that they have more expertise in other areas than they actually do. Several years ago I supported a large group of software developers. My supervisor warned me that although the programmers were experts in C++, they might wrongly assume that they had equal skills in networking and system configuration. This prediction was absolutely correct. I spent too many hours recovering data lost due to inadvertent erasure, fixing systems that wouldn't boot because of haphazard device driver installation, and reconfiguring systems that could no longer access the network because of changes that had been made to their configuration files.

These Power Users had simply bit off more than they could chew. I made it a point to remind them that each of us had particular skills and we should complement each other's abilities. Look to resolve these types of situations by clearly defining the areas over which you should have the ultimate authority. In this case, I simply requested to have control over only those files and settings that enabled the users to access the network servers and printers. If those capabilities were ensured, then I cared little about what else was changed on the computer. This type of compromise worked very well. I was confident that everyone could use the central resources that I administered, and the programmers enjoyed the freedom to tweak the rest of their machines to whatever degree they wanted. It is important to note that this compromise was worked out with the programmers' own boss. Policy is much easier to make and implement when those in charge get fully behind it.

Watch Out for Conflicts

If anyone questions your methods and network configuration, it is sure to be one of the Power Users. In past jobs they may have been network administrators themselves or worked in computing environments vastly different from what you are supporting. Comparisons are inevitable as the various merits of UNIX versus Novell NetWare versus Microsoft NT Server are debated between you and the Power User. Conflict can ensue if they confront you with reasons why their networks would be superior to what is currently in use.

Your response to this type of provocation requires wisdom and patience. You could be confrontational, explaining to the user that it is your responsibility to manage the network and so there is an inherent need for you to make all the decisions in its design. This is a legitimate tactic to apply in this situation, but remember that listening is sometimes the best way to learn. Ask for detailed suggestions and configuration settings and make a diligent effort to study them. Perhaps this strategy will yield some solid solutions and make your job easier. It will sometimes help to involve the Power User in the growth of the network.

Ultimately, be sure to strengthen the communication between you and the Power User. In many companies, Power Users behave as consultants to the company leadership. Their opinions can have a great deal of influence because their level of skill garners a great deal of respect.

IT REALLY HAPPENED: A large number of users on my network were suddenly failing to get their hard disks recognized during the nightly back up. My examination revealed that they had made some major modifications to their config.sys and autoexec.bat files for the sake of some minor utility program. Of course, they made no mention of this installation to me before doing it. The users simply assumed that they knew exactly what they were doing. If some simple testing had been done beforehand, we could have avoided the backup failures.

The Big Bosses and their Minions

Every company has an elite group of decision-makers and their immediate support staff, and IT managers use a different set of rules when handling their problems. It is no surprise that these people should expect and receive a higher level of attention than everyone else. This is not simply because they preside over entire companies and divisions; they don't deserve special treatment just because they are the ones signing the paychecks. In a nutshell, it is precisely these users that require the most timely access to data. Since the actions that they take in response to data guides how the business operates, it is vital for IT to maintain their ability to gather and process data. If the IT staff caters to the vital organs of a company first, the rank-and-file employees who form the limbs of the organization will be clearly directed toward common goals.

Good bosses will recognize that their needs are sometimes not as critical as those of the people who work for them. Intelligent leaders recognize that they can wait for a memory upgrade or similar service if an entry-level worker in Order Processing has a dead monitor. They may also recognize that their assistants require more powerful computers than the ones at their own desks. It makes little sense to provide the CEO with the fastest computer on the planet if all they do is send email and browse the Web. This is true especially if their secretaries handle large spreadsheets and databases yet suffer with a system that is slow and antiquated.

The Importance of a Good Relationship

The most critical goal for any IT specialist when dealing with Big Bosses is to make them your ally. Remember that you are developing policies for delivering service and support to an entire company. Without the backing from the top for your ideas and approach, it becomes rather difficult to achieve significant implementation of your plans. Again, communication is a key ingredient for success. Make every effort to learn exactly what issues are most critical to the company's leaders, and plan to address these concerns head on. In return, impress on your bosses the need for them to support your efforts in every way possible. You'll have a much easier time dealing with Demanders and other difficult users if your methods for handling requests are blessed from the very top levels of an organization. Imagine how much easier it would be, both personally and professionally, if a frustrated user's ire were directed not at you but at a centrally created policy requiring that specific steps be followed when IT service is requested.

Another point to remember is that you may often find it difficult to deal directly with certain people in highly visible positions. Their time is precious and it may be hard for them to sacrifice the time to help you solve computer problems. Frequently, it is the executive's aide who takes responsibility for handling issues with the boss's system.

Data Bosses

While it may be easy to identify company leaders based on title and office size or location, there are also folks at other levels who should be given the same level of attention. There are numerous people in any organization whose work is critical to the function of many others. I call these people the Data Bosses, a special subset of the Big Boss user classification. The efforts of the shipping clerk or receptionist, among the lowest-paid workers, are often vital to the entire company's functioning. Learn who these key people are and develop techniques to handle their critical system needs.

Special User Roles

IT staff must not treat users simply as people that require support. It is vital to form interactive partnerships between IT and company system users. Power Users and others can fulfill important duties as liaisons in a variety of ways.

There must be someone from within the user community that can be relied on to assist in the testing and evaluation of new products. Developing documentation, including user guides and help files, is much more effective when done in conjunction with those who rely on them. Front-line technical support is often handled best by designated individuals within departments. New user orientations can be most efficient when done with a buddy system.

IT specialists must also encourage feedback and establish systems to gather comments and suggestions. In order for the systems that you design to grow and evolve, you must have strong involvement with your users. In the next two chapters, I will explain the many formal and informal ways that this interchange of ideas and actions can be optimized.

UNDERSTANDING USER RELATIONSHIPS

While it may be convenient to think of users as distinct entities, each with their own abilities and needs, it is also important to characterize them in terms of corporate hierarchy and organization. It is critical to envision users and their data not as isolated units, but rather as a web of connected nodes and responsibilities. Appreciating how each member of an organization interacts with others will enable you to design more robust support systems to address problems that affect a cross-section of people and departments, rather than resolving them in a piecemeal fashion.

See How Data Gets Shared

In the same manner that you might examine TCP/IP traffic within a LAN with a Trace Route utility, the savvy IT specialist will determine how data is moved about within a company. You need to learn who shares data with others and in what manner this communication takes place. Remember that there are myriad ways to communicate data. Sneaker-Net trafficking, in which floppy disks are passed back and forth, is an ancient and still practiced method. Shared network drives, email, Notes servers, and many other sophisticated products are designed specifically to enable groups of users to work together. Whatever methods are employed, learning what they are and how they are used will be necessary not just so you can provide support but also so you can optimize and streamline the lines of communication. While it may seem adequate to take care of existing data transmission structures, you should always look for ways to improve them and make your users more efficient.

Place Users into Groups

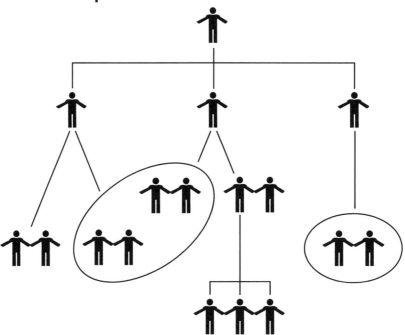

There are several reasons for placing users into groups. One obvious purpose is to organize email distribution lists and server access. A more subtle benefit, understanding which people share information and how they do it, can prevent real problems from occurring. Imagine what would happen if an upgrade to a word processing program suddenly prevented certain people from sharing files.

Having a complete understanding of how informal groups work together is just as important as recognizing more formal structures.

There are some simple methods you can use to clump users into larger groups. The most apparent ones are job function and departmental relationship. People performing similar tasks and working in the same department form a natural group and will typically require access to the same applications and network resources. Job titles and corporate organizational charts can be ready resources for determining which users should be treated as a unit.

Groups of users are often spread between various departments. While they may not work for the same manager, the nature of their work requires that they share data and common applications. For example, a sales force needs access to inventory data, as will those in Purchasing, Shipping, and Marketing. Providing consistent access for the many departments involved in a common task will make supporting the disparate users easier.

Watch Out for Sibling Rivalry

Whenever there are groups of users in the same job category, there will be two trends that you must be aware of. The first is that they will each view other's systems with envy if there are differences between them. While it may seem petty to compare screen size and megahertz ratings, users are notorious for making these distinctions and drawing inferences from them. Schoolchildren who have the 48-color box of crayons will always be envious of the kids with the more elaborate 64-color box. I am convinced that human nature changes little as we reach adulthood, except that the measurement changes from how many crayons we have to how much RAM is in our computers. There is probably little that you can do to change certain users' perceptions, but be aware of the problem and make every effort to address these types of concerns when they are raised.

Make it a point to listen to a user who expresses a need for a faster system or a larger display. Perhaps they have just assumed a new or more time-sensitive responsibility that would benefit from a more potent computer. Beleaguered users often call upon IT to be their advocate if they are saddled with obsolete or inadequate equipment that their own department is unwilling or incapable of upgrading. Sometimes you just need to offer a sympathetic ear as users vent their frustration.

Depending on your role in budgeting and requisitions, you should always make purchasing decisions that reflect the most obvious needs. Your opinion is vital to identify users most in need of newer systems. If IT only has advisory power, make sure to bring your observations to those who control the purse strings.

There often is a legitimate complaint when someone notices that another person in the same job position has a much more capable computer. While I don't advocate upgrading a system simply because someone feels slighted, it does make sense to create policies that address this issue. The simple solution is to always look to bring the slowest and oldest machines up to modern specifications first. More RAM or a bigger, faster drive will often bring more performance to older computers at a fairly modest cost. However, the most important consideration is whether or not the system is up to the task at hand. If the computer is indeed not capable of doing the job, then the user's gripe is legitimate.

A USER'S BILL OF RIGHTS

I firmly believe that it is the responsibility of IT specialists to be aware of what every user they support should expect from them. Chapter 7 will examine IT department structure, the different types of positions, and the responsibilities that come with each job description. However, no matter what type of function you perform in your company, remember that your main goal must be satisfying the needs of those who depend on technology.

Throughout my professional life, I have striven to understand the problems and expectations of those I support. Based on my own experiences and extensive feedback from my users, I have developed what I call a User's Bill of Rights. While I don't expect that all IT specialists will pin this list on the wall, I know that you will be much more effective if you at least study and guide your efforts by these guidelines.

1. Problems with systems should be handled in a quick and timely manner.

2. "Break and fix" is only half the job.

3. Users are always treated with respect.

4. Support staff should listen carefully to complaints.

5. Suggestions for services are carefully considered.

6. Service calls are never closed until the client is satisfied.

7. Explanations of what work was done should be offered.

8. Support staff must respect the deadlines of those they are supporting.

9. Plans for disruptive work should be broadcast well in advance.

10. Alternate solutions must be considered.

Handle All Systems Problems in a Quick and Timely Manner

Nothing is more frustrating than sitting in front of a dead computer and waiting for help to arrive. Even if the person reporting a problem cannot be helped immediately, she should at least be given a call and told where she is in the support queue. Specific goals for answering calls should be made known to the user community, and efforts to improve response times should be made if support staff fails to meet them.

Remember—Break and Fix Is Only Half the Job

"Break and fix" is the primary way that many support departments focus their efforts. After a computer is delivered to a user, that is the end of the interaction between IT and the system user until something breaks. A much better method is one in which users are shown the tools and techniques of keeping their system healthy. Automatic software Wizards that defragment hard drives, scan for viruses, update drivers, and report system status are all wonderfully proactive tools that not only make end users' systems more reliable, but reduce support calls as well.

It is certainly vital that broken systems be returned to health quickly and efficiently. However, if you limit the interaction between IT and users to only this type of scenario, then you are not providing all of the support that should be given. As I explained earlier, you should enable your users to better understand and control their computers. Alerting them to some simple operating system functions will help them keep their own systems in top shape.

Always Treat Users with Respect

While this rule seems like common sense, users often complain that tech support people treat them with an air of superiority and disdain. Consider that the person experiencing a problem may at first think that they themselves are the cause of the problem. Often this is indeed the case. No matter how well trained and experienced they are, people can create problems by simply forgetting a step or entering the wrong command. Treating this like a normal everyday occurrence is precisely the way it should be handled.

Even when the problem is simple and solved quickly, spend a few extra moments to ask if anything else is the matter. Many times, there is another issue that did not prompt a call for help but that does indeed vex the user. Address that issue now and neither of you will feel like it was a wasted trip. Look upon every contact with the people you support as a precious opportunity for users to learn more efficient ways to use their computers and for you to learn more about the people you support and the tasks they do.

Listen Carefully to Users' Complaints

When you respond to a call for support, make an effort to listen to exactly what the problem is before plunging in and banging away at the keyboard. First of all, you can't always assume you know what the situation is based solely on a support call. Allow the user to demonstrate what caused her to request help and make every effort to trace the steps that she takes. Ask before closing down applications and saving file changes. Always remember that you are working on someone else's system. Frustration with applications and balky networks will fray anyone's nerves.

Allow people to blow off some steam and understand that you will be an easy target. Part of the job description for every IT support specialist is being a patient listener. On the other hand, you shouldn't accept abuse. If the situation gets heated, calmly remind the user that you are there to help.

Carefully Consider All Suggestions for Improving Services

I've often heard comments about how applications should behave from users frustrated with cumbersome menus and cryptic error messages. Since your ultimate goal is to make programs easier to use and support less necessary, make an effort to listen to such suggestions and to record them for future consideration. While it may be impractical to make changes when responding to a service call, collect user comments and see what can be done to improve the systems in use. Communication of this type is easy and really goes a long way in helping support staff to understand what users want from their applications.

Never Close a Service Call Unless the Client Is Satisfied

Perhaps nothing upsets people more than being told that their problems have been satisfactorily dealt with when the opposite is true. IT support specialists should never close out a service call until the user who logged the complaint is satisfied. Often all that is required is a simple follow-up call a short time after the repair has been rendered to verify that the problem has been rectified. This should be a standard quality check for IT managers as well. Check with some of the clients that your department helped and see how well the problem was handled. This is an opportunity to improve service and strongly illustrates how seriously user complaints are taken.

Always Explain What Sort of Work You've Done

There are several reasons to explain exactly what is being done to someone's system during a service call. The most obvious is to educate the user as to the extent of the problem and what methodology is being used to address it. Perhaps the user will retain some of the information and be able to handle a similar problem independently in the future. If another problem occurs and a different technician responds, the user may be able to relate what was done the previous time. I consider it a sound policy to educate those I am assisting as I fix their computers. While some people would rather take a break when work is being performed on their system, I usually ask them to stay and answer my questions about the specifics of their problem. This provides another opportunity to take care of any other problems not included in the original request.

Respect the Deadlines of Those You Support

One of the easiest ways to earn the disdain of users is to intrude on their work by forcing your work upon them. Of course, a completely dead system should be addressed quickly, but not all service calls are for nonfunctional equipment. Often, IT service calls are made to update programs or to install new applications. In most cases, every effort should be made to schedule work when it is least intrusive to the person getting the service and those who depend on that individual's work. Virtually all jobs have busier and slower periods that vary by the day, week, or month. Look for a time that works best for the people you take care of.

When an IT person is working on a client's machine, it can have the same impact as the computer being down or the worker absent. Taking users' schedules seriously will earn the IT department kudos for respecting the needs of the people they support. You must balance this need with the urgency of the work being performed and the estimated time that the work will require.

Broadcast Any Disruptive Repairs or Services Well in Advance

A corollary to the previous rule is that any planned outage in services for system upgrades or similar maintenance should be announced well in advance to all affected users. Providing such information will allow those you support to better plan their day to work around your projects. When a service advisory is issued that indicates that work will be done in only a few days, it will likely be taken as an edict and will be sure to raise the ire of those affected. Giving ample warning and a full explanation of the work will permit everyone to absorb the disruption in their schedules and minimize any impact.

Staffers in a well-run IT department should be aware of what days present the most concern for the other departments in the firm. The last days of a fiscal year or similar key dates should be red-flagged on every IT manager's calendar and never even considered for work that will interrupt system availability.

With any large corporate infrastructure, there are bound to be certain occasions when data services may be interrupted or threatened by a wide variety of factors. Loading patches on network operating systems, enhancing server hardware, upgrading computer room power, or installing new data communication lines can seriously limit network availability. All of these activities must be scheduled well in advance to ensure that IT and any contractors can coordinate the work effectively. Alert those you support of the dates and extensiveness of the work you are planning so they can voice any concerns with the schedule that you are considering. You may not want to modify your fax servers the same week that marketing is planning to launch a new campaign, for example.

Provide Alternate Solutions

It is inevitable that workstations and servers will suffer from breakage and other problems that render them unusable. While you may make every effort to repair and restore systems, there will be times that your efforts are not successful and nothing works correctly. IT must make a concerted effort to provide a backup solution for this type of situation. This can be as simple as keeping a spare system to loan to a user with a broken computer. In addition, IT should plan and test disaster recovery and similar systems before they are needed. This may require that extra equipment and services (such as ISP connections) be purchased and sit idle, but insurance of this type can be easily justified when the alternative is a total loss of productivity.

CHAPTER 4

Formal Support Structures

The "User's Bill of Rights" in Chapter 3 promotes an acceptable minimum standard for supporting individuals in your corporation. There are several levels of structure that need to be established in order for your company to meet that standard. IT is responsible for creating instructional documentation, providing technical support, and training users.

These areas are just as critical to maximizing the investment in technology at your company as the latest servers and hubs are. Building a solid foundation in these key fields will create a positive environment where users will thrive and IT can respond to problems efficiently and quickly.

FORMAL SUPPORT STRUCTURES

One of the biggest aids to providing client support is the development of resources and tools that permit the easy dissemination of instructional information and guidance to your users. Successful IT departments make every effort to provide all employees with detailed, step-by-step guides in a variety of formats. In conjunction with these tutorial materials, you must also maintain support systems that users can rely on whenever your instructions are unclear or something breaks. In addition, ongoing training should be offered, in a variety of formats, to build both users' competence and comfort with the equipment they use.

Some of these support structures should be familiar to most readers of this book. Corporate help desk and training centers are common, but like any tool, they must be used correctly and maintained to ensure their effectiveness. There are also some terrific strategies that are not widely used which address many of the challenges that IT managers grapple with daily.

Reading this chapter will reinforce what should be the most important elements of your technical support infrastructure. Securing a solid support foundation will allow you the freedom to pursue new projects and build on the investment your company has made in technology. It is almost impossible to make your network better if most of your time is spent redoing the same jobs in a wasteful manner.

The guidelines to follow when building these solutions are rather clear. First, you must determine what information and instructions should be documented for every user interaction with the systems you support. There are many ways to present this data. Second, there must be assurances that technical support structures are tailored to meet the demands of the users. Lastly, training should be provided on both core competencies and subjects that expand users' capabilities.

Getting New Hires Started

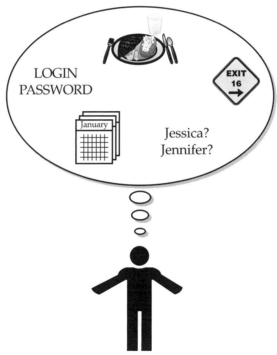

One of the best ways to identify all the information necessary to understand, support, and instruct in the use of your network is to appreciate the needs of newly hired employees. If you can satisfy all of their needs, then you can certainly support everyone else in your company. Try to anticipate all of the details a new employee will need to learn in order to effectively contribute to their department.

Common to any company is the constant flow of new hires and transfers. Each is saddled with the same problems. In order to be effective, they must assimilate a great deal of information. While existing skills in the use of particular programs or network operating systems are usually helpful, every network will have its own unique personality.

People have to quickly learn the use of corporate email, directory structures, login procedures, and proprietary applications. This information has to compete with the new employee's struggle to learn names, directions to the nearest mall, and how to use the mammoth copier down the hall. Taking care of the needs of people at this time of transition can easily consume an inordinate amount of your attention.

Share the Load

Rather than shoulder the entire burden, it makes sense to share responsibility for orienting new employees with the department that they work for. Partnering in this way enables the department to develop a better employee faster and also helps you understand what that particular department does. There are some things that the IT department can handle best by itself, but your most important job involves building solutions that meet the demands of those you support.

As I discussed in Chapter 3, there are certain special users who can act as liaisons for IT. People already within the department should be familiar with all the applications and procedures that a new hire will need to know how to use to be effective. By combining their experience with IT's documentation and training, you can take an effective team approach to making the new hire comfortable and productive.

Setting Up a Buddy System

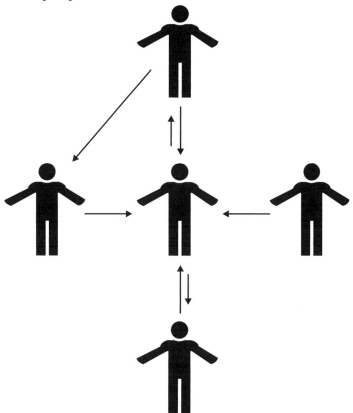

One of the easiest and most effective plans to implement is the buddy system. Simply request that someone in the department familiar with the operation of the network be assigned as the first line of contact for the new hire. As I stated in Chapter 3, when considering groups of users, you will likely find them all sharing the same general setup and applications. It's those coworkers who are most familiar with all the specifics of computer use for their jobs.

The buddy should be able to quickly outline the various procedures that are in daily use. Even the most astute IT specialist will never be as familiar with a particular department's environment as its users are. Each work unit will have unique responsibilities and will exploit specific features of your network and applications.

In the next chapter, we will examine the importance and structure of the relationships between IT and corporate organizations. I strongly emphasize the need to assign a technical liaison who can elucidate the needs of individual departments as well as functioning as a single contact point for the IT staff to communicate with. The buddy system is one example of this relationship.

New Hires and Their Buddies

One of the most effective strategies is to allow new hires to work closely with their buddies during the first day on the job. This is a critical period, because everything is new to them and they'll be asking the most questions. Allowing the buddy to demonstrate typical procedures on a one-on-one basis can be the fastest way for a new employee to learn how their department gets its work done.

Even after the initial period of adjustment is over, there are bound to be additional problems that will arise in the first few weeks of employment. Having a departmental liaison provides a safety net for IT and adds to the new user's sense of security. Being able to turn to someone nearby for assistance with chores like printing, email, and application use is often the fastest way for a new employee to get their questions answered.

Train the Buddy

It is no small responsibility to be a buddy for a department. Aside from the commitment of time, the buddy has to be willing to act as a technical support person when that role is not their primary responsibility. IT must be careful to cultivate an environment of mutual assistance. Users in a department get faster access to help, buddies gain valuable experience, and IT benefits from a virtual expansion of staff.

NOTE: You do not want a situation in which the buddy is perceived as a proxy for others who should bear the brunt of support. IT must retain the ultimate responsibility for providing assistance.

While the designated buddy may be talented and eager, be sure to remain aware of their efforts. Work with their managers to ensure that buddies are not being saddled with additional work that detracts from their primary functions. There certainly should be active quality controls to verify the effectiveness of this arrangement at your company.

TIP: See if you can get several people to be the buddy for a department. It is good to rotate the responsibility and not burden a single person with the job. You also gain exposure to different perspectives and abilities.

Set Clear Limits

Make sure that there are clearly demarcated levels of responsibility for the buddy and IT. There must be limits on the length of time that the buddy can be called upon by the new hire for questions. Create and enforce a policy that dictates a reasonable yet flexible commitment on the part of the buddy. While the policy should not be confining, it should be reasonable enough so that the buddy can perform his or her own work without being constrained by time-consuming hand-holding chores.

While each company is different, there are some subjects that are sure to be common to most networks. Make sure that your designated buddy and the IT department are prepared to address them, and you will be well on your way to getting new hires off on the right foot.

TIP: Everything that you encounter should be recorded in detail. The documentation that is created will be key to providing technical support in the future. It makes sense if both those you support and members of the IT department can refer to the same instructions and setups when tackling problems.

Documenting Procedures

Creating documentation can be a complex and time-consuming undertaking. IT needs to account for all of the steps a user will take to perform a particular task. Breaking each interaction with the systems you support into modules will greatly ease this job. Try to identify the most common or critical procedures used in each department and record the steps needed to complete them. A modular approach makes future updates or additions easier to make. All of the information that you create should be used to create system user guides and corresponding support materials for IT.

Login Procedures

The first task faced by any user when sitting in front of their keyboard each morning is a successful login to the network. Like a well-choreographed dance, every step needs to be done in correct order for the user to have access to the necessary resources for their job. There have been numerous occasions in my career when a reported problem with printing or a failure to receive email was simply due to the user having logged in improperly.

Each step should be recorded and added into your master guide for system use. Screen shots of typical login sessions are a great visual addition to these materials. At a minimum, show where and when the username and password should be entered. If your network has elaborate login scripts and displays informational messages when a user attaches to servers and print queues, provide some clues so the user can interpret the results.

Be sure to highlight typical error messages and methods for overcoming them in your documentation. Password expiration warnings, disk quota limits, and other problems should be outlined, along with the appropriate solutions for each problem detailed. By highlighting steps that users can take to recover from a problem, you help reduce support calls to IT and create a more self-sufficient body of users.

UNIFIED DIRECTORY MODES   It is not uncommon to find networks that require separate logins for access to file/print servers and email. Since this creates both frustration for your users and an additional administrative chore for IT, you should look to adopt products that permit single sign-on. This technology allows authentication of accounts across your entire infrastructure from a single point.

Novell NetWare's NDS is a popular choice, merging the management of user accounts in NetWare-centric environments. Microsoft's competing scheme, known as Active Directory, provides the same functionality. Be aware that various vendor products may not be compliant with all directory management systems.

Printer Configuration

Be sure to note the memory size, paper-handling capabilities, and default print job setup. Also check network print queue assignments. Different queues will affect print job priority, and these are not always uniform within the same department. Be aware that some departments may have special output devices that require some extra instruction time. Large pen plotters, digital image setters, and solid modeling equipment often require precise setup information to operate correctly. Since these are most often used by entire workgroups inadvertent errors in usage by one user can cause the device to fail for everyone. Coping with interruptions to these expensive devices should be avoided.

Your documentation must show how a user can check printer queues for print job status. If appropriate, detail the steps for selecting special printer features, such as specific paper trays or output sorting options. Point out the method for selecting an alternate printer so that users can still be productive if the primary printer fails.

You may also want to add instructions for adding paper or toner to departmental printers. Simple maintenance tasks should not require a call to IT and are often handled quickest by those who use the printer daily. On the other hand, critical printer errors that sometimes appear on status displays may require more than just casual user intervention. Include information on these in your documentation to help prevent well intentioned but pointless efforts by users to fix things themselves. Highlight what these errors may show and, more importantly, direct users to the appropriate contact methods when IT must be reached.

Application Use

While there may be corporate standards that control the variety of software programs installed, every department will exploit different features of a given application. Integrated office software suites, such as the many flavors of Microsoft Office, Corel WordPerfect, Star Office, Linux Office Suite, and Lotus Smart Suite, contain a dizzying array of programs. It is not uncommon to see one group heavily involved with spreadsheets and another with Web publishing. There are various types of computer use throughout a company, and knowing which are the most typical will allow you to develop better support tools.

Knowing how the applications are used, you should emphasize particular features in your support and training. Word processors can be utilized to create simple memos or complex online documents. Don't obfuscate when creating user guides; concentrate on the tools most often required by the majority of your company's employees.

Server Usage

Find out which network directories and specific servers are in use. Make use of the documentation described in Chapter 2. IT specialists should be able to consult their own records for this information. However, since network drive usage is always changing, be sure to periodically check with your users for changes.

Shared network storage locations are regularly generated to account for new projects or to reflect calendar dates. It makes sense to designate new directories to handle work related to your latest projects, thus avoiding any confusion with existing files. Calendar dates are often embedded in directory names to mirror when the stored files were created.

Users are apt to create directories on servers for others. While IT specialists may desire to control server access rights and reserve directory creation for themselves, this can be a cumbersome and inefficient use of resources. As I stated in the previous chapter, the best way to handle this situation is to devise a logical naming convention for directories and make every effort to publicize and enforce its use.

You can often create and consult user templates or profiles that outline the common elements of users in a particular group. Login scripts, directory access rights, and printer queue and security permissions are typically shared by most people in the same department. Consulting with these guidelines makes account creation less error-prone and reduces the number of support calls to address problems with network access.

Email Assignments

When adding new users, it is important to place them on all the appropriate mail groups. Large companies can have extremely complex mailing lists, which makes additions or deletions an arduous task. Moving a user from one group to another is equally daunting. Use the profile for a representative within the same department and job assignment as a template for creating the correct email groupings.

Custom or Vertical Product Solutions

Many specialized and highly customized vertical market software systems are used in today's businesses. Inventory management, sales, and customer service applications are often designed to meet specific company requirements. These are especially troublesome to support if they involve legacy equipment, unusual interfaces, or highly customized access methods.

Many companies continue to rely on homegrown applications written when MS-DOS was the prevalent operating system and graphical user interfaces were virtually unknown on most computers.

These programs often rely heavily on CONTROL and ALT key combinations, and learning how to use them is a study in repetition and careful consultation with documentation. Many older systems are still retained due to the tremendous investment in equipment and the high cost of converting to modern hardware and software.

Network Orientation

If the new hire is reasonably computer savvy, all that he or she may require is a simple introduction to your network. Clearly demonstrate where printers and other shared resources are located and can be used. Explain corporate security and email policies and prepare handouts that spell them out clearly. Pictured in Figure 4-1 is an example of the email guidelines I've used at several locations.

XYZ Corporate Email Policy

This document is a statement of accepted policy for the use of our email system. Please familiarize yourself with the guidelines.

1. Email is expressively designed only for communication within XYZ Corporation and our customers. Sending messages for other purposes is strictly forbidden.

2. Refrain from the use of abusive or profane language.

3. Don't "reply to all" when responding to a message unless absolutely necessary. Sending out dozens of unneeded messages will only clog up mail server storage and slow down the network!

4. Avoid the sending of attachments! Report any virus warnings from your antiviral scanners to the IT Department immediately.

Some quick tips:

To send a fax message, click on Fax in the To field and follow the prompts.

Your Internet email address is rendered as follows: Firstname_Lastname@XYZCORP.COM

Help for all mail program functions can be reached on the XYZCorp intranet site. Click on the Mail Help button on the Help Files pages.

For additional questions, send an email to MailHelp@XYZCorp

Figure 4-1. Sample Corporate Email Policy

As I've stated before, users on any network tend to struggle with the same problems. Access to shared data resources, printing problems, and routing tasks like logging in can all be areas of extreme frustration and lost productivity. Be proactive, demonstrating correct procedures and providing detailed print or online instructions, to ease the new employee's transition to your work environment. Laying out the ground rules first will pay off with fewer support calls and more confident users.

Working with the HR Department

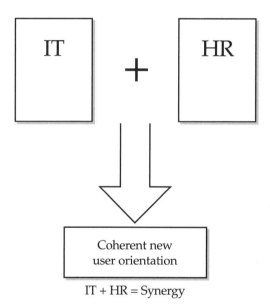

IT + HR = Synergy

The Human Resources department should be consulted and vigorously lobbied to support the institution of a buddy system where you work. Departments can be asked to rotate assignments for the buddy position or request volunteers to fill the role. Of course, certain personalities and temperaments are better suited for this responsibility. With the innumerable questions that new hires invariably have, it makes sense to promote a structured response to this need. Local knowledge of ones peers is useful for both IT questions and ones that involve finding coffee in the morning. The same people who know which email groups to address reports to will also know where the closest donut shop is.

There are certainly advantages for the designated buddy. This is an opportunity for them to become more involved and learn about computers and networking. They may become critical members of decision-making groups that evaluate and purchase new technical solutions for their departments. These people are not necessarily Power Users; rather they are the ones who can most effectively translate their department's needs and computer use patterns to IT department staff.

Designated buddies get special computer training and status, which can be a compelling reason for them to take on the responsibility. They are the ones who the IT department depends on to communicate the function and needs of a particular workgroup. The buddy is trained to understand and manipulate the most common configuration settings and application commands. In a sense, the buddy may become a field representative for the IT department, creating a symbiotic relationship that can be extremely beneficial for everyone. However, never allow a buddy to shoulder the burden that rightly belongs on your shoulders.

Augment Corporate Information Packets

Most companies prepare elaborate reams of material that they distribute to new employees. Common to them are information on various benefits, stock purchase plans, health insurance, life insurance, and numerous other important topics. You should look to augment these handouts with instructions specific to your network.

Work with the various departments to make sure that information specific to the department the new hire will be working in is included. For example, outline the specific email groups that the particular user should be familiar with. As I've stated before, you want to equip those you support with all the tools they need to do their jobs effectively. Having instructional materials specific to their daily tasks makes everyone more productive and less apt to request help for routine matters.

New Hire Advisories

HR departments excel at making sure that new hire start dates are transmitted to payroll before the employee starts working. Alas, my experience has been that IT departments are often given little or no advance warning when a new person is starting. Impress upon your HR department the importance of passing this information to you as early as possible. New network accounts, equipment, and email lists will all have to be established and tested in order for them to work effectively.

Documentation for Users

There are several methods for making instructions readily available to those you support. The most common is the simple printed document. It can be readily reproduced, and many appreciate being able to thumb through papers at their leisure, not tethered by a computer keyboard and mouse. Screen shots that show dialog box settings and similar information are often very helpful.

Electronic hosting of files is increasingly popular. Documents can be distributed in Adobe Acrobat format so that complex graphics and text can be stored in small files with search capabilities. Intranet servers provide an excellent repository for this data as well. A quick and dirty approach is to simply dump copies of all your support documents in a designated network drive and grant everybody read-only access to them.

Custom Help Files

Most operating systems and application programs permit creation of and access to help files without relying on external resources. In other words, you can document information on a particular use or feature by using standard Windows .HLP or application-specific HTML help files or a format common to your operating system.

You can create help files with a simple text editor such as Macintosh Simple Text or Windows Notepad. These files permit the user to access company-designed documentation that relates precisely to their particular duties. Designate a specific network location to centralize these help files for employee use. Create a shortcut, Web page link, or drive mapping that permits easy access to this data.

Using an Intranet Server

Many companies now use hyperlinked HTML pages to create unique help files. The company intranet server is an ideal candidate to host this information. Create files that cover all your programs and resources. You may also create a special Help link on the corporate intranet server that opens a Web page with a multitude of other help file links.

You can augment your help files with additional links to vendor Web sites. Encourage your users to seek help directly from vendors' support servers. Make the links directly to the support sections of the Web sites to avoid excessive browsing by your users. Be sure to update your links as vendor sites change or become available. Users can also be encouraged to maintain their own private list of bookmarks to access useful sites.

Remember that the content on Web servers does not have to be static text files. Companies rely on streaming media players like Microsoft NetShow, Real Networks Real Player, and Apple QuickTime to combine audio and visual information. Presentation software such as PowerPoint can also be used effectively.

Creating Content

Training or documentation materials can be presented in a wide variety of formats. Traditional print materials have been supplanted with Internet-based solutions. While some may argue that the snazzy and modern approach of Web-based training is the best way to go, traditional methods still have their merits. Paper-based manuals allow the reader to make comments in the margins and don't require the user to be sitting in front of a computer to access the material.

Virtually any competent word processor can be used to produce satisfactory user training guides. Using a screen-capture program like HiJack, you can create high-quality materials that include pictures of all the different screens a user will encounter as they navigate through your system. Printing and binding of these materials can be a simple staple in the corner or a more elaborate effort that includes fancy binders and indexes. The amount of time you can devote to the project and your budget, artistic ability, and intended audience will influence the nature of your documents.

If the IT staff is generating their own HTML content for distribution on corporate WWW servers, then they need to be familiar with the tools for creating usable help files. Fortunately, there are numerous tools available for easily authoring Web documents for viewing in a browser.

One simple approach would be to use a product like Microsoft FrontPage to create Web pages. Its close integration with MS Internet Information Server and similarity to familiar products like MS Word promise a short learning curve and easy publishing. Freeware and shareware offerings are also available and produce similar results.

More sophisticated presentations that include features like intense multimedia effects require more powerful tools. Macromedia's Authorware and Director are very popular for the creation of Web sites. The Shockwave browser plug-in is a great way to integrate video clips on your Web pages.

Real Networks G2 Producer is a wonderful way to develop streaming video or audio content. IT departments can create training materials that include active displays showing actual program operations, not just passive screen shots. Combining screen images with narration can make for some powerful lessons.

There are also products specially designed for the generation of training materials. MicroMedium Trainer Professional can create lessons for distribution on corporate intranets or CD-ROMs. Asymetrix Learning Systems ToolBook line of products can be combined with their Librarian application to provide centralized control of a corporation's online educational materials.

The entire field of "distance learning" has been going through an explosion of growth fueled by the rise of Internet technologies. Web-based training is an attractive way to bring information to users through their browsers.

HELP DESKS

In many companies, the first line of formal contact between users and the IT organization supporting them is the corporate help desk. The help desk may be called on to simply catalog and submit technical requests to the appropriate support staffer's job queue. More elaborate schemes include problem resolution as an intrinsic function of the help desk. Whatever platform your company uses, its proper operation is vital to ensuring prompt and accurate support.

Your help desk can be dependent on elaborate call management systems purchased from systems integrators or a homegrown solution built with off-the-shelf products. Many companies will outsource some or even all of their help desk operations in order to concentrate their precious IT resources on specific issues. Providing direct telephone support is an intensive, and thus expensive, activity.

Companies and their IT department philosophies vary. Chapter 6 details how IT departments interact with the corporations they support. Chapter 7 explores how IT departments should be constructed to meet various needs. I hesitate to recommend a single "best" strategy, because I doubt that one can be found. It is important to tailor a whole range of solutions to meet the diverse needs of your users. The most successful support strategies call for maintaining a mix of approaches, each geared to specific groups of users.

It may be impossible to contract with vendors to support custom applications that have been designed in-house. Companies that rely on common off-the-shelf programs will find a large number of suppliers willing to provide services to your users. While certain environments are well served by strictly telephone support, others demand that direct hand-holding be done for anyone with a problem. A careful review of the requirements of your users and their expectations for support must be balanced with the possible support scenarios and budget limitations.

Attitude

The single most important quality, after technical competence, for the person handling support calls is the right attitude. You must be prepared to deal with people in states of despair or panic as critical files are lost or their system misbehaves. Being able to offer a calm and compassionate tone while absorbing the nature of the problem requires patience and a thick skin. Telephone support agents are often targets of the pent-up frustration and anxiety of vexed users.

While some IT specialists find a great deal of satisfaction with helping people with problems, it can be a stressful job. No one ever calls a support line to register kudos and compliments on a server that never crashes. Be sure that those handling calls in your organization are placed in an environment where they can blow off some of the steam they accumulate and that they can relax periodically.

The Check-Back

No matter which type of help desk system your company uses, it is critical that you ensure that users are satisfied with the resolution of problems. Rating your help desk on the total number of calls handled is meaningless unless you can prove that each call taken has indeed fixed the problem that prompted it.

WARNING: Never permit the closing of support calls to be made immediately following an interaction between the user and support person. Allow some time to pass before declaring that a problem is indeed rectified. Certain issues that appear fixed will only resurface again after a computer is rebooted.

For all support calls, institute a mandatory check-back with the person placing the help request. Even when a user reports that a problem has been resolved at the point of contact with the IT support person, make it a habit to verify the resolution at a later time. I've often "fixed" computers only to discover later that an error had returned. It is a sound policy for the support technician to call a few hours later or the next day.

I always caution those I support that there are many ways to fix computer problems. I try to adjust the most likely setting or install an upgrade that I think will solve the error, but it is not always the first attempt that fixes a balky system. Alerting users to the uncertainty of some repair techniques and promising to verify that the repairs are indeed working will allay apprehension if a user's problem returns.

Don't forget that your own satisfaction with a program's operation or a system's configuration may not mirror what your user experiences. While they may cause their own crashes with incorrect usage, users are likely to encounter situations that the IT specialist will not experience.

IT REALLY HAPPENED: A group of QuarkXPress users in an editorial layout department were upgraded to new Number Nine video cards and Windows 95. Everything seemed to work well, and I assumed that everyone was happy. Only during a routine walk in their area several days later did I hear a complaint that page layout grid lines would disappear from their displays at high resolutions. The video cards were installed using an 800x600 display size and the users had later reset the cards to 1024x768. While it would have been easy for me to insist that they stick with the lower resolution, it would be better if I found a fix to their problem. I installed a generic S3 graphic chip driver from a CompuServe support forum and everything worked perfectly.

Escalation

There must a clear policy of problem escalation if the help desk worker cannot rectify the situation. Not every issue can be resolved by a phone call. Systems that have died in a puff of smoke will demand hands-on replacement of failed components.

Certain problems will likely lie beyond the scope of materials that the help desk relies on. New software and hardware products take time to be added to the database of supported products. Also, the issues raised with the use of recently adopted items are likely to be unique and unanticipated. It takes time for bugs to be worked out and for support staff to become familiar with added features.

There are also users who are so flustered with the state of their computers that they are best served by face-to-face contact. It is pointless to attempt to work through problems over the telephone if the user is agitated or clearly nervous. Certain users are also faced with extreme deadline pressures, and their difficulties should be prioritized for immediate service. As I've stated before, you should be aware of the schedule under which groups and users operate and tailor your response accordingly.

IT departments in larger organizations generally have support specialists with different levels of experience and expertise. While an entry-level technician should be able to assist with printer setup and account password issues, more complex situations may call for the advanced help of IT specialists. As I advise in Chapter 7, when we discuss IT department organization, there should be a clearly defined chain of escalation that support personnel can follow if a problem is not easily solved.

Make sure that the affected user is informed that a problem is being escalated. There should be no shame for IT staff to admit that a situation is beyond their area of expertise. Modern medicine has many specialties available to handle specific illnesses. Today's networked corporation is equally dependent on specialists' abilities to handle the myriad complex technologies that exist.

Call Logging Only

The easiest help desk setup simply captures technical requests for later review by the IT department. A single email account or telephone mailbox can be established that all employees are instructed to use for all assistance messages. The email account and voicemail can be checked periodically and responses can be planned accordingly.

For smaller companies, this system can work well. With only a few requests for help being generated, it should be little trouble to sort issues and assign priorities. If the number of calls is manageable, then a single support specialist should be able to handle all the problems.

If the company grows and the IT department adds staff, there are two ways to control the increasing load. The first method is for all the calls to be screened by a single person who then assigns work to other staff members. Secondly, you can employ an honor system in which all of the IT specialists rotate checking the job queues. As soon as a support job is finished, the email and phone accounts are checked for new work.

INHERENT LIMITATIONS The most obvious shortcoming of this system is the difficulty of assigning a priority level to each submitted request. If the only way to reach a support specialist is to wait one's turn on a first-come, first-served basis, then real chaos can ensue. Imagine the frustration of a user who learns that someone who simply needed help formatting a floppy disk was helped before his or her completely dead machine was revived.

The honor system also presents the risk that only the quickest to solve problems will be attended to, because no one wants to take responsibility for the difficult ones. There is also the reality that a particular support person may not like everyone in your organization. You must make sure that these issues don't conflict with IT's primary responsibility to get the job done.

There is also the very real problem of a frustrated user slamming the phone down when reaching a machine. IT must clearly demonstrate that they will indeed respond promptly to calls or email if this system is to work. There is no faster way to sacrifice user respect than to ignore requests for help.

Call Logging and Assignment

A larger and more sophisticated help desk arrangement can capture each service request and then parcel out jobs to individual IT staff members. Assignments can be given in a variety of ways. Specific types of help should naturally be forwarded to those most capable or designated to handle them.

For example, a corporate network with many Windows PCs and relatively few Macintosh systems may designate a single individual to handle all Mac problems. Another support specialist may perform all modification and creation of network accounts, while another group may manage UNIX or AS/400-related issues. Application program problems may also be directed to a specific group of experts.

As with any call logging and assignment system, there must be careful attention to setting priorities. This requires an understanding of both the nature of the problem reported and the importance of the system and individual affected. Users that are most affected by deadlines or those who have many others depending on their work should be addressed first. Systems that are completely non-functional must be handled before those that suffer from a minor problem.

TIP: My manager once designed a three-tier rating for problem severity. The highest priority, Level 1, was assigned to any system that was unusable for any function. Level 2 calls were for situations in which a particular application or resource was faulty but the computer was still productive. Calls with a Level 3 designation typically were new application installations or other issues that did not involve loss of system functionality.

Call Logging and Attempted Problem Resolution

Certain help desk systems seek to have those taking support calls try to provide technical support directly to those making requests. This places those working on the help hotlines at the front line of support at your company. It requires a much more technically capable person than someone who just records and refers requests for assistance.

Companies that rely on this method usually have several tools at their disposal to maximize their support efforts. Support databases are available from a variety of vendors that can be searched for answers to common problems, driver updates, and numerous white papers. CD-ROM and Web-based products like Support On Site have proved valuable to me on numerous occasions.

While software programs have become more sophisticated, it seems that documentation has drastically shrunk. Help desks are an ideal candidate for the purchase of resource kits and other materials that expand on what comes with the programs you buy. There should be at least one full library of documentation available for everything a company is using. Books for hundreds of applications and operating systems are available. A well-stocked resource room is an invaluable tool for any help desk operation.

This type of effort may require that those answering the phone have access to the exact same software as those they support. It is obviously easier to tell a user what option to select if the support person can view the same screens the user is seeing. Standardization within a company will limit the number of applications on the help desk systems, but there are typically a few resource-hungry or expensive applications that may have to be installed on one machine that is shared by the entire help desk.

TIP: Make sure that your support materials are updated to reflect the constant upgrade cycle that applications follow. Keep close tabs on preinstalled software on newly delivered hardware and watch for purchase orders for program updates. Public beta introductions are a prime opportunity for IT to investigate upcoming products.

REMOTE CONTROL SOFTWARE

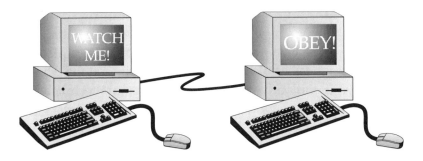

There are some programs that IT can use to take over direct control of another system remotely. Remote console programs permit full access to system resources from another computer connected via network or modem. CoSession for Windows and Timbuktu for the Macintosh are two examples of these applications.

Programs like these have an ideal niche for training and support settings, since they allow a confounded user to watch precisely what actions to take to perform a particular function. Remote console operators will usually have the option to disable keyboard and screen display on the end-user's remote computer if security-sensitive information needs to be used. Perhaps it is necessary to perform an action as a supervisor or root user; thus IT should shield the name and password data to prevent malicious use later.

Self-Help

Many companies have adopted a self-help model of technical support. In this environment, users' Web browsers or other client software is preset to access help files, drivers, and other information relevant to their systems. Essentially, people are provided the tools and basic instruction so they can first try resolving problems themselves. Here is a way to exploit your company's existing network to solve several challenges and take some of the strain off of valuable IT resources.

Users can be directed to various email addresses that handle a specific range of problems. These email addresses can be those of your own company's staff or of the support departments of hardware manufacturers and application software developers. For example, a user unable to use a particular feature of his Matrox G200 AGP graphic card adapter would be prompted to contact Matrox directly.

CONTRACTS FOR VENDOR SUPPORT   Most software companies sell premium support contracts that grant buyers the ability to contact product technical specialists for a given period of time or a certain number of incidents. This really makes sense for many critical and difficult-to-support products. Highly complex applications such as CAD/CAM and statistical packages require more subject knowledge than IT specialists are typically comfortable with. In a situation such as this, the IT specialist should invite the support of someone highly skilled in a particular area.

Managing and maintaining a stable computing environment is a demanding challenge, and mastering every application that your company uses is an almost impossible task. Support contracts can often be bundled with software upgrades during the contract period. Always consider this factor when considering the investment.

While bug fixes should be free, many vendors will only fix problems in their newest releases. Unlike cars, you are unlikely to see manufacturers recall older software and hardware systems for updates when problems are discovered. While patches and other updates are typically offered on numerous Web sites, the computer industry creates orphan products with every major release.

Outsourcing

Some companies outsource their entire help desk system. As with an internally developed and sustained call center, the scope of the outsourcer can vary widely. Support calls can be routed to a center that can handle simple logging and then either dispatch a technician or offer more detailed phone assistance in which the user is guided to a solution.

Information Services departments may find contracting with an outside vendor to be a very attractive scenario. Help desks are a very labor-intensive activity and the shortage of qualified support personnel makes adequate staffing a real challenge. While it fills a critical need, telephone technical support has never been seen as a glamorous or enriching job by many. Finding and keeping people in these positions is notoriously difficult.

Keep Your Identity

Many outsourcing solutions will dedicate a portion of their phone lines to your company specifically. Those answering support calls will identify themselves as being with the corporate help desk. This important distinction can only ease the anxiety a user feels if they sense that the one answering the telephone is not working for the same employer. This should be a fairly easy arrangement to make.

It may make sense to outsource only certain aspects of your help desk. You may wish to retain support only for certain applications, such as word processing and spreadsheets. Some companies can provide services such as collecting and assigning trouble tickets from users, while internal IT staff respond directly to all requests. A combination of services can be purchased for a limited time. For example, you may want to hire some temporary help to coincide with a physical relocation of workers and their computers or to anticipate heavy demand during peak times of the year for your particular business.

Feedback

You can only judge the effectiveness of any user support system—whether internal or external—if you actively seek feedback. Not only do you need to know if problems are being attended to in a timely manner, but the quality of the support given is even more important. A rapid response is useless if the computer system attended to remains inert or unstable. You need to learn which response systems are perceived to be the most reliable and easiest to use. This is the best way to modify and grow your help desk to address the demands placed on it. Figure 4-2 is a sample form that can be used to measure help desk abilities.

There also must be some way to gauge the effectiveness of those IT specialists actually doing the direct support work. Does anybody have a brusque telephone manner? Which one of your staff has the best command of operating systems, and who seems to have a knack for fixing printers? All of these questions can be answered by providing and soliciting input from the users at your company.

Never assume that an elaborate help desk management tool will automatically boost user confidence or satisfaction. Getting an

---

IT Department Feedback Form

You recently requested support services from the IT Department. As part of our constant effort to improve and gauge the effectiveness of our work, please take a few minutes to answer the following questions.

Name:
Department:

1. How did you contact support services?

| Email | Telephone | Printed |
| Request | Hotline | Form |

2. How long did IT take to resolve your problem?

Less than 1 hour   Within 4 hours   Next day   Still pending

3. Did you receive a call back checking repair status?

Yes   No

4. Please rate the quality of service rendered.

Excellent   Adequate   Poor

5. In the space below, please record any comments you have on IT services for this incident.

If you have any additional concerns or questions, please address them to the IT Client Service Manager at HelpManager@XYZCorp. All of your comments will be handled in confidence.

Figure 4-2.   Help Desk Feedback Form

automated email stating that a problem has been recorded and dispatched to a technician will give little comfort if the user waits for help that never comes or if the help fails to fix an error condition. Spending money on elaborate hardware and software may bring a perverse joy to any IT manager, but results are only measured by the satisfaction of the users in your care.

Random Surveys

It would be cumbersome and unnecessary to request feedback on every incident your staff responds to. Instead, institute a random sampling of closed technical support calls on a regular basis. Select a range of problems from a variety of departments. You should also make sure that various members of your support staff are represented. This type of information can be useful when making judgments on worker effectiveness.

Ask users if they were generally satisfied with the service received. Make sure to protect users' anonymity so that they can respond more openly. Users are often reluctant to be perceived as complainers. In addition, users' negative experiences with systems may affect managers' perception of their job performance. Certainly balky computers can affect productivity, and users suffer if their machines keep crashing.

Determine the average time it takes to get recognition of problems entered into your response system. How long does it take for a technician to be alerted to a user request and then to actually respond to it? Once contact between the support technician and the user has taken place, see how quickly the problem is resolved. Only this quantitative data will help gauge how effective your staff is in handling the demands of users. Exceptionally long response times may indicate the need for more staff or highlight areas in which employees would most benefit from additional training.

Be sure to peruse your data for trends, such as products that generate far more help requests than others do. This may indicate a need to hire more people to handle the most troublesome applications. There may also be a valid need to evaluate which products are relied on by your company. In future purchases of new equipment and services, you should have some basis for eliminating those products that cause the most headaches.

TRAINING

Too many corporations pay only lip service to end-user training. Since training is often perceived as a costly expenditure, managers are reluctant to budget adequate funds for their department. Requests for employee time away from the desk to attend classroom sessions are often only grudgingly granted.

Providing entry-level and continuing training is one of the best practices to be promoted by IT managers. Adequate instruction in the use of company applications and procedures is one of the most cost-effective methods to boost productivity and gain more knowledgeable and valuable workers. Reducing the need for direct technical support also frees your time to pursue other demands.

Economic Benefits

While it is typical for managers to argue against incurring the very real costs associated with training, advocates for additional funding should respond with equally sound financial incentives to invest in training. It should be argued that direct gains in employee productivity will more than offset the price of every dollar invested in instruction.

It can be difficult to determine the exact value gained by training, but here are some guidelines. Question employees who have attended classes and determine how much time per day or week the skills acquired in that class will save them. For example, learning how to use Microsoft Word's macro features can save two hours per week for people who do repetitive word processing operations.

Multiply the hourly savings by the workers' hourly wages over the course of a year and you will quickly see the money accumulate to a very appreciable level. Spread these savings across your entire department and company and you should see some substantial contributions to the bottom line. Of course, the many training companies will each tout their own formulas for determining similar savings.

Gains in Abilities

A less tangible benefit of training is the new skills employees gain that are not directly applicable to their jobs. Comprehensive training budgets allocate funds for ancillary instruction. You may wish to offer Web page authoring classes to all employees, not just the ones responsible for maintaining the corporate Web site.

Web browser-based front ends are steadily becoming the norm for business databases and other data. It is much easier to have departments adopt new technology and spur its development in your company if those at the front lines are familiar with the skills required. I always encourage enabled users to develop new systems to perform their jobs better. The widespread distribution of Web authoring tools included in modern office application suites will only fuel this trend.

The Many Faces of Training

There are many different types of training available and each has its own benefit and purpose. Choices vary from a traditional lecture to Internet modules and self-directed study. Sessions can be held in well-equipped centers dedicated to computer training or they can be casual brown-bag meetings in your lunchroom.

It would be incorrect to assume that any particular format is most beneficial. Rather, a variety of methods should be employed that match the particular subject matter and time constraints of those taking classes. One great resource for those seeking in-depth information is the magazine *Inside Technology Training.*

Dedicated Training Centers

The best-known type of training facility is one that hosts nothing other than professional computer training. Designed to accommodate a wide variety of classes, these centers feature classrooms that usually hold less than 20 students. Most will dedicate a single computer to each student and have an instructor's machine equipped with an oversize monitor or projection screen.

These centers typically provide many different forms of vendor certification training. For example, attendees can take courses in preparation for Novell NetWare network administration (CNA, or Certified NetWare Administrator, classes) or for A+ service accreditation. Classes of this type must typically be followed by an exam to verify a mastery of the subject matter.

Courses vary from a few days for a single subject to several weeks if one wishes to attain a particular certification. Be sure to use centers that meet vendors' criteria if you want to obtain a recognized certificate. Microsoft and others will demand that instructors pass specialized training for each class taught. Minimal standards for equipment, student materials, and class size must also be met.

These centers are ideal for companies that don't have facilities of their own or that train employees in insufficient numbers to justify holding classes on-site. There are several benefits to those attending, as well. Being free of workplace distractions makes it easier for students to concentrate on the material. There is a definite psychological boost to one's feeling of self-worth when they attend a class at a specialized training center. Most people appreciate the company's investment in training classes and strive to learn as much as possible. Furthermore, the interaction with others taking the course is usually as stimulating as the training itself. It is always a good learning opportunity when you can share similar experiences with those in different fields and industries.

One of the largest companies in this field is New Horizons Computer Learning Centers. New Horizons has over 200 training centers worldwide and offers courses in hundreds of subjects. Productivity Point International and CompUSA teach a similarly broad array of classes. Each of these larger firms has a presence in major metropolitan areas around the country, which is important for firms that need similar training opportunities in geographically dispersed locations.

Quantity pricing is one of the surest ways to reduce costs. Training classes can easily run in excess of $300 a day. IT managers should always try to negotiate a volume discount if numerous users will be taking courses at the same training center.

RATING A CENTER   Always tour the training facility before spending company money on classes. See if the equipment used is well maintained and modern. Make sure that the classrooms are comfortable and that parking and public transportation are convenient. You should be able to audit a class for free and judge how well the entire center operates. Check the fee structure and cancellation policies. Also find out which type of guarantees are provided. See if students are allowed to retake classes if they are unable to digest all the material the first time.

IT REALLY HAPPENED: One of my own managers hated training. He believed that people would take classes to better their resumes and look for work elsewhere once they achieved certification. The local CompUSA Training Center extended a warranty on all their courses. If I left the company less than one year after completing my class, they would offer the same class to another employee for free. This guaranteed that even if I took my new skills with me, my company could then send another person to the same class. This provision gave my boss the comfort factor he needed to approve my attending training classes.

In-House Training Centers

Large corporations often maintain a single classroom or elaborate facilities that are always available for employee training. The same range of vendor-certified classes can be taught in such centers, as well as courses dedicated to specific company applications. Training materials can be purchased or developed from scratch. This high degree of flexibility is one of the best features of this arrangement.

If you have the facilities available, it certainly makes sense to offer a core curriculum covering typical user applications on a regular basis. Word processing, WWW searching, and spreadsheet classes are sure to appeal to most in your company. Advanced classes in program development and other technology should be offered with a frequency that matches user needs.

TIP: Look to develop an in-house certification and training recognition program. Employees should be rewarded for their learning with certificates that recognize the classes they have taken. These typically are prominently displayed in the employee's office or cubicle. Human Resources departments should also acknowledge workers who complete classes. Financial incentives, quarterly lunches, or similar perks can be extended to those who complete a certain number of courses.

OUTSOURCING TRAINING   Having adequate facilities does not require that you hire anyone to be a regular instructor at your firm. Certified training instructors can be used to provide training at your own site. This can be a very economical choice for companies that only have occasional demand for instruction. It can also be the only way to offer classes on new technology or programs that your own training staff is unfamiliar with.

All the training requirements for your firm can be fulfilled with products you buy off the shelf or contract for. Thus, even the smallest firms can obtain high-quality instruction on the entire range of technologies required by modern corporations. The tremendous variety and competition in the training industry is truly amazing. Generating more mail to my office than any other particular piece of hardware or software (although my title is usually listed as IT *Manager*) are offers for training. You should never have a problem finding available training options for all but the most esoteric technologies.

Computer-Based Training

One of the most popular forms of instruction is self-paced computer-based training modules, or CBTs. The software is often bound into books that cover particular products such as Microsoft Internet Information Server, Visual Basic, Cisco routers, and numerous popular application programs. The CBT usually includes one or more CD-ROMs with a variety of multimedia presentations and practice examinations for those seeking vendor certification.

The per-person training cost of CBTs is often very modest, because typically they can be used by more than one person. The software can be loaded on a specific computer designated as a training system, signed out for use on individual workstations, or borrowed for use at home.

Since these are self-paced materials, they are much easier for some people to use than courses that require all-day attendance at a training center. Managers who are averse to having employees out for an extended period may be much more accepting of solutions that minimize this impact.

BOOKS WITH CBTS   It is very common to find books on operating systems, networking, or popular applications that include a CD-ROM loaded with simulators, certification preparation, and helpful utility programs. Osborne/McGraw-Hill publishes several titles that address the need for Microsoft, Novell, and Cisco networking certifications. Because they can peruse such books in a piecemeal fashion, employees can do their training during off hours or while at home.

Simulators are the best way to experience operating a file server or router without actually having all the software and hardware running. It's also a *really bad idea* to try learning how an operating system works on an actual production system.

TIP: Here is a great reason for IT managers to push for funding of an experimental network. The safest way to gain experience with new systems is to have dedicated testing facilities. You can play all day with new toys and protocols and never put your users at risk.

The variety of courses available in this format is staggering, and there are many vendors to consider. See if you can acquire samples of various CBTs from vendor Web sites, and evaluate them in the same manner that you would other training methods.

Internet-Hosted Classes

There has been a tremendous growth in companies offering training materials based on Web browser clients. Web-based training (WBT) is sure to continue gaining favor as the Internet explodes in popularity. This allows workers with access to the Internet to take online classes easily. For example, Ziff-Davis University runs an extensive selection of classes hosted on ZDNet.

This type of learning has much of the same appeal as CBTs since the learning is self-paced and does not require workers to travel out of the office. Again, the price is relatively low because there is little overhead. The major drawback to any kind of self-administered training is the lack of interactions with fellow students and the difficulty in getting answers to questions with no instructor present.

Videotapes

Instructional videos have been a valuable tool for many years. Basically nothing more than highly advanced animated cave paintings, they allow anyone with a VCR to sit back and absorb information from their TV. The main drawback is the lack of interaction that this format offers.

The biggest pluses are the low price and the fact that almost everyone has a VCR in the home. One doesn't need special equipment to view a videotape, whereas a complex CBT may require capabilities not found in older, slower computers.

Traveling Road Shows

Training companies typically hold classes in area hotels and conference centers. This permits them to host courses in a variety of locations without the expense of maintaining a full-time center. Many of these classes can be highly specific and present information rapidly and in a densely packed format. For example, there may be a three-day class on TCP/IP networking that contains instruction specifically geared toward companies that rely on Cisco routers.

WARNING: Technology classes presented in this format are typically not designed for the casual user. They are best suited for those with specific needs for highly specialized training.

Holding classes in hotels allows these companies to attract individuals from more rural areas that are not served by local training centers. Living in the heart of downtown Boston, I am somewhat spoiled by the wealth of training opportunities available in my vicinity. However, I've often met people at hotel-based classes who were from parts of Maine and New Hampshire that were many hours away by car. These courses are especially convenient for them since the training companies typically reserve rooms in the same facility for attendees.

Free Vendor Seminars

Larger technology manufacturers often host free training and informational seminars, especially in major metropolitan areas. Microsoft, Novell, SUN, IBM, and others often partner with each other to tout new products to existing customers. A typical offering will be a hardware vendor such as Compaq demonstrating the newest business software products from Oracle running on Compaq servers.

Being a registered user of a particular product is a sure way to get invited to these events. Scour the various vendor Web sites you are involved with and register to attend some of these events. Besides accumulating the usual T-shirts, hats, and pens, you can also gain valuable insight into new products. White papers and evaluation copies of software can be excellent resources for projects at your own companies.

Trade Shows

While you might have to pay to get in, industry trade shows often run intensive seminar series concurrently with show floor displays. It makes sense to provide training opportunities at events that attract many highly qualified people, but huge shows such as Comdex, held in Las Vegas, may not be the best choice for a learning atmosphere free from distractions.

Focused shows such as Seybold for the publishing industry or LotusSphere for Lotus Notes enthusiasts are prime spots for focused courses. You may have the opportunity to learn directly from company developers and engineers. This is also a great place for a manufacturer to hear directly from their customers. This type of two-way communication is almost impossible to get any other way.

CHAPTER 5

Individualized Client Support Strategies

Certainly the most visible role that the IT specialist has is providing direct support to computer users in an organization. While you may be justifiably proud of the advanced and powerful servers you have running, it is the productivity of the workers with their individual systems that requires the most critical attention. Only when you satisfy all the diverse needs of your user population can you be judged as having done a good job.

STRATEGIES FOR CLIENT SUPPORT

There are numerous methods one can apply when providing technical support. Creating and deploying FAQs, generating custom help files, and designing problem-reporting mechanisms are all important skills to master. However, the successful and effective IT Specialist must also understand that human relationships need to be nurtured.

With tremendous frequency, those who depend on your technical acumen will call upon your expertise whenever anything fails. It is critical to appreciate the degree to which your ability is seen as a safety net. No matter which error condition appears, what application is being used, or which network resource is required, your capability to provide the correct answer quickly is vital to the optimal functioning of those you support. Never underestimate the psychological boost that confidence in your skill gives. People you support will always be much more effective if they feel that they can trust your competence to help them when required.

This chapter will explore the ways of providing exceptional customer service and support. Using a proactive approach, you can implement many wonderful techniques to dramatically reduce the time required to answer the same queries over and over again. You will also learn how to maximize your presence both to satisfy users' needs to see your involvement with their systems and to respond to problems before they get worse. The emphasis in this chapter will be on the many informal and personal ways that support should be handled. Chapter 4 will focus on more institutionalized support structures. By combining the methods in both chapters, you can create dynamic and highly effective strategies to maximize your users' capabilities. Not only will your users become more efficient, but you will also greatly reduce your workload.

Central to supporting users are the methods you use to protect their data and make their systems stable. The last part of this chapter will give an overview of typical user problems and the classic approaches to troubleshooting. Later, Chapters 12 and 13 will give more detailed coverage on the subjects of technical support and system repair.

Making Your Presence Felt

There is perhaps no better boost to users' confidence than seeing that IT staff plays a visible role in their department. In the same way that the presence of a police officer can make you feel safer in a threatening environment, knowing that the IT specialist is nearby and readily accessible makes for a more comfortable computing experience. Remember that for many people who use computers, there is a good deal of fear and uncertainty. The mystery of how computers work and the terror of losing a file conspire to make users wary. It is your job to anticipate and minimize this apprehension.

Even when users are highly capable and can use their systems with little assistance, there are still numerous areas that will require your input. People who use stand-alone machines don't have to be concerned with network access rights, printer queues, shared data folders, and centralized administration. All of these areas require a network administrator to configure settings and, more importantly, to convey that information to network users.

Walk the Floor

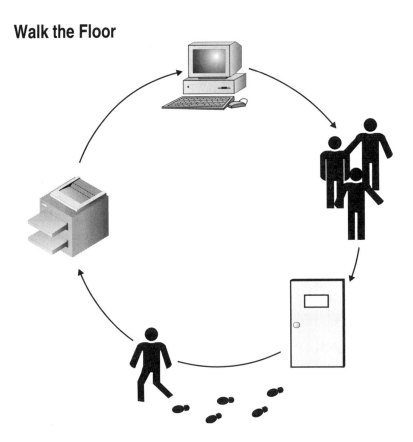

One of the simplest and most effective actions you can take as an IT manager is to make regular walks around the offices you support. It has proven to me to be one of the greatest habits to develop and I cannot emphasize strongly enough the importance that it plays. There is no better way to develop an appreciation for the jobs and needs of your users. Also, it is the soundest way to create a reputation as someone who truly cares about the user population.

If the only time that a support person and a user interact is when a problem occurs, then you have missed opportunities to make both of your jobs easier. Technical support should be an ongoing process, with a constant flow of information between IT staff and system users.

Depending on your daily responsibilities and the physical layout of the company, your sojourns should be planned so that you visit everyone at least once a month. I advocate that those who work in smaller companies or departments make an appearance daily if possible. These walks around all the cubicles and offices should be made part of a regular routine. You should exploit this contact with your users within both a structured and informal format.

There is a significant amount of work that should be handled in a formal manner. One typical task is to check the health of all your printers. Make it a daily habit to inspect the status lights and operational readiness of all your output devices. Check to see if the toner levels are sufficient. Make sure that paper is loaded and that there are additional reams available nearby.

Pay careful attention to details. Letterhead and other special stationery should be correctly oriented so that print jobs will come out correctly. If multiple input tray printers can be set up to use specific paper in each tray, verify that the configuration is correct. Company logos and other information such as phone numbers can change, so make sure that you discard obsolete paper. If this work is assigned to a user within the department using the printer, make sure they are instructed in proper paper tray use. Some companies assign this task to mailroom or facilities staff.

Depending on how heavily the printers are used, you should also tailor weekly and monthly maintenance routines. Paper and toner dust will affect print quality and increase paper jams. Dedicate one day per month to giving each printer a thorough cleaning with a vacuum and other appropriate products. Not only will cleaner equipment last longer and perform more reliably, but people will notice the care you give the printers. This may inspire users to approach their own equipment with greater respect.

DISTRIBUTED ORGANIZATIONS   There are many companies that have multiple far-flung sites, precluding a particular IT person from visiting every desk, let alone every location. However, IT specialists charged with providing front-line support in a large organization should be assigned responsibility for specific users, grouped by job description or location. I have always believed that attaching specific technical support staffers to certain departments has many benefits. First and perhaps most importantly, it fosters a team atmosphere that closely ties the users and IT together. Users get to know "their" support person and feel more comfortable knowing that she is assigned specifically to their needs. The IT specialist benefits by becoming more familiar with the technical requirements and work of the users in her care.

It is the IT director's responsibility to make sure that all users feel they are being given the attention they deserve. While you cannot lavish personal attention on everyone, make sure that you create an appreciation in every IT professional on your staff for the important role that direct support plays.

MOBILE AND HOME WORKERS   A special population of clients that require IT support are mobile or home workers. These can be salespeople who only occasionally venture into the main office, spending most of their time traveling to client sites with dial-up laptops. Many companies also have contract employees who work from home. Still others work from home part of the time and in the office the rest of the time. Whatever the situation, mobile and home workers typically have special needs for the IT manager to address.

Laptops are both expensive and fragile. Optional advance replacement warranties are a good investment when loss of a computer for any length of time is a threat to productivity. Some companies purchase extra systems and maintain a pool of backup machines ready to be sent via overnight express to users that lose their use of a laptop due to damage or theft.

While you can easily replace a system, more critical is the data that can be lost. Remote users that only access centralized data on corporate hosts may not face this problem. Applications like Lotus Notes provide tools to create replicas of data on several servers and workstations. However, IT should provide the capability to back up local data to corporate hosts. STAC Inc.'s line of Replica products is one of the best solutions to data archiving of highly decentralized user machines. Another recommended application for mobile workers is from utilities giant Symantec. Its Mobile Update software helps keep data synchronized between the home office and those in the field.

Supporting home users is always made more complex by the variety of systems that they use. One sure way to ease the support headaches is for IT to provide and install computers for remote workers. This is the only way to ensure that IT is familiar with the hardware and software used and that the correct versions or custom templates are being utilized. An alternative is to have home workers bring their computers in to a central office so that IT can install and test the systems for compliance with corporate standards.

IT may desire to accommodate users that have cable modems or other high-speed connections to the Internet. Routers can be configured with VPN (Virtual Private Network) to allow speedy access through corporate firewalls. Analog dial-up users can be handled with in-house remote access servers or via outsource connections with an ISP. Always make sure that the connection speed is appropriate to the tasks the user has.

WATCH WHAT'S GOING ON   There is so much one can learn just by observing. Go in early a few mornings and see who comes in first. Then stay late a few evenings to learn which users are last to leave. If you have network-monitoring capability and can ascertain user account activity, be sure to add this information to your observations.

This practice will make you more sensitive to the work habits of others, and they will undoubtedly appreciate your concern for their schedules. When you need to bring the network down for maintenance or upgrades, gently explain to those who arrive early or stay late why one time of the day is better than another. Only in this atmosphere of communication and knowledge can you get the happy cooperation of your users.

Having this information can help you plan system outages for upgrades and similar short-term work. Getting a sense of who is on site and what work is being done during the "edges" of a workday lets you minimize impact. If you are contemplating any network changes, it is best to approach people when you already know who is most likely to be affected.

IT REALLY HAPPENED: I was supporting a substantial software development effort that involved many programmers who loved to work exceptionally late hours. Several made it a habit to stay well past midnight because they found it the most productive time for them to work. My memories of late-night programming sessions in college involved prodigious amounts of cola, coffee, pizza, and beer. Writing programs was as much a social event as it was an academic endeavor. This made it extremely difficult for me to undertake any major or minor network maintenance without impacting anyone else's schedule. In fact, I even got an irate email from a user who was adamant that the only acceptable time for a network outage was "from midnight to 5 A.M. weekdays and 9 P.M. to 6 A.M. weekends." I defused this seemingly inflexible requirement when I enlightened the user to what my condition would be if I honored his request. I wrote back, "I don't want to commence upgrades or similar minor work when I will be tired from unusual hours and more prone to errors. Also, my ability to reach vendor technical support centers and get more than basic help would be reduced after midnight." I made sure he knew that I appreciated his need for network access and he was more aware of what conditions I faced.

SCAN FOR NETWORK BEHAVIOR   Certainly one of the best methods to "watch what's going on" is by monitoring the network wires themselves. With network scanning software an IT Specialist can determine when the network is busiest and which nodes broadcast the most information. A skilled observer can spot "choke points" or malfunctioning cards and address poor performance issues.

There are several good products that can fulfill this need as well as aid in more complex network monitoring and diagnosis of problems. You want to be able to gauge how much bandwidth is being utilized at different times of day. Knowing which nodes are the busiest makes it easier to upgrade and reconfigure, maximizing LAN throughput.

One of the best-known high-end choices is Network Associates' line of Sniffer products. There are models appropriate for virtually any cabling topology in use. A Sniffer can perform trend analysis, allowing the network administrator to chart network baseline behavior and generating alerts when utilization or other errors reach certain thresholds. While a fairly expensive solution, the Sniffer provides an incredibly broad range of protocol support and can even draw up troubleshooting guidelines based on LAN analysis, making it an invaluable tool for large and complex networks.

Linux and UNIX users can discover a wide range of open-source programs on the World Wide Web. One such tool is MRTG, the Multi-Router Traffic Grapher. This is a fully SNMP-compliant product that generates HTML pages for easy viewing of network performance. It is distributed under the Free Software Association's GNU General Public License, and there is even code available for Windows NT servers. This software is highly customizable, but you'll need Perl programming skills. While free programs are sometimes more powerful than commercially available products, they may lag in ease of use and lack slick interfaces.

EtherPeek by AG Group is a software-only analyzer that fills the void between a more expensive Sniffer and products like MRTG. Not only will it capture, decode, and display traffic information, but it can also be configured to email an administrator if certain events occur. While it doesn't handle as many protocols as a Sniffer, most popular ones can be captured. There are versions for both Windows and Macintosh systems.

ASK FOR PROBLEMS   When walking your beat, make it a point to tell people why you are walking around rather than "fixing something somewhere." I always find people who will work around problems and suffer from some generally frustrating aspect of their computer behavior, yet never report it. Sometimes they simply think that I have too much other work or that their situation is unimportant and can be ignored. Remind them and yourself that what some perceive to be a minor error can become serious if ignored.

I've heard people say, "I just clicked on OK or Continue and everything seemed to boot up fine after that." These error messages that had been clicked through could easily have indicated that a hard disk failure was imminent. There have been times that only my presence prompted users to ask me what the error message was that they had seen every day for the past week. People often misinterpret messages from virus scanners, mistakenly believing that they are protected when the opposite is true.

If you encounter minor problems, fix them immediately. What a great and simple way to save yourself grief if a disk were to later fail or a virus continued to propagate. More complex tasks can always be scheduled for later attention. While users should and usually do request help when something appears to be wrong, the number of times I have witnessed balky systems that users were simply living with convinces me that you will uncover lots of problems by canvassing those you support. This proactive approach is one of the best ways to raise user productivity and satisfaction.

EXPLAIN HOW TO RECORD SYSTEM PROBLEMS The support specialists' job is made much easier when users can convey precise information about their problems. *The first rule is to insist that every error message be captured VERBATIM.* Error messages are often cryptic and don't convey much to the untrained eye. For the IT specialist, however, every error message should provide a clue to fixing a misbehaving computer. Almost any troubleshooting tool requires that the exact error code be entered to get the precise repair instructions.

It is nearly pointless to attempt to fix a problem if all the user can convey is a vague recollection of some screen messages. It makes sense to create a specific problem report form that can be distributed to everyone in the company, such as the example shown in Figure 5-1. With some simple instruction, users can be shown exactly what information to capture so that it's easier to resolve problems. This form should be tailored to the specific needs of a company and reflect the type of network and desktop operating systems in use.

While many IT departments rely on electronic filing of complaints via email or similar mechanisms, it still makes sense to distribute paper forms to everyone. That way if the system locks up or email is not available, the user could still record the information required. Also, whenever problems do arise, users are less apt to launch another application for making a service request.

I would urge that a single electronic system be maintained as the ultimate repository of all technical support requests. When requests are submitted on hard copy, they still should be entered into the master database. This can be done in a few different ways. The IT specialist can record the information via electronic means after

Systems Support Problem Form

Name: Date:
Location: Time:
Phone:
Department:
System ID Number:

Description of problem:

Best time for contact:

Please record the following information:

Operating System:

Computer Model:

Applications Used:

Figure 5-1.   A sample problem report form

addressing the problems posed by the user. Handwritten requests can be forwarded to help desk personnel, who can check that duplicate records are not being created by cross-referencing the problem reported, date, and specific user.

The information in your central support logs can be exploited in various ways. You can examine which departments generate the most help requests and redistribute support resources from less busy areas. The usefulness and reliability of applications or systems such as fax servers can be judged by the frequency that they generate problems for users. Unreliable solutions only frustrate those that use them and bog down IT with calls to fix the same problem repeatedly. IT staff appraisals should consider the number of calls handled by each support specialist in a given period.

ALWAYS LOOK FOR TRENDS   It is vital that a centralized database of support requests be maintained so that important information can be gleaned from it. IT should know which applications or specific computer models generate the most complaints. Being able to identify the most common issues will allow you to focus greater efforts on preventative measures such as increased training or targeting less reliable systems for replacement.

Code your help calls to categorize them easily. For example, all printer problems can be type A, password problems could be type B, etc. Hiring additional support staff for particular trouble spots is more easily justified with a clearly demonstrated need. Raw data that shows the total number of problems responded to is more valuable if you know the exact nature of the problems reported.

IT REALLY HAPPENED: One department that I supported had been upgraded from Compaq Prolinnea 486/66 desktops to Hewlett-Packard Vectra VL4 Pentium 166 towers. Everyone seemed pleased with the increased speed and capacity of their new systems until there was a failure of a hard drive. While the loss of a single hard disk was not alarming, two more hard disks crashed in a similar fashion in the next few weeks. Since all the systems were purchased at the same time, they all were equipped with the same Western Digital hard drives. While normally a rugged and reliable component, an acknowledged problem during manufacturing had plagued HP and other vendors that installed the same model hard drive. Rather than wait and hope that my other systems had reliable drives, I had Hewlett-Packard replace every single drive in every computer. Be sure to look for similar trends where you work. Address them proactively and don't wait for everyone to have a problem.

LEARN PEOPLE'S NAMES   This is a simple task that can have lots of benefits. People will always appreciate you a bit more if you make an effort to learn their name. Providing support is more effective if there is at least a professional relationship already established. Users are calmer and more patient dealing with someone who knows them than with an anonymous worker sent to rescue them from their troubles.

Of course there is a lot of other information about your users that would be useful to know. Once you become familiar with the names and faces of those you support, you can begin to learn their skill levels and their work habits. Informal conversations will reveal who works with others and can aid your understanding of group dynamics, discussed in Chapter 1.

While not every IT specialist is gregarious and outgoing, the best support people generally are. They make an effort to create friendly relationships with everyone they support. Being able to discuss someone's pets and children is a welcome change from discussions about megahertz and disk drives. Many system repairs and program installations require a great deal of time to complete. I have always relished this time to learn about the people I support. It is often an excellent opportunity to discover additional problems or to offer advice and instructions on other areas of computer use.

Provide Ready Contact Information

IT support staff should function as much more than trouble-shooters who only show up when problems require their expertise. Your goal is to maximize your users' abilities to exploit their systems easily and confidently. Being available to strategize and brainstorm will allow you to build more capable solutions that answer the needs of your company.

Large IT staffs will include people with varying abilities and specialties. Inform the people in your company about which members of the IT staff are best suited to handling database inquiries or word-processing issues. You want to funnel requests to the people best equipped to handle them.

ESTABLISH OFFICE HOURS   Whenever possible, IT staff members should maintain office hours and dedicate some time each week for face-to-face contact with users. Be sure to publicize these hours and explain what this time is designated for. Setting aside one hour twice a week should be enough for most company needs.

TIP: A good use of this time would be for HR or department managers to inform network administrators about new hires or department restructuring. This allows you to collect and then process similar requests all at the same time rather than in an inefficient piecemeal fashion.

Establishing office hours is a great way to avoid the countless interruptions that waste your time when you are trying to give attention to other projects. If users understand and accept that a particular block of time is dedicated to answering their myriad ad hoc requests, then they will make an effort to follow these guidelines.

IT specialists are recognized as the experts in an organization for the use and development of computer systems. It certainly makes sense to make this expertise available to the general company population. Being available to answer questions or just to talk about technology can provide an excellent atmosphere to brainstorm about problems that vex the users you support. Chapter 1 examined how IT specialists can make the most positive impact on their companies' use of technology. Being available and welcoming queries is the best way to start making a contribution.

LIST ALL CONTACT METHODS   Modern technology has spawned numerous ways to contact someone who is not in shouting distance. Many IT specialists use an office telephone, pager, cell phone, and email. Make sure that all of the numbers for reaching you are correctly cataloged and distributed to your users.

It makes sense for you to rank these contact methods for both purpose and time constraints. For example, let users know that high-priority emergency calls should be directed to your pager or cell phone and that less important jobs can be communicated by email. Make sure that specific hours for use are listed as well. IT departments typically rotate weekend and evening coverage, so be sure that these assignments are well publicized.

Larger IT organizations will integrate their help desk systems with messaging systems. Alphanumeric pagers or more elaborate PDAs can handle dispatching technicians to a particular user's desk. The obvious time savings in getting jobs to support specialists will make your entire IT department more efficient.

Special Challenges of a Hostile Environment

One challenge that IT professionals sometimes face is encountering organizations where users harbor strong negative opinions on the state of customer service. You may experience this atmosphere when undertaking a new position or when your company acquires a new division. It is vital to get off to a good start and make those you support recognize your efforts to turn things around.

A history of unresponsive technical support and unreliable systems can make for a very hostile user community. Regaining users' faith in IT must begin with a clearly demonstrated attitude that their needs come first. Whenever you begin a new job, it is a wise investment of your time to gauge the current state of affairs and methodically plan a response to remedy the situation if necessary.

Assess the Crucial Trouble Spots First

The first step when encountering a dissatisfied and angry user community is to determine where the most obvious problems lie.

Undertake your investigation by first stating your goal, to return users' faith in the ability and desire of IT to maintain a reliable and usable network. Next, hold a series of brief meetings with department managers or other representatives who can identify the most pressing issues that users are facing.

While you can gather similar information with email, having personal contact will reveal much more about the true nature of the situation. It allows for a free exchange of ideas and will help you assess the extent of problems. There is also an added benefit: making IT highly visible. Rather than retreat into your computer room or office to read reports or scan server consoles, position yourself to personally grapple with and appreciate the plight of the users you support.

Set Priorities

Identify a few key areas where you can make the fastest and most visible impact. Even repairing a simple yet nagging problem will go far in restoring user trust, meanwhile buying you time to address more complex issues. You must restore stability and reliability to your network before you undertake any expansion work.

Make a project list that clearly indicates each particular task that IT is working on and provide a method to indicate progress. I use a project board in my office and color-code various entries so I can quickly scan items for status. For example, I code emergencies in red, continuing projects in blue, and non-critical issues in brown. In another column I record each entry's submission data, the target date for resolving it, and the actual completion date. All of this information is eventually transferred into my master system logbook. It is important to review records occasionally so you can spot trends and identify issues that are common or those that are more difficult to rectify.

Use a calendar to signify when a project has begun and when it has been completed. Complex projects should have a series of interim steps and clearly demarcated deadlines so that users and IT can gauge progress. Make this "scorecard" visible so users can see how much headway is being made. Weekly updates via email on system-related work are also a good idea, giving users periodic reassurance that their issues are being addressed.

Stress Client Service

Making a visible commitment to listening to and then addressing system problems is the best way for IT to demonstrate concern for users. By exploiting the techniques outlined in this book and emphasizing the User Bill of Rights in Chapter 3, you demonstrate your commitment to client services. Follow up your initial efforts with a canvassing of users to see how well you are meeting their needs. Invite suggestions and comments so you can better focus your attention to problems.

COMMON COMPUTER PROBLEMS

No matter what type of NOS and workstations your organization uses, there are certain problems that will inevitably surface. Troubleshooting specifics will vary depending on the particular computers used, but there are some general rules I recommend for approaching any of these problems. Using the tools and procedures discussed in the following sections will help you respond to common problems more effectively.

While the range of problems is quite extensive, certainly the vast majority of help requests center around four broad themes. The first type of issue is the simple inability to access a network. Secondly, printing problems have always ranked near the top of my list of frequent, frantic calls. Despite the promises of a "paperless office," anyone working in a modern office will report that use of paper is way up from twenty years ago. Computers make it much easier to process and transmit data, which invariably gets printed.

The third type of problem you will frequently see is a user having trouble accessing or finding files. Large networks with dozens of servers display a dizzying array of choices where people may inadvertently save their data, which then lies buried in some obscure directory. Of course, retrieving deleted files is another vital part of the job.

The final major concern is system stability. While the previous chapter delved into matters of network reliability, you must also pay attention to making individual workstations perform better. Don't forget that making your users' systems work better will make your job that much easier.

Check Status Lights

Most network cards have a status light that indicates packets are being transmitted. A blinking light normally indicates that data is flowing through the NIC. Some Ethernet cards also indicate the speed of the connection by showing different status lights for 10MB versus 100MB operation.

You may also want to check the connection of the workstation to the hub. Virtually all hubs have indicators that signify if signals are being sent over each port. Different colors or blinking conditions can indicate speed or if an error condition is present. All of these checks test for the existence and quality of the physical connection.

A correct physical link between network card and hub does not guarantee successful communication across the LAN. After your checks of the physical layer is complete you must next verify that a logical connection can be made. The software for doing so is explained in the next section.

Oh Say, Can You Ping?

I have found that the single most useful troubleshooting tool, especially with UNIX systems, is the ping command. It essentially allows you to verify that a viable TCP/IP communication path exists between the computer you are checking and another host on the network. Since UNIX systems almost always utilize TCP/IP as their default protocol, the ubiquitous ping command provides a versatile program for testing communication between nodes on a network.

The rapid growth of the World Wide Web has made TCP/IP a common feature for virtually all corporate networks. Microsoft- and Novell-based networks are gradually migrating their default networking protocols to more standard TCP/IP rather than proprietary ones. This makes integration of disparate systems both easier to manage and to troubleshoot. The adoption of a single protocol standard is sure to help make IT more efficient.

TIP: Ping the address 127.0.0.1 from your system prompt. This special IP address can be used as a loop-back test. If you can successfully ping the loop-back address, then you know that your TCP/IP software is installed and running. Next, ping your gateways. See if your IP packets can reach the next hop in a transmission. Another static destination to check during network troubleshooting is the DNS server's address. Using the ping and TRACEROUT programs allows administrators to get an accurate picture of the network's health and configuration.

Windows Network Neighborhood

Windows systems have a Network Neighborhood icon on the desktop. Double-clicking on the icon should reveal all the available servers on the network. A failure to see any servers may be caused by lack of the correct protocol being loaded.

Use the Control Panel to access the protocol settings for your NIC. NetWare environments most often use IPX/SPX. NetBEUI is the preferred protocol for NetBIOS compatible networks such as Windows NT Server. Having the wrong protocol active will render the computer blind to the network servers.

Use the included troubleshooters to help pinpoint the problems with your computer. A failed network connection will normally trigger the troubleshooter whenever a user attempts to access servers. It may also be invoked via the Windows Help program.

TIP: There are different flavors of Ethernet that can be used. Having the incorrect frame type selected can cause a network connection to fail. Make sure that the servers and workstations are all using the same type. This setting can be found in the Network section of the Control Panel on Windows systems.

Macintosh Chooser

The Chooser is a Macintosh program that is used to access all network resources. A failure to see File Servers when selecting the

Appleshare icon may indicate that your system is off the network. If your hub status lights are showing connectivity then you must then check the Appletalk Control Panel.

A Macintosh computer can use a variety of ports for connecting to a network. There may be a built-in Ethernet port or Localtalk port that can be used. Always make sure that the Appletalk Control Panel has correctly selected the correct port for your LAN. Sometimes a dial-up session may have the computer incorrectly thinking that the modem port is the active network port.

I Can't Print!

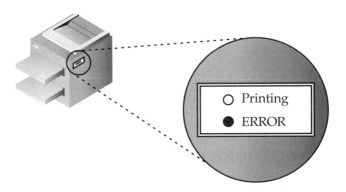

One of the most frustrating situations for users, and thus one of the most typical complaints to IT specialists, is an inability to print. As with any problem, it is best to approach this one from the most basic level and then to add layers of complexity to try to determine the exact problem. There are many elements that need to be checked when faced with printing failures. To locate the source of the problem, first check the underlying physical devices, next look at the network and operating system, and then move on to specific applications.

Check the Status Lights and Configuration Pages

Savvy IT specialists make it a habit to check equipment status lights and other display indicators during normal operations. Familiarity with a printer's proper functioning conditions will make it much easier to spot errors when they occur. Most printers will also report configuration and operating parameters via dedicated printing routines. Manipulating various switches and menus can force this information to be printed for analysis.

TIP: Make a file where you can store configuration and status page printouts so that you can refer to them when a problem occurs. Having access to a setup known to be good will make repair faster and easier.

Check the Server Queues

Network printers typically service print queues on file servers. Use your network utility programs to check whether submitted print jobs are actually reaching the server. If print jobs are piling up and no output is being produced, you need to check the connection between the server and printer.

Make sure you are familiar with the software that your NOS uses to manage and monitor network printing. You may need to bypass the network completely and attempt to print using a standard parallel cable to verify correct printer operation. Novell servers can use the PConsole utility to check queue status. Microsoft Windows network users can access queue status by clicking the appropriate printer icon in their Control Panel.

UNIX systems may vary widely in underlying hardware and employ different GUIs, but there are ubiquitous command-line utilities that are designed to verify printer operation. The LPSTAT and LPQ programs report on outstanding queue jobs. Show your users how to use the command-line switches to check queue status and the default printer. Proper configuration of the system must also be verified. Check the /ETC/PRINTCAP directory for the printer setup files. Your users may have the wrong driver specified or an incorrect port captured.

Is the Problem Isolated?

Always ask if anyone else who uses the same printer is experiencing similar print failures. If the situation is isolated to a single user, then you can safely assume that the problem is localized. This is always preferable, since the failure of a shared network resource has much more serious consequences, as many are affected.

If there is only one user who cannot print, verify that he or she is indeed logged in to the network and has selected the printer correctly. Network accounts normally grant printer access, and not being logged in is a common cause of printer problems. Demonstrate to your affected users how to correctly access network printers and verify their network activity status. With Windows systems, users typically go to the Network Neighborhood desktop icon to browse and select network resources. Macintosh users rely on the Chooser to accomplish the same function.

Print Using the Operating System Only

If you have verified that the user having the printing problem is correctly attached to the network, the next step is to attempt to print using only the workstation operating system. You want to eliminate any conflict with application programs. Macintosh computers allow the Print Desktop operation. This simply prints all the folders and other icons on the system desktop. If this step completes correctly, then you can assume that the fault is with the specific application program.

Windows 95 and Windows 98 workstations allow an easy printer test page to be generated. If this outputs correctly, then it is safe to assume that the problem is not with the individual computer or network printer. You should always verify your connection with the simplest operation possible. You can produce a test page from the Properties setting for each installed printer in your Printers folder. Double click on the "My Computer" icon on your desktop and then double click on the "Printers" folder to display all your printers. Right click on the desired printer and the Properties selection will be displayed. The Print Test Page option will then be displayed.

Verify That the Correct Drivers Are Installed

Epson, HP, IBM, Apple, and other manufacturers continually introduce new and updated models of their printers. Individual printers will also vary on their features, such as support for

PostScript or the amount of installed memory. Both these factors make the correct selection of the proper printer driver critical to proper operation. One user submitting a wrongly formatted print job can cause the printer to freeze or spew out reams of random text.

Here again is an area where documentation and training can save the day. Make sure that you know exactly which driver is the current and correct one to use for each of your printers. The settings for paper size, font usage, memory, and numerous other parameters should be recorded in an easy-to-decipher form. Using a screen capture program will allow you to create documents that show the precise use of every dialog box and the correct option settings. Make sure your users know how to select the appropriate printers for their operating system.

Maintain a central library of driver files and be sure that all your computers are consistent with the corporate standard. Don't ever assume that newer drivers should automatically be installed. Always pass them through some rigorous testing to prove their stability. One of the advantages of network operating systems like Windows NT Server is that you can store printer driver information on the server for automatic download to most Windows workstation clients. Sometimes the safest option is to use a generic or older version of a similar printer driver to ensure compatibility.

Use System Troubleshooters

Microsoft has done a fairly good job of writing problem resolution routines right into the operating system. To make sure that you know all the required steps, deliberately move through all the procedures that the self-help Wizards prompt you to undertake. The worst time to become familiar with these programs is when you're dealing with a frantic user whose print job is hours late.

Being able to use operating system Wizards with confidence requires that you become familiar with their actions. Perform trial-and-error investigations to learn exactly which menus and options should be checked. Practice the problem-resolution scenarios and you will be able to quickly respond when there is an actual emergency.

UNIX systems distribute documentation for virtually every command in a series of MAN, or manual, pages. MAN pages list all the myriad optional switches associated with every command. Linux users should exploit the numerous how-to pages on the World Wide Web that contain similar information. A great starting point is the Linux Documentation Project at http://metalab.unc.edu/mdw/linux.html.

A proactive IT department will produce custom guides for users that highlight the most common activities and provide examples of their use. Demonstrate how to read MAN pages, directing users to information specifically geared to their network. Be sure to update your users' search paths so they can go to the same place for support information.

Check Individual Application Setups Last

Many programs have detailed print configuration settings that enhance or supplant the controls available within the operating system. Desktop publishing programs such as QuarkXPress utilize their own drivers to take control of printers. Make sure that you are familiar with these files and their settings.

If you can successfully print using OS-provided tools or a simple program like the Windows Notepad, then you assume that your problem is with the specific application. Distribute a small ASCII text file for testing to avoid problems with fonts and complex graphics. As discussed previously, you should check for other problems before addressing problems with applications, which depend on everything beneath them functioning correctly in order to operate. Always check that you can print something through other means before manipulating program settings.

Where Are the Files I Need?

Stand-alone systems typically have only a few local drives and thus a minimum of drive letters being used. However, networked computers need to access data storage resources on one or several servers. Because of this added complexity, users are much more likely to misplace a file. Only the most capable users seem to be comfortable and knowledgeable handling network storage.

Data stored on file servers typically requires that many workstation drive letters be used, each one pointing at a particular server location. It has been my experience that most users never seem to associate a particular file server resource with a location they need access to. They will refer to the X drive and have no inkling that it really is SALES_SERVER1\\DATA. It is particularly difficult to respond to a service call when a user cannot describe which server he or she cannot utilize. The user will complain about the X drive not being present, never realizing that the problem is lack of access to a specific server drive volume.

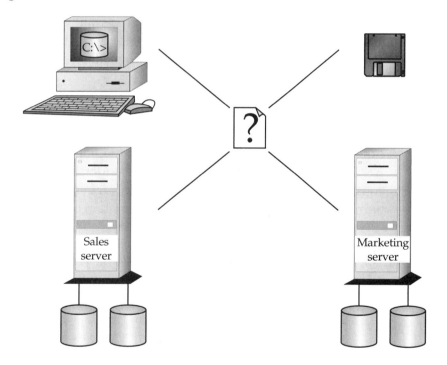

To address this situation, there are a few simple steps you can take. The first involves training. Teaching users the concept of how server storage equates to drive letters can be difficult. One technique that works well is to provide each user with a printed cross-reference outlining the drive associations that they use. Users in the same department often use identical network resources, making this type of documentation simple to create.

Keep a copy of this information available for IT staff to reference when responding to help requests. Encourage those you support to keep this documentation handy and to study it occasionally. Always remember that an educated and informed user is much easier to support. IT can handle support calls more swiftly when users can convey precise descriptions of errors.

Manage Your Directory Structures

Too often, file server directories are created without any particular consistency. Naming conventions are not standardized and usage is rarely specified. While older systems and certain applications place limits on the number of characters for naming a directory, the more robust operating systems provide much greater flexibility. It makes sense to use longer directory names to make complex trees easier to comprehend.

Directory names should be meaningful and a standardized pattern should be established for the entire company. A directory called SLSNE98 is much more confusing than one called SALES NEW ENGLAND 1998. Rarely will one person understand the naming convention used by another. Distributing suggested guidelines will permit users to follow a template and maintain consistency.

WARNING: Remember which operating systems your directories will be used by. Overly long directory names can be cumbersome to decipher. In particular, DOS legacy applications can often get confused when one strays from the 8.3 limitations of DOS. Macintosh, OS/2, and UNIX users have long enjoyed the luxury of longer file and directory names that users of the latest versions of Windows can now exploit.

USE PLACE MARKERS   Major or root-level directories should be organized to store specific types of files. Grouping data files by function or type within directories is key to efficient storage. Keeping your Sales files separate from Personnel data is a simple example.

You may want to create a small text file in each major directory describing its function. Figure 5-2 shows a sample placeholder file.

The text file can be used to record who created the directory, to explain its purpose, and to detail relevant account access information. Of course you will want to adjust the file attribute settings to prevent accidental erasure and modification of these descriptive files. Documentation is certainly one of the most important yet neglected tasks to perform. I've found that placeholder files are a valuable resource to the general network user community and that these files serve as the best reminder of what all my directories are for.

Demonstrate File Search Techniques

Looking for files should not be an arduous task. Windows puts the Find function right on the Start menu. Macintosh computers have sophisticated file location programs built into the operating system too. Showing users how to use these tools well is time invested wisely. UNIX system users should be given a demonstration of the WHEREIS and FIND programs. These command-line utilities provide a quick way to search an entire system for a specific filename, and wildcard characters can be used when only a partial filename is known.

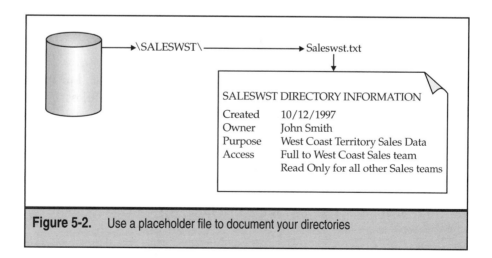

Figure 5-2. Use a placeholder file to document your directories

This is another task that can be more clearly illustrated with a screen capture program. Create a sample search job and use the resulting screens to make an excellent template that others can follow.

Keep Critical User Data Files on Your Servers

File servers should be equipped with highly reliable drives that enjoy regular backups. Typical workstations at people's desks will rarely have any fault-tolerant features. Under these circumstances, storing valuable files on servers is a prudent move. Servers may also take advantage of clustering and fail over technologies for maximum uptime and data availability.

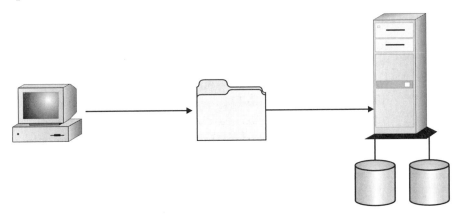

Most network operating systems allow creation of user home directories and login scripts that permit easy access to them. Educate your users as to their location and purpose. Stress that this disk space is intended for the storage of their most important files. Understanding that certain space limitations on the server and user demand may warrant setting limits on how much each user account can store.

Server disk quotas can prevent a single user from using all available space on a disk designed for shared access. Downloading of graphic files can quickly use up network storage. Multimedia data such as *South Park* video clips takes up scads more room than less complex text files. Products like Knozall File Wizard can clearly illustrate which users are the biggest disk hogs on your network.

IT REALLY HAPPENED: Someone I supported was charged with the responsibility of editing a complex user manual. Multiple revisions, screen shots, and sample code files had exceeded nearly 75 percent of the capacity of the shared home directory volume on his workgroups server. He alone had effectively prevented many others from storing data on their home directories. If I had placed a quota on his usage earlier, it would have prevented this problem. I established a dedicated area for the manual on a spare volume and migrated his data there.

There may be concerns about security for particularly sensitive files. Be alert to these concerns and carefully review what barriers to access are in place. Many popular applications give you the option of encrypting and password-protecting individual data files. In addition, only the laziest network administrators will grant universal access to directories intended for private use. Be able to demonstrate to skeptical users how user account privileges can be employed to block or grant access to directories.

You may want to create a system policy document for users to consult that outlines security arrangements. Make sure that Human Resources is aware of your security arrangements. There are some occasions when the system administrator must secure an immediate shutdown of network accounts and access to data, such as when an employee is terminated. I have had the uncomfortable experience of personally supervising the removal of users' personal data files in such cases.

Learn How to Recover Lost Files

Losing a file is one of the most alarming experiences any computer user can have. The best solution is to prevent accidental loss in the first place. Many programs such as Microsoft Word have the capability to automatically save files on a timed basis. You can even specify that a certain number of backups be created so you can successfully return to an earlier version of a document.

Putting such safeguards in place and showing people how they can be used will certainly prevent a great deal of future anguish. While you may play a small penalty in performance and disk usage, the end result will be a much safer computing environment. Emphasizing that a simple program setting will prevent the loss of work is sure to allay the fears of many anxious people.

File recovery programs such as Norton Utilities should be part of every IT specialist's arsenal. PGSoft markets a product cleverly named Save Butt. It provides Windows systems with a great deal of security by automatically making backups of every changed and deleted file on the system. This provides a wonderful way to "go back" to almost any previous state of your hard disk. Make sure you are familiar with how these programs operate *before* you need them. Also be sure to check the settings that your NOS uses. Novell NetWare, for example, has a setting to immediately purge deleted files. While not the default setting, it can be invoked to boost performance, but it makes file recovery a difficult process.

Windows users should also check their desktop Recycle Bin settings. Right-click on the Recycle Bin and go to Properties. In the Properties dialog box, you can adjust the settings for automatic deletion and the maximum amount of space reserved for tracking deleted files. Ensuring that this safety net is activated is a small but important step.

Extend Network Backup Systems to Workstations

Products such as ArcServe from Computer Associates can be used to back up individual computers, not just file servers. The investment in equipment for backup becomes much more attractive when it can serve multiple needs. Often, the files on users' systems are just as critical to your company as those stored on the servers. Data created by one person can be vital to someone else's job.

Workers often turn off their computers at night, which can defeat centralized nighttime backup. Many network cards and motherboards now support Wake on LAN features. This permits a network signal to turn a computer on remotely to perform a specific function. This can include installation of system updates or scripted copying of files to another location.

As I mentioned earlier when discussing remote user support, STAC manufactures an excellent suite of data-archiving products in their Replica line of software. Intelligent backup operations make sure that only unique files are copied; for example, there is no need to make multiple copies of every instance of the same executable program found on several computers. Combined with high compression of data, this makes for a very efficient solution for many networks with widely dispersed clients. An added benefit is end users' capability to easily search for and retrieve data from tape without network administrator intervention.

Tape capacity considerations and the impact on network bandwidth during backup sessions should be carefully reviewed. It may be most practical to designate a specific local directory as the only target of nightly backup. However, making a full backup of each workstation, and especially mobile users' systems, has some wonderful benefits. It is the single best way to ensure that you can recover from a total disk failure or other catastrophic data loss.

IT REALLY HAPPENED: A user trying to free disk space on his Gateway workstation had accidentally deleted a directory instead of a file. Dozens of important files were lost. What made the problem more acute was that several other programmers in his department were dependent on the code he had lost. I was able to rescue all of the data from the previous night's backup, enabling everyone to go to work. This perfectly illustrates how the loss of one person's system can affect many people's productivity.

SHARE A PORTABLE TAPE DRIVE   There are many parallel port devices that can be used to facilitate workstation backup. A single unit can be shared among many systems. Purchase a new tape for each user and make sure that everyone uses it on a regular basis. This is also an excellent product for use with portable computers not connected to the corporate network.

TIP: Permit users to sign out portable backup equipment and provide all the software required to do the job. Create a detailed instruction sheet and include it with the hardware. Periodic email reminders can be used to prompt those who have not done a backup in a while.

My System Keeps Crashing

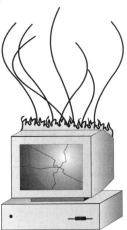

Nothing spooks a computer user more than an unstable system. Frequent crashes are sure to put data at risk. As I discussed in Chapter 3, users often form groups and share data between them. Never think that a misbehaving system is an isolated event. While there may be only one person's computer crashing, there are inevitably others who somehow depend on the work being done by that person.

The soundest method of making systems stable is summed up in the acronym KISS: Keep it simple, stupid! Computers that run the most standard setup with the smallest reliance on third-party add-ons to the operating system will be the most robust and also the easiest to service. Every single OS vendor preaches that a stripped-down configuration is the only way to track down problems.

Avoid System Enhancements

Fancy screen savers, performance monitors, and numerous other programs are marketed to help make any OS "better." Every one of these tools can raise the potential of conflicts with the core operation of a computer. Every extra line of code, especially ones that peer under the hood of the OS, robs performance and eats memory at the very least.

I have always run my work systems as bare bones as possible. Never relying on any optional programs has forced me to become intimately familiar with all the foibles and work-arounds that exist with any OS. This gives me a distinct advantage when doing support as well. Imagine how difficult it would be to help a user if I were only accustomed to working on a highly modified system. All of the hot keys and killer utilities that I relied on would not be present.

There will always be the need for well-written and powerful additions to your OS. For example, Quarterdeck's memory-enhancement program QEMM was an invaluable tool for users of DOS and earlier Windows systems. However, any of these programs will introduce their own unique problems. Why invite extra trouble when it can be avoided?

Create a Corporate Standard

While personal computers are wonderfully customizable, trying to support a myriad of setups is an open invitation to problems. Try whenever possible to create a standard profile, one that provides the functions your users demand and that most of the computers you support can share. This requires the purchase of similar systems with comparable features.

The many reasons that I outlined for server support apply here as well. The ability to share parts and drivers and to utilize the same utilities will lessen the burden on IT specialists' time. It is preferable to apply fixes and updates to a broad range of machines rather than to create unique ones for small groups of computers.

Standards should apply not only to the hardware used but also to the applications and operating systems installed. Reducing the number of variables will make repairs and support less complex. If all systems are supposed to subscribe to a particular setup, you can spot anomalies quickly.

Network administrators have a great deal of flexibility in limiting the scope of control (and damage) users have over their environment. Careful control over login scripts and file access rights can prevent the use of specific programs. Obviously reducing users' options for running software or changing system settings should make for an environment that is easier to support. An old DOS trick was to remove the RECOVER, FDISK, and FORMAT commands on a user's system just to prevent accidental hard drive erasure.

TIP: Build a system that works reliably and that contains installations of all the applications your company requires. Use a drive clone utility to make a disk image of a working system. Restoring malfunctioning systems can be quicker with a brute force restore of all files. The more elegant approach of a meticulous debugging of all settings and programs will often take more time than it is worth.

The Primary OS Troubleshooting Techniques

Every operating system has a method of running in a stripped-down fashion to aid in troubleshooting. These methods vary but all seek the same goal, to reduce the OS to its bare essentials and only then add extras one step at a time. If your OS can execute a minimal setup, you can add in software drivers and activate hardware components one at a time to see exactly which one causes a problem. This is the same philosophy that applies when working on printing problems.

The other method for troubleshooting requires disabling the more advanced features of the operating system. Many of the settings intended to boost throughput are turned off to throttle back performance. For example, you can disable video hardware acceleration with Windows computers. While speed is desirable, stability is more important.

MACINTOSH OPERATING SYSTEM   Perhaps the most elegant operating system for handling troubleshooting is the Mac's. Its Extensions Manager displays all Control Panels and OS extensions in a pick list that permits easy selection of which files to load or skip. You can even create and name customized startup settings that reflect a choice of system files.

The Extensions Manager has only been available with the most recent versions of Apple's OS. With older systems, you must manually move programs into and out of specific folders. This is perhaps the single most important reason to upgrade older Mac computers.

One of the nicest features is the predetermined set of boot profiles that include only Apple OS features. Using them is the surest way to identify the third-party program that is causing crashes. Start with a base OS setup and then manually add an extension or Control Panel in a piecemeal fashion.

WINDOWS   Anyone who has system crashes with Windows is familiar with Safe Mode. This is a system condition that disables many of the advanced features in the hope of creating stable operations for further diagnosis. With Windows 98, you can hold down the F8 key during system startup to force a Safe Mode boot.

You will not be able to access all of your devices and the screen will be using a standard VGA driver. The same 640×480 VGA mode is typically used on Windows NT Server for troubleshooting too. Video drivers seem to be the biggest cause for unstable operations. Using a standard, feature-bare setup usually allows the system to successfully load and display its desktop.

Windows has several ways to throttle back performance. All are reached with the Control Panel application. Within the System group, go to the Performance tab to change settings for the file system and graphics adapter. Disable certain features and reboot with the new configuration, and then attempt to run the crashing applications.

While users may be leery of options that seem to rob performance, the overall penalty these settings exact is rather small. Even if benchmark programs can measure a difference, I have never seen any user complain of a noticeable lag in system responsiveness. Most importantly, the stability gained more than compensates for the modest reduction in speed.

LINUX   The best friend a troubled user of a damaged Linux system can have is a system boot disk. These can be created during the installation process of Red Hat Linux, for example. Slackware distributions typically contain bootable disk images that you can use to access a system if the root partition has errors. The most important step when installing any UNIX-like operating system is to create an emergency boot disk. It is the single best way to resuscitate a computer whose file system has gotten damaged or corrupted.

Clearly label the diskette with the complete information. Indicate the version of the operating system and the kernel level. You should record the specific hardware involved for the system, paying particular attention to hard disk parameters such as partition configuration. I always make a copy of the rescue disk and store it centrally with my other software archives and keep another copy with the system it was created on.

UNIX systems have almost always been designed with networking as a central function. File servers are rarely shut down except for upgrades or similar maintenance. When I stressed to my users that leaving their computers on overnight and weekends was the preferred practice, it was somewhat difficult for them to grasp. I found the best way to illustrate this concept was pointing out that people never unplug their clocks or refrigerators. Some equipment is designed never to be shut down but instead to run continuously. A further point that reinforces this concept is stressing how a lightbulb tends to fail when first turned on. The sudden burst of power and heat causes the filament to fail. In the same way, electronic equipment is aged slightly whenever it is turned on.

BOOT WITH A CLEAN SYSTEM DISK   In the old days prior to the prevalent use of GUIs, the best troubleshooting tool was a DOS disk. By using a floppy with just a COMMAND.COM file in the A:> drive, you could start the computer and bypass all of the CONFIG.SYS and AUTOEXEC.BAT functions. With the use of Windows 95, Windows 98, and Windows NT, it is impossible to boot from a floppy disk and have access to the computer through the GUI. The number of large files required to start up a modern GUI system is just too much for a single floppy to store.

However, while you may not have access to all of the fancy features of a GUI, you can still run diagnostics to verify your drives' integrity or to scan for a virus. Always make sure that all of your systems have ready access to an emergency startup disk. This is an item that every IT specialist should keep handy. Some of the newest Windows computers and most Macs have the capability to use their CD-ROM drives for booting an OS. Some versions of Linux also permit this feature.

TIP: Make a Windows 95 or Windows 98 boot disk through the Control
Panel. The Add/Remove Programs icon will take you to a Properties window
where you can select the Startup Disk tab and with a single click make a
bootable floppy.

Access to a boot disk is critical to the use of configuration and other
utilities. Network cards such as the ubiquitous NE-2000 Ethernet
adapter use DOS command-prompt executable programs to select
Interrupt and I/O addresses. Be careful not to confuse a windowed
DOS prompt under a GUI as equivalent to the DOS environment
you achieve with a boot disk. Your access to hardware can be hindered
or otherwise shielded by the presence of the Windows interface. You
almost always want to run diagnostics and setup programs with
as little interference from the operating system as possible.

CHAPTER 6

Your Company and Technology

B y definition, IT specialists are supposed to possess exceptional technical skills and vast experience with many types of computing systems. They must also have a varied arsenal of other abilities. Key among them is a keen understanding of the business their company is in. The IT staff rarely decides on its own priorities; instead we are responsible for addressing the needs generated by the numerous demands of the company we work for.

While the company where you work can manufacture myriad products or provide diverse suites of services, the challenge for IT is making sure that all the data to support these transactions is readily available. Sales figures, production schedules, and financial information are only a small portion of the data required to run a modern corporation.

Intertwined throughout the operations of any company are computer systems that handle reams of data. Information is the lifeblood of any organization. It must be created, stored, modified, and transmitted on systems that IT develops and supports. Data may also be created for use by your customers or accessed from your suppliers' computers.

Being able to develop the correct system solutions for an employer requires that IT learn as much as possible about all the activities going on in each division of the company and how these processes are affected by computers. Only through familiarization with corporate operations can you adequately address the diverse needs that exist. Rather than presenting generic solutions with a generalized approach, you should develop the skills to quantify exactly what the users at your company demand. Then you must create targeted tools that truly maximize the efforts of the people at your firm that depend on computers.

This chapter explores the many areas that you must learn about to completely manage the depth and scope of actual and potential computer use at a company. It is especially important to grasp the concept of potential computer use. IT has always been expected to know how to leverage expertise with information technology into solving real business problems. You must always be vigilant in identifying new opportunities to exploit technology. By functioning as a consultant to your own company, you can make a tremendous impact on the ability for your company to grow and boost profitability.

BUSINESS CHALLENGES FOR IT

While some companies regard IT's primary function as simply "keeping the servers running," this is a myopic view and severely limiting. Technology has become the single most important element shaping modern business operations. Enabling the company to wield technology with precision and to respond nimbly to new opportunities is clearly the most valuable contribution that IT can make.

I have always advocated an involved and proactive role for IT. Computer systems and related technology have had a profound and revolutionary effect on how our economy and businesses function. The evolution of commerce has truly accelerated during the past 20 years through the advent of personal computers, high-speed communications, and the Internet. Even the most pessimistic analysts see a steady increase in the influence of computer systems. IT has a unique role to play in every corporation. We are the only people capable of translating raw computing capacity into tangible tools for solving business problems.

Data Is a Resource (and It Costs Money)

The core belief that must ground all of your activities is that corporate data in all its forms is a vital resource. Every business activity—sales, purchasing, facilities, taxes, payroll, and other functions—generates or is driven by data. By providing the tools for employees to understand and manipulate this data, IT can dramatically affect how a company behaves.

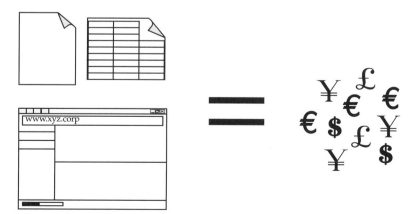

Data must be treated as a precious commodity. While it may be fairly simple to calculate the cost of raw materials and depreciate capital on equipment, companies rarely view data in the same way as they do hard goods. Placing a value on corporate data simplifies your job when proposing new systems or justifying budget expenditures. If IT can clearly demonstrate that money invested in computer technology has tangible fiscal benefits, then winning approval from the CFO and other "bean counters" is much easier.

The continuous investment in new computer systems and related technology is driven by the need to process greater amounts of data more quickly and in different formats. Information that was once held strictly in proprietary database formats, requiring dedicated terminals in order to be viewed, is now accessible with Web browsers via virtually any platform. Multimedia applications permit data to be displayed with compelling charts and recorded comments rather than dry tables of numbers.

Calculate the Cost of Data

I must admit that no adequate formula for determining exactly what data is worth can be found. Certainly every company will value differently the information held within its databases. By providing each department within a business fast and easy access to the data they need, IT will boost productivity and hopefully profitability. Assessing exactly how much value can be given to individual data records will vary greatly at every company.

Perhaps the best way to frame this calculation is by accumulating all the costs associated with the storage, presentation, and interpretation of data. This will include all the physical hardware, operating systems, application software, network infrastructure, training costs, support staff, maintenance contracts, telecommunication links, and numerous other factors. The other side of the equation could be every sales transaction that the business conducts on their systems. In other words all the costs of handling and creating information would be compared to revenues generated.

Some companies place a great deal of attention on ROI or return on investments. These corporations want to be sure that their expenses associated with deploying technology solutions are producing tangible benefits. I have examined this concept in more detail in Chapter 9.

THE VALUE OF DATA VARIES   While both large and small companies treasure their data, the differences among companies makes calculating the worth of data difficult. It is hard to associate a real dollar value with access to information. An enormous manufacturer like Boeing has vastly different requirements than a local independent hardware store. Both will certainly agree that meeting customer needs is important and can be facilitated by computing systems, but selling an aircraft is vastly different than selling a screwdriver.

Another possible way to value data is by measuring the cost of replacing it. The Colorado Memory System division of Hewlett-Packard makes the following claim on its Web site: "Industry analysts estimate that it costs $2,500 to re-enter one megabyte of lost data. According to some estimates, re-entering lost data costs U.S. firms $5 billion and 25 million business-days annually."

The Keys to Understanding Your Company

Corporations approach technology in a variety of ways. Some businesses readily embrace computer systems and willingly invest money and time into building large and dynamic IT departments. These companies give great latitude to IT, allowing it to influence the company's structure and its performance in the marketplace. In these organizations, IT is expected to contribute expertise and guidance at the highest levels of the company hierarchy.

The opposite side of the spectrum finds IT managers and staff laboring within companies that only grudgingly allocate funds to technology and the people that support computer systems. For many reasons, IT is simply looked upon as a "cost center," and minimizing expenditures is the first priority when budgets are created. While you may be relegated to a caretaker roll at your company, there are ways to gain influence and build a presence that becomes perceived as vital to corporate fortunes.

If you can identify choke points in business processes and address them with technology solutions, you can gain respect for your abilities and the potential power of computers. The best way to gain influence is by demonstrating that your solutions will save money and boost efficiency. You should strive to make IT proactive and not simply wait for trouble to land at your door. An effective IT manager is approachable, eager to hear problems and suggestions and inviting more work for her staff.

In some cases, the best advocates for increasing the roll of IT are satisfied users. Simply by addressing the daily routine needs of people, the IT specialist gains visibility and appreciation for a valuable contribution. Take every opportunity to go beyond the problem at hand and find ways to make users more productive. Look to translate informal proactive work into a core part of the role IT plays at your firm.

No matter whether your company embraces or shuns technology, IT staff members must firmly grasp the type of business that they serve. While I don't plan to offer a treatise on industrial organization or corporate economics, in this section I will explore the major factors that you should consult to better understand your influence on a company. Once you have identified which areas are most relevant to the input of IT, you can begin to determine how IT can meet these demands and make your company more prosperous.

The following subjects are not exhaustive. There are simply no universal rules that can be applied to every situation and company. However, a savvy IT specialist should be able to use this information as a baseline starting point for their investigations.

Look for every area in your company where data is produced and shared, both within and outside your business. Learn as much as you can about the company you support. While you cannot be an expert in every operation, you must cultivate an appreciation and understanding of the range of activities performed by those you support. The best solutions are ones clearly created to meet the demands of end users, business partners, and customers. Look for opportunities to apply your expertise with hardware and software to the most vexing and frustrating tasks at your company and you will garner adulation and respect for a job well done.

What Products Does Your Company Offer?

The first question, and the easiest one to answer, is exactly what your company sells. For example, your company may be the world's third-largest producer of widgets in the world. IT in this case should learn everything there is to know about sales, marketing, production, distribution, and all related activities in the world of widgets.

While manufacturing physical goods is fairly straightforward to understand, many companies don't actually produce physical products. Instead, they provide services that other businesses purchase. Express freight carriers are an example of this type of business. Companies in this field provide a service—rapid distribution and delivery of products to customers—rather than manufacturing goods. No matter what type of firm you are employed by, timely access to data is vital to corporate health.

If your company provides services you must be completely schooled in the depth and breadth of their offerings. Whether producing physical products or services there are similar structures for marketing, distributing, and sales. Familiarity with your employer's business must include more than just knowledge of the computer systems they utilize.

CHECK SALES MATERIALS   The fastest way to see what your company sells is to consult any sales materials that are given to customers. Perhaps there is an online catalog or a hard-copy price sheet that lists all the products offered. Obviously the Sales Department must possess a very clear image of exactly what products and services are offered. Spend some time with Sales staff management and get a sense of how they envision the company.

SALES CAMPAIGNS AND SLOGANS   Advertisements and product catalogs typically feature tag lines that give the most distilled version of the corporate image. Microsoft's current slogan—"Where do you want to go today?"—evokes a sense of technology enabling users to face any challenge that presents itself.

While investigating catchy slogans and other marketing efforts may be foreign to many IT experts, you must use every means available to understand and appreciate how your company reaches out to clients. Once you gain familiarity with how sales are made, you can make more informed decisions when designing technical solutions for marketing efforts.

While your company may decide against using email campaigns to inform existing customers about new products, IT is certainly equipped to design or outsource the software and hardware to conduct mass emailings if needed. There may be other occasions in which IT needs to produce mailing labels for conventional mail appeals. Perhaps a centralized fax server needs to be maintained for mass fax distribution of sales materials.

At the heart of almost any customer outreach effort are databases of information detailing purchasing habits and demographic data. IT holds the keys to unlocking the data and extracting the most pertinent records. While contacting all clients en masse can be useful in some cases, it is often better and more economical to target a specific subset of all customers.

Consult the Corporate Mission

Many companies have a credo or mission statement that clearly outlines their goals and corporate identity. Almost all mission statements contain words like "first," "best," or "largest," attempting to convey an idealized image of the business. When you design initiatives to address challenges where you work, make a concerted effort to address the points raised by the company mission. By demonstrating that you're paying attention to what the senior executives prize most, you can win their support more easily.

While publicly stated goals and missions may sound impressive, realistically the most important factor in many executives' minds is how well their company is doing compared to the competition. Naturally, most companies want to grow market share and prevent customers from choosing another vendor. The free marketplace in most industries is populated with voracious competitors that look for any advantage. Computer systems can often provide an "edge" to many aspects of companies' operations. When you design technical solutions that can be used to improve efficiency or better serve customers, corporate decision-makers should be quick to support your initiatives.

Many IT projects require a good deal of capital and commitment of personnel. While it does not guarantee their endorsement, making certain that you purposefully target solutions to further the companies' stated goals is much appreciated by corporate decision-makers. If technology is particularly foreign and intimidating to the residents of the executive suites in your company, then couching IT ideas in business-relevant terminology and evoking the greater company mindset is the smartest strategy for gaining budgetary and other endorsements for your approach.

Learning Your Industry Vernacular

Acronyms are so popular with manufacturers of technology products that it is not uncommon to discover new acronyms accompanying each new release of hardware and software. Industry-standard terms like SCSI, DAT, TCP, and UDP are bandied about freely by the digital crowd.

In fact, every field has its own unique language in which slang terms and sets of initials make a shorthand reference to commonly used procedures and products. Viewers of police and medical dramas on television have all been exposed to actors requesting APBs, CAT scans, and numerous other procedures by spouting a string of acronyms at a rapid clip. You must become familiar with the lingo common to your workplace.

Learning the language of your company can be eased with several resources. See if there is a dictionary relevant to the industry. Dictionaries of legal, medical, biology, and other distinct lexicons are available in most bookstores. Textbooks designed for introductory course work in your industry can be another terrific source of common terms and definitions. See if there are any professional societies or organizations that your coworkers participate in. These associations may maintain Web sites or produce other publications that can be a useful reference.

IT REALLY HAPPENED: One of my responsibilities at *PC Week* is supporting the Editorial Production Department. Because the staff comprised people with journalism and publishing experience, I needed to learn a great deal about magazine terminology. For example, I found out that terms like "ears," "legs," and "ankles" referred not to human anatomy but to the location of elements on a printed page. Making sure I understood the staffs' lingo was key to my effectiveness in understanding the dynamics of their jobs.

Become a Student of Your Industry

In previous chapters, I stressed the need for IT to learn exactly how those that they support use computers. While it is critical to be familiar with the spreadsheets, word processors, and other applications your employees use, that knowledge is incomplete until you understand the nature and scope of the problems that the software and hardware needs to address.

Using the same methods that I suggested for acquiring knowledge about the specific computer use of those you support, you must also learn about the general business challenges and responsibilities that face everyone in the company. This can mean spending time with other departments in order to appreciate the scope of their jobs. Remember that limiting yourself to just the computing aspects of employees' work is not adequate; you need to understand the entire picture.

While you can certainly catalog which people use Microsoft Word and who relies on Adobe PageMaker, it's important to remember that each of these tools is exploited to address certain needs. Strive to go beyond simply knowing who uses each program and instead try to grasp the challenges of those that use the software are trying to meet. Knowing the context and scope of computer usage is critical to truly understanding how to best design IT solutions.

How Does Customer Communication Take Place?

Another key to understanding how your company functions is to learn about the dynamics of its customer relationships. Successful companies continuously strive to better meet the needs of their customers, and technology provides many opportunities to achieve this goal.

What types of data does your company need to share with customers? Certainly every client will want to know their account status, and they may have questions regarding how much money is owed, when the payment is due, the status of their order, and so on. The variety of questions that can be asked will certainly vary at different companies, but it is easy to see that your clients may request all types of information.

Vendors also need to gather data from customers. The ability to identify past purchasing habits allows the seller to better mold the relationship with a client. E-commerce sites, for example, have built a reputation for permitting highly individualized shopping experiences. There is an emerging niche of products called Customer Relationship Management systems. Companies like ActionWare try to automate the capture and distribution of customer information. Such tools are vital for sales campaigns as well as for technical support issues.

How Is Distribution Handled?

Getting products into consumers' hands quickly is one way to foster a positive relationship. Computer systems are often called upon to speed shipping, inventory, and other aspects of product delivery. Sales forces must be able to keep abreast of orders and verify that products are being sent to the correct location.

Our fast-paced society has gotten people accustomed to next-day delivery and "just in time" manufacturing, and customers often want feedback on their order status. Many company Web sites allow clients to check delivery status. Providing customers with the tools to track shipments themselves is emerging as a standard practice for many businesses.

How Are Sales Transacted?

Before the Internet, the most prevalent way to purchase products was to physically go into a store and interact directly with a merchant. Catalog sales and traveling sales staff were a valuable adjunct to traditional sales channels, yet they account for smaller percentages of total transactions every year. The demise of the famous Sears catalog and the collapse of retailers like Service Merchandise helps to highlight the dramatic changes that have taken place in the retail sales world.

Sales today increasingly see merchant's Web servers interacting directly with buyers' browsers. One of the most well-known examples of this sales model is the online bookseller Amazon.com.

The astounding success of Amazon has sparked online competition from traditional retailers like Barnes & Noble and Borders.

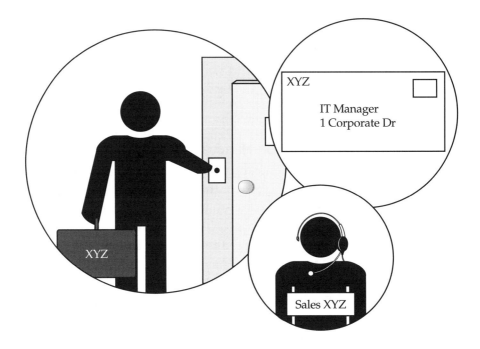

Today many sales forces are equipped with portable computers. This technology provides a way for salespeople to carry a tremendous amount of information and to access corporate data on faraway hosts. Laptops and other mobile devices, such as personal digital assistants, have revolutionized the way sales are handled. This direct way of bringing computer interactions to the customer is a valuable addition to more traditional selling methods.

Even if they aren't doing sales over the Web, companies recognize that having a presence on the Internet is a critical element of their overall strategy. It is a wonderful method for buyers to get information directly from a manufacturer. Alerts about new products or innovative uses for existing purchases can be very valuable to customers. In addition, providing an easy means for consumers to give direct feedback can be a boon to your company.

Where Does the Company Advertise?

While advertisements in traditional formats such as print, radio, television, billboards, and the sides of buses is sure to continue, the Internet provides another channel for advertising dollars. Television ads for virtually all products now contain references to Web addresses that customers can visit for additional information.

Being able to exploit the Internet in particular has become increasingly popular recently. The banner ads on Web sites almost always link back to the advertisers' own sites, where transactions can take place. These ads are the splashy vendor advertisements that hawk products and services along the top border of your browser window attempting to entice a mouse click from a Web site visitor. The ability to sell over the Internet is sure to make the Web an increasingly vital advertising medium. It is the only form of advertising that permits near-instantaneous interaction directly between vendors and consumers.

TIP: Keep aware of the rapidly changing face of e-commerce. Taxation and concerns for privacy will fuel the passage of laws as governments struggle to understand and control the changing nature of our economy.

OTHER METHODS OF CONTACT While the role of computing technology is clear in Web-based advertising, there are several other ways that computers can be used to reach consumers directly. Email inboxes are a prime candidate for the reception of sales pitches. By using mailing lists culled from visitors to your company Web site or purchased from numerous vendors, you can assemble a large number of people who may want to receive information from your company.

WARNING: Spam, or junk email, is a scourge to many users and I certainly never encourage its use for reaching customers. Always provide an easy way to permit recipients to remove their accounts from any automatic mailing systems. Clearly indicate on mass fax or email messages how recipients can prevent future correspondence.

It can be difficult to draw a distinction between mass email campaigns and spam. Many people clearly believe that any unsolicited messages constitute spam. I have found that messages I get from certain vendors are valuable alerts to special sales or new product announcements. I find that I harbor the most animosity towards companies that I have never done business with before or offerings for goods and services I would never consider. Remember to be considerate and permit visitors to your Web site or with other contact to request that their email not be used for any unsolicited messaging or sold to other companies.

IT should embrace listserv technology to conduct email campaigns and carry out other data distribution tasks. Dedicated specifically for managing massive lists of mail addresses, listservs are a great way to send out sales offers, technical update notifications, white papers, and other materials of interest to your customers. You can also outsource these services; firms typically charge a sliding-scale fee depending on the number of emails sent.

Fax machines are another common tool used to foster communication with customers. Software and specialized servers for managing vast databases of client contact information and multiple fax lines are often used to send all types of data. Remember that some companies and countries only subscribe to Telex or similar legacy or proprietary technologies. Never lose sight of a "technology gap" that may exist between your company and its customers.

How Is Customer Feedback Sought and Received?

Companies readily admit that getting information from their clients is a key to business success. Designing new products, setting prices, and fixing problems with existing purchases are good examples of issues that depend on adequate communication between sellers and buyers. There are many ways in which an IT department can maximize its company's ability to collect customer data and analyze the information.

While most companies have retained traditional methods of gathering customer comments, such as phone help lines, many firms have broadened their efforts considerably by reaching out via the Web. Virtually every consumer product manufacturer and seller has a Web site that is heavily promoted in their advertisements. This unique medium provides a nearly instantaneous and consistently available forum for customers and vendors to share information.

Communicating with Your Suppliers

Whether your company acquires raw materials in railroad boxcars or finished components from manufacturers, open communication with your suppliers is crucial. New orders for additional units, changes in pricing, and other requests must all be handled quickly and efficiently among many parties. These lines of communication are among the many systems that IT supports and maintains.

Both office supply companies that furnish products like pens or tape and computer manufacturers like Dell maintain elaborate electronic ordering systems. By enabling their customers to place orders with a secure Web browser or via a proprietary interface, these companies allow customers faster and easier ordering procedures than standard telephone sales can provide.

Maintaining a steady flow of information is the only way to ensure that your company can function properly. Data that is shared with a supplier must normally meet certain criteria to be used efficiently. While your company may standardize on Lotus 1-2-3 for spreadsheets, your accounting firm may demand files formatted with Microsoft Excel. Being aware of data incompatibilities and taking appropriate steps to mitigate conflicts will certainly save your company time, money, and aggravation.

IT REALLY HAPPENED: At *PC Week,* digital files are transmitted to our printer every day. Not only are we concerned with ensuring that our files reach the printers' network quickly and intact, but the type of files transmitted is also important. While we can send standard PostScript files generated by QuarkXPress, costs go down tremendously if we preprocess the PostScript files into another format (CT/LW) that can be readily digested by the printer. After learning what format our printer preferred and calculating the savings, we decided to purchase a Raster Image Processor, or RIP, to create the desired file format.

Working with Your Partners

For purposes of this discussion, I define "business partners" as other companies that your business must rely on to function. After all, no company can survive or flourish on its own. Services like electrical power, telecommunications, construction, payroll, and many other outsourced functions are provided by others for a fee. Each of these transactions generates or requires an important data exchange.

Every company has a standardized method for doing business. For example, Ford's automotive manufacturing systems and McDonald's food preparation processes both demonstrate quite clearly the benefits of consistent and uniform operations. Working within a set structure makes ordering, pricing, and manufacturing less complex. These companies' customers are fully aware of their options and can tailor their behavior to that supported by their suppliers.

Seek Common Ground

Always strive to make your systems compliant with your business partners'. Meet regularly to determine what can be done to ease the sharing of data. Determine whether there are automated methods that can translate preferred file formats back and forth. Try to alert partners well in advance of changes to your infrastructure that might impact the flow of data. Also, be cautious when adopting new products to avoid generating new incompatibilities.

Efficiency gains should always be matched by lower costs. IT work is difficult enough without the complication of incompatibilities; avoiding them should always be high on your agenda. A financial incentive is perhaps the best method to encourage subscribing to standards. Consider spending (or charging) less whenever you can find a way to utilize similar capabilities with less work.

The pricing and purchasing of computer services can be especially perplexing, and the movement and massaging of data will only continue to grow in importance. Keep these rules in mind, and we will investigate this important topic more closely in Chapter 9.

Tracking Your Competitors

It is a rare corporation that exists without any type of competition. Even if a firm is the first to introduce a product and it seems to dominate the market, other companies eventually emerge and vie for the same customers. The most likely scenario is a marketplace where several players of different sizes and capabilities vigorously compete. Understanding how your competitors operate is key to ensuring that your own company remains healthy.

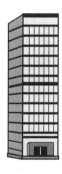

If a competitor releases a new product or service, your company may want or need to respond with a similar offering. Since technology is typically needed to support new initiatives, IT must be aware of what "the enemy" is up to at all times. Monitor their Web sites and subscribe to news sources that cover your industry to keep abreast of the marketplace.

Understand that competition can be a vicious example of Darwin's law, survival of the fittest. Companies that lack the agility to compete in the new economics of the Internet age are doomed to failure. Retailing is changing perhaps more rapidly than any other industry today. Established stores that have missed the opportunity to exploit the Web initially may have become threatened by year-old startups driven by modern technology.

Certainly some industries are more susceptible to online competition. Books and records have been relatively easy to market with browser equipped consumers. Clothing or furniture sales are still areas where customers want to browse physical store aisles and touch the fabric or try things on. However, startups like

Furniture.com have been making forays into this arena. Catalog sales stalwarts such as Land's End have also made major commitments to e-commerce. There is most assuredly going to be more emphasis on electronic sales even for companies that have yet to examine its scope and impact.

Competition Causes Change

IT must frequently augment or design new systems to respond to challenges created by competitors. New features or services are constantly being offered to woo or retain customers. When your company identifies competitor offerings that demand a similar capability, IT must be able to quickly determine what existing systems can be modified to offer similar features. Perhaps an already established automated technical support "Fax-Back" system can be adopted to offer price quotes.

Being able to stay a step ahead of your competitors requires a proactive approach. Always look for ways to extend the existing capabilities of your systems. Be especially mindful of new releases of software that your company uses. Updates typically include new features that can be exploited to your advantage.

WARNING: Don't automatically embrace the newest technologies and applications. New features are rarely appreciated if they render existing solutions obsolete. Forcing upgrades on customers who may not require any new capabilities is a sure way to earn scorn and alienate clients.

Understanding Your Company's Personality

Companies have personalities that are as diverse as people. Workplaces may require formal business attire daily from all employees or permit casual Fridays during the summer months. There may be a strict hierarchy of titles and a clear chain of command or a more flat organization in which dialog and cooperation is encouraged between all workers.

Many companies spend tremendous amounts of research and consulting dollars to establish and project a particular image to their customers. A large corporation may wish to appear approachable, friendly, and small enough to devote individual attention to those buying its goods and services. Smaller firms often wish to appear bigger to garner the attention that would normally go toward their larger competitors.

You should understand that the corporate philosophy has a tremendous effect on how Information Technology is applied at a particular company. Part of making yourself an exceptional IT specialist is having a deep understanding and appreciation for the role that you are asked to fill at your company.

Your work may involve interactions (or membership) in union shops. Familiarize yourself with any contractual obligations that need to be followed.

Does the Size of Your Company Matter?

IT professionals love to answer yes-or-no questions such as this with a vague, "It depends." Certainly the sheer size of a company affects the number of functions that IT takes on. However, a small Internet start-up with ten employees and a single server in a broom closet generally has a much more frantic attitude toward system availability than a 200-member law firm does.

While head counts are a useful indicator of IT's workload, the number of network nodes yields a more accurate picture. There are many people who use several computers daily, especially in high-tech firms. Don't forget my descriptions of the many types of computer users earlier in this book.

I sometimes refer to certain employees I support as "Dog Users." In the same way people calculate the age of their dog relative to humans' years, I calculate these users' demands in relation to those of normal users. Who could forget the commercial with Lorne Greene saying, "Sparky is 13. That's 79 to you and me!" This analogy has led me to say things like, "That damn Joel! Supporting him is like supporting seven normal people!"

Dispersion Definitely Matters

While overall user numbers give you an important indicator of IT's responsibilities, an even bigger influence is the physical distances between company locations. Having a widely scattered workforce to support and design solutions for makes IT's job much more difficult. Longer lines of communication and vastly different needs at various locations make centralized decision making and network management problematic in even the best circumstances.

A large corporation is typically constructed of different divisions acquired over a long period of time. Newly acquired branches are especially likely to possess different systems and IT philosophies that developed locally. Being able to effectively merge information between disparate systems is one of the major challenges facing IT.

Geographic differences can also account for difficulty in obtaining certain equipment or services. In rural locations, you'll have more difficulty obtaining high-speed data communications equipment than you would in a large city. Authorized service providers for hardware and contract programming and networking specialists are much more difficult to find away from major markets.

INTERNATIONAL CORPORATIONS   The challenge of maintaining corporate infrastructures across borders is particularly difficult. Data communication infrastructures can be radically different when dealing with nationalized industries. While ISDN and T1 lines can be simple to obtain in certain areas, other countries may only permit Telex or Switched-56 circuits. Federal statutes may also affect encryption standards for digital communication. Export law can closely regulate limits on the level of encryption that can be sold to foreign-based corporations.

The difficulty involved in usually simple tasks, such as making equipment compliant with local voltages and phone lines, has spawned a large market of suppliers of adaptation equipment. Tariff and government export controls may limit the types of software and file types that can successfully and legally be exchanged internationally.

Legal and Contractual Obligations

Certain industries operate under strict governmental rules for conducting business. Financial institutions such as banks, credit unions, insurance brokers, security dealers, and others must keep accurate records of operations and transactions and are often subject to reviews and audits. Telecommunication firms, broadcasters, and others must adhere to local, state, and federal laws.

Make sure that your IT department gets the legal advice it needs to ensure compliance with applicable statutes. Have your company's legal team make periodic reviews of your procedures to account for changes in law. Issues of privacy and protection of financial information of customers have become increasingly sensitive with the boom in electronic commerce.

Check the Rules

IT must always be aware of any state, federal, or other laws that require their computer systems to report and record data. Not only must compliance with governmental legal statutes be verified, but contracts made with your companies' clients must be strictly followed as well. Special deals that change pricing based on purchasing levels or other criteria can vary from customer to customer.

For example, a bank may issue credit cards in a number of states, but each state may enforce different rules for how interest can be calculated and how long a grace period can be. Since holders of cards in different states must be handled in distinct ways, this makes programming the systems that handle these types of accounts fairly complex.

The Company's Age and History

Many new firms have embraced computing tools from the outset. Knowing that a competitive advantage can be afforded by adopting modern telecommunication and data processing equipment, they have always had a strong commitment to the use of technology.

In contrast, some staid and established companies continue to resist the adoption of much computing equipment except when absolutely necessary.

IT REALLY HAPPENED: During a visit to my lawyer in 1998, I noticed that his secretary was using a vintage IBM PC-AT with a monochrome monitor and a DOS version of WordPerfect. The obvious look of astonishment on my face was countered with a quick reminder that everything worked and it served its limited purposes well. In stark contrast, my cab ride home was with a taxi firm that was utilizing a computerized dispatch system with terminals in every car.

Many firms continue to rely on the record-keeping methods they devised decades ago. Workers in medical offices and law firms are likely to consult paper records in color-coded binders rather than accessing data stored in electronic files. The comfort level with familiar procedures and the extensive efforts that would be required in order to translate old typed and handwritten documents into electronic form make the adoption of computing systems a difficult proposition.

Past Experiences

Previous experiences that decision-makers have had with computer systems and IT professionals, both good and bad, can greatly influence the future decisions that company will make. Vivid memories of an investment in an expensive system initiative that resulted in a costly fiasco will temper most enthusiasm toward new projects that you propose. Bad memories take a long time to fade, and you must confront them every time you want to address the same problem that an earlier approach failed to service properly.

IT REALLY HAPPENED: The editorial production department at *PC Week* was anxious to adopt a robust work-flow administration system to aid in the tracking of MS Word documents from reporters to editors to the copy desk and finally to layout. A clumsy user interface, poor performance, and a crashing database server doomed the ambitious project. Subsequently, every time a rival system was evaluated, disgruntled users raised the specter of the earlier disaster and strongly resisted the exploration of a new solution.

You may also encounter companies where previous experiences with IT staff and management have left users horribly tainted. Arrogant IT directors and incompetent support specialists can sour a person's opinion toward the entire IT profession. While the failure of computers and software can be expected and forgiven, it is much more difficult to overcome problems due to human factors.

OVERCOMING A NEGATIVE HISTORY   The expression "hit the ground running" is perhaps the clearest way to describe the attitude you need to assume to deal with prior IT problems. The quickest methods to win back the trust and respect of the company you work for is to quickly and clearly demonstrate the ability and determination to fix nagging issues.

Corporate Executives' Attitudes

A critical factor to weigh when assessing how your company approaches technology is the differing levels of commitment and interest that high-level decision-makers possess. CEOs who have always relied on secretaries for dictation, letter writing, typing, and other chores may never entertain the notion of using a computer to get their work done.

While mainframes have been part of corporate infrastructures for decades, the personal computer revolution of the late 1970s completely bypassed scores of executives in many industries. Having learned how to manage without a computer and risen up the corporate ladder devoid of personal familiarity with computing systems, older executives are less likely to grasp the importance of investing in technology.

IT SPECIALISTS AS CONSULTANTS

There can be few higher aspirations for an IT specialist than to be a valuable consultant for their own company. With a combination of technical expertise and a thorough understanding of the complex structure and business of the company you support, you have the unique ability to shape and foster the growth and direction that your business will follow. Computers have demonstrated the unique ability to truly transform how commerce is conducted.

By following the guidelines earlier in this chapter, you can get a firm grasp on your company's current uses of technology and what can be done to augment them. You should know what your company's general attitude is toward technology. Some companies will seek to exploit every advantage computers can offer while others adopt grudgingly only a minimum of systems. Another factor to consider is the relationship within the corporation of those producing data and others using it.

Once you have quantified the various items that define the internal usage of computer systems, the next steps involve investigating how data is shared with customers and suppliers. Melding your company's systems so they can order products, track shipping, and react to various customer requests is an exceedingly complex task. Compliance with government regulations and contractual obligations must always be carefully considered.

IT Consulting and Project Management

In Chapter 12, I will expand in much greater detail on project management. This section of the book is more concerned with gathering information on corporate use of IT and the general business structures that generate the need for specific projects. Certainly issues will be added to your docket by the direct request of corporate management. However, many other projects are generated directly by IT for itself. By observing company behavior and computer use and researching other factors, you should be able to readily identify numerous opportunities for your expertise with computing technology to be used as an impetus to create new tasks for IT to boost corporate efficiency and user satisfaction.

Composing a Mission Statement for IT

Many companies expend a great deal of effort and money to create a mission statement. The ideal is to produce a clear and focused document that defines the goals the entire company is striving to fulfill. Typically they contain a number of bullet points that evoke the standards the corporation seeks to meet. High on all of these lists are a commitment to customers and a desire to continually raise the performance level of the corporation.

While sometimes filled with lofty "marketing-speak" language and vague objectives, as discussed previously, mission statements can help a company define what it does and help focus efforts toward a common goal. For this reason, I think it is important for IT departments to create a mission statement of their own. Not only will it reinforce the goals for those who work in IT, but it will convey to others at your company exactly what IT seeks to accomplish.

You want to convey an image of professionalism and dedication to all levels of the organization. Your entire company should be aware of the wide scope of IT work. While this cannot be adequately conveyed by a single document, it is useful to provide a context for

IT department activities. The following is a sample IT mission statement:

1. Provide all the technological tools required by the XYZ Corporation to excel in the market.

2. Commit to developing the best solutions in a cost-effective manner.

3. Listen carefully to user needs and address problems in a timely fashion.

4. Explore new products and technologies to maintain a competitive edge.

5. Maintain a focused and enjoyable environment for all IT staff.

6. Demonstrate an ongoing commitment to technology education for end users and IT workers.

Defining Priorities

Once you have established that IT should function as an agent of change at your workplace, you must specify a direction for your efforts. The formula to follow when setting priorities is first to make sure that all of the primary obligations to company needs are met. These are all the systems and processes that clearly require consistent attention. Obvious concerns are keeping the servers up and maximizing users' ability to access data.

While there should be a core set of requirements that IT pledges to address, once attention has been given to basic computing needs, IT can focus on solving problems. These may be nagging issues known throughout the company or other problems that are discovered via user questionnaires and interviews.

Beyond the known problems and minimum requirements for system support, a proactive IT specialist should strive to find areas where computing can be wielded with greater precision. An exceptional IT department applies technological innovations in a way that boosts profits and enhances efficiency.

Computers have certainly boosted productivity in many areas. Word processors revolutionized the creation and editing of documents. Spreadsheets signaled a drastic revolution in the way financial calculations are performed. Networks and the Internet have altered how people and companies share data and conduct commerce. However, none of the technologies that permit these modern workplace activities are nearly as effective if there is not a clear focus and direction for using them.

Only IT can truly provide direction and technical leadership as to how computers can best be used at a firm. We are the experts with the tools of technology and we must figure out exactly how to tailor the systems so that those using them can do so with speed and confidence. IT also must make ongoing efforts to spot new opportunities and vulnerabilities. Never forget that a hot product from last year can quickly become obsolete and costly to maintain.

TIP: Think of your management role in IT as being the head coach of a team. You need to assess the abilities of all the players and determine how to maximize their effectiveness. Your strategy is to stay responsive and flexible enough to react quickly to your competitors' actions. Finally, your clients (or fans) need to be pleased by your efforts or they will look for another team to root for.

Basic Concerns

This category is for items like server maintenance and backup. IT must competently cover all the obvious needs at a company. You should define a precise list of items that form a strong basis for building your IT departments' "charter" with your corporation. IT must pledge to cover all the computing technology necessary to keep a company in business.

Always be sure to emphasize these core concerns. While new projects and products have a strong appeal, your attention to basic maintenance must never take a back seat. IT certainly must explore new areas, but you must never neglect the factors that satisfy the bottom line. A company that cannot complete a sale is marked for early extinction.

New Opportunities

Once core responsibilities are met, the real fun for IT begins with going beyond them. This means researching and proposing new technology to solve the problems that you have discovered or been assigned to address. Updated vendor offerings and emerging technologies can have potent capabilities that warrant serious consideration for your own network.

At companies where there is an extensive list of everyday activities that need attention, it will take a great deal of time to get new projects off the ground. Other companies, strongly lured to high technology, may be very aggressive and want to adopt everything new that comes along. In these cases, it is incumbent on IT to apply the brakes when necessary and promote a slow and careful approach.

PROBLEMS WITH NEW STUFF   Projects are likely to fail if proper attention is not paid to the inherent risks of new products. If IT has not tested and does not have experience with a certain program, it is difficult to optimize its performance or react to critical errors quickly. While new stuff certainly is enticing, its introduction does not automatically invalidate every product that was released earlier.

Pick your upgrades carefully and move with a great deal of caution whenever a critical component of your existing systems is targeted for replacement. Never believe all the hype and hyperbole the vendor marketing firms spout forth. Every solution that you propose *must* address a specific issue and promise to yield tangible results.

WARNING: Virtually all IT specialists have a big ego when it comes to selecting computing equipment. Remember that not all issues can be solved by installing new computers and software. Spending money simply for the sake of getting the newest toys is not the way to go. All of your efforts must be directed at finding the best solutions. This often requires subtle tuning of existing applications and hardware. While not as sexy as upgrading to the newest server, this strategy is certainly effective.

Learn How to Find Problems

While anyone with IT experience will claim that problems always find us, I still advocate looking for trouble. Answering regular calls for help with application errors and failed hardware will always be part of our job, but IT must go beyond simply dealing with the situations that float into our nets. Instead we must actively fish for any areas that have not been adequately addressed with computer systems.

In previous chapters, I have discussed ways to focus on computing issues that plague individuals. The type of information you need to gather for this purpose is different. IT must investigate larger overall system problems that affect whole areas of a business.

The first step is to seek out any areas that are begging for IT help. For example, you may identify departments that lack adequate systems to do the job. If a company upgrades its hardware every five years and installs new software every two years, trouble is bound to occur. I've often found people with 486/66 systems on their desks complaining about how slow their Windows 95 programs were running. Slower processors, small hard drives, and paltry memory capacity are particularly noticeable when comparing older systems to the current state of the art. Perhaps only the Russian ruble depreciates more rapidly than computers.

Workers that are inadequately trained are another common problem. Many IT departments are guilty of simply dropping new computers on user desktops and walking away. After installing new applications, you must follow up with instruction so that users understand and can exploit the additional features available to them.

Ask Questions

While Chapters 3, 4, and 5 explored user support issues with an emphasis on meeting the needs of individuals, systems consulting requires an overall, or macro, view of the company. Meeting with department heads and other company leaders should help you gather a sense of the kinds of needs your systems are expected to fulfill to meet broad objectives.

Be especially alert for calls for expansion and other changes. Supporting a company that is stable in terms of its head count and business model is much simpler than working with a growing firm. Press executives for early notification of acquisitions and divestitures. While the financial obligations of these transactions may be the foremost concern discussed in the boardroom, system work to support these decisions can be considerable and costly as well.

TIP: Your IT budget may not address all the technology needs you discover within your company. You can often draw on individual departments' funds to finance new initiatives.

HOSTING USER FORUMS   A simple and effective method to gauge actual and potential computer use is through holding informal user forums. Meet with a whole department to learn firsthand what types of problems people in a single area are facing. Make this an opportunity to gather information that can be used for future projects. Perhaps you can organize a brown-bag lunch session in which IT invites users to raise questions on any computing subject.

Don't promise to fix everything or to address every issue that is raised, although you should certainly gather every comment and treat each person with respect. The main goal is for IT to gain an appreciation of how computers are used by a particular group or to address a specific business issue.

When you bring many people together for a discussion, you may find that one person's comment stimulates others in the group to remember past problems or nagging concerns. This can help IT gauge which issues carry the most resonance with others. The most efficient use of your time is to address problems that affect the majority of users. Don't dismiss what may be perceived as an inconvenience to a few as unimportant. As I've stated before, those who do a particular job are infinitely more familiar with their computing requirements than is the IT specialist charged with supporting them.

There is always the possibility that the synergy between various users in a group will bring out issues that some individuals gloss over. The importance of sharing data among themselves highlights any difficulties with communications, file formats, and numerous other areas. Encourage the interplay among groups and you are bound to gain valuable insights into computer use at your firm and ways to improve it.

TALKING WITH THE DECISION-MAKERS   Department heads and senior executives are usually anxious to reduce costs and raise efficiency. Help them to see computing technology as a tool to meet these goals and IT as the master mechanic in charge of applying the tool correctly. Allow them to highlight whatever areas they harbor the most disdain for and which areas they see as most critical for improvement.

Look for existing systems that everyone likes and find out which features are most popular. While ease of use and reliability are always key components of successful technology solutions, the particulars of each industry will dictate what other factors should be embraced. The best solutions should reinforce previous popular decisions.

Ask what aspects of general business practices cause the most concern. Don't immediately assume that computers can solve every problem or that you can always identify a clear path to change things for the better. Systems work is often as much an art as a science, and IT must often weigh several options that could be applied to a particular situation. Sometimes it's best to leave existing solutions in place rather than embarking on expensive and complex transitions to new products.

Investigate Computer Use

IT must make a continuing effort to learn how computers are being used at a firm. You should also be vigilant to stay aware of any changes in the nature of your business. Most companies are constantly evolving and looking for new market opportunities. Technological advances will also present new options that didn't exist just a few months earlier.

Meet with users and their bosses regularly to stay abreast of changes. Be a continual student of your company and the industry. In order to influence your company's future, you must constantly be on the lookout for ways to save money, boost efficiency, and position the infrastructure to take advantage of new and emerging technologies.

IT must never be afraid to look for opportunities to offer its technical expertise to improve company operations. Changes challenge the status quo, and a fear of the unknown can make company leaders hesitant about adopting new products.

IT must also be alert to new technology and upgraded products. Replacing legacy systems with their modern counterparts can offer many advantages. While solutions for certain issues may not be available today, vendors that listen to users' requests for new products or upgrades may soon introduce something that satisfies your particular needs.

Whatever proposals you advance at your company, make sure that they satisfy the need to increase efficiency and boost sales. Consult the following list for guidance when looking for ways to influence the company where you work. Not every solution will be successful or accepted, but IT should understand that its systems are always going to need some sort of tuning if the business is to become or remain profitable.

▼ Does the proposal save money?

■ What processes can be changed to save time?

■ Will adopting new products provide a better path for future needs?

■ How will your partners and clients be affected by your changes?

■ Which current products cause the most headaches?

■ What systems will you need next year? Two years? Five years?

■ Have your partners or customers demanded any changes?

■ Does compliance with contracts and statutes need to be addressed?

■ Are any existing contracts for services or equipment set to lapse?

■ What will make your environment more fun?

▲ How can you make your company more competitive?

CHAPTER 7

IT Department Structure and Management

In order to make a strong contribution to a company, the IT department needs to be organized and run correctly. You must assign responsibility for the many different IT tasks to people with a range of work experience and ability levels. Merging the efforts of teams of specialists requires people management skills that programmers and system administrators are rarely taught. Often the need to mitigate friction between various staff members or between IT and other departments can consume more of your attention than time spent on server issues.

IT departments have differing structures and missions depending on the corporations that they serve. As discussed in Chapter 6, your company's attitudes toward technology greatly influence how you assemble your teams of programmers, server jockeys, desktop support specialists, and other workers. Remember, IT's mission is to satisfy the needs of the business it serves.

Managing IT requires much more than just making people work together effectively in teams. You must also pay attention to critical issues like attracting, hiring, and retaining workers. Ensuring that your staff members can develop both professionally and personally is a premier way to increase their value and contributions to IT.

This chapter details the various concerns of IT department managers. First we will examine the types of positions and the types of people best suited to them. This section should answer your questions about which skills and personalities complement each other best. Next we will explore the challenges of building an efficient department and a staff that can work confidently and proactively as a team. You'll learn many strategies for developing compensation plans that both attract and retain talent.

IT DEPARTMENT STRUCTURE

IT departments can vary considerably depending on company size, industry, and numerous other factors that we explored in Chapter 6. Your department may closely mirror the prevailing hierarchy in other company units or appear much flatter. Pyramid, or "top-down," organizations with many levels of responsibility and clearly defined lines of communication are a familiar setup for most people.

The ideal IT structure is one that enables people at all levels to exchange information easily. Systems work is difficult and often time-sensitive. Minimize the time spent making decisions and give feedback quickly to foster a more nimble and responsive technology infrastructure.

Company Size and IT Department Structures

Both the size of a corporation and how geographically dispersed it is directly affect how IT departments are constructed. Some of the reasons are quite obvious. Certainly large corporations can have major installations in cities throughout the globe. In any situation you can either strive for a tightly controlled IT structure or construct one that is more diffused.

Concerns in Larger Companies

Larger companies with worldwide operations and major offices in many cities often rely on a highly distributed command structure. Dictating policies or administering accounts is much more difficult with a workforce that spans many time zones and may not share a common language. Centralized management may also quash the freedom to innovate or to take advantage of localized services.

Every company takes a different approach to centralization of authority, but I have always felt that the most effective IT departments are those that encourage innovation and flexibility at the local level. A large corporation may be best served when all of its divisions commit to using a single email system or network directory structure. However, if IT specified every detail of permitted software application use, it might squelch creativity. A flexible approach to challenges typically yields the best results.

While hardware and software vendors often make their products available worldwide, it may be more difficult to find certain parts and services in some countries. One of the major strengths of Hewlett-Packard and IBM products is that they are supported with local resources around the globe. You should know the availability of key services in all the regions that your company conducts business.

Telecommunications standards and tariffs differ in many countries from those found in the United States. For example, ISDN may be unavailable in certain areas. Costs for phone and data services can vary widely, and there are often long waiting periods for new installations.

In addition, some products are more popular in one region than in another. During its heyday in the 1970s, Massachusetts-based Wang was much more likely to be found in New England companies than in the South. Once a product makes a foothold in a region, it tends to gain a great deal of momentum as name recognition and collective experience builds its reputation.

UNIQUE ATTRIBUTES OF LARGE CORPORATIONS   The sheer size of Fortune 500 corporations results in IT subdivisions that many smaller companies would view as a luxury. Not only does their purchasing power help secure better pricing, but vendors also take extra steps to please their biggest accounts. Customization of software, dedicated support mechanisms, and extensive beta testing opportunities can be mutually beneficial: large companies get the solutions they need and vendors gain real-world experience with their products in large-scale environments.

Larger IT departments tend to be more highly specialized, comprising dedicated units for software development, client support, purchasing, and other purposes. The complexity of the large corporate infrastructure demands this degree of compartmentalization. The sheer variety of systems utilized in a company of this size makes it impossible for IT to have expertise across all supported platforms.

The major benefit of working in an environment such as this is that you can learn about and work with all types of technology. Opportunities for advancement within the firm are more plentiful than they would be at a smaller business. Another plus is the amount of resources that can be devoted to certain projects without sacrificing in other areas.

Issues in Smaller and Mid-Sized Companies

Because they have fewer employees and are less geographically dispersed, small and mid-sized firms are more likely to maintain centralized control. It's much easier to share information and enforce central policies when there are no time zone differences or political barriers to contend with. Simultaneous, coordinated work is possible even in a company with branches spread across the U.S.; the time difference between units is only three hours or less.

Another advantage for IT is that there are fewer business units and less equipment in smaller companies. IT can respond more quickly to new technology because the infrastructure is less complex and there are fewer desktops to upgrade. In a smaller company, IT specialists can be more in tune with the entire business operation and have more control over computing processes.

The One-Man (or One-Woman) Band

One of the most unique IT opportunities exists in environments where a sole individual constitutes the entire department. Like the carnival performer that plays many instruments, the "one-man band" must be versed in all manner of computer system use and administration. This type of position can be found in both the largest and the smallest companies.

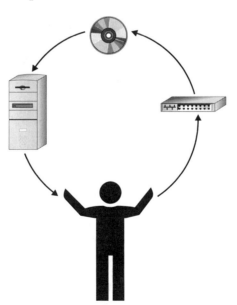

People that end up running their own IT departments often never contemplated a career in IT but suddenly found the position thrust upon them. Perhaps they were the first person in their firm to learn how to format a floppy disk. Soon everyone else in the office began to take every computer question to him or her. Having proved their prowess with a single task, with each passing day they are given more responsibility.

Small companies may not be willing to fund a full-time position for IT but are sometimes willing to have an employee split their responsibilities. In this type of arrangement, the person's primary job shares bandwidth with system administration or similar tasks.

WARNING: Business managers frequently underestimate how much time is required to support computers. This can cause problems if one has to divert attention from other projects to do IT work. Keep a log to demonstrate clearly how your time is being consumed and try to be as flexible as possible.

A one-person IT operation can make for an exciting career. You have a tremendous amount of freedom since there is no one else to debate strategy with. There is also some measure of prestige that accompanies being *the* IT specialist for a company. The opportunity to influence every aspect of a business's operations is not available to many other people within the company.

Problems and Headaches

Problems with the one-person operation are also apparent. Simply taking a vacation or sick day becomes complicated when there is no one else to cover your responsibilities. Perhaps a bigger issue is the lack of alternative opinions when you consider various technical challenges. For example, deciding whether to build a company intranet server strategy on an existing NetWare system or to purchase a dedicated Cobalt Qube is not simple.

If you are contemplating one of these positions, you must enjoy working independently. There are few opportunities to shunt workloads to others when a crisis is brewing. Learn how to pace yourself and avoid burnout! You must learn how to take advantage of educational and peer support opportunities such as user groups. Online support forums can often be your only option when you need to consult with experts on a particular problem.

A technically savvy person who desires the challenge and reward of managing the entire system infrastructure can certainly flourish in many small companies or in independent departments. Being free of detailed supervision and able to pursue an individual agenda can be a very attractive work environment. A talented person in this situation can be indispensable for a company and may be granted a great deal of latitude in their work. Innovation is often a plus when providing technical solutions. A culture that promotes an experimental nature can occasionally reap great benefits.

An Independent IT Department in a Big Company

The one-man band concept is not limited to small businesses. There are many huge companies that have small satellite offices. Geographically dispersed company units receive a higher level of service when dedicated IT specialists are kept on-site rather than dispatched from a central location. Not only can service be rendered more rapidly, but an IT specialist on-site allows a more intimate professional relationship in which systems can be designed to meet the individual needs of a particular office.

I have continually stressed the importance of establishing close ties between IT and those that we serve. The best solutions are reached when IT can respond directly to user needs. Certainly central offices can best negotiate volume purchase contracts and should exert control over companywide resources, but it is unlikely that a central office can fully comprehend its distributed needs better than a local staff does.

SPECIAL DEPARTMENT NEEDS   Sometimes an individual department's system requirements are so unique or demanding that they require dedicated IT personnel. Small groups of programmers, engineers, or marketing professionals may demand specific hardware for their jobs. For example, architects may rely on large-format pen plotters and digitizing tablets to create complex drawings. These types of devices are not typically found throughout a company.

Central IT can be expected to manage corporate email and file services, since these are common needs among all network users. However, it may be a stretch for a centralized IT department to provide expertise for the unique products in various units. While you may be a jack of all trades, it is difficult to be the master of more than a few.

Small companies that have sophisticated needs may find it difficult to attract IT talent that can fulfill specific needs. It's often hard to hire people who can manage file servers or run an intranet site; many of them perceive a small company as an unexciting atmosphere in which they won't enjoy the IT challenges that a bigger workplace can offer. For this reason, small companies must sometimes rely on outsourcing to find the talent necessary to fill a gap in experience or to handle a specific project.

IT REALLY HAPPENED: When I worked as a system engineer for system retailers, I often encountered firms that fit this model. The person in charge of systems was usually the senior secretary at the company. This makes a great deal of sense. Secretaries were the first to embrace the technology of dedicated word processors and, later, personal computers. Having extensive experience with the systems on their own desktops, they naturally became the most appropriate people to be given jurisdiction over the entire firm's computers.

IT People

While every organization is unique and has different requirements, there are some general rules to follow for IT staffing. Only a few people make exceptional IT specialists. The qualities that most of the best people in our field have are not rare; they must simply be combined with a gift for understanding how computers work.

One of the strongest qualities for an IT specialist is a good memory. While this sometimes means being able to recall certain IP addresses, more often it means remembering how similar problems were resolved before. Users tend to repeat the same errors time and time again, so recognizing these behaviors will make you a much more effective person.

Organizational skills are another important prerequisite for IT. You must be able to neatly label cables, document systems, and not misplace disks. Keeping a neat computer room and workplace makes it much easier for others to work with the systems that many have to support. Following directions carefully means that centralized guidelines for system configurations and setups are properly administered.

Good time management must also rank high on any list of IT attributes. There are often multiple projects and deadlines that we face every day. You must be able to juggle everything vying for your attention and make snap decisions as to which are most critical. Chapter 12 covers this subject in great detail.

TIP: No matter which type or size department you work in, the single best way to build quality IT is by ensuring that people at every level communicate effectively with each other.

Value Everyone

Encourage all IT employees to share information and influence decision-making. Even the newest hires with the least experience should be told that they are welcome to contribute their ideas. The greatest hindrance to building an agile and exceptional IT department is by underestimating the potential of any employee.

New hires often bring a wealth of experience from other positions that can be directly applied to challenges they confront at your firm. While broad experience is certainly the most coveted attribute for IT specialists, not every position is suitable for an IT veteran. New hires fresh out of college or training academies may not have lots of experience, but their enthusiasm can be a great asset.

One of my favorite sayings is, "Why invent the wheel if all you need is a car?" Take advantage of the expertise others have gained by struggling with the problem you currently face. It is infinitely easier to adopt a known solution than to custom design a proprietary one. In Chapter 8, methods for enhancing peer training within a firm and taking advantage of external learning opportunities is discussed. You should work with proven "best practices" whenever available.

Traits of Successful IT Specialists

The single most attractive trait in an IT specialist is an ability to work well with others. While this is a fairly broad statement, there are several key attributes that constitute this trait. The first is the confidence and clarity that you can display when discussing highly technical issues.

The best IT specialists resist the temptation to spout "technospeak" and convey information in easily understood terms. While a large percentage of your time may be spent in conversation with other computer-literate professionals, most corporations are not populated with people who are highly technically proficient. Providing IT services requires explicit instructions for implementing solutions that are understandable by users who are not programmers and who may indeed be intimidated by computers.

Just as important as skill in explaining and instructing others in system use is the ability to listen well. The people who use your computers often lack the technical understanding or vernacular to describe precisely what they need. While listening to various types of harangues, well-defined requests, and horror stories about lost files and other problems, IT specialists need to know how to filter the issues users raise and turn them into specific actions.

A friendly attitude and abundant patience are keys to good listening. Maintaining an approachable demeanor will make it easier for those you support to bring you questions and proposals. End users and department managers alike appreciate IT specialists who don't hide behind their mastery of technology.

Another important quality for IT is creativity. Most technical challenges have many possible solutions. Designing an elegant solution often requires brainstorming and discussing different ideas to arrive at the best for your current needs. Try to inspire the creative juices of those you work with and maximize the exchange of ideas between all IT staffers.

On the other hand, some aspects of IT work are routine, and being able to maintain strict adherence to schedules is vital to many industries. Ensuring that data is available in a timely manner is often required by law or other contracts. Strict attention to detail is essential for keeping ahead of deadlines.

Programmers

When we talk about IT, we must first talk about programming. Computers would do absolutely nothing if there were no software. Hardware is the muscle, bone, and sinew of computers, but programs are the storehouse of instructions that make everything work. While I have always stressed the importance of hardware knowledge, the best servers or workstations are only as useful as the programs they run.

Programmers can be found doing a wide range of work at many different types of firms. Some are responsible for the creation and maintenance of application programs. By utilizing high-level languages such as C++ or Cobol, they can create virtually any type of software required by a firm. Other programmers work strictly with database or middleware applications such as Oracle, SAP, and PeopleSoft. Software experts may also specialize in augmenting end-user applications by creating sophisticated spreadsheets using Microsoft Excel, for example.

The revolution spurred by the Internet and the Web has focused again on the importance of programmers to industry. Perl, Tcl, HTML, Java, and numerous other languages and tools are critical skills that you need in this area. Those who best understand the configuration of Web servers like Apache and UNIX operating systems have more than just elementary programming abilities.

WHY THEY GET TOP BILLING   Programmers were the first people called upon to make one computer perform a variety of tasks. While analog computers can be configured to perform different tasks, the true revolution in technology was the ability of a digital computer to run a stored program. This gave people tremendous power: They could take a fairly generic system and have software written to do a specific task.

The critical limitation of analog computing is that it is relied on for mainly single-purpose applications. For example, the fire control systems on battleships contain complex gears and wheels that calculate trajectories based on the curvature of the earth, ship movements, and distance to targets. When taken out of mothballs in the 1980s, these computers built in the 1940s were retained rather than replaced with modern digital systems. However, the analog computer on a battleship would be ill-suited to hosting a payroll application or inventory database.

A little understanding of the history of computing technology shows the importance of programming to the use of computers. Ancient systems like the ENIAC were active for many years. While the hardware was certainly improved, clever programming reaped the real benefits of the system.

I've found that most people unfamiliar with the vast spectrum of IT jobs tend to believe that everyone employed in the computer field is some sort of programmer. An explanation that you write software is not easily digested by those who are technically unaware. My parents will never understand what I mean when I tell them I am overseeing the upgrade of the network topology for the Sales Department, for example.

AN ECLECTIC BUNCH Having dealt with many types of programmers in various environments, I am convinced that they are the most ethnically and culturally varied group of people in IT. Some wear designer suits and expensive shoes while others opt for open-toe sandals, T-shirts, and ponytails. Since programming is a very creative art, it can attract free and independent spirits.

IT REALLY HAPPENED: One of the developers in my office used to commute to work every day by unicycle. He would take his unicycle on a commuter train to North Station in Boston and then ride the final mile to the office in Cambridge.

Some are prone to work odd hours. It is not unusual to find programmers hard at work in the middle of the night, on weekends, or on holidays. Since their activities don't always depend on others being present, programmers can be more productive when free of normal daily distractions. Of course, an ample supply of coffee makers, soda machines, and pizza delivery only helps to fuel this schedule.

One of the wonderful benefits of working in IT is your exposure to people of many different nationalities. In many companies, IT is the most diverse department. Learn to revel in this atmosphere and you'll often find that a cultural outlook different from your own is not only refreshing but can provide new insights into how computers are used by various people.

The difficulty in finding enough people with the critical skills required for exploiting computers' capabilities is well known. Corporations have long turned to oversea talent to address the shortfall. Programmers who lack conversational English skills may still be terrific IT workers if they have a strong command of Perl or C++, for example.

WARNING: American idioms can often be misunderstood. Make sure that people understand exactly what you are saying. I still remember the puzzled look on a coworker's face when I told him that a server had "kicked the bucket"!

Server Room Jockeys

The specialists who build a company's IT infrastructure have to love building computers, playing with hardware, and dealing with issues such as cabling, hubs, routers, and protocols. They must be familiar with the many types of disk controllers, RAID configurations, memory module types, and any other components that go into modern computers.

Along with their hardware expertise, they must have an intimate appreciation for network operating systems. Knowing how to correctly configure driver support for the many types of hardware is vital for running servers. Keeping abreast of system patches and firmware updates is also an important aspect of this job.

Server room jockeys must really love taking things apart and putting them back together. The digital equivalent of grease monkeys, they revel in the thought of setting dip switches and disk drive configurations. Being mechanically inclined is not something that can be taught. Knowing when something is stuck and yet not stripping screws or breaking components takes a careful touch and patience.

FILE SERVER WORK   Working with servers entails three broad areas of responsibility. The first is installation of the actual systems. The initial hardware configuration must be melded with the setup of the operating system. Bringing the server up and making sure that it interacts correctly with existing systems requires a careful and meticulous approach. You must always be aware of network addressing schemes in order to avoid IP problems and similar conflicts.

A second level of responsibility deals with daily maintenance and tuning. This can include providing tape backups and monitoring performance parameters. Operating system settings must often be tweaked to boost throughput or to correct aberrant behavior.

Finally, there are times when IT must troubleshoot and repair failed components or entire computers. Since these problems are often accompanied by frantic users and impending deadlines, you must always maintain clear thinking and a calm approach.

NETWORK ADMINISTRATION   Establishing and maintaining user accounts is another major task for IT. You must be sure that your users can log in to the network and reach the necessary files for their work easily. Providing security and warding off viruses or hacker attacks requires diligence and a willingness to scour system log files for unauthorized access.

While those who physically install and care for the servers may enjoy managing network accounts, this work may be best reserved for dedicated administrators. Network administration involves the human side of the equation, so both sides must cooperate closely.

Administrators know who needs access to which resources, and they are usually the first to hear users' complaints if print jobs disappear or servers stop responding.

HUBS, CABLES, AND SWITCHES   Linking all of the servers and users together are the miles of cabling and connecting equipment in your server room. It's worth repeating the old adage that most networking problems can be traced to bad cabling. Not only must the cable that connects workstations to the network be of high quality, but IT must also be careful to document and record how each cable is used. No one should have to play "yank the cable" to figure out where each strand is going.

An important part of this work is the installation and maintenance of switches, hubs, and routers, the components that actually provide the pathways for data to flow both inside and outside a company. IT specialists with expertise in protocols and routing architectures are best suited to these tasks.

Designing efficient and productive networks requires knowledge of how to best segment network cabling systems to maximize bandwidth. Someone who knows how to track traffic patterns and arrange systems to minimize hops between communicating devices can greatly boost overall network performance.

Server room jockeys usually handle firewalls or devices that control exactly what type of data or user can access the network from the outside. As such, those administrating the firewalls must closely follow the security settings done by network administrators. This is just a single example of the need to maintain good communications amongst all the different people in an IT department.

Desktop Support Specialists

Support staff are the front-line troops in an IT organization. They are the people who deal most directly with users. Being the first to respond to problems makes them the most visible part of your department. The entire success of IT can often be measured by how well support is performed at this level. Remember, those shiny new servers with gobs of storage are of little interest to a user frustrated by a broken monitor.

People that excel in these positions must really enjoy working closely with others. A thick skin is a valuable asset since there are times when anxious users bombard you with complaints about failed equipment or cryptic error messages.

When confronted by a distraught user, the first step is calming him or her down and giving assurances that the problem is being given close attention. Sometimes the mere presence of an individual dedicated to client service is enough to calm a frustrated user. IT specialists responsible for desktop support must also exude confidence in their own ability to understand and repair computers.

TIP: Not every problem can be readily repaired. Often IT must research and test various solutions before installing a reliable fix on the failing system. Preach patience to your users and demand dogged determination from staff members charged with finding answers. When users see the effort being put forth, they will appreciate the time being spent to address their needs.

Clerical Assistants

Not all IT work involves configuring servers or responding to calls from frantic users. As with any division of a company, there are numerous clerical activities that need to be done to ensure the correct functioning of IT. Skilled technical staff can devote their time to more pressing issues if they can delegate clerical duties. Non-technical support staff can free you from paperwork and let you pay attention to the more computer-oriented tasks at hand.

For example, purchasing new products requires someone to place the orders and then make sure the correct products are delivered. Matching purchase orders to packing slips and then to the actual items in the boxes is a critical task. Managing returns of defective systems or tracking which units are out for repair requires someone with good organizational skills.

Being able to figure out if the requested item is indeed the right one for the intended purpose can be rather tricky. The myriad of computer models and infinite number of options make the seemingly simple task of ordering memory a study in patience and detective work. I've often had to return products that were inappropriate to the required application.

SCSI cables come in many flavors and present a similar challenge. Even experienced IT people can get flustered when trying to determine the exact type of cable required for certain hardware. Internal or external, SCSI 1 or FW-SCSI 3, and numerous other specifications each require a unique number of pins and connectors. Always make sure that you provide the most explicit instructions possible when asking someone to order products who doesn't have the background knowledge to discern the specific options.

Trainers

Instructing people in the use of complex electronic systems is indeed a difficult challenge. Not only must trainers possess a certain degree of technical acuity with specific applications or hardware, they must be able to lecture effectively as well. Even if you understand a technical matter perfectly, that does not help anyone who cannot fathom your explanation of how it works.

Apple computer made a tremendous effort to train computer sales and systems engineers in the use of their products. One of the more interesting aspects of the training I used to take was the high percentage of elementary and secondary schoolteachers who were hired to do the training. The ability of good teachers to articulate information to a classroom full of confused and distracted people can be leveraged with both third graders and middle-aged office workers.

Companies with large training budgets may be able to hire experienced teachers and provide them with the tools to teach technology issues. IT specialists can also make fine instructors if they have the right personality and a desire to teach. Classes in public speaking and documentation writing can help experts in systems administration become effective lecturers.

Team Leaders

Every firm is made up of people with varying levels of experience and ability. Most IT departments designate certain individuals as leaders with supervisory roles. There must be someone that bears the ultimate responsibility for any team effort, and that person must be given some degree of authority.

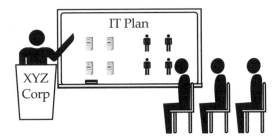

Those with the most experience are usually the most familiar with corporate standards, so they can ensure that accepted best practices are followed when dealing with user issues. Leaders' years of experience often means that they have dealt with issues similar to new problems that arise. Running a problem by a team leader can often save precious time if an existing solution has already been discovered.

Being able to delegate authority relieves the burden on IT department managers. Putting leaders in charge of certain activities may make sense in your company. You may want to designate someone to take charge of all tape backup activities and place another in command of all cabling issues, for example.

DESIGNATING TOPICAL SPECIALISTS   By assigning certain people responsiblity for specific areas of IT service, you begin to create advanced pockets of expertise within your company. Delegating authority allows you to concentrate on important tasks and not be distracted by minutia at every turn. The sheer volume of information and breadth of subjects that need to be addressed in most computing environments demand a good deal of specialization.

Those IT specialists with clearly defined expertise should be carefully assigned to appropriate tasks. An expert in Cisco routers is not as effective dealing with NT Server troubleshooting as someone dedicated to server maintenance. However, when LAN segments suddenly cease passing packets, the router specialist should be the first person contacted.

Technical Recruiters

IT skills are in such high demand and comprise such specific areas of capability that many companies dedicate HR people to filling all jobs in this area. Make sure to give these recruiters a detailed understanding of the exact set of requirements for an open position. A programmer who is thoroughly skilled in developing device drivers may be the wrong choice for a company that needs a database application written. This type of specificity is probably alien to many general-hiring managers.

Another difference in IT hiring is that compensation and work rules for IT may not mirror those in the rest of the company. Shift differentials for late night or weekend work may be available, but stock options may be of particular interest as the fastest way to make money. Balancing the unique situation that IT professionals enjoy—unprecedented demand and lucrative pay—with the needs of the company is especially critical.

Department Managers

Sitting at the top of every IT department is the IT manager. Some companies use a title such as CIO (chief information officer), CTO (chief technology officer), or a similar designation. Being responsible for the entire technical infrastructure of a business places the IT manager in one of the most critical spots of all the executives. As stated previously, a company's use of data and technology is vital to its ability to conduct business.

In my many years in the business, I've had my share of both good and bad managers. While not every good manager has the same personality, there are clearly some characteristics that contribute or detract from a manager's effectiveness. Often it is not their level of technical prowess that is the most important feature, but rather their ability to make the most out of the resources and skills of their staff.

Sometimes the single most important attribute that the manager can have is technical expertise in a broad array of areas. There has to be someone at your job that acts as the ultimate decision-maker on major projects. While you may not be as comfortable with Novell NetWare as you are with Windows NT Server, you must be able to adequately weigh the various features of each. Being a well-rounded IT specialist is better than being an expert in a narrow range of skills. Computer systems are so diverse in both their construction and usage that good generalists are the most effective in understanding them.

BAD MANAGERIAL TRAITS   Like many people, nothing upsets me more than a manager who fails to respect ability. Second-guessing and reviewing every step an employee takes does little to demonstrate confidence and will make your employees resent you and your constant oversight. While trust may be difficult to grant, people are much more effective when given the freedom to get their jobs done. Don't worry too much about your subordinates making mistakes that might go undetected as they're being made. A job that is done incorrectly will not remain hidden for long.

When you have difficulty with someone who works for you, be sure that they are told quickly and privately. There is no need to berate anyone in front of others. IT departments are best run as teams, and deliberately singling out one person before their peers shows little judgment or class. Problems should be handled in private and kept in confidence.

GOOD MANAGERIAL HABITS   Be sure to reward good work with all types of reinforcement and recognize your employees for their contributions. While you may not have an effusive personality, there are quiet ways to acknowledge quality work. Perhaps you can present a monthly reward of a gift certificate for a good restaurant or bookstore, or you can award movie passes.

Granting freedom to your workers to pursue solutions is the fastest way to gain their confidence. Remember that you will never have all the answers nor immediately grasp the single best solution. Computer problems are common, and having your staff learn the approach to fixing things themselves is many times more effective than having them come to you for guidance every time something breaks.

Be a mentor whenever possible! Your knowledge and experience is much more valuable when shared with others. Be pleased to take questions and to help your staff when they need it. Those that work for you will only respect you more if they see your willingness to pitch in and contribute.

Finally, accept that people sometimes make mistakes. Be sensitive to the pressures that others face and be willing to give them space and time to regain composure and focus.

NON-TECHNICAL MANAGERS   Not every IT specialist reports to a technically astute person. Some companies may place the financial or facility wing of the company in charge of IT. For the same reasons stated earlier, this can be either a good or bad arrangement. If the bottom line is getting your job done correctly and your manager does not unduly obstruct your efforts, then everything should work out fairly well.

It may be difficult in this situation, but try to keep your boss well informed about exactly what you are doing. I found that the most trying situation was justifying budget expenditures for hardware and additional staff. Some managers insist that you explain everything to them and account for your activities during the day. While keeping a log may seem tedious, you should accommodate the requests of your boss whenever possible. Perhaps your manager will develop a greater appreciation for your efforts after seeing the diversity of work that you accomplish.

IT REALLY HAPPENED: At one part of my career, I had to report to the CIO of a company. When many new clients began to strain my server, I wanted to purchase a new system to off-load the additional clients. My manager thought it would be sufficient to simply add new disk space to the server. Only when users began to complain about slow performance did he heed my advice and allow me to requisition an additional server.

WINNING AT THE HIRING GAME

As I touched upon earlier, IT professionals are commanding better salaries and perks, and there is no end to this trend in sight. The continuing rush to adopt Web technologies and exploit the myriad opportunities of component-base n-tier architectures will keep companies hungry for qualified workers. While cash is perhaps the biggest inducement to attract skilled people, there are many other ways to lure talent and, more importantly, to retain it.

Remember to use off-the-shelf software, if possible, since this makes it easier to hire people with prior experience. Temporary and contract workers can become productive quickly when they deal with standard solutions. You'll also find it easier to obtain technical support and secure training for standard software.

TIP: Many of the perks and benefits I write about are not just intended to attract new hires. Most of them can be useful for retaining current staff as well, and keeping good workers is often more critical than locating new employees.

Hiring Practices

The first step in hiring involves developing a clear definition of exactly what type of position is available and what minimum skills are required to fill it. Too often, the specifics listed in a want ad cast too broad a net or fail to clarify what expertise is being sought. You waste both the candidates' time and your own if you interview people who clearly are not qualified for the available slot on your team. Many firms will screen by telephone to help weed out candidates before holding a more formal interview.

Along with the skills the position requires, consider what type of temperament you are seeking. For example, while interpersonal skills are desirable for any hire, they are more critical for client support specialists and others who'll work directly with people. Meet with your HR representative to clarify the job description properly.

Define the Position

Be sure that you, or the recruiter doing the hiring, clearly understand exactly what the new hire is expected to do. Someone with several years of experience as a UNIX system administrator will be miserable and overqualified if hired to manage a tape backup rotation. Be absolutely clear about what the position entails and how much relevant experience you desire. The following list is an example of breaking down the components of a positions' responsibilities so that both the hiring person and the applicant are clear about them.

▼ Network administrator for Marketing Department

■ Manage tape backup

■ Configure and support marketing desktops

▲ Maintain imaging equipment

Describe the Skillset

Once the exact responsibilities of the job have been quantified, the next step is to list the qualifications a prospective candidate should have. It is critical to use specifics whenever possible. When crafting a job description, make sure to consult with everyone who will rely on the new hire. Selecting the right person for a particular position often means making several people happy.

The tasks you need performed by a Web administrator are a good example of the specifics you should indicate on job advertisements. Asking for someone with experience as a Web administrator is sure to bring in a lot of resumes. However, a more precise requirement might be that potential candidates should have two to three years of experience managing an Apache Web server within Linux configurations. Narrowing your search in this way will yield a more refined group of potential candidates.

Consider how many years of experience and what type of background your new hire should have. Previous supervisory experience should be mandatory before someone assumes control over a large department with many individuals. Only through experience will a network administrator be able to handle maintenance or emergency routines quickly and confidently. If a position calls for managing multiple servers under time-critical conditions, your hiring criteria must be more demanding. The need for new hires to "hit the ground running" is best served by finding people with experience in the field.

Startup firms that want to embrace the latest technology may want to attract only recent college graduates. These new companies are often populated by single people who relish (or simply don't mind) the long hours and weekends spent perfecting their products. Stock options are often an attractive lure for someone just starting their professional career, but more mature workers may place a higher value on flexibility and stability to balance the demands of marriage and parenthood.

Entry-level positions should ideally be designed to attract intelligent people with a desire to learn. Under the correct supervision, a rookie system administrator can be slowly nurtured and eased into having more responsibility and independence. Try not to get overly frustrated by those whose understanding is less than complete. Reserve your wrath for times when people are lazy and don't seek out the information they need. Encourage new hires to ask questions and request help if they need it. Take every opportunity to teach techniques and procedures, and your newest hires will gradually become savvy veterans. The following list shows you can clarify your hiring needs by compiling a list of specific skills and experience.

▼ Knowledge of Windows NT Server on Intel platform

■ Familiar with Computer Associates ARCServe

■ Support 35 desktops running Windows NT Workstation and four laptops

▲ Experience with Agfa scanner, Adobe Photoshop, and QuarkXPress

Look for Candidates

One lesson I will never forget from my meetings with employment counselors in college is the "one-third" rule. They stated that only one-third of all candidates came to a firm through traditional want ads in the classified section of the newspaper. Another third were recruited at various events such as visits to college campuses, job fairs, open houses, and similar "meet markets." The balance of the positions were filled with people referred by employees of the hiring firms.

While there is some truth to these old guidelines, I would add some additional categories to that equation. The tremendous growth of the Internet has added a new element to the job recruitment process. Monster.com (www.monster.com) and dozens of other online services allow employers to display job offers and job seekers to post their resumes for the entire world to see. In many industries, companies now place job postings alongside the other information of their Web sites.

The final listing you post, on the Internet or in a newspaper, should contain details about the position and the required skillset as shown in Figure 7-1.

INTERNAL RECRUITING   Perhaps one of the best places to look for workers is among those already doing other jobs for you. Often someone who has gained experience with computer systems while working with them makes a perfect candidate for handling desktop support services. Using a buddy system, as described in Chapter 4, is a prime way to develop new talent for IT.

The XYZ Corporation has an exciting opportunity for an experienced Windows NT Network administrator. Our Marketing Department has recently expanded and needs someone that can manage a new state of the art production facility. The ideal candidate has a minimum of three years of experience supporting Windows NT Server and Workstation. A definite plus is exposure to Computer Associates ARCServe tape backup software.

Candidates familiar with desktop publishing are encouraged to apply. We rely on Adobe Photoshop, QuarkXPress, and Agfa scanners to produce our attention grabbing sales brochures.

Our dynamic workplace strongly values the contribution of every employee. Numerous opportunities for training and career advancement are provided. We provide health club benefits, stock options, and competitive salaries. Travel is not required with this position.

Please send your resume in PLAIN TEXT or Word 6.0 format to xyz_hr@xyzcorp.com

You may fax your resume to (321) 555-1234

Snail mail address is XYZCORP
            ATTN: JOBS
            111 XYZ DRIVE
            Big Tech City USA 01110

Other job listings are at www.xyzcorp.com/employment

XYZ is an Equal Opportunity Employer

Figure 7-1.   Sample want ad

IT specialists often keep in touch with people they have met at previous jobs, and these ties can help you in hiring good workers. Trusting the judgment of your own staff can be a great way to find qualified people. Many companies recognize the importance of this recruiting mechanism and offer hefty bonuses to those whose referrals get hired.

Business card exchanges at trade shows or at training centers is another way to meet people in the IT industry. Chance meetings at sports events, on vacation, on a commuter train, or even in the supermarket can provide opportunities to find workers.

WARNING: Most people don't attend classes so they can be recruited. Exercise extreme caution when approaching people about jobs in this setting.

EXTERNAL RESOURCES   Sometimes the best or only way to locate talent is with the aid of an employment agency. Using a professional technical recruitment agency that understands your industry and desired computing skillsets can be a wonderful way to find new hires. Large agencies can draw resources from a number of offices, increasing your chances of getting the right candidate.

Agencies normally charge a fee if they help you make a successful hire. While this can be expensive, it may be cheaper than leaving a position unfilled. Some agency contracts call for a percentage of the candidate's annual salary during the first year or a payment equivalent to several months' pay. A company with a small HR department may find this the easiest way to augment its capability. You may need to work with an external employment agency when hiring for satellite offices, seeking hard-to-find skillsets, or if HR lacks a local presence.

TEMPS, CONSULTANTS, AND APPRENTICES   Temporary and part-time workers often want to become full-timers. The lure of more pay and expanded benefits can be very attractive. Hiring a temp gives you the advantage of getting someone you're already familiar with and who has demonstrated their worth on the job.

Consultants and contractors sometimes become regular employees too. This may happen when contracts expire or if they simply express a desire to change their status to full-time. I consider using consultants to be a case of renting talent, not buying it. The subject clearly demands more attention, and I will discuss it in detail in Chapter 9.

Apprentices are available from a variety of resources. Many colleges and occupational training facilities have internship programs in which students are placed in a workplace both for pay and to gain experience. With the severe shortage in qualified IT workers lately, these programs have even been extended to high school students.

When 12-year-olds can start successful Web design firms, it seems logical that there are some that have the maturity and intelligence to work for a living at an early age. Reaching out to these prodigies is not something I actively encourage firms to do, but it does help to remember that capable IT people don't necessarily have college degrees.

Compensation Packages

IT Compensation Menu	
Column A	**Column B**
Travel	Flex-time
Training	Stock options
Growth	Trade shows
Flexibility	Fun, fun, fun

There are many ways to attract people to work for you, but the most prominent is pay. However hefty, though, pay is not the only incentive for most people. Other factors that create a challenging, fun, and exciting career while respecting the unique needs of individuals, should also be appreciated.

Company cars, cell phones, high-speed data lines at home, awesome laptops, health club memberships, stock options, and many other perks are often part of the equation when calculating employee compensation. You must work closely with HR departments to see what monetary and other arrangements can be made for IT hires.

The current state of the economy and notable lack of job applicants has made IT a unique unit within many companies. Starting salaries and raises for qualified individuals are often the highest among all company departments.

MONEY   Everyone wants and needs to know how much they are getting paid. The monetary compensation your firm offers is determined by several items. All jobs in your organization should have a salary range that reflects years of service, levels of responsibility, and the relative importance of the position. Your budget must account for raises and new hires in advance, so be certain that you plan for additional positions early on.

The amount of experience the employee has is an important consideration. The more senior a person is, the higher the level of skills they should possess. You must also consider geographic differences when putting together a compensation package. The cost of living in one major metropolitan area might be higher than in another. IT salaries in New York or San Francisco must therefore be higher than those in Peoria or Ogden.

Provide some wiggle room for your offers. While you don't want to overspend to acquire talent, you also need to be able to attract certain people. A small amount of extra money may be all that is needed to secure the right person.

There are several resources that should be checked before making or accepting a job offer. You need to make sure that the compensation plan is fair for the job responsibility, experience, industry, and geographic location. Most major news and business magazines publish annual salary surveys. Government job descriptions typically give detailed information on qualifications and pay levels.

The Internet is another repository of this information. You can scan job postings on literally thousands of Web sites; www.datamasters.com and www.wageweb.com are two good starting points. The U.S. Bureau of Labor Statistics provides detailed salary and related information at stats.bls.gov. Some commercial sites also offer subscription services if you want to buy more in-depth reports.

COOL ELECTRONICS   There are many "toys of technology" that IT specialists like to use for both work and entertainment. Allowing the use of company equipment for personal reasons may not work in every situation. Often, when items like laptops are taken home, there is a sense that it is "owned" by the user.

You don't want people to utilize company assets for profit-making ventures. For example, using corporate servers to establish a money-making Web site would be an inappropriate use of equipment. However, allowing workers to use scanners and printers to create materials for a school project is usually fine. As a general rule, you may simply ignore the private use of equipment as long as it does not violate company policy.

TRAINING   Most companies state that they support employee training. I advocate that IT staff be given a specific allotment of time that they can devote to technical classes. A fair policy could provide for five days of training for every six months of employment, for example. Classes can be selected at either the company's or the employee's discretion. Most companies will approve training classes only if the skills being taught are appropriate to the job description.

Your workers will be excited to see that there is a definite commitment to employee skill-building. Permitting a certain percentage of classes to be of the employee's choosing can broaden everyone's capabilities. Avoiding stagnation requires learning and doing new things, and employees should be strongly encouraged to study new topics.

TRADE SHOWS   There are computer-oriented trade shows almost every week. With exciting cities like New York, Atlanta, Las Vegas, and San Francisco as destinations, the appeal of fun outside the convention halls is very strong. Obviously there are wonderful learning and networking opportunities to be found at conventions.

Giving your employees a reasonable expense account and airplane tickets for trade shows can be a good benefit to promise your workers. The opportunity to get away from the office and be entertained on the company's money is certainly a nice option for a week. Try to allocate everyone at least two shows a year. Some can be local affairs that only last a single day while others require a longer commitment.

EARLY REVIEWS   Because many companies wait a year before reviewing salaries, promising a shorter waiting period before the first pay raise can be a good incentive. This can also help you avoid offering too much for a worker who proves to be a substandard performer. Also, a new employee may work harder when more money is looming on the horizon.

MAKE THE WORKPLACE FUN   IT work can often be a frustrating and time-consuming undertaking. When nerves are frayed and your last good night's sleep is a distant memory, the importance of taking a break to recharge becomes apparent. There are simple steps you can take to give at least a small measure of balance to the workplace.

Some companies install foozball, darts, table tennis, and similar attractions in common areas for employee use. Planning pizza parties and buying a few six-packs of beer can provide an occasional respite from the stress of projects. Trips to the ballpark or the movies can also be a nice change of pace.

FLEX-TIME   Offer your staff the opportunity to work extended hours four days per week in exchange for an extra day off. Many employees are happy to work four 10-hour days instead of five 8-hour days. As long as the workload is shared equitably and other issues don't fester, this arrangement should work at most places.

The lifestyle of the modern family often involves both spouses working and a great reliance on daycare. Allowing workers to come in late on particular days or leave early on others to accommodate childcare or similar needs is a sound policy. I certainly believe that my family comes first, and I would resent any company that would make me feel guilty if I wanted to arrive one hour late one day to attend an event at my son's school or to take him to a medical appointment.

TIP: Whatever arrangements you make at your company, be sure to maintain consistency. For example, keep a calendar that indicates which days people are coming in late; this will show everyone that there is no favoritism.

Gauge Candidates

Once you have found someone you would like to interview, there are certain steps you can take to assess the person's abilities and demeanor. Traditionally, every job seeker submits a resume, which gives you a general idea of whether they have the skills you need. The purpose of the interview is to better gauge the applicant's depth of experience and to validate the skills cited in the resume.

Three other areas are also used to bolster the credentials of a candidate. References from previous employers or colleagues may have some value. IT specialists often acquire an alphabet soup of certifications that should be considered. Finally, many hiring managers love to conduct real-world tests of the candidate's knowledge and problem-solving ability.

RESUMES   I think of a resume as an expanded business card. After working in IT for many years, a comprehensive resume that would list all of the systems and projects I've worked on would take several pages. The result would be nothing I would want to read.

When reviewing a resume, I tend to look for the type of work done rather than a laundry list of the technology used. It is more impressive in my estimation to read about someone who supported a staff of 75 computer users on a NT network than someone who cites every application he has ever printed from and every computer he has booted up.

There are instances where you need to find specific expertise indicated on the resume. Again, the most important thing is how the skill was applied. Experience with a similar business or with equivalent systems is almost always a big plus.

INTERVIEWS   Interviews provide an opportunity to get a better understanding of the person behind the resume. If I will be working with the candidate, I need to know how comfortable they are with the work environment and the expectations I have for them. Personally, I look for people with an engaging manner who demonstrate a sense of humor and an inner faith in their ability.

I try to ask questions that highlight the candidate's strongest points. For example, when hiring a desktop support specialist, I always want to hear a story about a serious problem and how it was fixed. Not only does this reveal what types of products were involved, but it gives great insight into the type of methodology the person used to address the situation.

Interviews should never be one-sided. Ask open-ended questions of the applicant, listen carefully to their responses, and answer all their questions truthfully. Candidates often want to know about career path and other opportunities. The types of questions they ask often reveal what is most important to them.

This is also the time to determine whether any special arrangements would need to be made. Some employees need to be home certain days at certain times for personal or religious reasons. Avoid surprises later on: Make certain that the work hours for the job are mutually agreeable.

REFERENCES   I only check references when the hiring process gets serious. Due to threats of litigation, many companies won't give references but will only confirm that the person worked there. Another drawback with references is that, since the candidate suggests these contacts, it is improbable that they would supply damning witnesses to their prior failures.

There can be some value in honest appraisals, but I doubt that any reference would convince me to hire someone I had reservations about during the initial interview.

CERTIFICATION   Today there are myriad certification programs provided by many of the largest players in the computer industry, including IBM, Microsoft, Novell, Red Hat, Sun Microsystems, and Cisco. Several third-party firms and colleges also offer certification programs in one or more technical disciplines, such as network administration using one or more network operating systems. Each of these companies and institutions attempts to provide some assurance that those passing the qualifying examinations have some mastery over particular technologies.

Experienced IT specialists have a wide range of opinions on the value of certifications. Some feel that they are completely worthless and are merely scraps of paper. This thought is reinforced by the belief that courses are designed for people who are being reimbursed by their employers for taking the classes. Making sure that the majority of those who take the course pass the certification exam is one way to encourage students to enroll. Others believe that having achieved certification is a sign that employees have a serious and professional attitude and are capable of making an immediate contribution.

I have a middle-of-the-road opinion. There certainly is some value to taking classes. They can prepare you with the basics or core knowledge needed to understand some particular technology. Certification can augment the other skills that an employee has, but it is no substitute for experience.

TESTING   One of the best methods to quantify competence is with testing. You can generate your own tests to verify that candidates possess the skills they need to do the type of work you need done at your firm.

Tests should be tailored for the particular job applicants are vying for. People applying for positions on a help desk could be asked to answer some typical calls that you select from your logs. Programmers can be instructed to examine some code and quizzed as to its content and purpose. Network administrators should be able to demonstrate mastery of user management utilities. There are also firms that have tests you can purchase for this exact purpose.

Several companies provide Web-based certification testing. QWIZtek (www.qwiz.com) offers exams on popular applications, programming languages, and network administration. The Advanced Computer Testing home page (www.adstaff.com) gives information on its line of Prove It! competency tests. Take advantage of online demos to gauge the quality and appropriateness of the offered examinations. Remember that hiring someone who turns out to be under-qualified is both costly and time-consuming.

Opinions of various certifications quality will vary. Some applicants may have barely squeaked through the testing process retaking exams several times while others quickly mastered the materials. There are no grade point averages or class rankings that can be used to weigh various candidates that possess the same certifications. Tests can help quantify their abilities. These same tests can be useful when dealing with people with similar quantities of actual work experience. The type and quality of experience will vary depending on the dynamics of the company where candidates previously worked and the degree of responsibility they had.

IT REALLY HAPPENED: My test at *PC Week* consisted of a completely disassembled computer that I was asked to put together. After I installed all the hardware and the operating system, the IT director made sure that all the system functions were normal. This was a great test for the position of hardware support specialist.

Make an Offer

After you have decided that the candidate can and will do the job, and you want them to join your team, make sure that they know it. Don't just say, "We would like you to work with us. Will you do so for *x* dollars a year?" Instead, approach the person with a great deal of enthusiasm.

Tell them exactly why you want them to work for you. Explain why their skills, experience, and personality are perfect for the job. Describe how and where they will make a contribution and the importance of their position to the entire organization. Make them aware of all the other opportunities that await them and all the things you can provide for their personal and professional growth.

Seeing your excitement and desire will help them decide more quickly. Whenever I spot the right candidate, I want them to know of my interest right away, before someone else grabs them. Allow them to mull over your offer for a while, but place a firm deadline on their final decision.

WHEN THEY SAY NO   Of course, not everyone will accept your job offer. Competition is fierce and you can't always win a bidding war. While it can be frustrating not to hire a strong candidate, there is little you can do sometimes. Don't take it personally and keep interviewing. There are so many IT people in the world that the next resume you receive may be exactly the one you need.

If the candidate is so desirable that losing them is a significant disappointment, make sure to tell them you will arrange another position if they change their mind. Many in the IT field change jobs every two years or so, so you may get another chance to hire them before long.

CHAPTER 8

Exploring IT Skills

One of the biggest challenges facing any IT specialist is staying ahead of all the new products and technologies. The complex nature of our industry generates bodies of knowledge that are enormous and often quickly outdated. In order to learn new things and anticipate where technology is heading, you must constantly study and investigate the latest offerings.

Enhancing your knowledge and abilities has many benefits. Raises or other bonuses can be contingent upon obtaining new certifications. Promotions or new job responsibilities are often dependent on achieving qualifications. There is also the personal challenge of mastering additional technologies to complement your existing competencies.

Thankfully, there are many ways to acquire and maintain the skills necessary to excel in IT. Traditional training classes and CBT lessons are good ways to gain exposure to popular products. The Internet provides many resources via Web sites and other information delivery systems. Computer Science has gained stature as a distinct discipline in colleges and universities, and computing classes have spread throughout most other academic departments as well.

Trade shows, computer magazines, books, and other printed materials can all be useful learning resources. Television and radio programs that cater to the computer industry are growing in variety and popularity. General interest publications such as weekly news magazines and daily newspapers have greatly expanded their coverage of technology issues, recognizing the increasing role that computers play in people's personal lives and the economy at large.

There is no single strategy that best satisfies an IT manager's voracious appetite for news and information. Rather, you must survey the entire slate of offerings and construct a menu of options to meet your unique needs. This chapter examines the types of resources that can be used to build IT skills. Additionally, the sharing of information among all the professionals at your firm is another process that deserves your attention.

THE NEED FOR BUILDING SKILLS

It is hard to imagine any other field that changes as dramatically or as rapidly as IT does. The huge heaps of discarded computers and software that every company generates attest to the ephemeral nature of technology. Experience has shown me that subjects I once had to master are now passé and largely forgotten while the breadth of knowledge required to do my work has expanded dramatically. The same is true for nearly all IT personnel.

New technology continues to motivate industries to reinvent the way they conduct business. The capabilities that new systems provide often allow companies to reach their customers and sell products in different ways. Whatever IT specialists can do to enhance their companies' capabilities should be explored.

Professional Licensing and Organizations

  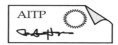

Unlike numerous other professionals, IT specialists do not have a well-known, nationally recognized sanctioning or licensing body that grants certification. American lawyers have to pass the bar exam and meet other state licensing requirements. Electricians, plumbers, beauticians, and teachers require testing and sometimes apprenticeship to practice their craft. But there is virtually nothing to prevent someone from claiming that they are a "computer professional" when dealing with the public.

Don't confuse professional licensing with vendor-approved certifications. Programs like Novell's CNE and Microsoft's MCSE are well-established and respected certifications. However, these are specific to certain products or technologies and are not granted by independent societies or governments. The expertise that these certifications confirm is critical since they concern widely adopted products. Certifications will be discussed in greater detail in the next section of this chapter.

Several groups are striving to raise the level of professionalism in IT. If these efforts achieve the goal of higher standards and accountability, then they are certainly worthwhile. I am continually astounded by the lack of ability exhibited by many of those I meet who are charging exorbitant fees for their work.

IT REALLY HAPPENED: A consultant was having trouble getting a network to remain stable. All of the servers and hubs kept falling off the Token Ring LAN and beaconing problems were common. Some investigation revealed that the consultant had been making his own station cables but was paying zero attention to polarity issues. After I demonstrated the correct wiring scheme, he spent hours remaking all the cables in the server room.

Perhaps because computers have risen only recently to such great importance and prevalence in society, licensing was never before considered a high priority or desired goal. The quality of service being provided by IT departments in many companies is certainly below where it should be, judging from the types of letters I receive. As our industry and profession matures, there may indeed be a rise in the need and desire for IT specialists to possess a professional certification that verifies certain minimum standards of performance and expertise.

In my opinion, there are only two ways in which the professionalism denoted by certification will actually occur. Governments may want to respond to problems related to unscrupulous, unqualified thieves who masquerade as computer experts by demanding that certain designations be earned by anyone doing business with the state or by those offering certain services to the public. The other scenario would be for those of us in the field to recognize the need to police ourselves and raise the level of expectations for anyone calling themselves an IT specialist. We would then have to convince the public that these

organizations are reputable and that members have earned the
respect of their peers.

Institute of Electrical and Electronic Engineers

Perhaps the most widely known professional organization for those
in engineering and computing fields is the Institute of Electrical and
Electronic Engineers (IEEE). Among the many activities run by the
IEEE are the committees that debate and establish standards familiar
to every IT specialist. For example, the 802.3 family of specifications
governs how implementations of Carrier Sense Multiple Access with
Collision Detection (CSMA/CD) or Ethernet networks are constructed.

Members of IEEE are encouraged to participate in the formulation
and extension of the many standards in use today. Membership has
several other benefits. The society's publications cover many of the
issues that confront users of computers and networks. With over
300,000 members in almost every country around the globe, IEEE
has an unparalleled reach and influence within our industry.

IEEE also offers a tremendous set of educational resources.
Courses on a wide variety of subjects can be taken on the Web, on
video, or with other media. The ability to network with others in
your particular area of interest is another compelling reason to join.
For more information on IEEE, go to their Web site at www.ieee.org.

Association of Information Technology Professionals

The Association of Information Technology Professionals, or AITP,
was established in the 1950s. It began as a knowledge store exclusively
for accounting professionals that enabled them to share information
on the evolving mechanical computing technologies that were then
being introduced. The organization has grown to embrace the entire
range of IT professionals with a variety of programs.

There are online discussion forums for members to share
experiences and ask questions. Publications and conferences that
target IT professionals are also run by the organization. Local chapters
provide a forum for meeting with peers in your area. Members are

asked to subscribe to a code of conduct intended to raise the degree of professionalism in our industry.

One of AITP's most important activities is its involvement with colleges and other educational institutions, where it addresses the shortcomings in technology training today. Collegiate representatives and college-based chapters seek to raise the level of competence of those preparing to enter the workforce. For additional information on this association, visit its Web site at www.aitp.org.

Institute for Certification of Computing Professionals

The Institute for Certification of Computing Professionals (ICCP) sanctions the Certified Computing Professional, or CCP, examination for experienced IT people and the Associate Computing Professional, or ACP, test for entry-level workers. The examinations are not specific to any particular vendor's offerings but rather reflect the broad spectrum of knowledge required for a career in IT.

People that earn these designations are expected to pass both a core competency exam and tests in specific subject areas such as data communications or management. ICCP certifications also require a minimum of four years' industry experience, and members are expected to pledge allegiance to a code of conduct. You can find out more about ICCP at www.iccp.org.

A+

One of the few vendor-independent certifications that has gained widespread recognition is the A+ program. Under the auspices of the Computing Technology Industry Association (CompTIA), it certifies basic competence in the servicing of computer hardware and basic operating system functions. Those passing the examinations should be qualified to seek entry-level jobs in the IT community. You can explore this certification at the CompTIA Web site at www.comptia.com.

In my own history as an IT professional, I started as a systems engineer at the Heath/Zenith computer chain in the mid-1980s. I have always felt that a solid foundation in hardware was best for anyone tackling system upgrade and installation problems. The A+ certification clearly charts these skills as a solid entry point to an IT career.

The certification is certainly biased toward WinTel architecture, with tests focusing on Windows and DOS operations and PC hardware. While these do not reflect the broad range of computers used in the industry, the need for technicians with at least the minimum set of skills is enormous. The new Network+ certification seeks to bring similar competence testing to those seeking network-centric jobs.

Aspirants for A+ designation will discover a tremendous number of books, interactive CDs, and other options for learning the necessary material. Want ads are starting to mention A+ as a desired feature on candidates' resumes. While such a certification does not guarantee performance, there are certainly reasons to favor independent testing of IT skills.

Registered Communications Distribution Designer

The Registered Communications Distribution Designer (RCDD) certification was developed by BiCSi, a telecommunications association historically known as Building Industry Consulting Services, International. Holders of the RCDD are skilled in the design, installation, and support of network and telephone cabling systems. An RCDD is trained to build the important infrastructure of a company. Cabling is one of the most expensive and long-lived components that you will ever install, so making the correct investment requires informed guidance. Compliance with numerous federal and local codes demands strict attention to relevant laws and standards.

BiCSi produces a wide variety of publications that are useful for network design specialists. Those who obtain an RCCD designation are required to keep up their skills with various training and continuing education. The organization also maintains an active trade show and exposition calendar. You can find out more information directly from their Web site at www.bicsi.com.

VENDOR CERTIFICATION

Virtually every major player in the IT industry has some form of certification program. These usually require the passage of a number of examinations relevant to the technology that the vendor identifies as most critical. To maintain certification over time, the designee typically must take additional exams to prove that they've gained skills to work with new products that are introduced.

Most vendors offer extensive schedules of classes especially geared toward preparation for exams. People interested in gaining certification are often looking for the fastest way to gain employment in the IT industry. Someone with the motivation and money can take all the classes and exams in a boot camp environment and get a Novell CNE or Microsoft MCSE certificate in three weeks.

While it does take a certain level of intelligence to obtain a certificate in a short time, most IT professionals with hiring authority view an "instant network manager" with a healthy degree of skepticism. Although a person may have mastered the sample exams in books and passed them on the first try, that does not necessarily mean that they possess enough relevant experience. However, a fundamental background in the breadth of technologies covered in most certification courses does prepare one quite well for most entry-level positions.

The certification industry is very lucrative, with many authorized centers giving classes. There is a certain incentive to have students pass qualification exams, and most instructors can give lots of tips and techniques to maximize the passing rate of their students. Many attendees have their tuition paid for by their employers, but some are reimbursed only if they pass the exam. This provides an additional incentive for the centers to make the tests passable. This atmosphere can tarnish the stature of these certifications.

Not everyone that takes the certification curriculum is seeking to gain a vendor-sanctioned stamp of approval. IT specialists are often simply interested in exploring new technologies or updated versions of products they already have. For example, those familiar with Windows NT Server administration may want to take a course on Microsoft Internet Information Server when their company decides to build an intranet.

In my opinion, vendor training can be very valuable. Through classes you can gain exposure to the accepted best practices for the most common applications of certain systems. While the perceptions of certification value may vary at your firm, I would rather hire a person who possessed a certificate than someone with equal experience who did not.

IT REALLY HAPPENED: The single most popular form of junk mail that I receive every week is related to training course offerings. The variety of classes is astonishing, and new ones are frequently introduced.

Microsoft

Not to be outdone by any sanctioning body, Microsoft has spawned a veritable alphabet soup of designations. One can become a MOUS, or Microsoft Office User Specialist, by demonstrating capabilities with the widely popular Office software suite. An MSS is a Microsoft Sales Specialist, certified in meeting the challenge of being a sales professional versed in Microsoft products.

Most IT specialists will be interested in the variety of high-level designations such as Microsoft Certified Systems Engineer (MCSE), Microsoft Certified Database Administrator (MCDBA), and Microsoft Certified Solution Developer (MCSD). All of these designations center on both a core curriculum and specialized classes. Examinations and a minimum passing grade on them are required to achieve these goals.

As with other designations, there are certain perks to achieving full certification. One gains a certain status and perhaps self-esteem by gaining Microsoft's endorsement. People often add Microsoft's various letter designations to their business cards as a sign of their achievements. An increasing number of hiring managers in certain industries look for resumes from those with the stamp of approval from various vendors.

One of my first hires now works for a worldwide consulting firm. His company places a great deal of emphasis on its employees' certifications, believing that customers will have more confidence in their competence. Another added benefit is access to premium content on the Microsoft Web site and in various other publications.

Novell

One of the most well established and best known certifications is that of Certified NetWare Engineer, or CNE. Obtaining this designation requires a strong background in computer hardware and broad knowledge of Novell software installation and administration. As new software products are introduced, certified CNEs must take refresher courses and additional examinations to maintain their designation.

Over the years, additional programs have been developed to broaden the number and type of designations that can be earned. For example, a Certified NetWare Administrator, or CNA, is ideal for anyone who is charged with doing the daily chores for a file server and workgroup but not interested in the more esoteric concerns of cabling and storage system installations. More advanced specialists can achieve Novell's Master CNE designation.

As with Microsoft, there are also certification paths for sellers and developers of NetWare products. Novell resellers are given premium status when their staff includes a certain number of certified individuals. Companies that rely on a strong reseller base for support of their products must have some method to guarantee the quality of those selling and installing them.

IT REALLY HAPPENED: I gained my CNE certification in 1989 so my employer could sell Novell NetWare products. Later the certification gained a prominent spot on my resume and was cited as a compelling reason that I was initially considered for a position I landed at a MicroAge store. Conversely, it was considered unimportant by the IT director who originally hired me for *PC Week*. As I stated earlier, opinions about certification vary widely.

Cisco

Cisco developed the Cisco Certified Internetwork Expert program (CCIE) to qualify people charged with the installation and support of Cisco products. Not only must candidates pass written exams, but they must also demonstrate their ability in a lab environment where various products must be made to function to meet specific requirements. Cisco's leadership role in routers, switches, VPN, and other markets makes this designation very desirable.

The importance of the Internet, intranet, and extranet technologies has made companies increasingly dependent on Cisco products. There are numerous related certifications that reflect the area of expertise and level of experience achieved. The needs of more complex networks with extensive switching or routing schemes or ISPs with enormous dial-in capabilities are addressed by one of the two Cisco Certified Internetwork Expert certifications: CCIE—Routing and Switching, or CCIE—ISP Dial.

Other Designations

There are well over 100 different designations available to the IT professional. Manufacturers such as 3Com, Compaq, IBM, and others have programs that support the sellers or users of their systems. Companies that have substantial investments in particular brands of equipment or software should investigate all of the training opportunities appropriate for their systems. A visit to the various vendor Web sites will quickly highlight the various certification programs.

Because there are such a wide variety of hardware and software certifications being offered, listing all of them and their requirements in this book would be impractical. In addition, certifications change with the development of new technologies, and it takes vigilance and persistence to maintain one's designation. Keep informed as your vendors introduce new programs and remember that your certification may lapse within a few years if you do not take refresher courses and examinations.

As your career progresses, you should always look to gain new skills that are coming into vogue. Programmers who grew up with Cobol and C have more recently been working with Java and Perl. Network managers with extensive backgrounds in Microsoft Windows NT have become increasingly interested in the capabilities of Linux. Read magazines, scan want ads, and interact with your peers to see which skills are expected to be the hottest in the future.

TRADITIONAL ACADEMIC PROGRAMS

Most universities now confer degrees in Computer Science. Certainly a substantial percentage of those working in the IT field have this academic background. Colleges have responded to student and business demands for more instruction in the computing fields. A chronic labor shortage and promises of a well-paid job upon graduation should be making IT an attractive academic option. However, as my college Fortran professor wrote me recently, "Not many graduate because they have to get through physics." A degree in Computer Science is a difficult one to complete.

Thus the vast spectrum of IT specialists includes people with all types of degrees, and even those right out of high school. A four-year bachelor's degree is not the only path one can follow to acquire IT skills. There are many students in a variety of academic programs who use computers as a tool for study and become quite adept with technology. As I have stated throughout this book, the range of skills needed to excel in IT encompasses many disciplines.

Computer Science Degrees

The field of Computer Science is certainly rich in options for those interested in exploiting technology. Programmers, systems analysts, computer architects, network administrators, and other IT professionals possess this degree. But compared to other disciplines such as English and Economics, Computer Science is an infant on college campuses.

Many schools have Mathematics or Engineering professors teaching Computer Science classes. Both by tradition and necessity, these older, well-established departments have wielded control over campus use of computers. Engineers have been the designers and users of much of the technology in computer hardware. Mathematicians have an analytical background that is well suited to careers in software development.

Common Requirements

The type and number of courses that students must take to achieve the B.S. or B.A. in Computer Science vary by school, but there are some general guidelines. First is a strong background in mathematics. Courses in calculus, linear algebra, statistics, and applied mathematics are often core requirements.

Specific computer classes include programming, data structures, algorithms, operating systems, and hardware architecture. These classes create the foundation in most curricula, which is then reinforced by upper-level classes in more specific tracts. The last two years of a college career in Computer Science stress learning additional computer languages, gaining knowledge of computer systems and networks, and exploring areas such as graphics, artificial intelligence, and other subjects.

Business Degrees

Many schools offer business students the opportunity to take a set of computing classes to bolster their general business backgrounds. Some programs confer a degree in Management Information Systems. Graduates of these programs directly address companies' needs to harness computer systems.

Students are introduced to the construction and use of computing systems in the workplace. Rather than concentrating on technical subjects such as programming, these programs emphasize the design and management of information and database systems. Additionally, students explore the capabilities of telecommunications to power a company.

Things They Don't Teach Engineers and Programmers

Management is one of the primary subjects taught in business school. Running a company takes skills in budgeting, industrial relations, accounting, marketing, and numerous other subjects that are not part of traditional engineering or computer science programs. But these business skills are crucial for IT professionals, with the many challenges we face.

A problem some companies confront is having technically skilled people who are neither trained nor particularly well suited for the roles. Wonderful technology without equally skillful business acumen will rarely satisfy user needs in the long run. While it may be tempting for a seasoned application support specialist to scoff and snicker as an MBA struggles with a spreadsheet, who is the person best equipped to define a corporate business plan?

Engineering Degrees

Engineers have historically had a close relationship with computers. Electronic engineers design and build most of the systems in use today, and engineers in all fields have always been among the groups that exploit computer capabilities. Some colleges have introduced specific Computer Engineering degrees.

Degree Requirements

Many of the required courses in an Engineering program mirror those taken for a Computer Science degree. Programming, algorithms, and similar classes occupy several semesters of study. Engineers also take many courses in mathematics, physics, and analog and digital circuitry. While being able to quote Ohm's law in your sleep may not win you many bar bets, designing computers takes a tremendous understanding of how electrical current can be controlled.

Look for schools that are accredited by the Accreditation Board of Engineering and Technology (ABET). During the first two years in these programs, students concentrate on electrical and electronic engineering courses. The final years of study feature classes in digital signal processing, VLSI design, and other computer hardware-specific technologies.

Non-Computer-Centric Degrees

Computers are so pervasive in academics and the workplace that there is perhaps no discipline devoid of their influence. Indeed, many students in "non-computer" programs are extensively versed in systems and their operations.

For example, some English departments offer majors in Technical Writing. It is almost impossible to write intelligibly about complex computer programs and hardware without grasping the fundamentals of their use. Documentation is a critical component of any system, and well-written manuals are too often a scarce commodity.

Philosophy programs teach logic and the organization of thought processes. Being able to construct software requires the same type of conventions and discipline. Perhaps the difficulty of getting employment as a philosopher is a strong impetus for Philosophy majors to seek a job in the IT field.

As I stated earlier, mathematicians have historically been tied to the development and use of computers. The term "computers" used to refer to humans who performed calculations. During World War II, many math majors were tapped to work in cryptography and ballistics research. Mathematicians may work as actuaries, processing vast quantities of numbers through sophisticated statistical analysis. In both applied and theoretical arenas, those with a math background are almost required to have computer skills to get their work done.

These days, virtually every college student in any major is expected to learn how to use computers. The school systems in every state recognize the need for computer literacy in every grade as important for economic growth. Computers are no longer reserved for the special few in Engineering or similar disciplines.

Graduate Degrees

People pursue advanced degrees for several reasons. Some simply wish to expand on the background they gathered during their undergraduate studies. Many universities grant Master's and Ph.D. degrees in Engineering, Computer Science, and Business.

Graduate school is an opportunity to probe subjects more deeply and widen the scope of your knowledge. Freed from unrelated coursework, you can immerse yourself in intense study with specialization in a particular field. Programmers may progress from writing programs based on packaged software to designing their own compilers, operating systems, and languages.

Many of the computer technologies we use today were developed in academic institutions. UNIX owes much of its character to U.C. Berkeley grad students. Linux was the brainchild of then-student Linus Torvalds, who rewrote the freeware Minix operating system. Students at Columbia University worked with their professors on the construction of the operating system-independent Kermit file transfer protocol.

Partnerships between universities and industry have been a major impetus in computer development. The investment that businesses have made in funding academic research has been repaid many times over by the commercialization of technology discovered and perfected in the classroom. There has also been a tremendous amount of investment in research by federal and state governments. Graduate students usually have the opportunity to work closely with industry when striving to make products for the commercial marketplace.

Career Changers

A large percentage of those in graduate degree programs are people seeking to change their careers. Accountants, lawyers, and other professionals dissatisfied with their current jobs often enroll in MBA programs that stress high-tech instruction. A two- or three-year program can help prepare a person for a career in IT, but only if it adds to other key qualities that they already possess.

In my opinion, no academic program can manufacture outstanding IT professionals, no matter how varied and demanding the classes are. IT will always demand more than can be taught in a classroom. Programs that place an emphasis on internships and co-op hours prepare the most well-rounded individuals. It's far better to experiment in the campus computer lab than to make a costly mistake in an actual business setting.

Career Enhancers

Many of us who work as IT professionals may find that a graduate degree is the best way to secure a higher-paying future position. People often write about a "glass ceiling" that prevents advancement based on race or gender, but there also are barriers to those that don't have a computer-centric degree. Mid-level IT professionals may find that the best way to revitalize their careers is through securing an advanced degree.

"Engineers feel most comfortable hiring other engineers" is a line I often heard when I first began looking for work in the computer field. My B.A. in Geography did little to enhance my perceived value as a programmer and computer problem solver. I am certain that an advanced degree in a computing field would have helped me secure a job quickly.

Non-Degree Programs

Not every college student is interested in pursuing a degree. Some just want to take classes to gain a specific skill or refresh their existing knowledge. Many schools permit people to take classes as a non-matriculating student. Selecting a single course from the school catalog and paying the registration fee may be all you need to do to take a desired class. This may be a good option when your time or budget are tight or if you just want exposure to something new.

Certificate Programs

While a full degree can take a significant amount of time and money to acquire, there are alternatives available. Many universities offer continuing education programs that grant certificates in many fields, including Computer Science.

Non-faculty members often teach these classes. These are often professionals in the field who may not have advanced degrees of their own. The usual emphasis is on the instructor's practical knowledge and real-world experiences.

Programs of this type can often be completed in less than two years. Classes are geared toward the working professional and meet in the evenings and on weekends. However, the fees per credit hour may be only slightly lower than those charged for a traditional degree program.

Associate Degrees

Community colleges grant two-year degrees in a variety of programs, including computer-related fields. These schools tend to emphasize practical applications rather than theoretical study. There tend to be many courses of study, such as Web page design, that lead directly to employment opportunities. In many ways, the community college functions as an advanced vocational school for motivated students.

Community colleges often cater to working people by offering evening and weekend courses. These can be an excellent and cost-effective way to build your skills without having to enter a full-time program.

IT REALLY HAPPENED: During a summer break when I was an undergraduate at the State University of New York in Binghamton, I took a Fortran course at Westchester Community College in Valhalla, New York. The equipment was excellent and the instruction was first-rate.

Judging Academic Programs

There are many criteria to consider when ranking the quality of a school and its programs. If you wish to get career support from your academic institution, then investigate the quality of the counseling and job placement services offered. Look for on-site job fairs and established ties with area companies. Academic programs often funnel dozens of graduates to the same employers year after year. A strong track record is a great endorsement.

Compare the quality of the faculty and student body. What percentage of the students are from the top tiers of their high school classes, and what is the median SAT score? What is the student-teacher ratio, and how well equipped are the computer labs and classrooms? You should be able to determine this information from course catalogs or by asking questions at the admissions office.

Study the course catalogs and syllabi of the departments you are interested in. Audit some classes to get a feel for the classroom environment. Do the other students mirror your own aspirations and abilities, or will you feel out of place and overwhelmed by the expertise they display?

Which college to attend is a highly personal decision. Your success as a student depends to a large extent on your degree of comfort with and excitement about the institution. The tremendous costs involved should motivate you to make a careful assessment of the relative merits of any school you are considering.

NON-ACADEMIC LEARNING

Of course, not all of your knowledge growth will happen in a classroom. To be a successful IT professional, you must draw information from as many sources as possible. You need to know how to tap into the expertise of others.

Among other things, you can learn from others in informal user groups. IT departments also need to nurture teaching opportunities among their staff. One should be a voracious reader and exploit books, periodicals, and electronic delivery of information. You also need to attend various trade shows and conferences.

TIP: Many of the techniques I cover in the remainder of this chapter will be reinforced in Chapter 10. Technical support requires aggressively pursuing the information you need to fix a problem. This chapter gives you a firm foundation of knowledge that will help you understand the concepts presented later in the book.

User Groups

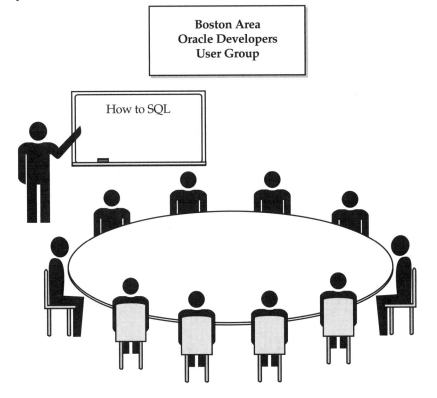

One of the oldest and most enjoyable ways of learning IT is through computer user groups. These are typically informal meetings of IT professionals who share common interests. They often convene monthly and last for a few hours. Membership is usually either free or inexpensive, and everyone is encouraged to share ideas, problems, and solutions.

Groups are formed to fill different missions. Some are general interest and virtually any subject matter can be discussed. Others are more focused and cater to specific interests. For example, there are user groups that address Oracle database programming, Web page design, and Linux server administration.

Most major metropolitan areas have several active user groups. Universities and schools often permit community-based groups to use their facilities for a nominal fee. Many computer vendors host meetings in their offices for those interested in their products. For example, in the Boston area, both Microsoft and Novell sponsor network user groups in their offices.

One of the best advantages of user groups is that you can meet people who use similar products in different ways. By talking with people who exploit hardware and software differently than you do, you can often discover invaluable insights and tricks. Groups generally encourage everyone to contribute, so be sure to share whatever knowledge you have.

Another benefit of attending user groups is interpersonal networking. You may find contract personnel or other help for your firm or learn about potential future opportunities for yourself. While some groups frown on recruiting at the meetings (after all, that is not the primary purpose of a user group), there are certainly a lot of talented people looking for new job opportunities. Sometimes it is the conversations in hallways and business card exchanges that yield the most productive and unexpected professional relationships.

IT REALLY HAPPENED: I used to work for Heath/Zenith and our store hosted a monthly Heath users group meeting. It was exciting to see the interaction between accountants, lawyers, software developers, and students. We had product demonstrations by Hewlett-Packard, Microsoft, Apple and others. These companies often extended special offers to group members.

Informal Training

While I have already reviewed the many traditional methods for learning, there are several less formal possibilities that you should explore at your company. Recognize that those you work with often possess a variety of experiences and skills that should be shared with others. Exploiting this knowledge is an inexpensive and effective way to boost the abilities of everyone else in your firm.

Look for those in your department who have recently taken a new class or attended a seminar or trade show and encourage them to brief others on the things they have learned. Others may have had experiences with previous employers that are relevant to technology options currently being explored at your company. Using the collective wisdom and training of your entire staff is a cost-effective, efficient use of existing resources, and a good way to build esprit de corps.

Brown Bag Meetings

You may want to host casual educational sessions during lunchtime from time to time. Invite or designate someone to give a ten-minute lecture or demonstration and then open the floor to questions and discussion. If your budget permits, pay for pizza or sandwiches. This is not only a way to boost attendance, but it also conveys your respect for your staff.

Rotate the responsibility for chairing the meeting so that everyone is encouraged to participate and all can contribute. Ask for topic ideas. This is a great way for people to learn about other staff members' skills and job requirements. For example, Java programmers can learn about the newest trends in network domain management and desktop support specialists can learn about Perl scripting or n-tier component-based development methods.

This can foster stronger working relationships among disparate members of IT staff who would otherwise rarely meet during a normal workday. The synergy that develops may yield other benefits; a rich exchange of ideas and experiences can often solve nagging problems.

Peer Training Sessions

People who demonstrate a natural affinity for teaching should be encouraged to lead classes for other IT staff members. Team leaders may be the obvious choice to run these sessions since they should command a greater degree of technical expertise and experience, but anyone with ability in a particular area should be prompted to share his or her knowledge.

IT is a complex field. Many discrete pieces of information and skills need to be blended together to run modern company infrastructures. It is absolutely impossible for anyone to obtain the complete depth and breadth of skills to tackle every need that IT addresses. Only a strong team effort will adequately address the demands of a thriving business.

WARNING: Keep a regular schedule for brown bag and peer training sessions. Failure to do so will likely cause attendance to drop and meetings to be put off indefinitely. Once everyone becomes accustomed to these meetings, they will look forward to the opportunity to learn and contribute.

Books

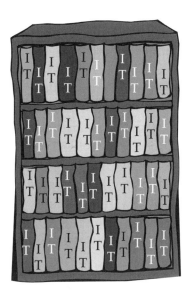

Unless you are new to the IT profession, your shelves are probably stuffed with books. This includes the manuals that came with your hardware and software, which are often inadequate. Most vendor-supplied documentation covers only installation and the broadest subject matters. While there may be a description of every command and function, the text is typically brief and often confusing.

The overall quality of vendor-supplied documentation is unfortunately fairly poor. Every software or hardware system has a multitude of commands that require explanation. Covering every one completely is difficult. The manufacturer usually decides which features are most typically needed and gives them greater attention.

Like me, you may get frustrated when the particular command or feature that you need details on is given only scant attention. But every system is used differently in a given situation, and there is no way for the vendor to anticipate every need. I've used router manuals that attempt to cover hundreds of configuration commands, each with dozens of options, by giving only minimal examples. It's times like these that I seek books to expand on what is offered in the vendor-supplied documents.

Printed materials are expensive to produce. Narrow profit margins for software means that manuals have become thinner and less informative. All of these factors have led to vigorous competition among book publishers to fill in the gaps with numerous offerings.

Products like Microsoft Windows NT Server, Novell NetWare, and Linux are extremely versatile. File, print, Web, proxy, and other services can all be run from a single system. It is almost impossible to address all of the detailed information for each of these processes in a single book. This is why books with a narrow focus are so important. For example, there are dozens of titles that concentrate on the use of Windows NT Server as a Web server.

Most IT specialists have several books on similar subjects grouped on their shelves. By utilizing several titles, you stand a better chance of finding answers to your questions in at least one source.

TIP: While new versions of software are constantly being introduced, don't assume that old books are suddenly obsolete. Most networks rely on systems for many years, extending the older books' usefulness. Commands may be augmented, but the core program functions are usually retained in all versions. For example, UNIX administrators can use old Awk and Grep documentation on the latest releases of their OS.

Find the Best Books

While I am somewhat tempted to write that anything put out by Osborne/McGraw-Hill (the publisher of this book) is wonderful, there are some things I always check for to see just how useful a book will be to me. Check for these features carefully and choose your books wisely.

Always scan the table of contents and book index to get a feel for the types of subject matter covered. While a book may tout itself as a "complete guide" to an application, anyone familiar with the program should be able to judge whether the book ignores or details its most important functions. Again, the author makes a judgment as to what the reader will need most.

When you find a particular book that interests you, read a passage that pertains to the particular subject you need to know about. Get a feel for the writing style and book design. The text should be logically organized and easy to navigate. Check if there are special features like a glossary or program listings, and see whether they are informative and helpful. If there is an area that you know particularly well, compare your understanding to the view the author espouses.

Consider past book purchases that have satisfied your prior needs. Perhaps there is a series with a solid reputation and a style you like. Many authors are quite prolific, so look for additional titles by those you have enjoyed before. Be sure that the book you purchase meets your current information needs. A quick start guide should be terse and abundantly clear, for example, and beginners' guides should not assume too much prior knowledge of the reader.

INCLUDED SOFTWARE   Many technical books include one or more CD-ROMs of supplemental materials, including software. Sometimes the programs are collections of shareware or freeware utilities that are appropriate to the subject matter. These CDs obviously vary in usefulness and quality, so be sure to check the contents list in the book to ascertain whether the software would be helpful to you.

There are some books that include complete compilers or operating systems. Many Linux books contain various distributions such as Slackware or Red Hat. The variety of available open-source software is certain to grow in upcoming years, and this type of bundling is likely to increase in popularity.

Many hardware and software vendors have active publishing groups that generate and distribute books for their systems. These are almost sure to contain software that did not make it into the original boxes with the shipping products. Time, space, and monetary considerations often place limits on what can be included.

Optional Vendor Documentation

Vendors often address their documentation limitations by issuing resource kits, additional documentation, or tutorial materials along with more extensive instructions and examples of product use. Often bundled as additional software, these can be a valuable addition to your library.

Some companies provide expanded manuals as part of the purchase of upgraded service plans. By subscribing to newsletters and CD-ROM knowledge bases, you can get tips and solutions that are used by the technical support staffs at the various vendors. If your company can include an initial budgetary line item, IT will be armed with extra materials that normally require a telephone call to access, creating tremendous savings over time.

Email Subscriptions

Waiting for printed materials to arrive in the mail or reminding yourself to regularly browse the Web sites of your key product manufacturers are not the fastest ways to get breaking news. Dozens of vendors maintain listservers, essentially an automated system that sends email to a database of subscribers, permitting anyone to get a variety of information feeds. You can select the type and number of automated emails you wish to receive.

While companies like Novell, 3Com, Apple, and Microsoft send out updates on a wide variety of subjects to listserver subscribers, vendors are not the only source of this type of information. Both print and electronic publications, such as *InfoWorld*, supplant their traditional and online information delivery systems with listservers.

> **TIP:** Establish a generic email account dedicated to your listserver subscriptions. By granting reader access for that email file to everyone in your IT department, you can centralize a great information resource. Periodically clean out the oldest data to keep the mail file manageable and current.

White Papers

White papers are an attempt by vendors to provide real-world analysis and examples of ways to use their products. For example, 3Com and Cisco's Web sites (www.3com.com and www.cisco.com) contain technical information on routers and network security. The various scenarios for installation of firewalls and proxy servers are described in great detail. While every network is unique, viewing illustrations of several security schemes can help you develop the plan most appropriate for your workplace.

White papers are the best places to check for explanations of new products and announcements of technology introductions. When acronyms are introduced along with products, these are a great place to learn about the features being touted.

> **WARNING:** Realize that the information presented in any vendor-produced material is likely to be influenced by the company's Marketing Department. Bragging about enhanced capabilities and one-sided comparisons to competitors' products are commonplace.

Press Releases

Technology companies frequently announce products, joint ventures, pricing specials, awards won, and numerous other news items. Users of these products who wait to read about product coverage in magazines can often miss opportunities or make uninformed decisions. IT specialists must aggressively pursue information about the products and services that their company depends on.

Avail yourself of the marketing machines at your suppliers and request that you be placed on any contact lists they maintain. Distribution by fax, email, snail mail, and other means can keep you up-to-date on technology upgrades and similar subjects. You can typically scan Web sites for archives of press releases, too.

Don't forget to check on your vendors' competition. Not only can you use this information as leverage during negotiations, but you also need to know what other options you have. Being informed is one of the best tools any IT specialist can have.

Most technology magazines illustrate product features with a grid. Features that are best used to differentiate a product, such as support for particular protocols, are denoted with checkmarks or with numerical rankings. This permits readers to quickly determine the suitability of a product for their environment.

Case Studies

Vendors are always looking to publicize users' success with their products. While you can assume that failures are never discussed and problems are likely glossed over, this information is normally quite useful, especially when the topics discussed closely mirror your network. Case studies normally highlight the most prominent features of the technology being employed and detail their application.

Developing truly unique and revolutionary solutions is much rarer than replicating or adopting proven solutions. Investigate ways that others have approached issues similar to yours and you will potentially save lots of time and money. Don't be afraid to contact the companies mentioned in a case study. Most IT professionals I know are usually happy to share their experiences so long as they don't betray trade secrets.

Magazines

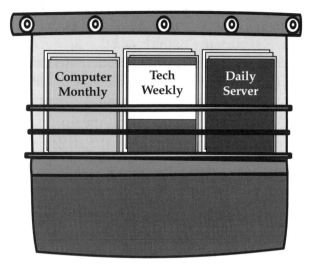

Weekly and monthly magazines can often be your best source of information, especially on rapidly emerging trends or new product releases. Vendors desperately want analysts and editors at these magazines to examine new products and highlight features for their readers. Also, many of the staff members at these publications, such as myself, either have IT backgrounds or do work for the magazine in addition to holding an IT position.

Magazines come in a variety of forms and cater to different needs. There are general-interest publications that cover a wide range of technology issues, such as *PC World* or *InfoWorld.* In these periodicals you are likely to find coverage of new IBM mainframes, Adobe software, AT&T service offerings, and Linux kernel updates. More focused publications like *SQL Server Magazine* target niche markets by covering topics such as Oracle database programming and Lotus Notes issues.

Tech magazines generally contain a balance of news, reviews, and analysis pieces. News items announce newly introduced products and services and attempt to assign significance to them. Reviews of a single item or a group of related products try to rank their relative abilities and competence for readers. A technical analysis is usually an attempt by an expert to explain or define the technology and its relative importance to the reader.

Most magazines also feature columns and editorials. Among these are advice columns similar to the one I write for *PC Week.* Other columnists, such as *InfoWorld*'s Maggie Biggs who is also the technical editor of this book, offer opinions on a variety of subjects that are often based on personal and professional experience. Editorials provide a way for the magazine management to both prophesize about and chide the industry they cover.

Read Several Magazines

There are many excellent print and online publications that cater to the IT industry professional. Weekly publications like *PC Week, InfoWorld, Information Week,* and others provide timely articles on numerous subjects. What distinguishes these magazines is the breadth and depth of their coverage.

Monthly magazines don't try to offer the wide range of breaking news coverage that their weekly brethren do. Instead they try to have more comprehensive and in-depth features. Whereas *PC Week* examines a few systems from a select number of vendors, *PC Magazine* covers dozens of vendors, from the smallest to the largest.

RATING MAGAZINES   In the same way that you scan books for content and clarity before buying them, pay attention to the magazines you rely on. Make sure that the editorial coverage matches your needs. Check the reviews for relevance and attention for detail. See how well columns are written and how easy it is to navigate through the various sections.

Magazines are very economical for the amount of content they provide. An investment of less than $100 per year can pay for several subscriptions. Create a library for back issues that is open to everyone and use routing slips to maximize circulation throughout your organization. Many magazines are also available as controlled-circulation publications, which means that they are provided at no cost to subscribers. *PC Week, InfoWorld,* and *InfoWeek* are distributed in this manner. Visit their respective Web sites to fill out their application forms for a free subscription.

Don't Skip the Advertisements

The numerous advertisements that appear in every tech magazine are another good source of information. Make it a habit to clip and store ads that feature products of interest to you for later reference. There may be new product introductions or pricing incentives that you want to remember next time your budget permits spending.

Online resources are often cited in ads. Use a sticky note or highlighter to make this information easy to find for future reference. Most magazines produce an index to the ads in each issue, so be sure to check there as well.

IT REALLY HAPPENED: At *PC Week*, there is a steady stream of CEOs and product managers eager to hear our opinion of their latest offerings. They hope that our close relationships with our readers will give us the knowledge to provide a highly tuned and critical appraisal. Any large media source can have a tremendous impact by providing indirect feedback to vendors about their products.

Use Reader Service Cards

Many magazines provide ways for readers to request additional information from vendors. These are typically postage-paid cards on which you circle the items you want to have mailed to you. Other magazines have forms that you can fill out and fax.

Visit the Companion Web Sites

Most technology magazines have Web sites, such as *InfoWorld* (www.infoworld.com), that augment their print products. These sites can contain back issue archives or more extensive coverage that was not included in the print version. The detailed methodology used in reviews and complete test results can give the reader information that they can interpret themselves.

Web Zines and Independent Sites

One of the best things about the World Wide Web is that it allows people to create and distribute editorial products without the time-consuming and expensive process that traditional print publishing involves. Web zines, or e-zines, are a rapidly growing segment of the Web. Magazines like Slate (www.slate.com) and Slashdot (www.slashdot.org) only exist in electronic form, yet they command a great deal of respect from their readers and vendors.

Electronic publishers often utilize various push techniques to get information to subscribers. Fax and email delivery of daily or weekly feeds to subscribers can be free or require a standard subscription charge. The quality of these offerings can vary greatly, so give them the same degree of scrutiny you would any other publication.

Today anyone with a computer and access to an ISP can get into the publishing business. Many people on the Web have created shrines to their favorite Star Trek or Teletubby character. There are many IT specialists who create sites dedicated to helping others to get the most out of their computers. I will cover some of the best places on the Web for technical support in Chapter 10.

Newspapers

Recognizing that technology increasingly plays a decisive role in business and the home, many general-interest newspapers have expanded their coverage of computing subjects. Product reviews, opinion pieces, and technical Q&A columns have become common. The *New York Times, Boston Globe, San Jose Mercury News, Wall Street Journal* and many others have broadened their technology coverage and dedicated staff to computing stories.

Virtually every major newspaper has embraced the Web to supplant or expand their print operations. There are often stories that only appear in the electronic versions of newspapers. While you may not get the in-depth product information or technical analysis, coverage of local issues can be critical.

Local Coverage

Changes to telecommunication and tax laws are often applied to local versus national markets. Having extensive coverage from a local news source can be invaluable to your company. Local newspapers also carry advertisements from area ISPs, vendors, and training organizations.

Scanning the want ads in your local paper is a good way of determining which companies are looking for particular types of talent. This information can come in handy when you are competing for workers with similar skillsets. It also illustrates which technologies are currently in vogue so that you can adjust your own learning priorities accordingly.

Trade Shows

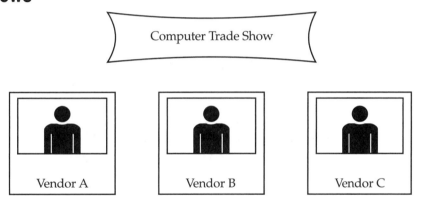

Sometimes it seems that trade shows are nothing more than an opportunity to collect as many hats, pens, T-shirts, mousepads, calendars, screwdrivers, and other trinkets as possible. While the windfall in free apparel may be an enticing feature, there really are great benefits to trade show attendance. They are terrific forums for learning a great deal directly from vendors and from other attendees.

Trade shows can be found in many forms. Annual events like COMDEX in Las Vegas are among the largest gatherings in the world. When hundreds of thousands of IT professionals descend on Las

Vegas, virtually every hotel room and conference center is booked. Cab stands are mobbed by throngs of people struggling under the weight of all the free stuff they just grabbed inside. Monster events of this scale attract the entire range of people and technologies used in companies today. You are just as likely to meet a CIO of a Fortune 500 company as you are a programmer who works out of his garage.

Other events are more sedate. They may be organized by local user groups or resellers and attract only a few hundred attendees. Small events may be designed for a very narrow focus, and organizers try to keep this boutique approach to enhance the interchange among those who attend. Academic institutions and government agencies also frequently host events. While you may be a consummate generalist, it is sometimes wonderful to attend an event that delves deeply into a more focused topic. You won't feel rushed to take in an array of information and instead can spend time examining a single subject in detail.

Maximize Trade Show Benefits

Approaching a trade show with the correct attitude and plan will allow you to maximize the precious amount of time you have. One should not enter the convention center blindly but rather invest some time in research beforehand. Find out who will be exhibiting at the show and what types of items you need most.

I always try to identify a few specific people or vendors that are scheduled to be at the show and make sure to contact them there. Set up appointments before the show to guarantee that those you seek will have the time to meet you. Vendors often have special private briefings that require prior invitations to attend. Contact company Marketing departments a few weeks before a show and see if you can secure the necessary credentials for the private sessions. This type of experience may be limited to Fortune 1000 clients, but it won't hurt to ask.

FLEXIBILITY Whenever I attend a trade show, I try to keep my schedule as flexible as possible since I never know what I will encounter or exactly how much time I will have to investigate particular items. Certain events such as keynote speeches and training sessions have stricter timetables, so work around their constraints.

Most booths that are running demonstrations indicate upcoming presentation times and their duration. Keep a notebook handy and mark off your day in 15-minute increments. If you plan carefully, you can attend all of the sessions you want.

BUSINESS CARDS Take an ample supply of business cards with you. Make sure all the information is up-to-date. Keep a pen handy to make notes on the backs of the cards you hand out. People working in the booths will no doubt collect hundreds of cards over a few days and will never be able to sort them all out easily. Jot a quick note that states exactly what you need, if appropriate.

Likewise, make notes on the back of business cards that you get from others. Record the exact reason you asked for the card and the area of responsibility the cardholder has. Be sure to follow up with them after the show before a new project dulls your memory of the interaction.

VISITING SMALL EXHIBITORS   I always love going to the small booths at shows. These people may be demonstrating the coolest technology that you have never heard of. Often the very entrepreneurs who have created the product staff the booth. If you have a compelling reason to be interested in their products, they will be just as interested in hearing your feedback.

Small companies often target market segments that have been ignored or underserved by bigger vendors. They sometimes introduce products that enhance the usability or administration of major products. Corporations like Novell, Adobe, Sun, and Microsoft now organize pavilions that showcase companies featuring enhancement products under their sponsorship flag. The endorsement of the larger company is a clear signal that these products are valuable and highly desired.

The technology industry is rife with stories of companies that began in a basement with a handful of employees. New competitors just starting out may one day challenge Hewlett-Packard, Apple, or

Microsoft. AOL has become an industry giant, swallowing up CompuServe, Netscape, and numerous other companies within the past few years.

ENJOYING THE CARNIVAL ATMOSPHERE   IT work can give you a headache. Take the opportunity to enjoy some of the more frivolous events at a show. While I don't remember exactly which company had a rock-climbing wall, ran a parody of "Jeopardy," or hired a bungee-jumping group, I try to take the opportunity to laugh and enjoy myself. Every presentation has an element of entertainment and P.T. Barnum mixed into the information the vendors are trying to get you to digest.

On the other hand, I make it a rule to avoid vendors that have obnoxious clowns or scantily clad women out front of their booths or that otherwise insult my intelligence with inane displays and blaring music. It should be obvious which products are being shown and how long the presentation will last. (I also want to see what kind of prizes I will get for my 15 minutes of listening!)

Attend Training Sessions

Trade shows often have training or conference sessions that run concurrently. These are typically held in neighboring facilities and may require a premium fee over the normal show admission charge. This gathering of industry and manufacturers' representatives can provide an excellent opportunity to learn directly from the experts as well as those producing and utilizing the same solutions that you need.

Conferences at larger shows are organized into tracts, with similar technologies grouped together. By staggering starting times, an attendee can take several classes and get a broad exposure to the latest in technology directly from those who produce it. Focused, stimulating sessions are often more valuable than any presentation on the show floor.

Vendor Expositions

Computer stores, hardware manufacturers, and software producers often host shows. These are typically done on a local level and don't attempt to draw attendees from all over the country. Oracle, Microsoft, Novell, Sun MicroSystems, Adobe, Macromedia and many other firms sponsor conferences that rotate to different cities a few days apart.

One of the better examples of this genre is the quarterly technical briefing held by Microsoft. The TechNet shows are a one-day affair with a morning briefing followed by a few focused sessions. There are often a few other co-sponsors that augment the presentations being given by the host. For example, a demonstration of Microsoft's Cluster Server might be shown on Compaq-supplied file servers.

These mini-shows are bound to be biased, since only one company is running the session and controlling the entire process. However, their value to those dependent on particular vendors can be enormous. Most companies will and should treat customers as a valuable commodity, and you should have an opportunity to give them your feedback.

CHAPTER 9

Winning at the Purchasing Game

Meeting all of a company's computing needs requires more than just providing dependable technical support and user training. Many IT specialists are also responsible for the purchase of all goods and services needed to meet user and customer demands. The list of products is exhaustive, and the goods are usually acquired from a wide variety of sources.

Making sure that you know how to manage the entire purchasing process is the primary goal of this chapter. We will begin with a brief examination of the major product categories that your budget will need to account for. By examining a sample purchasing situation, you will learn how to construct a Request for Proposals (RFP) and a Request for Quotations (RFQ). Next I will show you how to critique a vendor quotation based on a hypothetical purchasing scenario.

Your assorted options for buying products will be discussed and their various strengths and weaknesses explored. There are many steps to take to ensure that you maximize your purchasing power. The economics of leasing and incremental upgrades will be compared to the costs of purchasing new equipment on a specific cycle.

Another important part of this chapter covers strategies for dealing with consultants and consulting firms. At one time or another, most companies need the assistance of contract help. Services, including telecommunications links and other functions crucial to IT, are another budget consideration that needs to be studied carefully.

EVERYTHING IT BUYS

The variety of items that IT departments use to fulfill their mission is often staggering. Some of the products are basics that any IT specialist will be familiar with, but understanding all of the items needed to power a modern corporation means that you have to account for the entire gamut, from the smallest CMOS battery to the largest storage hardware.

While thoughts of powerful servers and VPN services may command your attention, you must be equally aware of network patch cable and competing disk formats of removable media.

Remember that a faulty $10 cable can doom a network just as easily as the most expensive router. Only by accounting for every component will you be able to create comprehensive budgets and ensure quality throughout your organization.

Hardware

The computers on users' desktops and inside the server room can comprise a major portion of yearly budget expenditures. Servers equipped with massive drive arrays, enormous RAM, and multiple processors can easily cost tens of thousands of dollars. Host systems designed for thousands of users often cost over several hundred thousand dollars to lease or purchase.

Along with the actual CPUs are the dozens of supporting components. Monitors, printers, mice, and other standard accessories are all part of the purchasing scheme. Less common devices such as plotters, CD-ROM burners, or digitizing tablets may be critical at your firm.

Furniture

You may be responsible for selecting the furniture used not only in the server room but also in employees' work areas. Ergonomic chairs and lighting are important considerations for a productive and comfortable environment. Companies such as Symbiote, Wright-Line, Zero-Stantron, and Steelcase manufacture custom, built-to-order units that may cost thousands of dollars per workstation.

TIP: While computers may be replaced every few years, LAN technical furniture can remain useful for well over a decade. Communications racks designed to universal standards are versatile and can work with just about any type of equipment. While initially an expensive acquisition, quality furniture is a long-term investment.

Networking Hardware and Tools

Telecommunications and networking hardware may form another significant portion of your budget. Hubs, routers, and switches for large networks are very expensive items. Remember that these units are typically used for a longer period than client machines, so careful selection of the correct product is critical.

While there are some computers and monitors that you purchase by the dozen, you may acquire only a single unit of some other important equipment, such as an expensive dye-sublimation color printer designed to be shared by large workgroups. Some IT specialists rely on sophisticated tools for network performance monitoring. A powerful protocol analyzer costs at least $15,000. Test equipment such as a Microtest Omniscan cable scanner is worth about $5,000. IT specialists also need simple screwdrivers and pliers. Remember to always account for the mundane needs as well as the high-end components when building your budgets.

Computers

Your essential hardware purchases are the systems that go on users' desktops and in the server room. Whenever I create a budget, I always consider the total number of units needed rather than calculating a specific dollar figure to be meted out during the purchasing process. Make sure that your systems are correctly outfitted before determining the per-unit budget amount.

Consider that your computers will each require a monitor and sufficient disk space and memory to do the required tasks. Network cards and other specialized options such as Firewire-capable video-capture cards can add significantly to the cost. As I outlined in Chapter 2, your servers can be outfitted with massive disk arrays and other expensive features. Intel-based servers may cost four to ten times more than a typical desktop PC.

BUSINESS VS. HOME COMPUTERS Virtually every major PC manufacturer designs computers for two distinct markets. The first is the home user. The second line of products, of most interest to IT specialists, is designed for business use.

There are several factors that differentiate the two distinct product categories. Typically, the home user has fairly generic performance needs and a tighter budget than a business buyer does. Many budget computers designated for a home user are built to run basic software programs, provide adequate game performance, and give users the ability to surf the Net. As such, they often are provided with 56K modems, speakers, a CD-ROM drive, and a minimum of expansion capabilities. While not blessed with numerous bus or memory slots for growth, they are certainly adequate for most students, small business owners, and recreational computer users.

Home computers often match their business counterparts in sheer CPU horsepower. Pre-installed software and generous hard drives can make them quite attractive given their cost. However, a system designed for the office market usually includes other features that a home user does not require. For example, instead of a modem, business users generally desire an Ethernet card. Network management features such as Wake On LAN (WOL) and Desktop Management Interface (DMI) are highly desired options for easing centralized control of LAN-connected PCs.

Workstation-level systems with cutting-edge features such as high-end 3D video cards can add considerably to overall cost and are not found in consumer systems. SCSI drives and RAID storage are normally limited to business-class computers. Multiple processor-capable machines are also not often required by or marketed to home computer users.

Included software also varies. Many corporate customers currently require computers that come with full versions of Microsoft Office. Casual home users may use the more cost-conscious Star Office or Microsoft Works. Games and other entertainment applications that are not needed in an office setting can be found in many home systems.

Home computer users typically get Windows 98 preloaded on their machines, but they may be able to replace it with Windows NT Workstation or various flavors of Linux if desired. Dell and IBM are among the many suppliers that offer non-Microsoft alternatives for an operating system. Whatever OS you select, be certain that it is appropriate to the computing tasks you intend to run. You may also be faced with a different acquisition cost when you opt for an alternative OS from your supplier's default.

Service options can also vary widely. Business users may desire extended next-day service plans for all their desktops. For example, the Compaq Deskpro EN is sold with a standard three-year on-site warranty. You must upgrade the less-expensive Prosignia system by an additional $99 in order to receive the same next-day service coverage. Always be conscious of these differences when making your budget decisions.

WORKING WITH HOME COMPUTERS   Even if your company does not purchase computers that are typically marketed to home users, you will certainly interact with employees who do. While these systems may be earmarked for Junior's homework and family budgets, people often use them to work remotely or when they bring work home. This scenario calls for software and hardware at home that is compatible with what is available in the office.

The use of DSL, ISDN, cable, and analog modems to access the corporate network via the Internet should prompt a proactive IT department to suggest certain standards for remote home-office configurations. One strategy is to develop with your normal vendors a list of recommended systems that users can buy with confidence and that IT can comfortably support.

TIP: If your department is responsible for managing remote access to the corporate network, develop special support materials for these users. Create documentation that covers setting up a dial-up connection and dealing with VPN security access. Also create and abide by a strict policy of involvement with these computers; you don't want to be responsible for rescuing a child's book report or debugging problems with Reader Rabbit. You must avoid a situation in which IT is unduly taxed by supporting dozens of different brands of systems. Establish a standard support policy that dictates which types of machines and software will be supported by IT or a third party.

Software

All of your computers require operating systems and application software to perform their functions. Commercial software licensing is another line item that can consume a significant portion of your budget. The appeal of open-source solutions is that you can achieve the same level of features and performance at a much lower cost. Major vendors such as IBM have embraced these open-source products and they will continue to grow in prominence in many corporations. Remember that acquisition costs for software is only part of the total picture. Service and support contracts for your applications and operating systems can form a major portion of your expenditures.

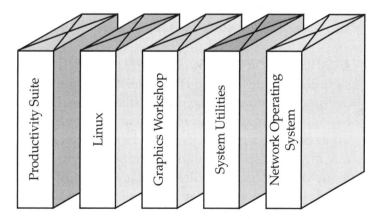

Later in this chapter I'll cover ways to break a software budget into several sections, which you can use as a general guideline for your own company's purchasing plan. Certainly your budget distribution will vary depending on the type of business you are in and the breadth of your purchasing responsibility.

Application Software

Running the gamut from word processors to programming languages, application software often comprises the largest segment of your software-purchasing budget. When popular office productivity suites carrying a $300 price tag are paired with virus scanners, custom applications, compression utilities, and numerous other titles, the cost of outfitting hundreds of computers can be staggering.

When the personal computer was still a new item, the number of applications that were run was fairly limited. Many users simply relied on only one or two programs for all of their computing needs. With revolutionary products such as Lotus 1-2-3 spreadsheets and the WordPerfect word processor, a user could accomplish things no one dreamed of only a few years before.

With the introduction of window-style graphical user interfaces (GUIs) first popularized on the Apple Macintosh, the steep learning curves associated with each new application were greatly reduced. Having a similar interface and standardized dialog boxes meant that computer users could now easily operate more than just one or two application programs. The combination of greatly expanded storage, memory, and processor power has dramatically increased the variety and complexity of software found on desktops.

ARGUMENTS FOR OPEN-SOURCE APPLICATIONS   One of the most significant issues that an IT specialist in charge of purchasing decisions must face is the impact that open-source products are making. Whereas commercial software licenses can exceed several hundred dollars per workstation, there are freely available alternatives that are increasingly gaining in capability and acceptance. There are many companies that will service and support open-source products, so it is less risky now to adopt these solutions for critical systems.

I think that the current trends in open-source systems will continue. Linux operating systems and server-based activities such as Web and proxy serving should see rapid growth among corporations where the need and talent to support the UNIX-based OS exists. However, desktop applications that are dominated today by Microsoft Windows PCs will require more time to accept open-source substitutes. Other corporations are carefully revisiting their approach to source-code licensing. Recent announcements by Sun indicate that they will soon be making the source code for their hallmark Solaris operating system available.

The ability to customize and modify programs is certainly an attractive feature for many IT professionals. However, I believe that stability and ease of use are the most compelling features for any technology product. The ultimate winner in any purchasing decision I make is the product that clearly is the easiest to install, monitor, and support. The money saved when acquiring a certain product can easily be lost in other ways, such as higher support costs or lower productivity.

Network Operating Systems

At the heart of your network are operating systems designed to handle the needs of anywhere from a dozen to hundreds of users. Products in this category include Novell NetWare, Linux, and Windows NT. Those with higher-end networking requirements may need to implement one of the many flavors of UNIX—Solaris, HP-UX, or AIX OS/400, or perhaps the big iron, OS/390.

The cost of these operating systems on really large systems can be well over $100,000, though they typically include higher-end options not found on lower-cost, lighter-weight network operating systems. The complexity of an OS such as this often demands that IT maintain a close relationship with the software vendor. Dedicated support contracts for these large systems are certain to be part of your budget. Recent releases of many of the higher-end network operating systems have implemented Internet-based standards so that support is lessened and connectivity with other operating systems is simpler.

NETWORK APPLICATIONS   The first tier of networked applications is the traditional file and print services. There are also processes that run as applications on your servers, many on a middle-tier server between the client and back-end network servers that usually house the company data. Some of these include application servers, host access services, and messaging servers.

You'll also need to account for the back-end databases that house the company operations knowledge. These may include Oracle8i, DB2, Sybase, Ingres, Informix, or Microsoft SQL Server. I would also account for any client server applications in this category. Groupware systems such as Lotus Domino, Microsoft Exchange, and Novell Groupwise qualify for this classification as well.

In addition, new permutations of some application categories require you to do a bit more additional research before completing your budget. In what ways could your company speed up e-commerce? Would an object-oriented database be of use? Do you need to build an application integration framework to link business processes? As I've discussed in other chapters, IT specialists should always be learning about the latest technology offerings and looking for new ways to support their companies' goals. Continued study of the changing network application market is a good example of this practice.

Upgrades

The conspiracy theorists who work in IT believe that what drives the software development cycle is not so much vendors' wish to release new features as it is their desire to produce a steady revenue. Whenever a newly released version of a program doesn't maintain data file compatibility with an established predecessor, this theory is reinforced. There has been ample evidence of this practice by software developers. For example, Microsoft is notorious for releasing new versions of Word that create files incompatible with their older brethren.

However, I believe that improving existing products is truly the driving force in the upgrade cycle. New features are the single most compelling reason to adopt the latest versions of applications and operating systems. Performance and stability enhancements form the other half of the incentive to upgrade. Make it a habit to periodically check vendor Web sites for bug fixes and patches.

TIP: Check your software license agreements carefully to find out about provisions for automatic updates. Some vendors permit users to get every upgrade for a particular product that is released during a specified time period following the initial purchase.

Sometimes software is updated in response to advances in hardware. For example, when the MMX instruction set was added to Intel's Pentium processor, vendors updated their programs to take advantage of the new multimedia capabilities. Adobe PhotoShop is a prime example of an application that was upgraded to exploit newer hardware. Developments such as the Universal Serial Bus (USB) required that users adopt the latest version of Windows 95 or Windows 98 to exploit its features.

WHEN TO UPGRADE   There are several factors that lead me to explore an upgrade. The need to fix a bug or add a necessary feature is the biggest influence when I contemplate adopting the newest code from a vendor. I try to avoid upgrades for the sake of upgrades. There should be a compelling reason to expose my systems to the inherent risk involved in installing program updates. The old adage "If it ain't broke, don't fix it" is one of my guiding principles even though it employs the dreaded double negative.

Always find out first what an upgrade is intended to address. Major releases often introduce new file formats or changes in program architecture, often making adoption a difficult process. Minor bug patches or "point releases" may not improve performance for your systems, and you may be better off simply ignoring them.

Software Support Contracts

As I mentioned in the previous chapter, software support contracts are often a wise purchase. The most compelling reason to purchase these agreements is access to prompt technical support. Large vendors often assign higher phone-queue values to customers who call in with a special access code.

Many vendors guarantee free product updates for a certain period of time or number of revisions. Subscribing to automatic updates can save time and frustration, giving your users constant access to the latest software versions. Vendors' Web sites often have a password-protected download area that allows subscribers to fetch file updates and patches.

Subscribers often receive special newsletters and magazines as well. News and information are often quite valuable to those who are heavily involved with an application. CDs loaded with utilities, white papers, and case studies are also part of many upgrade subscriptions.

LEVELS OF SUPPORT   Investigate the various options available for supporting your products. Some companies provide packages that cover a specified number of incidents per year. Others permit unlimited calls during a similar period. Vendors may provide customized Web-based content to those who subscribe to premium service contracts. Technical call lines with a shorter waiting time are often reserved for customers willing to pay more for a faster response. You can also find third-party companies that are willing to support your use of many popular applications and operating systems.

I typically purchase advanced support licenses for products used in critical production tasks such as maintaining the company Web site. Most of my license purchases are for a minimum of one full year versus a specified number of incidents. It is much easier to plan and budget for a yearly purchase than to get new funding when a contract has exceeded your allotment of calls. For operating system contracts, I feel more comfortable purchasing a three-year support commitment. A NOS will probably be used for several years with minor modifications, while applications are more apt to change.

Development

Companies often spend a substantial portion of their money on custom-designed software. Many mission-critical systems that were written in Cobol decades ago are still being used. Corporations that support large in-house programming staffs need to purchase software that may be unfamiliar to most IT specialists, who are generally accustomed to standard packaged applications. Version control systems (e.g. PVCS, RCS, Visual SourceSafe), compilers, code libraries, or development toolkits for programming languages such as C++, Java, Perl, Python, and Tcl are common in custom IT shops.

Software development at many firms is a continuing process. Programs that run the various facets of a company's business are always being modified to fix problems or extended to provide new capabilities.

Software Budgeting

Balancing all of your application and other software needs takes some careful planning. Tables 9-1 and 9-2 illustrate two approaches to defining your budgetary formula. The first table assumes you are following a traditional purchasing methodology in a firm using only commercial software. Table 9-2 depicts an n-tier Web environment in which a mix of development, commercial, and open-source products are being used. The budget allocation mix at your company may be similar to or dramatically different from these examples. You'll be able to arrive at the best percentage mix by analyzing how much custom development is done and how many commercial and open-source products you need.

Category	Percentage	Description
Application Software	40%	Includes only new software purchases used on end-user workstations.
Operating Systems	5%	Includes all client operating systems such as Windows NT or Macintosh OS.

Table 9-1. Sample Software Budget Allocation for a Traditional Network

Category	Percentage	Description
Network Operating Systems	20%	All server and middleware applications. I place client access licenses in this category. Workgroup collaboration products such as Lotus Notes should go here as well. Database purchases also come from this category.
Upgrades	20%	Money in this category is for all software upgrades. This includes end-user applications, operating systems for workstations or servers, and any utility programs.
Service Contracts	5%	These are only for the few key programs you must purchase optional vendor support contracts for.
Development	10%	This category is appropriate for any software development work done for your firm. Some of these funds are for construction of custom applications using traditional programming methods. The balance of the money is earmarked for production of tools using built-in scripting and macros of existing programs.

Table 9-1.   Sample Software Budget Allocation for a Traditional Network *(continued)*

Category	Percentage
Development	40%
Support	20%
Application Software	20%
Network Operating Systems	10%
Client Operating Systems	5%
Upgrades	2%
Slush	13%

Table 9-2.   Sample Software Budget Allocation for a Mixed-Use Environment

TIP: Try to earmark a portion of your entire budget for a "slush fund." Challenges *always* arise that you could not have foreseen when laying out your initial annual budget. Giving yourself a cushion will allow you to address these issues without unnecessarily sacrificing normal expenditures.

Services

Most modern computer networks must rely on the services of outside vendors to create a complete environment. ISPs (Internet Service Providers) and ASPs (Application Service Providers) are the most prominent of these expenses for IT budget makers. An ISP can provide access to the Internet for your company. An ASP may handle your e-commerce activities such as automated email, billing or manipulation of corporate databases. Many companies also require off-site data archiving, product testing, and other contract services.

Telecommunications

Once data leaves your office's physical location, you utilize the communication links of various telecommunication companies.

Contracts with ATT, Sprint, MCI, and other carriers can be categorized in the service portion of your budget. The importance of Virtual Private Network (VPN) technology is obvious to any corporation interested in providing remote access to central network resources.

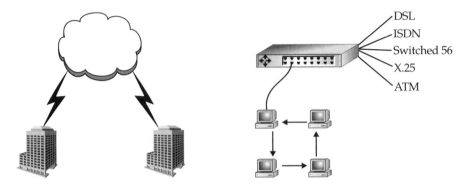

The alphabet soup of digital communication services includes various flavors of ISDN, T1, OC3, xDSL, and other circuit types. The different capabilities of these circuits must be matched to the needs and budget of your firm. As with the purchase of any service, you should carefully analyze the exact features being offered and the demands of the systems that will rely upon the service.

The extent of your communication needs depends on many factors. The number of employees, number and location of offices, and availability of certain circuits are all important criteria to consider. Redundant links and fail-over capabilities add to the number and complexity of the links you must purchase. Telecommunications providers such as Nynex, Sprint, and local services can provide detailed guidance for sizing your infrastructure. I err on the side of expandability and excess capacity whenever possible, because I never want WAN links to slow productivity.

Companies that have a presence on the Web often hire Internet businesses to physically host and maintain their Web sites. You'll often need to account for outsourced connectivity requirements as well as links between your locations and the outsourcer. In addition, many IT departments are charged with the management of all standard analog voice services. Familiarity with Northern Telecom

Meridian or SL1 systems may be as important to your job as competence with UNIX system administration.

Other Services

There is an almost endless list of subjects that require IT departments to work with outside service companies. I've already mentioned telecommunications and data archiving as two important areas to be aware of. Every corporation will require different services at different times, so try to account for all of those your business demands.

There may be occasions when you have to work with architects to design new computer data centers. Legal counsel may be needed when negotiating various contracts or reacting to litigation. I've had to purchase moving company services when relocating offices and roofing contractors when a leak threatened some servers located just below.

Consultants

IT must often rely on the expertise of outside consultants or dedicated consulting firms. The primary reason to deal with contract labor is to gain access to specific skills that are not available within your IT department. Special projects or emergencies are another prime occasion when hiring outside help may be prudent.

To some IT specialists, consultants are a necessary evil. While it's easy to feel resentment toward the mercenary existence consultants enjoy, it's important to acknowledge the talent they bring to a project. Few companies can afford the luxury of training every employee to have specific knowledge applicable to every job they undertake.

The fast-changing nature of technology means there are vast areas of knowledge that keep evolving. Making mistakes with new technology is inevitable, and there is great value in getting assistance from an individual or firm with prior experience in a certain area. For example, most of the companies that have developed a presence on the Web could not have done so without hiring outside help. Consultants have often worked on similar projects at other companies, making errors less likely. This is a key reason that consultants are so important.

Without consultants, some companies would be unable to satisfy the computing needs of their users. The difficulty in hiring experienced workers may require using higher-paid consultants to bridge the gap until permanent employees can be found. A healthy balance between consultants and full-timers can be achieved if some simple ground rules are laid out and followed. These will be discussed later in this section.

Why People Hate Consultants

My uncle once told me that a consultant is someone you pay to tell you what the time is on your watch. Since he is an engineer, I assumed he meant that if a subject is important, then you should make it a point to learn everything necessary to handle it yourself. I know that he and many others will never approve of "outsiders" doing vital work.

The resentment toward consultants may sometimes be based on the large hourly rates they charge. One Lotus Domino expert I know charges $100 per hour for her services. While this may seem steep, her track record and work ethic are flawless, and I know that her services are a bargain at that rate. In contrast, I've met other consultants who charge even higher rates, and I wonder how anyone would be satisfied with their work.

Certainly simple addition illustrates just how lucrative consultants' compensation can appear. IT specialists who perform similar work for a seemingly lower annual salary may naturally envy this arrangement. Pride in their own ability prompts some IT specialists to wonder why an outsider was brought in to address a problem that they feel they could have handled themselves.

Negative feelings about consultants can also have a more tangible basis. Sometimes IT departments get stung when a consultant suddenly goes out of business. I have had a company renege on agreements to develop software when I had already paid a portion in advance for their efforts. While this is a rare occurrence, it does point out the danger in paying a premium price when materials may never be delivered.

Many IT specialists can relate a story of consultants who were clearly unprepared and lacking critical skills to accomplish project objectives. You may be left to pick up the pieces if they abandon the work before finishing. As the following story illustrates, you sometimes need to force yourself into a situation rather than permitting a consultant to continue a process that is clearly failing.

IT REALLY HAPPENED: A consultant providing a custom publishing system was installing a Novell file server that ran incredibly slowly. Though he claimed to have tested the Compaq back in his workshop, there was something very wrong. After watching him struggle with changing SCSI cards and memory cards for a few hours, I decided to check the Compaq support forum on CompuServe and see if there were any answers to our problems. A note about NetWare and a possible conflict with a CPU speed setting in the server BIOS provided the information we needed to fix the server's performance.

Why People Love Consultants

As I have said many times in this book, the range of knowledge and experience required to perform all IT-related functions is entirely too broad to be handled successfully by a single person. One of the things that makes consultants truly worth hiring is the expertise they can bring to a problem. To supplement the "jack-of-all-trades" qualifications of many IT specialists, sometimes you need a person who clearly demonstrates significant ability in a specific area.

While you may be able to gain the expertise to rival a skilled consultant, hiring a specialist is the most timely way to address an immediate need. When a project has to be completed quickly, companies will gladly invest extra money in hiring consultants who can help the company meet its goals right away.

IT EMERGENCIES   Anyone who spends time working in IT will encounter situations that require immediate attention or repair; if you do not respond to the threat, your company will be at enormous risk. A virus attack, corrupted databases, damaged server hardware, and other problems can render an entire network inoperable. While you can practice emergency recovery procedures, it really helps to have someone with significant experience available to guide the process.

Remember that during a time of crisis, clear thinking and cautious troubleshooting can sometimes be forgotten. An impartial observer can often spot problems quickly and give focus to uncoordinated efforts. A consultant should be immune to any political or personal problems in the workplace and won't be afraid to state exactly what is wrong and how to address it.

SHORT-TERM PROJECTS Some projects are not technically challenging but require lots of personnel to complete. For example, your company may be in the midst of migrating network connections from 10 to 100 Mbps Ethernet. This can require opening every computer, replacing network cards, installing drivers, and replacing cables. While these tasks are rather mundane and well within the skill level of most IT specialists, the amount of time it would take to handle more than a few computers is a compelling reason to seek outside help.

Having teams of people come in to perform a product rollout can be the best way to handle ephemeral needs. There is likely to be a slew of problems accompanying any major upgrade or installation project. Having extra technical specialists available during the first few days of transition as insurance can help guarantee a smoother changeover.

COST SAVINGS The cost of hiring full-time staff members amounts to more than just their salaries. Health benefits, vacation pay, parking privileges, and numerous other expenses can all be substantial. Consultants normally pay for their own insurance and retirement funds. Sometimes explaining this fact to full-time staff helps relieve any animosity they may feel toward high-paid contractors.

WARNING: Some long-term temporary consultants recently sued Microsoft for benefits that they would have received as normal full-time employees. This is an area of labor law that is sure to see legislative attention in the coming years, and changes may be on the way for corporations that routinely utilize contractors.

If You Are a Consultant

The best consultants are the ones who clearly demonstrate loyalty and commitment to the company that hired them. This means showing respect for the job you are currently working on. I've seen people who are being paid large sums take long telephone calls from other customers on their cell phones when they should have been working on the project at hand.

While you may be an independent contractor and have several other accounts, your first priority must be the company paying your current wages. I certainly will not complain if one of my consultants needs to address other issues, but these should not interfere with the job I hired them to do. Showing courtesy means using an answering service and keeping a reliable schedule.

SHARING YOUR KNOWLEDGE   Satisfy the innate curiosity of other IT staff members and explain how and why you address the challenges you are working on. Since you may have been hired for specific expertise that the general staff lacks, your knowledge may be perceived as very valuable. The best IT specialists have an insatiable desire to learn more about the computer systems they support. Opportunities to learn from an expert are very appealing, especially when the subject is important to their firm.

If You Work with a Consultant

Consultants can be a valuable and energizing addition to your department. They can relieve stress when new projects are launched or quickly fix problems. Many companies find them an invaluable and irreplaceable part of their IT support strategy.

If you are the one hiring or managing consultants, clearly define exactly what their responsibilities are and who they report to. Effective consultants should blend seamlessly with other IT staff and there should be no questions about where they fit in the IT hierarchy.

Make sure that contracts for services avoid ambiguity. Dates and conditions of performance should be mutually agreed upon. It makes sense to have periodic reviews of project status to make sure that everything is indeed progressing as expected.

When consultants are working for an hourly fee, they may wish to extend their work and maximize their pay. While you should never abandon projects before they are completed, having a firm production schedule helps keep the contractor honest and allows your budget to remain consistent. On the other hand flexibility is always important, especially when unexpected complications crop up, so try to plan for some "give" in your relationship.

How to Find the Right Consultant

I wish that there were a simple formula or universal stamp of approval that could be used to measure the abilities of a consultant. This is one area in which your best guides are often the contractor's reputation and your own past experience with an individual consultant or firm.

Vendors have certification programs for developers, and there are numerous professional societies that a consultant may belong to. These are extensively covered in Chapter 8. Unfortunately, these are never a guarantee of true competence or professionalism. Ask others in your field for recommendations. Good technical consultants (like plumbers) rarely have to advertise; word of mouth from satisfied clients usually keeps them busy. Attending user groups can be another great way to find competent help.

Consulting Firms

While there are many independent contractors who perform consulting duties, there are also large companies that can provide a global reach. Such firms vary in size from a one-person shop to multinational conglomerates with thousands of employees. Each can satisfy the needs of your firm as long as they are used in the correct manner.

TIP: Request from any prospective business partners a contact list of clients that have used their services before. A short background check can reveal the abilities of a company very well. Make sure that they have handled other companies with similar needs and complexity.

If your company wants to roll out a Lotus Domino intranet for its 20 United States locations and 15 international offices, you need a company with a global reach and infrastructure. However, if all you need is someone to install a single NT server, then your needs can be met by a local outfit.

SMALL SHOPS   If your company is relatively small with modest needs, then you may be well served by a local consulting firm. These can be a vertical systems reseller or someone working out of his garage. These firms often excel in providing highly specialized product installation and support.

IT REALLY HAPPENED: Before Quark introduced powerful versions of its XPress publishing software, *PC Week* had to rely on a proprietary solution built by a consultant. He provided all of the application software, network design, scripting systems, and other components. It would have been almost impossible to get the products from anyone else.

LARGE CONSULTING HOUSES   Some of the most famous and profitable companies in the IT field today are consulting firms. Sponsoring golf tournaments and large advertising campaigns are such well-known names as Perot Systems, EDS, Arthur Andersen, and IBM. Their clients include a veritable "Who's Who" list of Fortune 500 companies.

Built and marketed to manage the largest and most complex IT challenges, large-scale consulting firms are most appropriate to companies with a global scope and significant budget. I want to emphasize the significant cost of using these types of firms. Remember that you are potentially hiring a firm to manage some of the most critical parts of your company's operations.

Many corporate heads will "force" IT to accept input from outside consultants. I have seen this cause friction many times, so be sure to conduct yourself with the utmost professionalism in such situations. Resist the temptation to undermine a consultant's effort in the belief it will add luster to your position. Try to work with any outsiders and make your relationship a productive one.

Infrastructure Support

As I have mentioned before, there are numerous key areas that support the computing systems at your firm. These special components are all necessary to build a solid foundation for technology, so IT departments often hire firms to conduct the work to their specification. Many of the subjects that are discussed briefly here will be explored in more detail in Chapter 13.

Cabling

Unless you are in the rarest of environments where all communications are done with radio waves or infrared, you will have cables strung to every workstation and server. Many of the network training classes I have taken have stressed the high likelihood that a network problem will be caused by bad cables. With the increasing speed of today's networks, quality cabling is more important than ever.

While I have strung cable and crimped the ends of many types of cable, it is time-consuming, physically draining work. Building codes and union contracts may require that licensed electricians perform any cabling work in your facilities. You may need to refer to your building lease to see what types of work rules are in place.

HVAC

Heating, ventilation, and air conditioning—collectively known as HVAC—not only make people more comfortable but also provide a stable environment for computer operations. As I have mentioned before, heat is one of the greatest dangers to computer systems. Excessive heat can cause malfunctions and data errors.

Most computer room HVAC systems both control the temperature and adjust humidity levels. By maintaining adequate moisture levels, they prevent damaging static discharges. Dust filtration systems and clean rooms may be another important part of your operations.

Alarm Systems

Heat and smoke detectors are commonly found in most computer rooms. To guard all of your electrical equipment against fire, you may also need to install fire suppression equipment. Sprinklers, water curtains, and inert gas extinguishing products may be part of your network protection system.

You may also need to guard against theft and vandalism of your computers. Building security guards may be instructed to inspect bags for stolen laptops and other products. Video surveillance and inventory controls are another way to address this concern.

Power Conditioning

Providing a stable and reliable supply of electrical power to computers is a vital function that requires a variety of electrical systems. An uninterruptible power supply (UPS) can support a computer during a complete power failure. Line conditioners keep the current flowing to your computers within a very close range of tolerance.

These systems must be closely matched to the demands of the equipment they protect. The major considerations are the amount of standby time that the systems provide and the amount of draw that the connected computers demand. These calculations should be based on formulas supplied by vendors such as Best or APC. Typically you need to determine the total amperage required for all the hardware being supported. UPS units are often a good measure to have in place in the event of a power failure, since they allow IT more time to bring down computer systems in an orderly fashion versus their closing down in an abrupt crash.

TYPES OF VENDORS

Purchasing equipment presents a myriad of choices for IT specialists. There are many different ways to spend your budget dollars. The ways that computers are sold and supported have changed dramatically in the past 20 years.

In the early days, it was common to purchase *everything* from a single supplier. This one source would provide all of the hardware, software, support, service, and consulting required to run highly proprietary equipment. While this concept may sound archaic, it was the only way to obtain many products.

When I was growing up, commercial computing systems almost always meant IBM. With its unparalleled global reach and influence, the company dominated the industry for decades. While IBM had competitors such as Sperry, Honeywell, Control Data, and Digital, their combined market share and resources were puny compared to those that IBM had at its command. In popular movies of that era such as *Desk Set* (one of my all-time favorites), which starred Spencer Tracy and Katherine Hepburn, IBM computers played a prominent role in the story. IBM had perhaps the most pervasive reach of any company in the economy. IBM has most recently remade itself into one of the premier vendors in e-commerce solutions.

A commitment to both applied and theoretical research has seen IBM produce countless patents and garner prestigious awards for their scientists. An unparalleled sales force with well-compensated employees ensured that IBM would be a player in many potential deals. But with the introduction of the personal computer, the entire reseller industry faced a tremendous transformation.

Companies such as Compaq and Apple grew to instant prominence and influence only a few years after their founding. Microsoft has ridden the client/server wave and today is among the largest companies in the world. This cyclical trend of vendor prominence is likely to continue evolving with the influx of Web technologies. Today computers and software can be obtained from many sources and via many methods.

Direct Sales

Eschewing brick-and-mortar stores of any type, direct merchants instead rely on magazine ads and the Internet as their only channels for reaching customers. While this approach may have sounded wacky to sales organizations in the 1970s, the concept has succeeded extremely well. Michael Dell, of Dell Computer fame, started his company in a dorm room and now commands one of the largest computer firms in the world. His main storefront since his dormitory days has been the back page of countless computer magazines, such as *PC Magazine* and *PC World.*

The explosion of the Internet and electronic commerce has greatly expanded the role of direct sales in most IT acquisitions. Purchase orders and quotations can be done without any direct human contact. Tracking the status of shipments and accounts is a simple process.

Advantages

The direct sales model is a terrific way to maintain the lowest possible costs. A direct business does not need to have showrooms across the country with salespeople offering their wares. Products do not need to be pre-shipped to distribution centers or sit on store shelves waiting for buyers.

Since orders are directed to the manufacturer, they can more easily build systems directly to buyer specifications. There are many ways to customize a computer, and it's great to be able to acquire exactly what you want.

High-volume purchases are usually no problem with direct vendors, whereas a traditional retailer can only stock a limited inventory of each product so they can satisfy the most customers. Direct vendors are also likely to maintain volume purchase plans for their biggest or most frequent customers.

Disadvantages

While you can walk out of a computer store with your purchase, it is darn near impossible to use a phone or a Web browser to get a computer on-site the same day, though many direct sellers now offer next-day shipping services. The buyer must wait for delivery of the computers. Shipping entire systems with monitors and other peripherals can also be quite costly when faster shipping service is required.

While many manufacturers give a lot of attention to quality control, there are instances when the buyer receives a product that is dead on arrival. Return and replacement policies differ from vendor to vendor. Some offer an "advanced replacement," which means they will ship a brand-new unit without waiting for the return of the failed product. Other vendors require that a defective component be shipped back for evaluation and repair or replacement.

These return cycles can be costly in terms of lost productivity, taking anywhere from 24 hours to a week or more. Remember that insuring your packages may be important to guard against shipping damages. Check your vendors' return and replacement policies carefully. Customer satisfaction surveys, a regular feature in many computer magazines, can be a great source of information about vendor service policies and performance.

Sometimes it's important to evaluate a system hands-on prior to purchase. The quality of a keyboard or monitor cannot be determined over the Internet or telephone. See if your vendor has a trial period for their products so you can return something you find unsatisfactory.

Vertical Marketers

Many computer sellers have dedicated themselves to serving a particular market segment. For example, there are companies that specialize in providing all the hardware and software needs for medical offices.

Because they cater to the same class of customers, these vendors can build a standard configuration of products and services and offer them at a set price to many customers. Many vendors seek certification in specific product offerings and sell their services to customers along with the actual sale of hardware products.

One of the best resources for finding a vertical marketer is through hardware and software vendors. Their Web sites often provide information on authorized resellers and integrators of their products. This assures that these vendors have both technical and sales expertise in particular products.

Advantages

Because they specialize in a particular industry, these companies provide a depth and breadth of expertise not found in a more generic reseller. There are often specialized software packages designed for specific industries that are only sold by authorized vendors. These retailers typically permit "one-stop shopping" for companies that need their solutions.

Being able to contract with a single vendor for all your needs can be desirable, especially when a company does not currently have nor wish to develop extensive in-house IT support structures. Florists, insurance agencies, lawyers, dentists, chiropractors, funeral homes, and hundreds of other small- to medium-sized businesses may find custom packages suitable to the type of work they do.

There are instances in which IT departments will want to use the special capabilities of these vendors. If unique software solutions perfectly fulfill the needs of one of your supported departments, it is much easier to simply purchase these products than to attempt to build them yourself. Being able to get a quick resolution to a challenge at your firm often requires using the expertise of a specialized retailer.

Disadvantages

Perhaps the most visible shortcoming with these types of vendors is the lack of competition, which usually means higher prices. Any time there is only a single source of a particular product, the vendor has less incentive to cut costs for the customer. Always check any contracts carefully for unwanted provisions. Vertical market resellers may require that any software purchase be accompanied by a purchase of all the related hardware.

In this situation, all of the equipment required to run the custom applications must be purchased as part of the whole package. Hardware sold in this fashion is usually much more expensive than products purchased on the open market. Since the reseller is selling a "total solution," the buyer is essentially hostage to whatever hardware choices the seller makes. Even when existing hardware can be used, the fees for installation of software and integration into the larger network can be very high.

IT REALLY HAPPENED: When I worked as a systems engineer for Microage, there were several occurrences of companies requesting comparative quotes for products being sold by vertical market firms. We could easily beat hardware pricing by hundreds of dollars per system. However, the installation fees charged by the vertical market vendors would be significant for computers they themselves did not sell. This invariably tipped the equation in favor of the vertical market companies.

Traditional Computer Stores

For a long time, mainframe computing required systems built and sold by large corporations such as IBM. The introduction of personal computers (and now mobile devices) has created a new retail marketing opportunity that was not available previously. Unlike mainframe systems costing tens of thousands of dollars and designed for use by hundreds of people, the personal computer was designed to be used by one person and to be somewhat affordable.

Purchasing a personal computer 15 years ago meant traveling to a dedicated computer store. That was just about the only place to purchase computers, monitors, printers, software, and all the related products required to get a system running. Service areas and training classrooms were almost always part of these stores.

Back then, computers were sold in almost the same fashion as cars. You would go to a dealer that carried a particular make of system, and that vendor was the single source of support and accessories for your purchase.

IT REALLY HAPPENED: I got my very first computer while I was in college in the early 1980s for about $2,200. For my parents' money, I got a Tandy 1000 with 384K of memory and dual 5 1/4-inch 360K floppy disk drives. My system was complete with a Star dot-matrix printer and 13-inch color monitor.

Retailers with names like Computer Town, Microage, Bit Bucket, and Computer Land dotted the landscape in strip malls all over the country. Radio Shack had numerous Tandy Computer Centers, and even Sears built a large retail chain of dedicated computer stores.

While many of these chains and franchises have faded from memory, some have survived through specialization.

Advantages

The traditional computer store offers several attractive features for IT buyers. Since these resellers tend to cater to a corporate clientele, they usually carry manufacturers' business line of products. As discussed previously, most of the major PC manufacturers produce two types of systems, one designated for the home user and another for the corporate environment.

Some computer stores managed to survive by addressing a particular market segment. For example, architects and designers who rely on AutoCAD software can purchase these products only from authorized dealerships. Companies that perform network installations operate in a similar mode. Sun Microsystems, Novell, and Microsoft all certify resellers for their products.

Another compelling reason to use a traditional store is that they usually maintain a local repair facility, which can be the fastest way to get a system repaired or upgraded. These service facilities are most responsive to their local retail customers. Warranted computer-repair service has always been a lucrative business. By offering quality service, these shops provide a bigger inducement for IT buyers than simply a competitive price. Most of these stores also have systems engineers dedicated to providing technical support.

IT REALLY HAPPENED: I had a question about configuring a 3Com Superstack Netbuilder router. A quick call to my vendor placed me in touch with an on-staff technician who sent me a PowerPoint presentation of the exact procedures needed to set up my hardware.

Disadvantages

The most obvious shortcomings of traditional retailers are higher prices and a more limited variety of products and vendor offerings. Their lower sales volume also translates into higher wholesale costs that must be passed along to the customer.

Superstores

My Sunday paper is stuffed with ads from electronics superstores. Retailers such as Circuit City, Best Buy, and others sell computers along with VCRs, televisions, cameras, dishwashers, and vacuum cleaners. While these superstores are clearly targeting the home computer market, they also offer some products that satisfy the needs of the corporate buyer.

Advantages

Clearly the greatest benefit of shopping at electronics giants is the low prices for the equipment they sell. While they may or may not sell the business line of computers you desire, they do offer monitors, printers, software, and other common items you need. These stores are a great place to quickly purchase a needed cable or hard drive without having to wait for overnight delivery.

Disadvantages

These stores are what I used to call "box-pushers." They succeed by getting a lot of products out the door as quickly as possible. They are not designed to generate revenues through service offerings or by providing technical support. If they can provide the necessary products at a good price, then they have served their purpose well.

I would not go to one of these stores if I needed dozens of computers to outfit a new department. Don't expect much customization of the hardware or any customization of installed software. These firms should be capable of installing memory chips for a small fee, but they generally lack the expertise to set up network clients.

Office Supply Stores

Companies like Office Max, Staples, W.B. Mason, and others have expanded their product lines from paper clips and pencils to include much of the computing equipment used in businesses. Most of the items sold are intended to appeal mostly to the small office/home office (SOHO) market. These stores can be a good source for toner cartridges, software, and cables, but don't expect the staff to have much expertise in areas like Windows NT, Linux, or remote connectivity.

Many stores in this category are a good place to go to purchase high-volume printers and copiers. These have become increasingly popular in many businesses. Authorized Canon, Panasonic, Hitachi, and other major brand dealers offer one-stop shopping for all of your printing needs. They may have dedicated fleets of minivans driven by service technicians and ready parts availability, which can be critical to some companies.

Independent Computer Sellers

Some of the more interesting sources for computer equipment are the numerous independents that sell house-brand systems. Sometimes called "pliers shops," these stores assemble computers in the back room and sell them over the counter, via direct mail, or over the Internet. The computers they sell often have colorful names such as Tornado, Hurricane, or Mighty Web Browser Master!

The reputation and quality of independent sellers' work can vary greatly. If they use quality components and install them carefully, their systems can be an excellent value. In the next section of this chapter, I will discuss the build-it-yourself approach to computer procurement. Many of the same customization decisions I describe can be applied to these retailers.

Building It Yourself

One of my favorite activities is constructing computers from parts. I purchase every single component separately, from the memory chip to the floppy drive. This lets me get a system that has exactly the characteristics that I desire for a particular job.

While many vendors claim they can "build to suit," there may be limitations on the components they use. For example, if I need a system that has video-capture capabilities for producing training videos, then I need a premium card with lots of extra I/O ports. Sometimes a system vendor will not sell a computer with a specific video card or will limit you to products from a single manufacturer.

Most people only consider hard disk size when purchasing a computer. However, there are other factors that must be considered if top performance is a vital requirement. Drive rotational speed can vary from 5400 RPM to 7200 RPM and faster. The fastest drive will almost always have the higher speed rating. This advantage can be important when you are building a system that will really tax its drives. Back-end database servers, middle-tier application servers, and Web servers and systems that demand high performance or transaction processing truly benefit from the greatest bandwidth available for disk file I/O.

Bundled systems may include features that you don't want or need. Pre-installed copies of Windows 98 or Windows NT are useless if your company relies on Linux or Novell NetWare. Application program suites can be helpful, but they may not contain the standards needed for your network. You want to avoid a situation in which the latest pre-installed copy of a word processor creates data files that none of your older systems can access without a costly upgrade.

Included hardware may be equally inappropriate for your needs. Network cards may be unnecessary or not meet the cabling design of your company. For example, not every network has upgraded to UTP cabling and you may still need RG-58 thin net to connect. Sound cards are not needed for print and file servers and can sometimes be perceived as a time waster, since they are generally used only for games.

Motherboard Options

Today there are dozens of motherboard manufacturers producing a wide variety of designs. Companies like Abit, Soyo, Tyan, Intel, and others make many different models for inclusion in simple workstations or complex file servers. These are often the very same designs and chipsets that go into mass-produced computers.

A good single-processor-capable motherboard can be purchased for between $100 and $175. Most of these boards will accept around 512MB to 1GB of main memory. They will also support dual-IDE drive controllers, allowing you to install up to four disk drives. Along with the floppy disk controller, there will normally be twin serial ports, a parallel printer port, dual USB ports, and keyboard and mouse connectors.

More sophisticated boards support features such as "Wake on LAN" to enable better network management. This feature permits a network manager to turn a computer on remotely and perform program loading or other system modifications. Other popular options on some of the costlier boards are integrated sound cards and SCSI controllers. Additional expansion slots and support for higher processor clock speeds are other nice features that will boost the cost.

Motherboards that can accept more than one processor are also available. These are typically used for file servers or high-performance workstations or network clusters. Generally, network operating systems like Windows NT, Solaris, and Linux take advantage of multiple processors.

Processor Speeds

Speed and socket designs are the most important factors to consider when choosing a processor. If your motherboard is equipped with a Slot-1 socket, then you are currently limited to Intel products such as the Pentium II, Pentium III, or Celeron designs.

Socket 7 and its variants can accept chips from Intel, AMD, or Cyrix. Performance between various vendors is fairly comparable. The more critical factor, compatibility with operating systems, is almost guaranteed with every vendors' products. While Intel's competitors have primarily been concerned with lower-cost alternatives, the introduction of higher clock speeds and products like the Altheon prove that Intel does not have a lock on the fastest technologies being sold.

Video Card Interfaces

Video cards come in a variety of interfaces. ISA, PCI, and AGP bus types are all commonly supported, but the venerable ISA slot will soon fade from the scene. While PCI cards can be fast, your best bet today for performance is an AGP-style card.

Memory capacity is a good indicator of the board's capabilities. More memory is required to display high-resolution color graphics on larger screens. Fast graphics processing chips are most critical to real-time animation or engineering users.

Rating Your Sellers

No matter which types of vendors you use, there are several factors to consider when judging their ability. A quality seller will gain your loyalty and become an indispensable partner to the IT department.

There is no magic formula to determining the best vendors for your firm. The best strategy is to exploit all the channels available depending on your needs. Augment the offerings of the mail-order chains with the products you can purchase quickly from a local office supply store. Buy a product directly from a vendor's Web site, but turn to an authorized service center for any repairs.

TIP: Price should never be the only factor you consider when deciding where to purchase equipment. Pre- and post-sales support can be critical to your success. Also remember that your seller is entitled to a profit.

Retail Staff Specialists

Many hardware and software manufacturers have extensive training programs for those selling and supporting their products. Selling computer equipment is a complex and challenging profession because of the constantly evolving mix of products and technologies. Staying current with the various vendor offerings is a constant challenge.

Repair Services

While computers are generally highly reliable tools, there are still problems that require a trip to the shop to fix. Upgrades to existing equipment are often done by authorized service centers. If you anticipate having a substantial amount of service work performed, ask what turn-around time can be expected.

Take a tour of the service center. See if there are ample parts neatly stocked and ready to go. Make sure that work areas have static suppression mats and that they are being used. A professional service area should be clean and well organized.

Loaner Equipment Pools

Some vendors keep a few systems ready for use by customers in the event of a major hardware failure. Even with extended repair contracts and next-day delivery services, there are occasions when a system needs to be replaced ASAP. Perhaps the parts are back-ordered from the factory or the failed computer needs to be repaired during the weekend and the work cannot wait until the first delivery arrives on Monday morning.

If your company is unwilling or unable to purchase redundant hardware for its entire infrastructure, then using your vendor as an extension of your parts closet can be a sound strategy. Keeping a spare server, hub, or router and delivering it to a customer in time of crisis can be the single greatest boost to client loyalty that a vendor can offer.

I've had vendors proudly proclaim their commitment to maximizing my system's uptime by pledging next-day delivery of configured computers directly to my server room. Since they had set up the systems I purchased, they would be able to replicate the exact hardware and software configuration that was originally installed. With a quick tape restore, my department could be back up and running with minimum disruption.

Negotiating a Price

IT buyers normally ask for several companies to submit bids for needed equipment and services. The typical strategy calls for awarding the purchase order to whoever submits the lowest bid or the best overall price, service, and support package. However, you should *never* ignore the hidden costs involved in using some vendors versus others.

Will your vendor simply deliver a product to your door, or will they take the time and effort to configure it to your specifications? Installing memory and hard drives may be simple, but it is also time-consuming. Installation of a router can take many hours of tweaking settings to tune performance and adjust for the correct security levels. You must always weigh the value of the time you would need to spend on setup versus having the vendor complete the work for you and charge more accordingly.

Requests for Proposals

Think of a Request for Proposals (RFP) as an open invitation for a company to bid on supplying goods and services to meet your particular need. An RFP allows a fair amount of latitude on the part of respondents. You are essentially outlining a problem and asking for a vendor to construct a solution.

Vendors will almost always propose different configurations based on their prior experience and products they normally carry. IT specialists must sift through all proposals they receive and determine which best satisfies the needs of their company. Remember that the cheapest solution is not always the best one.

XYZ Corporation

Request for Proposals.

Vendors are invited to submit proposals for the construction of an intranet system for the Human Resources department at XYZ Corporation.

Scope: The intranet server will be a central repository of information and resources for employees at the Corporate Headquarters Building in suburban Boston MA. Approximately 200 users on an Ethernet-based LAN will be given access to insurance forms, investment information, and vacation tracking.

The entire HR department staff will create content on the Intranet site. As such, they need all the appropriate tools for creating Web pages on 8 Windows NT–based systems.

Interested vendors must submit a complete proposal outlining the entire system required for meeting this goal.

Figure 9-1.   Sample RFP for an intranet server

As you can see in the sample RFP in Figure 9-1, I have not specified the hardware or software platform desired for my needs. You should expect that each competing vendor will propose a slightly (or vastly) different solution based on their own experience. By leaving the proposal open-ended, you can be assured of selecting from a wide variety of suggested configurations. You can also be more specific if you want to limit selections to particular hardware or software.

Requests for Quotations

When you know the exact solution you desire, you can use a Request for Quotations (RFQ) to invite vendors to submit bids. Figure 9-2 shows an RFQ that asks prospective vendors for a price quote on a specific item.

Vendor Quotes

The best vendor quotes are easy to decipher and clearly list every item being offered for purchase. One of the worst practices, in my opinion, is to provide a single price for an entire system. I always want to see the exact line-item cost of every component. In responses to the RFQ shown in Figure 9-2, I would want to be informed about

XYZ Corporation

Request for Quotations.

Vendors are requested to submit bids for the following item:

IBM Model 600 ThinkPad Laptop Computer

Configuration:

64MB RAM
4GB Hard Disk
CD-ROM
56K Modem
10/100 PCMCIA Ethernet Card

Figure 9-2. Sample RFQ for a laptop

the price of any piece that was not part of the standard package manufactured by IBM. In this example, the network card is not standard equipment and should be listed as a unique item.

Good quotes go beyond simply listing the price for the items being requested. Good sales professionals list other options that are likely to be needed by the buyer. Most laptop users also want a carrying case, extra batteries, and an advanced replacement warranty if their laptop is broken. An experienced salesperson should be knowledgeable enough about related accessories and services to give more complete quotes.

I seldom think that a salesperson is simply trying to boost their profits by indicating "suggested" items on a quote. I would be more upset if a commonly needed item were not listed, leading me to buy an incomplete system.

How to Haggle on Costs

Anyone who has purchased a car knows that the first price quoted by the salesperson at the dealership is usually higher than the price you will finally agree upon. The MSRP (manufacturer's suggested retail price) is only a starting point. Computer system manufacturers have adapted, giving "street price" estimates rather than an unrealistic MSRP when quoting prices.

If you understand that sales professionals have some flexibility when setting prices, then you should be aware of certain rules that will help you secure the best deals for your company. Don't be hesitant to ask for a better price, but don't ignore the need of the seller to turn a fair profit.

VOLUME PURCHASES Buying multiple units at the same time is a great bargaining chip. Resellers are normally willing to offer a discount based on the volume of products purchased. If you are buying dozens or hundreds of a particular item, ask for a discount. If there is a set level for discounts, you may wish to slightly increase the number of units you order to qualify for a price reduction of several percentage points.

COMMITMENT TO FUTURE BUSINESS   Technology purchasing is an ongoing task, and IT departments order new hardware and software all the time. Some vendors offer a discount on all your purchases based on the entire activity of your account, not just a single sale. If you are willing and able to commit to a particular vendor for a certain level of expenditures during a specific time period, they are often willing to give you a set discount.

LEASING VS. BUYING   Deciding whether to lease or purchase products is a complex matter. If you purchase new systems every three years and are willing to discard or write off the obsolete equipment, then gauge the cost of a purchase every three years versus the lease payments during that same period. Products such as hubs and routers are typically used for a longer period, so leasing may not be a viable option.

BUY-BACKS AND TRADE-INS   Some vendors accept trade-ins of old equipment as a way to get their products in your door. By offering you a small financial inducement, the seller hopes to replace your current stock with his or her own. Hewlett-Packard has run programs in which they gave buyers a $100 discount for turning in any old laser printer if they replaced it with a new HP printer. Cabletron has offered to buy old competitors' hubs in an effort to capture my business.

OTHER SAVINGS TIPS   Sales quotas often need to be met by the end of the year, month, or quarter, making those periods a great time to buy. Salespeople are often given incentives to reach a certain sales level, and when they only have a few days left to obtain their goal, they are much more "willing to deal."

Buying a set of bundled items can often lead to rebates and other discounts as well. While buying a single CPU probably won't qualify you for these types of programs, there may be special incentives to those that buy a monitor and printer at the same time.

Inquire about end-of-model closeouts. While a newer, faster product may have just been introduced, the older systems are still viable and often a terrific bargain. Some companies introduce price reductions on existing stock whenever a new model is introduced. Check your preferred vendors' Web sites periodically for these specials.

Sometimes refurbished units can be obtained at a great discount. These systems may have been customer returns, used in training classes, or shipped to trade shows or other events. If they are sold with full factory warranties, then there should be little risk in purchasing a used system. Most go through a rigorous quality check before being returned to the sales floor.

Planning IT Purchasing

Allocating budget money is a critical step in the acquisition of equipment. Products can be purchased for cash or with loans, and in some cases leasing may be the wisest choice, as discussed in the previous section.

IT specialists must determine how to allocate their money wisely. Few companies can afford to purchase new equipment every year, so acquisitions must be spread out over time to stretch the money available for technology.

The One-Third or Every-Three-Years Rule

One of the popular ways to plan your purchasing is to subscribe to the one-third rule. This calls for replacing the desktop computers throughout your organization once every three years. This method ensures that no user ever has a computer older than three years. Replacing a third of your desktops every year is the best way to stay ahead of the performance curve offered by the newest computer models.

TIP: Feel free to amend this rule to making replacements every fourth or fifth year if your acquisition budget is tight. However, bear in mind that a typical business computer is obsolete at the end of five years.

The dark side of the advances in computing hardware is the speed with which existing equipment becomes outdated. For example, a standard business computer that cost $2,000 in 1997 may have run a non-MMX Pentium at 166Mhz and been equipped with a 2GB hard drive with 32MB of RAM. As I write this book, a more potent 500Mhz Pentium III with several times the memory and storage is available for even less money.

While the older system can still run most of today's applications, the speed may not be acceptable to your users. When you factor in the cost of processor, hard disk, and memory upgrades, it may indeed be wiser to invest in an entirely new computer. Add to the equation the associated costs of maintenance contracts and the likelihood of breakage as components wear out, and the argument for a completely new system becomes even stronger.

Calculate the Return on Investment

Return on investment, or ROI, is of great concern to many budget managers. This type of calculation attempts to determine just how effective IT purchases and practices are in improving company performance. Products such as Renaissance Balanced Scorecard from Gentia Software and the CorVu suite of applications can help you determine which metrics to use to calculate the real costs and benefits of your efforts. Consultant firms such as Gartner and Meta can also provide guidance in this field.

Credit Concerns

Some companies can use cash to purchase equipment and software outright, while others rely on financing to pay for needed goods. Both options have benefits and drawbacks.

The best feature of using cash is that you save money by avoiding interest payments. Some vendors even offer cash discounts. Paying "up front" for your products is a great incentive to sellers, since they have to buy products from manufacturers themselves. If a seller can quickly pay off their wholesale costs, they too can avoid interest payments, and they may be willing to pass the savings along to you.

Credit is useful if you want to spread out the acquisition costs over a period of time. If you are buying massive amounts of products, loans may be the only way to finance the purchase. There may also be substantial tax advantages to paying over time, so be sure to consult with your firm's Finance department for guidance.

SHOPPING FOR CREDIT   You should select a business loan with the same care as you would personal credit, because rates and fees can vary widely. Many vendors can arrange financing for you. Banks and commercial lending firms have an active marketplace and will all vie for your dollars.

You must take into account the tax and interest involved in each purchasing option you consider in order to determine the most efficient solution to your budgeting challenges. Remember that the quoted cost of any product provides only a partial picture of what the final charges will be.

CHAPTER 10

Surviving the Tech Support Nightmare

It is a sure bet that every IT specialist has endured several nightmarish experiences involving technical support. Nothing is more frustrating than reaching out to a manufacturer for help and not getting the information you need. If you are reading this book, chances are that accessing support resources to address problems is a major part of your job.

Even the most skilled computer experts can be stymied by tricky problems. It is important at these times to understand the many ways to obtain help and to maximize your chances of getting the correct instructions to help you rectify the situation. Remember when you reach out to support personnel that there is never a guarantee of obtaining the correct information. It's possible that you have uncovered a previously unknown problem that a solution has yet to be engineered for. Unfortunately, there are also some errors that are so unusual or rare that a manufacturer will not devote resources toward determining a fix.

Dealing with hardware and software vendors' support systems can be an adventure in automated phone system hell. Once you finally reach someone, you may find that their assistance is useless or that you have been directed to someone inappropriate to your problem. There have been many occasions that I wanted to reach through a telephone line and throttle the person at the other end. Unclear documentation and bizarre user interfaces can often obscure the correct way to operate computing equipment.

The explosive growth of the Web has provided us with a rich trove of IT information that is essential to include in your technical support strategy. In this chapter, I will highlight some of the best independent Web sites that you should bookmark and discuss ways to use newsgroups and other discussion forums to find the answers you need.

This chapter covers all the ins and outs for getting the best possible support from your vendors. We will also examine the many other avenues that you can use to get the information you need, sometimes building on themes I have discussed in earlier chapters. The central idea we will focus on is how to develop a proactive approach to obtaining support.

DO ALL THE RIGHT THINGS FIRST

There are many things you should do *before* a problem arises. If you accept that system errors and questions about product usage are inevitable, then you must take a proactive approach. The worst times to find the guidance you need is when systems are crashing and users are organizing lynch mobs to punish the poor IT specialist in charge.

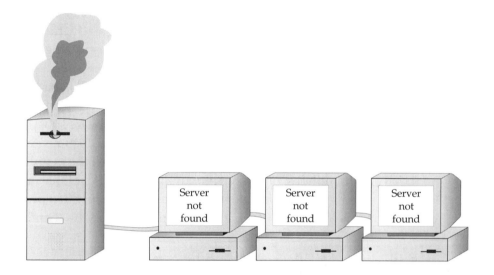

You cannot behave like a wise seer who lives on top of a mountain waiting for the confused and frustrated to bring problems to your attention. The best IT specialists familiarize themselves thoroughly with the products their company's staff members use so they can anticipate the most common problems and have solutions ready. You should locate all the available troubleshooting and FAQ information and catalog it for handy reference.

Of course, there are some problems you cannot plan ahead for. In those cases, you must exhaust all the other resources that a manufacturer provides for their products. This can involve doing research on their Web site as well as making direct contact with the vendor by telephone, email, or fax. You also should locate other Internet sites and sources of information that can provide answers to your quandaries. Certainly the company that actually sold you the products has a responsibility to help you.

Read the Full Manual

While some IT specialists have a slightly different definition for the acronym RTFM, the intent is exactly the same. Hardware and software manufacturers spend time and money creating online documentation and printing up user guides and installation manuals for their products. While the quality can vary greatly, the included documentation should be the first thing you consult when you buy any new product.

A corollary to this rule is to read *all* the manuals. For example, a file server often comes with many different manuals, each dealing with a different aspect of the system's operations or hardware subsystems. When you buy a Compaq server, you get separate documentation for the SCSI controllers, tape drives, hard disks, and all the many NOS drivers and utilities, plus a rack-mounting guide. All of the various components need to work together for a server to function properly, so don't overlook any of the information provided with them.

Don't Automatically Install Anything, Ever

I must admit that I have often violated this rule on numerous occasions when my bravado and curiosity were stronger than my good judgment. There is always the temptation to run an automatic installation routine with software, especially when a CD-ROM automatically loads the setup program as soon as you stick it in your drive. While a default configuration may satisfy the majority of users, there is always the danger that allowing such an installation to proceed unchecked can either mess up existing programs or change the behavior of your systems.

You may want to establish a rule for yourself and your workers that bans any activity with new products until after the documentation has been read and the registration or warranty information is filled out and submitted. A little homework up front can prevent big headaches later.

TIP: Assume that anything you are trying for the first time has the very real potential of damaging your network. Exercising caution at all times can protect your company from unplanned server outages.

Dangers of Software Installations

Hard drives can have multiple partitions and your computer may have more than one physical disk. Many users reserve their C: partition exclusively for their operating systems, placing applications and data on other logical partitions. This practice can make it easier to manage increasingly loaded systems.

There are other reasons to keep your boot partitions free of extra data. Virtual memory managers often place swap files on the boot device. These files can get rather large, and your system's ability to maximize its available memory may be compromised if data and program files consume large amounts of disk space. Print spooler operations typically need disk space on your startup drive as well. I've often resolved users' printing problems by clearing out their disk space.

Dangers of Hardware Installation

A ban on immediately plugging new hardware into your network is another good idea. Incorrectly configured network cards can bring down an entire network in certain circumstances. This danger is especially acute when you are dealing with new and unfamiliar systems.

Networking hardware often uses default settings that can potentially disrupt other systems on your network. For example, a particular danger can arise when you attempt to use Token Ring cards at different speeds on the same ring. Incompatible signals between 4 and 16 Mbps cards can corrupt ring traffic. Keep in mind any potential conflicts with existing computer configurations and you will have a much more stable environment.

Print Out All the README and Release Note Files

User manuals are typically written and printed before the hardware or software products are completed. While they may be mostly accurate, there are invariably differences in the shipping code or hardware that you actually purchase. Manufacturers normally include an addendum to account for the differences between documentation and actual specifications.

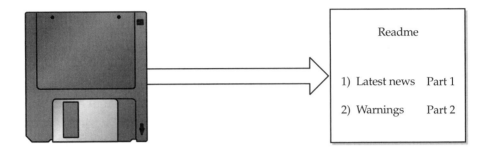

Common ways for information on these last-minute changes to be disseminated are via README.TXT or RELEASENOTES.TXT files. You should print out any such documents and file them with any vendor-supplied hard copy documentation. Read the information carefully, since there is a good chance that the initial documentation has errors that were not captured during its production. Even the best copy editors and writers make mistakes.

WARNING: Almost every compressed or ZIP file of updates contains a README.DOC or README.TXT file. When expanding these archives, take care that you don't overwrite existing files or you will lose information. Try to use separate directories for each archive and combine them later if desired.

Why There Are Last-Minute Changes

Testing of hardware and software is an ongoing process. Rigorous testing reveals bugs and incompatibilities that need to be engineered out of the products. The fixes for these problems can cause features that were intended to be in the shipping versions to be dropped if rectifying them will take too long. Vendors often prefer to issue updates to add features at a later date than releasing hobbled or unstable products.

Even days before a product release, compatibility and usability testers may uncover bugs. No matter how exhaustive and comprehensive prerelease examinations are, when actual users start working with new hardware and software systems, their real-world usage often reveals a plethora of new issues requiring vendor updates.

Not every problem can be addressed by code updates. Sometimes solutions are based on work-arounds. For example, aberrant or undesired system behavior may be fixed by making subtle changes to the program loading order. While skilled manipulation of the AUTOEXEC.BAT and CONFIG.SYS files have become somewhat passé, tweaking system registry settings in Windows operating systems is an even more complex and daunting skill to master.

TIP: Look for resolutions to similar problems to help solve the one at hand. For example, if you are experiencing difficulty using Microsoft Word with particular hardware, there may be similar documented problems with Microsoft Excel. Sometimes your search for technical support needs to be broad to capture the widest array of solutions.

Browse Through Online Help Files

While the graphical user interface has made function keys the least used on most people's keyboards, the F1 key should still be one of your favorites. Virtually all Windows applications activate their help files for your use when you strike the F1 key. These can provide a treasure trove of information that often surpasses the printed documentation. Index and search functions make them even more useful.

Many network devices can now be configured with a browser front end. The small Web servers built into printer and router firmware may also contain screens of instructions. Print these out and add them to the rest of the equipment's documentation. Spending some time reviewing the help files before users have problems can mean faster fixes when something goes awry.

Most Linux and UNIX releases rely on "MAN" pages as a standard way to provide documentation. Short for "manual," these pages are a great way to obtain access to the instructions normally provided in printed documentation. There are MAN references for system utilities, command shells, and other subjects. Using the command is easy. Just type in **MAN** at the command line followed by the name of the program you want help with.

Scan Vendor Web Sites

Supplanting all the information you get inside the boxes and disks of your products are documents posted on vendors' Web sites. An active site will consistently post patches and advisories that highlight newly discovered problems. Compile a list of your important programs and hardware and find their respective support pages on the Web. Add these pages to your bookmark file for quick access.

Send a Letter to Your Key Vendors

The worst way to get familiar with the technical support capabilities of your vendors is to wait until a problem cripples your network. A savvy IT specialist makes contact with manufacturers well in advance and finds out exactly who to contact and precisely what information they will need to get answers quickly. This is a critical step that can be easily accomplished. A letter template should be a key part of your toolkit as seen in Figure 10-1. You can use email to make contact, but standard snail mail is fine too.

Much of the technology that you purchase will be used for several years, so establishing a close relationship with your vendors should be high on your list of priorities. Manufacturers are always striving to make products stronger by offering more features and fewer bugs. Any company that values its customers should welcome reasonable requests from a committed user community. Linux and the open-source community are built around this simple principle.

Trade Show Contacts

One of my goals when I attend trade shows is to meet with product vendor support staff. Not only is this an opportunity for the vendor to get direct feedback from customers, it is also a chance for you to meet the people responsible for the design and support of your systems. Sometimes you can get help on a nagging question from the person who actually wrote the piece of code you find fault with.

At the very least, grab a business card and treasure it. Record on the back any relevant information about the person's area of specialization, if appropriate. If you submit your business card to them, make sure to make a note on it as well. It would be surprising

To: Megaboom Graphics Technical Support

XYZ Corporation has a large engineering department that relies on AutoCAD software for designing our award winning Widget line of products. The 30 engineers use Compaq Deskpro systems with dual Pentium II CPUs and Windows NT 4.0. With the desire to obtain the best possible 3D graphics capabilities, we are considering purchasing your latest Megaboom Pixel-Buster 5000 32MB video cards for all our engineers.

In the interest of avoiding future problems and addressing any errors that arise quickly we want to establish an open relationship between our IT services department and your support division. Please provide us with the following information so we can assemble all the necessary data before having to call for assistance.

1. What type of information about our environment and system does your support department normally need when handling a technical support request?

2. Is there anyone we can specifically direct our queries to? It would be terrific if we were provided with a telephone and email address for them.

3. Are there any newsgroups, CompuServe forums or other online resources that supplant the information contained on your Web site? We are particularly interested in faxback and automated voice support telephone systems.

4. Since drivers are constantly being updated for performance and stability, can we be placed on any automated notification systems so we can be apprised of new software?

5. What are your preferred methods of contact for handling support requests?

We look forward to working with your company to maximize the capabilities of your graphics cards on our mission-critical systems.

Thanks!

John Digital

IT Services Manager

XYZ Corporation

Figure 10-1. Sample letter to a Tech Support department

if the vendor could recall your particular problem when sorting through thousands of cards at a later date.

Send a quick email to the people that you met a short period after the show. Let them settle back in at work first and then send them a question. Most companies want to cultivate a positive relationship with their customers and won't mind this type of direct contact with customers. Remember, however, to appreciate the amount of time required to answer individual questions and limit your queries to those that you haven't been able to resolve by other means.

What Every Vendor Wants to Know

Having dealt for many years with technical support specialists and provided technical assistance to users myself, I know that there are some key pieces of information that are almost always needed to diagnose a problem. Some companies list in their documentation the types of data they want when a customer calls to report a problem. There may be specific information necessary for a particular product, but most situations call for the same general types of data.

```
Name:    Compaq Proliant 1600 R
RAM:     128MB
OS:       Red Hat Linux 5.2
HD:      6GB
Video:   16MB AGP
Network: 10/100 Ethernet
CD:       DVD-ROM
```

Every piece of equipment that your company relies on has specific characteristics. The amount of memory, processor type, firmware version, storage capacity, and other features all dictate the operational parameters of the systems. Technical support departments often want you to supply all of the specifications for the problem hardware.

Typically they will also want to know the status of software configuration settings. If you click on the Tools menu of a complex application such as Microsoft Word, you find that the Options submenu has ten different categories. Each of these categories has on average ten additional checkboxes and dialog boxes. Simple math reveals that there is a tremendous variety of setting options.

In the next chapter, I will discuss the best ways to adequately capture and reference all of your systems information for inventory and tech support needs. While it may sound time-consuming to gather all the different types of hardware and software data, it is well worth the investment. The data you gather can be used for support, purchasing decisions, and other activities.

Operating System Version and Supplemental Files

The operating system on the troubled equipment is the first thing Tech Support will need to know. Don't assume that it is sufficient to report that you are running Windows NT, Windows 95, or Windows 98. Each of these systems has been released in different flavors. Various service packages can dramatically alter the behavior of computers because they may replace core files.

Sometimes the particular file that generates a support call is not supplied with the core operating system. Application software packages often install additional drivers particular to their operation. Control panels and extensions on a Macintosh platform are a perfect example of these types of programs.

Brand and Model in Use

It is impossible to find many component matches between systems that a single vendor produces. Technical Support departments may have information on problems that affect only a specific make or model of a computer or component. Every year sees advances in technology, and manufacturers continuously add features to their newest products. It is inadequate to say that you have a problem with a Brand X system; you must specify the exact version.

Hardware Configuration

Vendors' support specialists invariably inquire about your hardware configuration. The obvious questions involve the amount of memory, disk storage, and processor type installed. Sometimes it is also important to determine the firmware revisions on all the expansion cards and the motherboard. Because manufacturing can take place at different times and in different countries, engineers constantly refine products, and various vendors' components are used for assembly, there are inevitably slight differences between batches.

The type of information requested will vary depending on what sort of question you are trying to answer. If you are having problems with a graphics program, the support person will target the video card and its capabilities. With network connectivity issues, he or she will focus on the installed network card and all the drivers necessary for its function. Your being able to paint a complete picture of the system will help support technicians zero in on the root cause of your problems.

Serial Numbers

Hardware and software products are usually tracked by serial number. Vendors can use this information to determine what exact model you are having problems with. In addition, many support services check product registration information and warranty contract provisions to determine whether a customer qualifies for free help with their system.

For software products on certain operating systems, you can sometimes display the serial number by choosing the About option from the Help menu. For hardware, the process is a bit more complex. You can find a master serial number on the back of most computers, monitors, and printers, but for hubs you may need to examine each individual card that is installed.

Another option is to use vendor-supplied diagnostics to determine system configuration. Third-party programs such as TouchStone's CheckIt have great inventory and detection applications to ascertain the hardware components on Windows computers.

Additional Options

The number of different hardware options for computers is staggering. Exotic video cards, hard disk controllers, sound cards, modems, and USB devices all vie for system resources. Some combinations of drivers can cause other components to fail. Whatever option cards your system has, make sure that you have the specifics on them when you request assistance.

The same attention to detail should be applied to all your networking hardware. Hubs and switch equipment can be equipped with various modules and amounts of memory to provide a given function. With servers that have internal options, such as multiple-port serial cards, you may not easily find the serial number without first removing the cover. It makes sense to record this information before you install the option and keep it handy for future reference.

THIRD-PARTY OPTIONS   Many components for servers and workstations can be purchased from vendors other than the computer's manufacturer. Network cards, video cards, memory, and SCSI controllers can all be obtained from a wide variety of sources. This is a viable way to build systems, but it can complicate technical support issues.

Vendors may excuse themselves from supporting any of their products if they have been modified with an unrelated company's components. In these cases, be prepared to coordinate tech support calls between several companies. Your best resource for getting answers is often the third-party manufacturer.

Network Configuration

Since computers need to communicate with each other over networks, the topology and server clients have a strong impact on configuration. The types of protocols that are loaded and their setup can affect how operating systems behave. Remember that many troubleshooting guides suggest disconnecting from any network to isolate problems.

KEEPING UP-TO-DATE WITH CHANGES   Remember that your systems networking environment is continually evolving. Some IT departments make sure that they are using only the latest drivers. Changes to the network security and directory schemas can force the adoption of different procedures and software for client systems. These modifications to the workstation configuration sometimes cause behavior changes in applications. Whenever you are troubleshooting system problems, be certain that you have correct, up-to-date information on the networking setup.

TELEPHONE SUPPORT

To many of us, the most familiar way of seeking help is to call the manufacturer directly. There is certainly a strong desire to make contact with an actual live human being when you are confronted by a problem. Just having someone else listen to your tale of woe is somewhat therapeutic. However, there are roadblocks and rules to follow when reaching actual support engineers.

Many companies struggle to justify the expense of running extensive telephone support centers. Using a Web server or automated phone system to address user calls is significantly cheaper. This desire to cut costs has also resulted in fee-based support lines and 900 services.

The biggest shortcoming when dealing with a vendor's support staff is that they often lack actual experience and product knowledge. At many companies, the entry-level jobs are often in the Technical Support department. While there are some people who enjoy handling telephone calls and have vast IT experience, there are many more who hate being on the phone with irate users and can't wait to get out of the call center.

In many support departments, there is a reliance on scripted troubleshooters to guide the problem-resolution effort. I have previously discussed the logic of relying on a similar technique to provide internal support to your users. Most people who use a particular product will be faced by the same errors, and concentrating on the most common issues makes sense.

Keep a Phone Log

Almost everyone who reads this book can recount a horror story of telephone message-loop hell. A call to a firm leads to listening to a recorded message that directs you to hit a specific number for sales, returns, support, and other departments. When you select the appropriate number, you are dropped down into another menu of choices and then into other submenus. At companies with broad product lines, you may have to wade through ten or more phone menus before you finally get into the right support queue.

Keep Track of Keystrokes

Keep close track of the keys you must press to reach the support section you want. If your phone call is cut off or if you need to get back to the same area again, then having a reminder of the correct sequence can save you time. The complex nature of many telephone systems can make this record a long and convoluted one.

WARNING: Some older or less robust office telephone systems may have problems working with technical support lines. The sheer number of responses to automated prompts can overflow the telephone buffer and prevent you from entering additional numbers.

Request an Incident Number

Some Technical Support departments automatically assign a tracking number to every support request. This permits them to track and index problems. If you are unable to fix a problem after the initial call, you can call back and resume troubleshooting at the point where you left off. The technicians who respond to your subsequent calls can refer to a record of your prior contacts, saving you the trouble of repeating the details of your problem over and over.

Ask for Contact Information

Often the repair of a problem requires several steps and intermediate tests to get rectified. You can't always expect the support person to hold while you try to apply a repair. Instead, ask for their name and a method of reaching them again, making sure that you can get back to them as needed until the situation is rectified.

It is especially important to be able to reach the same person if you think that he or she is particularly astute and helpful. You also don't want to have to describe a system error again to a new person. They will probably instruct you to go through the same steps recommended by the person who initially confronted your problem. To move ahead with a solution, you need a coordinated and methodical approach.

Give Your Name and Number

One of the first things I do when making initial contact with a support technician is to give them my name and telephone number. In case the connection is lost somehow, you want to be certain that they can reconnect with you. Some company support departments are trained to request this information automatically. I wish that all firms followed this practice.

VOICEMAIL REQUESTS   Some technical support departments only allow you to leave a message, and your call is returned by a technician when one becomes available. If you anticipate a return call, make sure that you inform the company of your hours and leave any other special instructions. I often request to be paged first so that I can make sure to be available for the call. Since I work all around the building supporting users, I can't simply wait by the phone. If you work across multiple time zones, the window of time in which both you and your vendor can communicate may be quite small, so let them know when that time frame is.

Be Patient

The most important attribute you can have when making a telephone support call is patience, since you may have to sit on hold for an hour or more. You can use this time to continue exploring other possible solutions to your quandary. Some support lines give you the option of listening to audio FAQs and tips while you wait on hold.

CALLING AT OFF-PEAK TIMES   There are periods of the day when telephone queues tend to be quieter. When I call from the East Coast to a company in the Pacific standard time zone, I attempt to make contact as soon as the offices open for the day. West Coast callers should aim to use the noon lunch break in the Eastern time zone, since there are usually fewer people actively attempting to contact help departments during this period. Fridays are typically a slower call center day overall.

Be Ready to Work

Most support situations require you to have access to the problem system as the support person walks through the steps to make repairs. Don't make a call if you are unable to work on the failed computer from the telephone's location. If you cannot transfer the conversation to the closest extension, then you may want to use a cellular phone when making contact.

WARNING: Some users will not want you to use their telephone for a support call. Since their computer system is down, they may feel completely cut off and unable to work if they also cannot use their phone. You may need to supply a replacement system while you work on their problems.

When Support Fails

Unfortunately, there are times when a technical support phone call is simply no help at all. You may be disappointed by unqualified people or dismayed to learn that you have had the bad luck of being the first one to discover a bug. There are still some methods of dealing with these situations. Stubbornness and persistence are often required attributes for anyone struggling to fix a problem with a computer.

Wrong Information Supplied

In the worst-case scenario, you may actually be given incorrect information. This sometimes happens because the person providing the support is inexperienced. The failure to ask the right questions and direct your attention to the problem area will doom any effort to help. With all the versions of software and hardware being sold, there is also the danger that a support technician may be consulting the wrong help guide.

IT REALLY HAPPENED: I was installing a brand-new NetWare server that would host a bunch of CD-ROMs. Whenever I attempted to bring the SCSI-Express NLM software up, the server crashed and the Dell server displayed the ROM BIOS setup screen. I spent a good hour on the telephone with a support specialist, going through several reinstallation and reboot cycles, before we finally determined that the problem was caused by a known bug in the drivers supplied with the CD sharing software. This information was readily available to the technician assisting me and was easily determined by checking the date and size of the offensive program. I won't quote the exact words I used when I learned this, but they were far from complimentary. My next call was to the technician's boss, with whom I expressed my disbelief. The technician could have informed me in the first few minutes of my support call of the known problem and not made me go through a reinstall of their product.

No Fix Available

You may uncover errors for which no fix is available. This can happen for numerous reasons, the first and most obvious being that you are working with a new or beta product. Until a product is actually released into the marketplace, users and their systems place stress on a product in ways that no test period ever can. In these circumstances, you must simply report that you have uncovered a bug and hope that your vendor will release an update to address it.

IT REALLY HAPPENED: One of my NetWare servers began to crash unexpectedly and required a cold reboot to restart. I opened an incident report with Novell support and went over the problem in great detail. Despite the technician's effort, he could find nothing wrong with my configuration and there was not a single existing report of a similar problem. I eventually determined that the problem was caused by a large print job being spooled to an AppleTalk-connected PostScript printer. The huge spool files seemed to overwhelm the server, causing the crashes. Since Novell could not answer my query, they did not charge me for the support call. They also said that the rarity of the error would likely mean that Novell would not devote any resources to fixing the situation. Relying on a dedicated printer server restored printing and alleviated the strain on the NetWare server.

If at First You Don't Succeed...

One of my favorite strategies is to conclude a support call that is not helpful and try to contact the company again in the hope of getting a different support person. This approach may only be available when you are dealing with the largest technology companies. Smaller companies may have only a small support staff, and you're stuck with the people they have.

If the company has an extensive support staff, you can just hit the Redial button on your telephone. You may want to call at a different time of day or later in the week to maximize your chance of getting someone new. With staggered shifts and outsourcing of technical support services, your likelihood of contacting a new person can be rather high.

CALLING THE SALES DEPARTMENT As I mentioned before, Technical Support phone lines can sometimes require holding for over an hour. As I sit in my office listening to music from my speakerphone while I wait for a technician to actually pick up the phone, I often get restless. I find it especially annoying when my original purchase of the problem product was handled in a matter of minutes by a telephone sales representative. Noticing the difference in telephone response times between the Sales and Tech Support departments has sometimes inspired me to use the following rare but often effective practice.

I call the same line that I used to acquire the product and complain that I have been unable to get anyone to answer the phone over in Technical Support. While some sales folks are trained or warned to never answer technical questions, they sometimes have valuable information that I can use. Many vendors have compatibility guides that sales professionals can use to determine which one of their products will work correctly with others. These documents may also include warnings, pointers to resources for work-arounds, or necessary software requirements.

Many sales representatives can forward your support request directly to the Technical Support department. Having someone call me back, rather than my waiting an interminable period for someone to pick up the phone, is vastly preferable. Don't employ this tactic until you have exhausted the normal vendor-recommended methods.

Going around existing structures by asking someone in another area of the company to intercede on your behalf may be frowned upon by many companies. But having worked in sales organizations before, I understand their desire to make customers happy. Part of the equation of pleasing clients is doing the unexpected for them. Exceptional sales professionals cultivate close relationships with support specialists. A quick answer to a technical question is one of the best ways to close a sale and retain past clients.

Technical Support Answers Are Not Always Right

The sad reality of dealing with complex technology is that even the companies that sell and support these products do not always know how to troubleshoot their own stuff. Since many problems are first discovered by users rather than in the developer's testing labs, it is reasonable to expect that many users will develop their own techniques to overcome system failures. Remember that it is impossible and unreasonable to expect any company to test their products on all the possible platforms and configurations that exist in business.

Technical Support departments attempt to answer every question with precedents. Most users tend to get caught by the same problems that others had before. These common complaints can quickly become familiar to those handling help requests and dispatched quickly. Truly irksome issues that are unique and unexplained are the ones that will forever be the measure of how effective Technical Support is. How well a vendor can assimilate users' problems and then determine the correct fix can vary widely depending on the company's size and the seriousness of the bug.

Systems Are Complex

A file server used by your firm can be purchased from a number of different vendors. Components like networking cards, hard drive controllers, and video cards can also be bought from a myriad of suppliers. Mixing and matching these items creates unique systems that cannot be easily duplicated in testing labs. The best you can hope for is a replication of a similar system with comparable configuration.

Be Persistent

When I am convinced that my judgment of a problem's cause is different from the vendor's, I continue to pursue a fix. This stubborn attitude is necessary for any IT specialist who wants to get solutions despite being told that there is no known fix for their situation. Often you must do lots of detective work to find a solution that works. The story forthcoming illustrates an experience I had while working on this book.

SUPPORT FROM SUPPLIERS

Many corporate IT departments purchase equipment from system integrators who take responsibility for the equipment they sell. If your company has purchased systems from these vendors, then they should be your first points of contact for any problems. The extra cost of purchasing from a vertical marketer is used to defray the higher costs of providing individual client support.

It should not matter which size or type of vendor you are working with. If your seller is not willing to assist your efforts to find a solution, then you should definitely look for another supplier.

It Really Happened: When Tech Support Fails to Provide the Right Answer

I had a number of non-MMX Pentium 166 Hewlett-Packard systems that were in need of a performance boost. While the budget did not permit replacing the computers, there were sufficient funds available for a processor upgrade. I had purchased some Evergreen 333 upgrades that replaced the Intel chips with a KMD K6-2 333Mhz processor. All of the upgrades went well on HP VL4 tower computers but failed on the slightly newer HP XA5 desktops.

My observations led me to believe that an electrical problem was at fault, since the system did not even power up completely. The technician who returned my calls to Evergreen support insisted that a BIOS upgrade was needed. In his prior experience, systems with bootup failures always pointed at a faulty BIOS as the culprit. Evergreen had successfully tested their chip on a variety of HP systems (not including the XA model) and thus I would need them to diagnose a system that they had never seen.

I dutifully followed the directions from Evergreen and updated the BIOS on the failing systems, but this did not help. The green power light came on, but the drives would never spin up. After relating this experience to the technician, he informed me that his company's product was simply not compatible with my computer and I needed to try a different model of upgrade processor.

I scanned technical literature at HP's Web site and found that a different voltage regulation module would be required for running an MMX chip on the XA motherboard. This information did not change the Tech Support engineer's stance, since the Evergreen product was supposed to be independent of the motherboard power supply. The only way to test my theory was to order the $40 part and test the new combination. The system then ran perfectly.

To the credit of Evergreen, they added this solution to their support database. Situations like these have happened before and I know will arise again. My sense of accomplishment is from finding a solution when none was offered. I am certain that anyone who spends enough time in the IT field will stumble upon problems that they will need to fix themselves.

Making sure that customers can utilize purchases should be central to their sales efforts.

The threat of a loss in repeat business should be the only incentive a seller needs. Do not be afraid to wield the specter of lost sales to your vendor. They should respect the business you have given them and provide sufficient after-sales support to ensure additional purchases later on.

Systems Engineers

As I've mentioned in previous chapters, I used to work as a systems engineer for retailers before moving to Ziff-Davis and *PC Week.* My job was to assist the sales force with both new and existing accounts. Every week I was called upon to respond to server problems, network errors, and general questions on system use.

Apple, Compaq, IBM, and other vendors gave me special training on their equipment. I was expected to attend periodic seminars to learn about the newest developments. This was also an opportunity for me to network with other support staff members and share war stories with them.

Many vendors maintain a dedicated support staff to handle their customers' problems. Many manufacturers' reseller certification programs require that trained technical personnel be available in order for the supplier to sell specific products.

Strength in Numbers

Remember that resellers serve many customers buying dozens of products. While you may have bought a single Cisco router, there may be another client who has purchased dozens. A good reseller should be able to leverage their buying power with manufacturers to get customer problems resolved.

Vendors often maintain dedicated support systems to handle reseller concerns. Diagnostic equipment that is not available to the general public is common in these repair centers. Service departments may also have access to high-level resources that manufacturers reserve for their use. A good vendor should be able to act as a liaison in these situations.

INTERNET-BASED SUPPORT

While technical support has evolved over the years, no previous innovation had changed it as much as the Internet boom has today. By connecting people worldwide with a multitude of messaging systems, the Internet permits almost limitless sharing and distribution of information.

While building a presence on the Web can be an expensive and complex project, the investment required is almost certainly smaller than the cost of staffing a Help department with dozens of support engineers. Web servers never get tired, work 24 hours a day, and can do a credible job of providing information directly to customers. It is usually easier to cut-and-paste specific program instructions from a Web page than it is to follow the verbal instructions of a technician who cannot see your keyboard and screen.

Vendor Web Sites

Most IT specialists begin the search for technical information on the Web sites maintained by their product vendors, as they should. Of course, the quality of these Web sites varies greatly, but vendors know that users who are frustrated and unable to use their products are likely to select other suppliers if they can't get the information they need. Web sites are simply the best and most preferred tools for supplying support directly between vendors and users.

There are thousands of hardware and software firms whose products can be found in corporate networks. Even a small company can easily rely on over a dozen firms for their equipment. Always make it a point to familiarize yourself with the organization and capabilities of your key vendors' Web sites and add them to your bookmark file.

Support Links

Virtually all technology-centric corporations provide links to their Technical Support section directly from their home page. Microsoft points users to their Product Support Services page (www. microsoft.com/support/) for access to drivers, a knowledge base, and other troubleshooting tools. Novell's Support Connection (support.novell.com) can be easily accessed via the Support button on the Novell home page.

Linux administrators can refer to the Web site of the Linux distribution they use. These are some of the major Linux distributors' online support centers:

▼ Red Hat Support Center: www.redhat.com/support/

■ Caldera Systems Support: www.calderasystems/support/

■ S.u.S.E. Installation Support: www.suse.com/Customer/
support.html

▲ TurboLinux Support and Services: www.turbolinux.com/
support/

Another useful site is the Linux Support Center (www.linux.org/help/index.html), which contains multiple support links.

Dell Computer

I wish all my systems vendors would model their support sites on Dell's. Simply put, it is one of the best resources I have ever used. The most distinguishing feature is that you can enter a computer's five-digit serial number and get support content customized for that specific computer. I've found support information for some of the oldest systems I have looked up using this service.

Users at the Dell site are directed to all the relevant files for their system. Drivers for video and other options for a variety of operating systems are a simple click or two away. FAQs and firmware updates are equally accessible. Of course, ordering new products and accessories is a quick and simple process, too.

Independent Web Sites

The majority of the Web sites I consult for technical support information are run directly by equipment vendors. They tend to offer the most complete and up-to-date drivers as well as extensive documentation. Once I have exhausted these primary sources, I usually turn my attention to the mass media sites maintained by CMP, C I net, IDG, and

Ziff-Davis. The mix of technology titles from these publishers covers the entire range of computers used at most firms.

Sometimes the most interesting and deeply technical resources are available from what I consider to be independent sites. These sites are typically targeted directly at "gear heads," those of us who really thrive on tweaking BIOS settings and debating the merits of competing video card chipsets.

Most of the sites in this category were begun and are maintained by people who want to share their knowledge of computers with others. They contain not only reviews and product news but also links to many other resources of interest to IT professionals. Some function best as a single point for browsing when you are looking for driver files from a variety of vendors.

Recommended Sites to Explore

Real World Technologies (www.realworldtech.com/index.cfm) is a cool site that highlights hardware reviews, a great resource for anyone interested in building and supporting PC systems. It contains plenty of articles on BIOS chipsets and diagnostic tools that form the major portion of the content. There are also lots of useful links to other sites.

Tom's Hardware Guide (www.tomshardware.com) contains several interesting editorials and lots of links to news stories. There are lots of in-depth hardware product reviews on chipsets and processors. The site also gives good explanations of esoteric BIOS settings and more to exact the best performance from your hardware.

PC Help Online (www.pchelponline.com) maintains extensive links to dozens of computer hardware manufacturers' Web sites, as well as phone numbers for sales and technical support. Service911.com (www.supporthelp.com) is another good site with links to files and discussion forums that can be very useful to IT specialists.

University Offerings

Colleges and other educational institutions are the hidden gems of technical information. There are many reasons for this quality and breadth of knowledge. Many of the products used in modern corporations are directly derived from academic development efforts.

For example, Berkeley was deeply involved in the growth of the UNIX operating system and Columbia maintains the Kermit communications protocol software.

Beyond software and hardware development, universities also need to support scores of academic users on the widest variety of systems. Therefore many universities maintain searchable archives of programs. One good example is the UIArchive (uiarchive.cso. uiuc.edu). Hosted by University of Illinois at Urbana-Champaign, the site gives you access to thousands of useful utilities for Windows, Mac, and other platforms.

Travel to the West Coast with oak.oakland.edu to discover the OAK Software Repository and you will gain access to dozens of excellent indexes of software. A project of Oakland University's Office of Computer and Information Resources, it mirrors the popular Walnut Creek CD-ROM Simtel.Net Windows and DOS archives.

Of course, Windows users are not the only ones who should be interested in these resources. Also available from the OAK Software Repository is the Hobbes OS/2 collection. Users of the venerable CP/M are directed to vast libraries of 8- and 16-bit programs and utilities.

WebRing

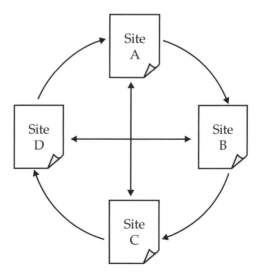

One of the more interesting concepts on the Internet is known as WebRing. It is essentially a collection of Web sites that share a common thread. Navigation tools on each Ring's home page direct users' browsers to the Ring index housed at the WebRing site (www. webring.com). This Yahoo-owned service does not serve as a host to any Ring sites; instead, it simply provides the code and indexing services to direct traffic around the WebRing.

It can be very frustrating to look for information on the Web using standard search engines. You enter a search term and then pick one of the sites displayed on the result screen. If you are lucky, the site you choose is perfect and you get the stuff you need. However, if the site does not serve your needs, you have to return to the search results page and try another link. This can be a very time-consuming strategy to pursue.

With WebRing, you can identify a Ring that appeals to your particular area of interest and limit your browser travels to only members of that Ring. Most technical computing-oriented Rings contain a mix of commercial and individual sites.

A Few of My Favorite Rings

In mid-1999 there were nearly 80,000 different Rings. The NetWare WebRing has over 40 sites; its home base is at HelpBoard.com (www.helpboard.com).

The Windows NT Professional WebRing (www.internexis.com/ mcp/ring) links more than 125 member sites, and Linux aficionados can link to over 90 sites from the Linux Users' Group WebRing (www. nlug.org/webring).

Newsgroups

One of the most useful features of the Internet is Usenet newsgroups, yet they are underutilized. These are typically focused discussion databases that can be reached with a newsreader-capable browser or a stand-alone newsreader product. Users of Microsoft's Internet Explorer can launch the Outlook application to read or post messages to groups, and those who use Netscape Communicator can use the Netscape Messenger to access newsgroups. Other free stand-alone newsreaders are available for most operating systems.

Whichever software you wish to use to access newsgroups, you need to configure the settings properly beforehand. Browsers access newsgroups using the NNTP protocol. Check with your ISP to determine the correct entries for adding news services to your connection.

News servers store the discussion threads and allow many people to post, read, and reply to messages from others. You can find groups of interest to you by using links provided by vendors, a search engine such as Excite, or an index like Yahoo. One of the best places to check for many computing-centric groups is on the World Wide Web Consortium site at www.w3.org/History/19921103-hypertext/ hypertext/DataSources/News/comp.html.

Another way to find newsgroups is by searching Deja.com (www. deja.com), one of the best resources for finding discussions about your particular interest areas. Try to familiarize yourself with the exact subjects that are covered in the particular newsgroups you subscribe to. Since there are so many different groups and most have a very specific focus, you don't want to raise the ire of others by posting questions that are off the main topics. Browse through the many postings and get a feel for the way responses are handled and which other users seem to be the best contributors. Never forget that using all uppercase letters is considered to be SHOUTING in the online world. Note that many computing topics are covered in newsgroups whose names begin with *comp*.

WARNING: Newsgroups are available on countless topics. The same cautions that apply to pornographic materials on the Web should also be used for newsgroup postings. Anyone who explores the many alt.sex groups will uncover many bizarre and troubling images. Networks that wish to block user access to "sex sites" on the Web should also pay attention to newsgroups.

Linux

Links to all of the following groups and many more can be found on the Linux Online support pages (http://www.linux.org/help/ index.html). For example, the newsgroup comp.os.linux.apps provides a general discussion about Linux software applications.

The comp.os.linux.networking forum is the place for discussions about networking and communications issues.

Windows

There are some groups under the comp.windows listings. Many more are listed under the alt.windows and alt.os.windows headings. Use your newsreader application to search for occurrences of the word "windows" and it should display well over 100 discrete groups to explore.

List Servers

As I discussed in earlier chapters, list servers are automated discussion systems that rely on email to distribute information between subscribers. They can be an effective and inexpensive way to communicate with others who share similar interests. Their modest server and client requirements were well-suited to technology conditions before the Web exploded in popularity.

Users can email the list server, and their message is then forwarded to all other subscribers. Readers of the posted messages can choose to respond to the entire list. An active list with many subscribers can generate a tremendous number of email messages. Check the instructions when you first sign onto a list server to see if you can get a daily digest of all messages rather than individual postings. The quickest way to grow disgusted with a list server is to become bogged down with hundreds of messages.

While some list servers permit the exchange of messages between subscribers, others function simply to distribute information. This classic "push" technique is great for the passive gathering of data, but it is not ideal for sharing among all list users.

Subscribe to a List

Getting started with a list server of interest to you is as simple as sending an email message to the correct account. The list server normally adds the name of the sender's address when it receives a message with the subject "Subscribe" in it. List server software varies, so check the specific commands for the service you wish to subscribe to.

There are some lists of particular interest to IT specialists, such as the one maintained by Novell. Send a message to netwarenews@ novell.com and you will get messages regarding product releases and similar announcements. Microsoft has many lists that you can learn about on their Web site. My favorite is the TechNet mailing list; see www.microsoft.com/technet for information.

TIP: Many of the publications in the technology field offer automated email delivery of breaking news and analysis columns, which can be a great source of information.

There are also many indexes of list servers that you can use. Some of the better ones are Liszt (www.liszt.com) and the index from Webpedia at http://webopedia.internet.com/Internet_and_Online_Services/ Newsgroups/newsgroup.html.

Your favorite Web search engines can reveal hundreds more.

OTHER SUPPORT SYSTEMS

If you limit yourself to Web sites and telephone support lines, you are ignoring several other important resources. The most successful information-seeking process is one in which you take advantage of every avenue that is available. Some of these may be alternative services run by vendors or Internet-based discussion forums.

Bulletin Board Systems

When I first started working in the computer field, many companies supplied electronic support through a bulletin board system, or BBS. Using a standard analog modem, users could connect with almost any communications package and be given a password to access the BBS server. This was the primary way to download files or post messages to the Technical Support department at the company.

Fairly inexpensive and easy to maintain, a BBS can be a viable solution for companies to provide a messaging and file transfer service that does not rely on the Internet. Using ultra-simple VT-100 terminal emulation, a very modest BBS server can handle several simultaneous sessions. Some companies may still maintain bulletin board systems, but I haven't used one for support in many years.

Don't be surprised if you uncover a company that maintains a FirstClass BBS. Much more sophisticated than text terminal servers, these require a special client. They are great for sending and receiving files using a graphical drag-and-drop interface.

Faxback Services

While I can always use a Web browser to locate the documentation I need, sometimes it is more convenient to use a fax machine to receive information. For example, when I need jumper settings for hard drives, I almost always want a printed document for reference. A plain-paper fax is ideal. When I am fixing a computer, I may not have ready access to a browser and yet still need a printout of the online documentation. Certainly if the computer I am fixing is down, then a browser is useless!

Companies that support faxback systems typically use an automated voicemail system to guide the ordering of fax documents. A caller is directed to enter their own fax number and the code for the desired documents, which are then sent to the designated fax machine. You are almost always directed to print out an index to all documents first and then order the specific ones desired with an additional call.

The vendor-supplied documentation that accompanies your products often indicates whether there are faxback services available for detailed troubleshooting information. In addition, many telephone support lines play faxback numbers while you are waiting on hold for a technician. Hard disk manufactures such as Maxtor, Western Digital, and Seagate have traditionally supplied faxed descriptions of jumper settings.

TIP: Collect indexes of faxback documents for all your systems. Keep them handy so you can quickly request the information you need.

Non-Internet Online Services

Before the Internet became the haven for manufacturers, file update libraries and support services on Prodigy, CompuServe, and AOL were the primary way to get technical information. Hundreds of manufacturers monitored discussion forums and responded to user questions. Patch and upgrade files were commonly distributed on these services also.

While millions of people rely on Prodigy, CompuServe, and AOL primarily as ISPs, they still provide viable forums worth visiting on their core services. I often used a CompuServe account to get assistance with major products like Novell NetWare or Microsoft Windows. It was also a good place to obtain support for more esoteric items such as Number Nine video cards. Even though most manufacturers have abandoned direct support forums on these online services, there are still many active forums that can be useful.

Low-Bandwidth Access

One can still access many of the features of CompuServe using only a low-speed connection and a text-based terminal. This capability may be critical if your company has branches in countries where there are few options for Internet access outside of CompuServe and high-speed connections are expensive and difficult to requisition. Users of operating systems other than Windows and Macintosh may have to rely on similar terminal-based access to online services.

Monitored Forums

I've noted that CompuServe and AOL forums have historically been fairly well run and active. Many forum participants are programmers and consultants who work daily with the products featured in the forum. A significant number of vendors help sponsor moderator accounts or have their own employees scan the discussion items. This can be a great source of feedback for the vendor and a terrific way for users to get direct support straight from the horse's mouth.

Technology Publications

While not the place to turn for an instant response, many computer industry publications have advice columns in which readers' questions are answered. The nature of the topics covered varies considerably from magazine to magazine.

By searching the archives on various Web sites from IDG, Ziff-Davis, and C|net, you can often locate previous reader questions that relate to your current problem. Don't be afraid to submit a query to the columnists. I try to answer every message I get even if the exchange will never appear in print. Of course, I can't guarantee that my fellow columnists will be so generous with their time!

Net Adviser

Please forgive this shameless plug. My own *PC Week* column, *Net Adviser,* has had a major influence in the creation of this book. Readers' demand for coverage of a broad range of issues clearly demonstrated the need for a general-purpose guide to address IT issues.

I've dealt with user questions on Novell NetWare, Microsoft Windows (every version), fault tolerance, Linux, virus eradication, hiring, education, network cabling, and many other topics. My intention is to write about problems that interest a broad segment of readers and to avoid technical minutiae. I hope that readers of this book find quality information in my biweekly column.

Test Center RX

InfoWorld has a column similar to mine that runs every week, written by Laura Wonnacott. Her answers to reader questions are often similar to my own, but there are certainly times that our opinions differ due to the experiences and habits we have developed during our careers. Competition among all the computing publications has all the editorial staffs vying to provide the most complete and relevant information to their readers.

Other Magazines

Take a trip to your local Barnes & Noble or Borders bookstore and you will find dozens of computer-oriented publications. Purchase a few that cover your areas of interest and see what types of reader forums they have. Of course, at the library you can browse many of these titles at your leisure. *PC Magazine* is not only the largest magazine in the technology field but has historically had many different columns dedicated to answering reader questions.

Virtually all computer magazines have an advice or ombudsman columnist dedicated to addressing readers' problems. I know from experience that we need reader-submitted questions to feed our writing efforts. Thankfully, computer users are continually finding new challenges or errors with their equipment. While I doubt that my readers enjoy having problems, it is extremely satisfying for me when I can solve their quandary.

Feedback from other readers has made me aware that problems are rarely unique. A steady stream of email shows that plenty of IT specialists suffer with the same errors.

TIP: Scan archives of past issues to see if your problem has struck someone else. I always maintain that most problems are not unique. Others have usually faced the same bugs and system behaviors that plague you.

Radio and Television

While Click and Clack's NPR car repair program has earned them a large and devoted following, no one has yet found similar success with a computer-oriented program. There are several technology shows that air on local radio stations, and I'm sure that syndicated programs will continue to grow in reach.

Most of these shows are fairly general in concept and deal with the kinds of issues that face home users and small businesses. Don't look for exceptional detail. Listeners may be interested in the benefits of various USB scanners but most will probably be lost if the discussion turns to IPv6 and NAT configuration.

IT REALLY HAPPENED: I have been a guest on several talk-radio programs and enjoyed listener calls on a variety of subjects. Most callers were interested in buying their next home computer or wanted to know which was the best anti-virus program.

Computer Chronicles on PBS, *Wild, Wild Web,* and CNN's *Digital Jam,* among other television shows, are populating the airwaves in increasing numbers. ZDTV is available on some cable and direct-TV systems and is strictly dedicated to computer-oriented programming. Most of these shows are targeted at home consumers rather than corporate IT professionals. I suspect that this trend will continue, and as computers further permeate every level of society, more of these shows will be produced and they will feature more technically involved content.

CHAPTER 11

System Security, Inventory, and Repairs

Maintaining a productive environment for your company demands careful attention to many details. While users may desire easy and open access to networks and other resources, freedom of access must be balanced by security concerns. Maintaining the privacy of all electronic communications and stored data is important, both to protect corporate assets and to ensure proper workplace decorum.

Beyond providing for a secure environment, IT professionals must track and maintain all of the systems in their care. Inventory control is a fundamental step in planning the budget for upgrades and equipment replacement. Having an accurate accounting of installed computers, peripherals, and software helps you coordinate service calls based on equipment age and current versions of firmware, operating systems, and applications.

This chapter explores three major subjects. The first section is an overview of the important techniques to ensure a secure environment. I will cover password-protected access and the many threats posed by viruses and hackers, as well as resources that are critical for countering outside threats to your users and their data.

In the second section, we examine the need for and methods of providing inventory management for your systems. The types of information you need to record will be discussed. There will also be a discussion of software management systems for the automatic gathering of computer and LAN hardware and installed applications.

Finally, we will explore in detail the requirements for providing system services. Repair centers, rolling crash carts, tools, and parts are all required to care for computers. I'll give tips to cover all of your network service needs, regardless of your company's size.

SECURITY

For IT specialists, preventing unauthorized access to data and application resources is only the first definition of system security. Many layers of protection may be required, depending on the company's needs and complexity. Password management, network account privileges, access control lists, server location, router configuration, network scanning, and virus prevention are all part of the system security equation.

You must not ignore any piece of a comprehensive defense strategy, since all of the components depend on each other. Secure system operation demands an integrated approach, with attention given to all avenues of vulnerability. An assessment of your own company's demands will help you determine the complexity and invulnerability of the security measures you need to install and support.

Levels of Access

Corporate security needs vary widely between industries. Companies that handle financial and other personal information need to zealously guard this data from unauthorized viewers. Banks and medical providers are two prime examples of systems that should maintain stringent control over access.

In general, companies should endeavor to protect their data as they would any other asset. Both customer and company data files can contain information to which access should be strictly limited. Most corporations keep servers that hold sensitive files on networks that are totally separate from any Internet connection. A physical barrier of any sort is the best method to ensuring data security.

Keeping prying eyes away may mean warding off those bent on industrial espionage or hackers just trying to gain access for the rush it provides. Instances of Web site defacement appear in the media regularly. Theft of credit-card numbers and other information has been a major concern as electronic commerce blossoms.

Ease of Use vs. Invulnerability

Virtually any step you take to increase security will make it more difficult for bona fide users to reach data. Most users can accept the need to enter a login name and password, but they may balk if the NOS demands frequent password changes and lengthy passwords, too. The use of smart cards and other technologies can only add to the "Big Brother" fears that users sometimes harbor toward IT-imposed policies.

Performance vs. Defense

Any security measures that are imposed for a network can impact overall network throughput. Firewalls, routers, and proxy servers work together to safely link users' systems to the Internet. The hardware and software implemented to support these services verifies that packets being transmitted are allowed to reach their destination safely.

Every packet of data that attempts to move into or out of a protected network may be checked for a variety of characteristics. For example, the type of data being transmitted is a typical factor to control. An administrator may permit users to view static HTML sources but block reception of Java commands. Certain sites deemed inappropriate to the workplace may be identified, and access to their content denied. Many companies prohibit access to porn Web sites and others that are both improper and unproductive for users to be viewing during the workday.

Each one of these network control decisions requires time for the filtering hardware and software to execute their commands. The more complex and restrictive the rules for data transmission, the longer it takes for communications to occur. Certainly these types of controls are important and necessary for a secure environment, but be aware that there is a penalty for implementing them. Try to carefully tune your exclusion rules to minimize performance degradation. Always work closely with your ISP to monitor bandwidth and security measures on a regular basis.

Firewalls

In the construction field, firewalls are barriers placed in walls to contain fires. Fires that would normally spread between floors or adjacent homes are stopped. Similarly, network firewalls control the flow of packets between your corporate network and the Internet. A big part of network security involves ensuring that unauthorized parties cannot access certain off-limits data. Firewalls control what types of data can be transmitted from a network across an Internet link.

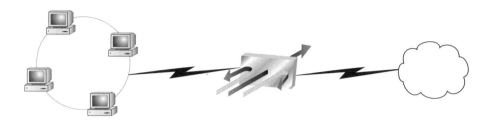

In a totally open network, all types of packets are allowed to move in any direction. Computer users outside your company could theoretically access your servers just as easily as users on your internal LAN. In addition, your users could access any type of services available on the Internet. Security policies demand that careful control be exercised over which packets are permitted passage.

Firewalls can be constructed totally with hardware products, and they are often built into equipment firmware, such as routers. Routers will be discussed in more detail in the following section. Other network administrators install firewall software on their existing file servers to provide security.

Routers

Most network specialists define routers as devices that connect one network to another and exchange data. For example, routers can allow a user on your Token-Ring LAN to access the Internet via an ISDN link. This can be accomplished by placing an ISDN interface directly in a file server. In this situation, the file server is responsible for the movement or routing of data from the LAN to the Internet.

Many networks rely on dedicated hardware routers. These are specially designed products designed to connect networks together. They can be equipped with a variety of serial interfaces for connection to T1 or DSL lines, for example. Ethernet or other LAN ports are provided to service network connections.

Most routers are configured to deny any data transmission unless it is expressly permitted. This is a more secure setup, since it assumes that any packet may have consequences if it penetrates the network. A more lax policy would be to permit all traffic unless there are rules against it.

Routers are ranked by the speed with which they can forward packets and make routing decisions based on their security rules. The number of ports and protocols can also add to the cost and complexity of these products. Some permit management by a Web interface, while others allow only text-based configuration with Telnet or a serial terminal session.

Routers may also be upgraded with software to provide firewall security. As one example of this approach, Flowpoint ISDN and DSL routers can be used with optional Flowpoint Secure VPN and Firewall software. With this combination, the network administrator can provide a high level of security to their company's Internet connection.

There are many manufacturers of routers offering a wide assortment of products. Cisco is the clear market leader, producing hardware that addresses almost any business requirement. The company overwhelmingly dominates the largest and most complex market segments. 3Com, Ascend, and others compete for the smaller and mid-sized markets.

Networks with an existing investment in management schemes such as Novell's NDS should look for routers that can utilize the same database of user accounts. This makes administration easier, since it means using a single control structure rather than having to learn and manage another one.

WARNING: Router configuration is a complex subject. Tweaking the operation of a multi-protocol router can require hundreds of commands and settings. Because the potential for security problems increases with incorrect router management, the person who configures these devices should have a great deal of experience and a meticulous approach.

Proxy Servers

Many networks permit all clients to directly access World Wide Web hosts when they request data. This means that all users can download data to their workstations, which can be an inefficient and insecure method of operation.

A proxy server intercepts users' requests for data and directs them to its own cache. If all your users wanted to scan the news from CNN (www.cnn.com), for example, it would be much less taxing on your routers if the data were made available locally. A proxy server can be directed to actively scan popular Web sites and pre-cache the pages for later user retrieval.

If users are accessing the Web through a proxy, this gives your company a great opportunity to control which sites they can reach. Administrators can deny access to pornographic sites or gambling servers, for example. A proxy server also shields user systems from Web sites that attempt to grab data from a browser's workstation.

Open-source aficionados can select from a variety of freeware proxy products. The Squid, available at squid.nlanr.net, is a good choice for UNIX-based systems. With funding from the National Science Foundation, the Squid Web Proxy Cache supports the controls and features required for most corporations.

Windows NT Server networks may utilize the Microsoft Proxy Server as part of the BackOffice suite of products. Its content caching and firewall capabilities make for a powerful solution. Novell offers BorderManager software for NetWare-centric shops.

Physical Security

One of the first lessons taught in any system administration course is that preventing access to servers is critical to ensuring network immunity. Whenever an unauthorized individual can touch a keyboard or access a floppy drive, there is a serious breach in system defenses. Locking a server into a secure area and limiting access to the smallest group of people is the best way to prevent unauthorized tampering.

A device that tracks each door entry can help you identify who entered an area and when they did so. Some companies use surveillance cameras to monitor critical areas, creating videotapes that can be used to review any room activity.

You may also wish to place similar controls over your electrical, cable, and telephone systems. Network lines can be tapped and phone systems are often a target of hackers. Don't forget that dumpster-divers can go through your trash and get sensitive information from discarded printouts and office memos. Many companies require that all discarded papers be shredded as part of their normal security routines.

ID Cards

Many companies require employees to wear ID badges when they access buildings or specific rooms. Doors to the computer room often have locks that open only if the person seeking to enter swipes a valid card. Building guards may also check for proper identification before allowing entry into certain secure areas.

Some networks use ID Smartcards to enhance security. Rather than just accepting a password and username, these systems also demand that users present an ATM-like card to gain access. The need to physically possess an object to gain access can block hackers who may have a list of stolen passwords.

Products like Litronic's NetSign use a card reader connected to a computer's serial port. Utilizing public/private key cryptography, these items can create a very secure environment. Voice recognition, finger-length detectors, and face identifiers are mostly experimental technologies that so far have met with minimal success in the market.

Headless Servers

While the name sounds somewhat macabre, headless servers can be a valuable security measure. Servers without a monitor are hard to penetrate, since they do not give feedback to the screen. Some servers are run without any input devices, either.

Without a keyboard and mouse to give input or a monitor to view system activity, it is exceedingly difficult to breach a server's defenses. You can avoid POST errors, which can occur when no keyboards are attached, by using hardware devices that permit you to boot servers by "emulating" the feedback of an attached input device.

Some of the keyboard eliminators also permit a user to simply plug in a functional keyboard and proceed to administer the system. An alternative arrangement would be to use a USB keyboard. One of the great features of the USB port is that you can hot-plug devices into running systems without special precautions.

Administrators can also access the system in other ways. Remote-control programs such as CO/Session or Timbuktu permit an IT specialist to use their local screen and keyboard to manipulate a remote system. The connection can be maintained over the network or through a dial-up connection.

Keyboard and Drive Locks

Schools and libraries often use physical barriers to prevent unauthorized use of computers. Locks and shields can be an effective choice for companies, too. A lock inserted into a disk drive slot prevents unauthorized loading of software or copying of data. A similar lock placed over the keyboard prohibits users from inputting anything.

These measures are most appropriate when servers cannot be placed in a physically secured area. Some small companies lack the space to dedicate to a network room. If you cannot guarantee that physical access to servers will be limited, then locks may be your only available choice.

Passwords

A password, combined with a valid username, is a common way to grant valid users access to network resources. It is highly important to protect passwords, and there are several tried-and-true methods you can use to boost security. Since usernames can be fairly easy to deduce from phone lists and other sources, I always assume that intruders can confidently assume which user account names are valid. Passwords are often the only thing hackers need to determine in order to gain unauthorized entry.

Require Frequent Changes

Making users change passwords frequently is the best way to avoid complacency. People tend to want to use the same password forever because it makes their life easier. Not having to constantly remember a new access code makes their login less daunting.

Balance the schedule for forcing users to change their account passwords against your company's security needs. Higher security requirements may dictate making changes as often as every month.

Use Different Characters

Make sure that user passwords combine both upper- and lowercase letters, and encourage them to mix in numerals to further frustrate hacking efforts. Also make certain that passwords are case-sensitive, so that BimBOB24 is a different password than bIMBob24. Some NOSs even allow the use of other characters in passwords; if so, encourage users to add those as well. The password Bi#bo*24 is even more difficult to crack than BimBOB24.

Create Longer Passwords

"The more the merrier" is the guiding principle here. When you increase the number of characters in a password, guessing it becomes more complex. I try to enforce a policy of a minimum of 8 characters for most environments. Moving much beyond 14 characters may be difficult for most users to accept. Remember that longer passwords are more challenging to remember, and thus users may be more likely to write them down.

A long password reinforces the appeal of single sign-on technologies, which permit users to enter a single name and password to gain access to all network resources at once. Many network administrators prefer this scenario since it is convenient for users. However, requiring discrete logins for each resource will be more secure.

Limit Login Attempts

Some networks are insecure because their administrators allow users unlimited attempts to re-enter passwords. These networks can more easily succumb to a brute-force attack, when a hacker enters a random password with a valid username. Just as an ATM can yank a bank card from a patron who fails to enter a correct PIN after a set number of attempts, you should block access to an account after there have been several unsuccessful logins.

Use NOS Policies to Enforce Standards

Most users attempt to abide by policies set by IT, but these types of rules must be enforced. Every NOS gives administrators the ability to control user accounts to a very fine degree. You can adjust login attempt settings for time of day, day of the week, MAC address of login station, and other factors to gain more complete control of your environment. These settings will be discussed in more detail later.

Beware of Special Accounts

Usernames like `guest` and `supervisor` have a special quality. Normally, the supervisor account has all rights everywhere on the network. Armed with the password for the supervisor account, a user can delete or view any data they please. The supervisor can also add new users, change existing passwords, or modify the access capabilities of other users.

One fearful scenario is a hacker creating a new supervisor account and disabling the old one, essentially holding the system hostage. Your IT staff would not be able to access the server as an administrator to lock out the stolen account. I'll discuss ways to prevent this scenario in the following sections.

IT DEPARTMENT ACCOUNTS   Some firms make the mistake of automatically granting IT staff accounts high access rights. Every account that has wide access creates another potential flaw in your security strategy. The simple act of granting directory modification permissions can make accidental deletions possible. User errors are still the leading reason that tape backups are so valuable.

SECURING THE SUPERVISOR ACCOUNT   Windows NT Server 4.0 does not permit a supervisor account to be deleted. The best practice in this NOS is to disable the supervisor's account after creating a new one designed just for supervisory duties. One can use this account to add or modify security settings. A hacker who cannot utilize the username `supervisor` and guess the password, because the account has been disabled, is thwarted with this approach. Linux and UNIX administrators are always cautioned to avoid the use of the root account whenever possible. It is much safer to use a regular user account as a standard procedure.

TIP: Create a `superuser` username and password, and lock them away. Only a select number of IT staff should be given the correct name and password. This account can then be used to rescue a system if a hacker takes over the supervisor account.

GUEST ACCOUNT SECURITY   Perhaps the best policy is simply to disable or completely remove any guest accounts from your internal file servers. While Web and FTP servers are often geared toward anonymous connections, there are few compelling reasons to maintain generic access accounts. Administrators have sometimes unknowingly granted generous system rights to guest accounts.

Account Access Limits

Most network operating systems allow an administrator to place a number of limits on any account. Certain logins can be permitted only from specified network addresses. With this scheme, even if someone has discovered the supervisor's account name and password, they would be unable to log in unless they were using a particular NIC address.

Time- and date-sensitive measures can also be applied. Users may be permitted to gain access only during certain times of the day. Accounts can also be set to terminate active sessions if the workstation is logged in after a specific time.

Monitoring Account Activity

IT specialists who are charged with enforcing security must maintain a diligent overview of their network. This requires periodically reviewing log files to see if there have been unusual attempts to gain network access. Failed login attempts that occurred during off-hours are a sure indication that an unauthorized user has been trying to get in.

Clear Out Old Accounts

I am willing to wager that everyone who reads this book has old network user accounts that should have been deleted yet still remain active. Whenever an employee's relationship with a company ends for any reason, their access to corporate computing systems should cease immediately. Delays in getting accounts closed or just plain oversights can leave these accounts active, potentially breaching your security.

CONFIRMING WORKER EXIT DATES   People leave companies for a wide variety of reasons. From the time when notice is given, an exit date can still be months away. I've made the mistake of terminating an account early for a user. I was given notification of their expected departure date, but a snag in a project they were involved in extended their stay an additional week. Before you click OK to confirm the deletion, check with the HR department to make sure the employee has indeed left.

TIP: Establish procedures with your HR department to ensure that employees' status is reliably reported to network administrators.

Data Encryption

Encrypted messages are created with a "key" before transmission, and the recipient then uses the same key to decode the data once received. If someone steals encrypted data, they will have a difficult time reading it.

Secret
Encoding
Key

Two of the more popular methods of data encryption are RSA and DES. RSA is named after its developers, Rivest, Shamir, and Adleman, and RSA Laboratories can be found online at www.rsa.com. Your company can purchase this technology for uses like electronic commerce. Data Encryption Standard, or DES, was originally developed at IBM. Many vendors employ DES security in their software and hardware products.

Key Concepts

When only one key is used both to encode and decode messages, there is a risk that the key could fall into the wrong hands. Anyone with access to the secret unlocking power of the key can read any stolen data.

To address these concerns, data encryption typically depends on a public/private key scheme. Each user who participates in this plan has a private and a public key. The public key is published and the private key is reserved for them.

When someone wants to send a message to a user, they can use the recipient's public key to encrypt the data. The recipient of the message then uses their personal private key to decode the data. Since the decryption depends on having the private key and it is only in the possession of the recipient, this can be a very secure method of handling communications.

A Master Key for the Government?

The U.S. government has been attempting to address the issues of privacy and their desire to be able to open encrypted messages. While I was writing this book, there were numerous reports in the press of Justice Department efforts to pass the Cyberspace Electronic Security Act. Armed with a warrant, investigators could potentially use their master key to unlock every document on a system.

Electronic Frontier Foundation

Libertarians and others who value privacy and other civil liberties should visit the Electronic Frontier Foundation's Web site at www.eff.org. With headquarters in San Francisco, the EFF is dedicated to ensuring that the Internet and other communication channels are free from government intervention. I consider this group the electronic equivalent of the ACLU.

Guarding Your Backups

Network server backups are often stored on tape or removable disk media. With a little ingenuity and the correct hardware, a determined hacker could restore the data from your backups and never have to worry about passwords. Don't be a lazy administrator and store your tapes in an unsecured area.

A fireproof safe in a locked office may be the solution for your company. Larger corporations should explore off-site storage solutions. Obsolete tapes and disks that are no longer part of your normal rotation schemes should be destroyed.

VIRUS ATTACKS AND HARMFUL PROGRAMS

Many IT specialists tend to attribute all unwanted program behavior to viruses. By definition, a virus has the capability of replicating and spreading to other systems, unlike other system bugs. Some of these virus programs destroy data, and others simply place ominous messages across your screen, such as saying that your computer is now "stoned." Harmful programs can steal your password and other sensitive data or wreak havoc with your data.

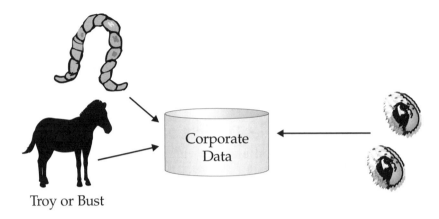

Troy or Bust

The explosion of the Web has spawned a new generation of programs that exploit security holes in browsers, office suites, programming languages, and network operating systems. IT specialists need to be aware of threats with Java and Active Server pages. IP-based file servers can be damaged by their own unique types of rogue programs.

While the strict definition of a program virus is rather limited, in this book I consider all unwanted programs to be viruses. The techniques of detection and eradication are virtually the same for all destructive code, and these programs can have harmful effects no matter what you call them.

Types of Pernicious Programs

The number and types of virus attacks are quite large. They have been affecting computer operations for the 15 years I have worked in this industry. Some are more destructive to your data than others, but the growing popularity of the Internet and electronic commerce makes all of these threats more ominous.

I've seen virus attacks on virtually every platform that I have supported. Early on, most of the viruses I experienced were found on Macintosh systems. Recently, most of the attacks have targeted Microsoft Word and Excel document files on Windows computers.

The popularity of the Windows environment has made it a favorite target of virus code writers.

The Trojan Horse

Anyone who read mythology back in high school knows the story of the Trojan horse. Fans of Monty Python's "Holy Grail" movie may remember the slightly twisted version called the Trojan Rabbit. In the context of technology, Trojan horses are programs that are embedded into seemingly innocuous applications; once these programs run, they can purge data or steal information.

Worms

Worms can penetrate your systems and cause damage, but these programs don't replicate themselves. Other than the fact that they don't reproduce, they can pose a threat equal to any virus program.

Logic Bombs

Halloween, Friday the Thirteenth, April Fool's Day, and other dates can cause system administrators to hold their collective breath. Many destructive programs are timed to go off when a particular date is reached. Since they lie hidden, logic bombs can be a favorite tool of the disgruntled employee, who sets them to go off long after their last day.

Thief Programs

Perhaps I can take credit for coining a term for all types of programs that attempt to steal information from a system. Many of these attempts center on exploiting "features" in Windows and Web browsers. When a computer accesses a Web site, the Web server sends program commands that get executed back on the browsing system. By allowing information to flow back from the browser to the server, your system allows itself to reveal data you may not want it to.

PROTECTING YOUR BROWSER   While the changes I recommend here can diminish the threat of data theft, they can also make browser use more frustrating. Simple steps like disabling Java can reduce the potential of harmful activity. You can also hide data by not exchanging cookies with servers when they request it. Many Web servers request certain information from clients, and you will get plenty of warnings from your browser if you select higher security settings.

When performing activities that involve commerce, you should only deal with servers that support secure transactions. The best known is the SSL (secure socket layer) protocol. The greater encryption capabilities of 128-bit browsers should motivate anyone using lesser 40-bit browsers to upgrade immediately. You should also rely on the software products I discuss in the next section.

TIP: Regularly check in with the vendors of your operating system and browser to see if security updates have been released. Make sure that both end-user systems and your servers are given equal attention. Products such as Microsoft Exchange have been the target for attacks on numerous occasions.

Virus Protection

Several companies market virus-scanning programs. Naturally, each vendor claims the fastest scan times or the most complete solution, but none of them are perfect. I've seen many instances in which a program detected a program but did not eradicate it. In other cases, one anti-viral application could not find anything wrong, yet another did.

My policy has always been to purchase a site license for a particular virus scanner and to use that solution on every machine.

However, I still own copies of another vendor's product in case the first one proves inadequate in a particular situation. New viruses are being written all the time, and it is unreasonable to expect that every scanner can detect and destroy every virus.

All virus scanners must be periodically upgraded to account for new virus threats. Normally there are updates for both the virus-scanning program and for the database of virus signatures used to identify particular viruses. Be sure that you keep your programs and signature files up-to-date to maximize system protection.

WARNING: If you find a virus, keep scanning for a recurrence in the following days. It is likely to return if it spread to other machines that your first scan failed to cover. I've had machines that were unused for a period of time suddenly infect a department when the user returned from vacation.

Symantec

The Norton AntiVirus and Norton Utilities programs are perhaps the best-known anti-virus products for Windows-based computers. The companion program Symantec AntiVirus, for the Macintosh platform, is more commonly referred to as SAM. There are specific versions of Norton designed for DOS, Windows NT, and other varieties of Microsoft operating systems. Make sure you get the right one!

On the Symantec Web site (www.symantec.com), not only can you purchase their products online, you can also download the latest updates automatically. They also provide links to an extensive set of virus information resources.

McAfee

The McAfee site (www.mcafee.com) is one of my favorites. Not only can I download the latest updates, I can also run anti-viral scans directly with my browser. McAfee's platform support is as broad as Symantec's.

Use a Total Solution

Make sure that you place a scanning product on every system you support. This obviously includes all end-user workstations, but remember to cover your file servers as well. Since a workstation and server scanner work slightly differently and use different virus signature files, you increase the chances of uncovering a virus by using both.

HACKERS

There are as many types of hackers as there are viruses, each one with different characteristics and methods of operations. They are sometimes given different names like crackers, "phreaks," and other labels, but hackers are best lumped into one big category. They are all people who wish to gain unauthorized access to your data.

Hackers   XYZ Corporation Data Center

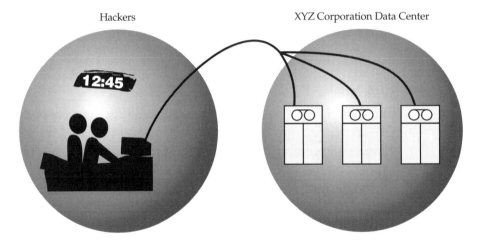

Some attacks are malicious, and can include corporate data being replaced or erased. There are hackers who take pride in bringing down a server or defacing a Web site. Other hackers simply want the thrill of getting into someplace uninvited. Like "gate crashers" at a party, they derive their satisfaction from finding a secret way in.

Protecting Your Networks

To begin with, you should use the security measures discussed earlier in this chapter to defend your network. Careful control over the use of passwords and accounts must be the first step. Making sure that authorized users are the only ones who are accessing your servers requires carefully checking server logs and file access journals.

The use of encryption and firewall technologies can make unauthorized invasion of your systems more difficult, but the single most important factor in network security is vigilance. Lazy administration is the surest way to leave holes in your security.

Hackers use many different tools to gain entry into protected networks. Most look for well-known weak spots in operating systems and exploit them. Administrators can sometimes use these tools to probe their own networks and shut down any discovered problems. IT specialists must always watch for code updates from vendors and religiously apply patches to fix security holes. If the worst happens despite your vigilance, there are organizations you can turn to for guidance and assistance when hackers have invaded your domain.

SATAN

I am not talking about the devil here. The Security Administrator Tool for Analyzing Networks, known as SATAN, is a great way for UNIX administrators to discover security-related problems on their networks. SATAN is turned loose on the tested network and checks for common flaws in security.

If irregularities are discovered, the SATAN program describes the problems and suggests a way to rectify the situation. It is available as freeware all over the Internet. Use of the program requires a version of Perl to execute the scripts. Remember that hackers can use SATAN to probe your network, so be sure to run it before they do!

Back Orifice

Another oddly named program, this one is a tool used by hackers. An open-source application developed by a group of hackers called the Cult of the Dead Cow, it is designed to let users take control of Windows NT systems. Administrators need to carefully monitor system files for modifications and date changes to see if Back Orifice attacks have been occurring. System files should not be altered during normal computer operations. These files should only be modified by administrators with high-level access rights. Unexplained changes are a signal that something fishy may be going on.

While it can be used perniciously, there are some legitimate uses for this program. It can be a good tool for remote administration of network servers. A full-blown Windows interface makes the program fairly easy to configure and run. You can download the program from the Cult of the Dead Cow site at www.cultdeadcow.com/tools/bo.html.

RealSecure

Internet Security Systems' RealSecure is typical of the commercially available products for scanning your network to identify hacker intrusions. Geared for TCP/IP networks, RealSecure is designed to detect SATAN scans and other attacks. You can learn more about ISS products at www.iss.net.

Abirnet

Part of the massive Computer Associates corporation, Abirnet offers another tool for securing TCP/IP-centric networks, called SessionWall-3. Expect to pay about $5,000 for the Abirnet or RealSecure products for a typical installation. You can find Abirnet's product information at www.abirnet.com.

ICSA

Based in Reston, Virginia, the ICSA (www.icsa.net) develops security products and certification programs for people interested in security issues. The organization seeks industry acceptance of security product designs that meet specified criteria for performance and capability. They also produce a range of publications and seminars for network security specialists.

Their TruSecure services attempt to guard corporate infrastructures from all manner of attack. They will monitor your network for hackers and scan for viruses, too. A periodic review of your security structure by outside experts is one of the best ways to guard against intrusion.

CERT

Based at one of academia's true centers of computer science, Carnegie-Mellon University, CERT grew out of the Computer Emergency Response Team, developed under a federal grant from the Department of Defense. CERT today functions as a center of services dedicated to dealing with Internet security problems.

The group publishes a wide range of security alerts, and over 100,000 individuals subscribe to their newsletter advisory list. You can discover more about CERT and its range of offerings at www.cert.org. The site provides a great deal of information on making your network more secure and includes numerous FAQs. You can report problems with your systems and read about other attacks that have recently occurred.

DEF CON

Point your browser at the DEF CON home page, www.defcon.org, and you will find a site dedicated to the hacker. Hackers, along with government and corporate network security experts, attend annual conventions in Las Vegas. The mix of people is interesting at these events—there are groups of people interested in getting into networks and others charged with keeping people out!

Not only will you be able to learn about the latest hacking tools and contests at a DEF CON event, you will also have opportunities to learn directly from those most capable of penetrating your network. It is interesting to note that a large number of consultants who now work to protect networks started out as hackers. In fact, a big focus of the DEF CON conference is on finding legitimate ways for hackers to get paid for their expertise.

CSI

The Computer Security Institute, or CSI, is a membership organization for IT specialists who are charged with providing network security. The conferences and exhibitions sponsored by the organization are another great way to learn more about this important field. Numerous newsletters and journals are offered to help members keep ahead of the rapidly changing threats to computer systems.

Their Web site, at www.gocsi.com, provides a wealth of links to resources about security threats and products. Perhaps the most interesting reading here is the variety of assessments made by numerous government offices. The overall threat to computer systems is quite serious and generally goes under-reported except when a popular Web site is defaced.

Know Your Ports

As I've stated previously, many network attackers exploit known flaws or common security holes that administrators leave open. In-depth knowledge of how TCP/IP services are maintained is critical for any administrator whose network is connected to the Internet. Most of the network scanning and security tools that you can use will look for well-known security problem areas and direct you to patch them up. Remember that these are the exact same tools and techniques that hackers can use to find any paths to your network. Be sure that you use them first before hackers get into your systems!

USER ERRORS

While they may not seem to pose as big a threat as the other ones I've discussed in this chapter, my own experience has shown that simple user errors are the biggest threat to data. Once your users have been given the right to change any directory file contents, they can easily lay waste to hundreds of megabytes of server storage or cripple their own systems.

Most times when I've been called to save a file or resuscitate a trashed directory, the problem was caused by someone inadvertently executing an incorrect command. In earlier chapters, I gave tips on how to give better support to your users. Along with performing these action items, you must always remember that the majority of your problems can be caused by simple user errors. By placing guards on your data internally and externally, you achieve a much safer and more secure environment.

Putting Things on a High Shelf

One of the keys to preventing mishaps with younger children is putting anything that could be dangerous on a high shelf in a closet. While a parent can reach the Drano when it's needed to unplug the sink, Junior can't try feeding it to Fido.

Treating users like children may sound somewhat foolish. But the blame all falls on you when someone finds that their system won't boot up after they've tried to clean up some disk space. Make your network policies reflect a cautious approach. By placing barriers that prevent users from destructive activities, you will prevent a majority of problems.

Hide Dangerous Commands

One of the original ways to guard against accidental destructive program use is to simply remove certain commands or use the operating system to hide them. Back in the days when MS-DOS ruled, many system administrators would delete commands like FORMAT, FDISK, and RECOVER from users' computers.

If you don't want to delete files, you can use the hidden file attribute to render certain programs invisible to casual users. Renaming programs is another way to achieve a similar result. Remember that Click-a-Holics often try to run any executable program they discover, so deletion is a more secure choice for them.

Use Autosave and Autobackup

Many applications can be configured to automatically save files at set intervals. Continuity of data can also be enhanced by automatically creating archives. Many programs permit the storage of multiple prior revisions of files. Every time a file is saved, the previous versions are retained. This allows users to readily return to a version that existed just before a mistake was committed.

Document and Train

The importance of providing your users with adequate training and documentation has been discussed in earlier chapters. This training is also crucial for preventing common user errors. Most employees can follow directions if shown how. The fear of losing files and perhaps damaging others' work has always been a powerful motivator. People are much better users when they can operate their systems with confidence.

Carefully Mete out Access Rights

When granting access rights to delete or modify files, IT specialists must be sure to limit the number and types of users that can perform these functions. There are many network administrators who take too lax an approach to security settings. Simply don't grant unnecessary access to users whose jobs never depend on modifying key data files.

IT REALLY HAPPENED: I was helping a friend upgrade his tax preparation office network server. To save time and administration chores, he had granted everyone manager access to the entire network. While he had not had a problem with this approach, my sobering warnings of the possibility of an accidental deletion of hundreds of client files motivated him to modify the security schemes that same day.

INVENTORY

Another important duty of IT specialists is keeping track of your systems. Knowledge of the current state of your computers is critical for planning any program installations, upgrades, bug fixes, budgeting, or training. The constant need to keep ahead of new technology requires ongoing efforts to retire less capable systems and bring in updated equipment. Very few IT departments have unlimited budgets, so maximizing your new system's budget demands a clear picture of installed computers.

What to Track

Tracking software typically requires only a version and serial number. Product license information is certainly another important factor to track to ensure compliance with your vendor agreements. Many applications and file servers can track the number of simultaneous users, so be certain that your network usage complies with the license agreement for the programs you rely on.

Master Inventory				
CPU Model	Serial #	Date Purchased	User	Location
HP UL4 5/166	USA 228 3196	3/24/97	Joe Kay	Sales
Compaq 1600R	K8586192B	1/12/99	Systems	Server room
IBM ThinkPad 600	BB728691A8	8/9/98	Sue Royce	Management

Hardware is significantly more complex. Computers that look identical from the outside can contain vastly different components. The pieces of information you need when you contact Technical Support, outlined in the previous chapter, are a good starting point. The processor, RAM, hard drive size and interface, video card, and network card physical address can be easily determined with scanning software or by doing a visual inspection and manually recording the data.

Usernames

Associating a particular piece of hardware or software with a certain person is a sound strategy. When upgrading applications, it helps to identify who will need the code and to issue an advisory prior to the update. This can also help you determine which users may require training when new features are added to existing systems.

Department or Cost Center

Many Accounting departments want to know precisely which company division has which assets. Fiscal responsibility may shift from one group to another, and budgets must reflect these changes. Mergers and acquisitions may necessitate the transfer of equipment from one company to another. The value and number of systems involved can be critical to assessing the total value of corporate capital.

Serial Numbers

Every piece of equipment that you own should have a serial number somewhere. An inventory database is a good way to track this information. Technical support calls and service advisories are sometimes issued for particular pieces of hardware. This is sometimes done to address manufacturing flaws that were not discovered until after the product was shipped to customers.

Buyers are often required to produce previous license numbers in order to purchase software upgrades. Since upgrades are almost always significantly less expensive than full-version products, having this information can be a great cost-saver.

IT REALLY HAPPENED: Tektronix manufactures a wide range of large-format color printers. A letter from their Customer Service department requested that I check the serial number on one of *PC Week's* printers that they thought might have a defect. Tektronix discovered that some units could heat up internally and warp the plastic printer housing, and they feared that a resulting loss of airflow could damage the printer even further. A telephone call to the Tektronix Customer Service department confirmed that my printer would need a field-installed upgrade, and one was scheduled.

Version Numbers

There can be significant differences between versions of software and hardware although the products may appear similar. Maintenance releases may only update a version number from 3.01 to 3.02, but program operations can vary greatly.

Hardware with embedded programs can be difficult to track. It is impossible to determine externally which one of your Ethernet switches has a particular version of firmware installed. Capture and record this important data for later use before installing the parts.

Insurance Needs

In the event of theft, fire, flood, or other catastrophes, you must have adequate documentation of any products lost. Remember that options may have been added to a computer after the initial purchase, increasing its value. You should also factor in the cost of replacing all the installed software.

Only an accurate picture of the exact configuration can yield proper information for an insurance claim. Be sure to have invoices to show proof of purchase. Remember that depreciation affects coverage with some policies.

IT REALLY HAPPENED: When I worked at the Heath/Zenith computer chain, I often had adjusters call for verification of costs for damaged products. They questioned the retail prices of items claimed by the insured. On one occasion, someone claimed that his Apple II was worth $3,500 when a brand-new system was available for less than $1,400.

Tracking Software

There are many ways to handle your system inventory. Some companies simply record each computer's information manually in a logbook. Other IT specialists rely on database applications such as FileMaker Pro or spreadsheets like Microsoft Excel to store the information. These manual methods require a lot of work. First you must determine which products you have, and then you need to enter the data.

The best solutions for busy IT departments that track lots of computers are automatic inventory-capture programs. These query your hardware and determine all of the installed options and software. You can copy the information to a floppy disk or across the network, building a comprehensive database of your equipment.

Large-Enterprise Solutions

Large companies with thousands of users typically rely on sophisticated management systems for many IT functions. Large companies often have a wide mixture of platforms, and a key feature of the more expensive and comprehensive inventory products is that they support a diverse blend of hardware. These solutions help flesh out and augment other system-management utilities rather than simply capturing data.

UNICENTER TNG   Computer Associates International is the world's second-largest software company. They have designed or acquired some of the leading products used by IT specialists. Offering everything from ArcServe for tape backups to Jasmine and Neugent tools for managing Internet business practices, they are a clear leader in the computer industry.

Not only will Unicenter TNG capture your inventory, it can also help IT departments manage client systems, security, help desks, and other areas of concern. Be aware that the scope and expense of these products requires a major commitment of time from your staff to fully exploit its capabilities and value. You can find more information about this product and many others of interest to IT Specialists from the CA Web site at www.cai.com.

TME Inventory

Typical of high-end inventory solutions, the Tivoli Systems product integrates with their existing TME 10 enterprise-management software. While not currently functional with Macintosh systems, it works well with most UNIX and Windows computers. An agent is installed on clients, and a server is configured to query and collect information on all nodes in a network. Tivoli can be found at www.tivoli.com.

Homogeneous Networks

Many companies don't need and can't afford the wealth of features in high-end programs like TME Inventory. If you are only supporting a mix of Windows, DOS, and OS/2 systems, then a less expensive product from Intel or Blue Ocean Software will suffice. While these solutions are not scalable to the large-sized networks that the high-end packages support, they should have all the features you require for a smaller network.

INTEL LANDESK   Providing extensive capture capability, Intel's LANDesk is designed for WinTel-based architectures. One version is optimized for compatibility with Novell NetWare or Microsoft Windows NT servers. The included capability to centralize management of clients is sometimes more critical than the inventory functions this software provides.

Its companion product, Device View, captures data from SNMP devices on your network. This is a great way to learn more about your switches, routers, and hubs. For LAN managers who rely on Intel brand networking products, the graphical management features are wonderful tools. Intel's Web site is www.intel.com.

TRACK-IT!   Browse on over to Blue Ocean's site (www.blueocean.com) and try a free demo version of the Track-It! program. It can perform automatic inventory of your hardware and software as well as capturing the contents of computers' startup files. Comparing these file setups to corporate standards can often uncover potential problems.

REPAIR FACILITIES

Companies that own thousands of computers and lots of related equipment typically maintain a center where systems can be repaired. These same facilities can also be used to set up and test new products before they are delivered to users' desktops. Even if you outsource your systems support, you should still have an area for storing consumables.

Large corporations may have dedicated workshops where system maintenance can be handled. Equipped with independent power and network connections, they are an ideal place to fix, upgrade, and test your computer systems. Small companies' system administrators may simply perform all repair work in their offices.

Service Centers

Workshops to repair and set up your computers can be elaborate, including dedicated power and network connections. Others are modest closets furnished with spare desks and bare lights. In either case, there are certain tools and test equipment that should be part of any service center.

You can spend less than $50 and have virtually all the tools you need to work on every system in your company. Some test and diagnostic equipment costs more than $5,000. Whatever budget you have to dedicate to these items, make sure you always buy high-quality components. Cheap tools are harder to work with. Your arms will tire more quickly and you'll strip screws, too.

Tools

The variety of hardware store purchases required to effectively repair most computing equipment is rather modest. When IBM introduced its PS/2 line in the 1980s, they promised that only two human hands were required to open and service the units. This was in stark contrast to the all-in-one Macintosh, which discouraged users from venturing beneath the cover. In fact, the older Mac systems required a special clamshell cracker to take the case apart!

SCREWDRIVERS   Any service technician needs some quality screwdrivers. You should have an assortment of types and sizes to accommodate the various types of screws used. Phillips-head screwdrivers are normally sold in sizes 1 and 2. You will need both. A variety of standard-slot drivers are useful for driving screws and to wield as pry bars. Finally, many manufacturers utilize Torx-head fasteners. Size 5 and 10 Torx drivers should satisfy most needs.

The one tool you can use to repair virtually all computer equipment is a single multiple-bit screwdriver. If you have Phillips, slot, and Torx bits, you can take almost any computer apart and put it back together. Available from Radio Shack and other places for about $10, multiple-bit screwdrivers are a terrific bargain.

ELECTRIC DRIVERS   If you are assembling multiple systems, then the speed of an electric driver is most welcome. I find it especially helpful when installing heavy servers and communications equipment on my server-room racks. A cordless model, which goes for about $25, is adequate for most users.

WARNING: Be cautious when using electric screwdrivers. With their high torque and lack of manual feedback, you can easily strip screw heads right off.

WIRE-HANDLING TOOLS   Wire cutters and strippers are necessary for anyone creating network cables. A good, clean cutting tool runs less than $10 at any hardware store. A spinning-wire stripper is the perfect device for stripping the insulation from UTP cable prior to crimping the proper end. These tools cost only a few dollars and are sometimes included free when you purchase bulk spools of cable.

Crimpers are designed to attach RJ-45 or RJ-11 male plugs to data communications cable. While most station cables are purchased in standard lengths, there may still be occasions when you need custom lengths or pin assignments. For example, you may construct crossover cables that connect transmitting and receiving wire pairs to link hubs together.

Installing fiber-optic cabling requires a unique set of tools. Cables must be carefully polished and terminated to transmit data cleanly. Most of the cable installation companies that I have worked with have designated technicians specially trained for fiber optic work. The delicate and precise nature of this work demands an experienced pair of hands.

PLIERS   Needle-nose pliers are extremely useful. For example, they can be used to retrieve screws that have fallen into narrow areas of computers. When placing Lilliputian jumpers on disk drives and option cards, they can be a lifesaver for those with stubby fingers.

Stronger pliers and vise grips may be necessary for assembling network room furniture. I've sometimes needed pliers to bend drive brackets back into shape that were damaged by shipping.

SOLDERING IRONS   There are very few activities in the support of modern corporations' systems that require the use of soldering tools. Component-level repair is almost never done. Instead, entire boards are exchanged, and the pieces snap together. However, there are some custom communication cables and electrical connections that may benefit from being soldered rather than crimped.

IT REALLY HAPPENED: On a few occasions, I've needed a soldering iron to do an emergency repair. In one instance, my manager's hard drive was intermittently failing. It seemed that the power connector had worked loose due to heat and vibration. A few quick touches of iron and fresh solder fixed the problem. In another case, a delicate circuit card was cracked when the printer was accidentally dropped. While it was an ugly-looking repair, I was able to fix the board with some wires and solder.

ANTI-STATIC MATS   Electronic equipment needs to be guarded from spurious electro-static discharges (ESD), which can fry delicate equipment. The same energy that leaps as a spark from your fingers as you touch a doorknob on a dry day can corrupt CMOS memory or damage sensitive chips. This is why computer components are shipped in gray or pink plastic wrappers designed to insulate them from static.

To prevent ESD, special work mats are often used when performing computer equipment maintenance. The mats are grounded and funnel excess charges away. Technicians, to ensure that they too remain electrically grounded, wear wrist straps. There are mats designed for large workbenches as well as portable units that a technician can bring along when making a field service call.

TIP: Always touch the power supply of a computer before reaching for any of the other components. This drains any charges from your body into a sturdy power supply rather than into the delicate motherboard.

SPECIAL TOOLS   While most computers can be serviced with only a modest assortment of tools, there are some products that demand specialized implements. Turning exotic star-shaped screws can require a unique driver. You need extra-long tools to reach the deeply recessed screws found on the backs of monitors.

Magnetic-tipped screwdrivers and pick-up probes should be used carefully, if at all, in IT work. Floppy disks can be sensitive to magnetic fields, and the wrong touch can ruin valuable data. See if you can substitute screwdrivers that use mechanical gripping fingers to secure screws to the driver head.

Some technicians use temperature probes to make sure that HVAC units are working correctly. Highly skilled engineers may employ oscilloscopes to diagnose the electrical properties of circuits. Any firm that uses uncommon technology may need single-purpose specialty tools and diagnostic equipment.

Test Equipment

Diagnosing certain computer ailments is much easier with dedicated test equipment. The cost ranges from a few dollars to several thousands. While not all of these devices are mandatory for a successful service department, their use can often save time and money.

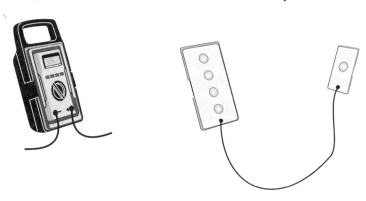

MULTI-TESTERS   A multi-tester is one of my favorite tools for its ease of use and versatility. I fondly remember a multi-tester as a handheld device with a large speedometer-type needle and a small dial to select the desired test. Two small leads (one red and one black) were used to probe the problem hardware. Today many multi-testers provide digital readings, but the principle is exactly the same.

These tools are perfect for checking continuity. By testing for resistance, you can determine whether a fuse is blown or a switch is actually closing. You can save yourself the bother and expense of replacing a functional $300 power supply if you discover that a $5 power switch is the culprit instead. When you check for voltage, a multi-tester can reveal whether a battery for a laptop is charged and how many amps an unlabeled AC power adapter is producing.

Various units that can be purchased for around $100 will suffice for most of the situations you are likely to encounter in IT. I've used Fluke products for many years and they have been reliable and easy to use. You can find their products in many computer catalogs and on the Web at www.fluke.com. A single unit should serve many technicians, unless you are running a computer service center for thousands of users and expect to do many repairs on printers and other more exotic equipment. Most companies opt to use outside contractors for systems that complex.

STETHOSCOPES   No, you won't need a stethoscope to check the blood pressure of overstressed programmers! Instead, these are used in noisy computer rooms to listen to suspect components like hard drives in servers. Servers with internal drive arrays may not have individual lights to indicate whether a particular disk is spinning. By listening to the drive, an astute IT specialist should be able to determine whether it is functional.

DATA CABLE VERIFICATION   There are basically two types of popular testers for qualifying data cable for a given transmission speed. Most use a two-part design. The master unit has all the dials and gauges to indicate test functions and results. The remote unit is placed at the terminus of the cable being tested. By either acting as a terminator or actively signaling the master unit, remote units can reveal a massive amount of detail about high-end products.

A basic, inexpensive tester just checks for proper polarity in the wire, which only reveals whether the cable pairs are correct for the given application. They should be available for under $50.

A more thorough cable diagnosis requires a significantly more expensive device called a time-delay reflectometer, or TDR. By sending a carefully modulated signal across the tested wire, it reveals not only continuity but also whether the cable can function correctly at high speed. Cross-talk and interference on properly paired wires can still defeat network communications.

Companies such as MicroTest sell units that range from about $600 to over $4,000. The more expensive products can test a wider variety of cable types and run more exhaustive tests. If all your network cabling is UTP, a more modest unit will suffice. Fiber-optic cables require the more sophisticated testing products that fall at the higher end of the price spectrum.

SIMM/DIMM CHECKERS   Memory chips can substantially add to the overall cost of a computer. Modern servers can easily hold a gigabyte of RAM. Making sure that your RAM chips are functioning correctly is most easily accomplished with a dedicated memory-testing unit.

A SIMM checker not only diagnoses chip health, it can also confirm the exact type of memory chip you have. One memory module tends to look the same as another, and there are few visual clues to help you distinguish them. Unlike disk drives, chips seldom carry labels indicating their design type or capacity. They have different designs and capabilities that can have drastic performance implications for your systems.

Memory speed can vary, and not all chips are capable of running at the 100Mhz or higher bus speeds in the newest motherboards. Features such as EDO (enhanced data out) and ECC (error-checking control) can boost computer performance and reliability. Many Intel and Macintosh systems require that memory be added in pairs of matched SIMMs. This can permit memory interleaving, which can greatly boost system throughput.

Over time, every IT service department collects bunches of unmarked SIMM or DIMM chips, with no indication as to their design or quality. A diagnostic unit costs about $1,500 and can test 72- and 168-pin memory modules. This investment is a wise move for any IT department that supports more than a few systems.

I have been using a SP3000 unit from CST with great success. It has been able to identify and test virtually every memory chip I have ever tried. You can find out more about CST products at www.simmtester.com.

Other Service Center Items

There are dozens of items that may be required in your environment. I've used an ultrasonic cleaner for maintenance of plotter ink pens. Telephone-line testers are necessary for anyone who handles telephony integration for their company.

HUBS AND SERVERS   I suggest that you use a small network hub to permit testing of NICs and cables. You don't want to link a system that you suspect is bad to the company network. A single bad card can crash an entire LAN, so assume the worst possible results from testing. An 8-port, 10-Megabit hub can be purchased for about $100 from 3Com and other vendors.

You can use an old server to test effectiveness of client software. With a modest number of licenses, the server should be able to handle the load of your service department network. It can also be an ideal way to store drive image files for rapid workstation setup.

FURNITURE   Solid workbenches with ample power outlets are a feature of most electronic repair rooms. Topped with anti-static mats, they provide a stable and safe environment in which to open up delicate computer systems. Companies like Zero-Stantron, Symbiote, and Systems Management Corporation manufacture a wide variety of technical furniture.

While you can always use cinderblocks and plywood, a professionally designed workbench is vastly superior. Pre-made benches with spacious drawers and built-in lighting can be purchased out of a catalog, but I usually buy benches that have been custom designed for my exact needs. These products are not cheap, but they will remain useful for many years.

Parts

Any IT service department staff needs to keep a ready supply of extra parts to service all of their computing equipment. Some of these parts can also be used to perform upgrades when necessary.

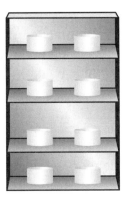  

While you may have on-site service contracts for all of your equipment, I believe that internal company IT departments should have the capability to repair any critical piece of equipment. A delay in service can be a costly penalty for a company to endure. The high interoperability of most computing components means that you won't necessarily need to stock an enormous variety of parts. Hard drives, network cards, and memory chips can easily be exchanged between dozens of different computer models and brands.

Disk Drives

You will encounter floppy, hard, removable, CD, and DVD drives at your company. Having a sufficient quantity on hand to deal with failed systems will ensure that you can return problem units to service quickly. Drawing from knowledge of your inventory, you should make sure that you could replace almost every single drive with a spare from a parts cache.

HARD DRIVES   Hard disks are the most critical components to have available. Loss of a hard disk can render any system unusable. I like to have at least four to six drives available for every 100 computers I support. Make sure that the interface and capacity of your extras match the types needed in your users' systems.

The performance should also match the intended application. You don't want to sacrifice the performance of a server with a disk rated at 5,200 to 10,000 RPM by swapping in a slow hard drive. With RAID 5 systems, you must normally match all disks in an array with identically designed units to ensure smooth operation.

TIP: It's a good idea to purchase a few larger disks than the ones currently installed in workstations. This permits you to perform a capacity upgrade if necessary. User problems are often caused by lack of disk space.

FLOPPY DRIVES   Unless you are using thin clients and diskless workstations, most of your computers will have a single floppy disk drive. Almost every system today uses the standard-size drive to accommodate a 3 1/2-inch, 1.44MB capacity disk. While the drive's mechanical format is a universal standard, many computer manufacturers use a slightly different cable or power adapter to connect a drive. Make sure that you have the correct faceplate and mounting rails for your systems.

CD AND DVD DRIVES   Most modern computers also include a CD or DVD drive, which is used to load programs or access databases of information. As with hard drives, there are differences in the interface and performance rating of these drives. Most computers use an IDE interface for CD and DVD drives, but some systems rely on a SCSI interface.

REMOVABLE MEDIA DRIVES   Zip, Jazz, and DVD-RAM drives are all used for archive and primary storage. While not as ubiquitous as other storage devices, they are increasingly becoming standard equipment for power users. These drives can be fairly expensive compared to non-removable storage drives that provide the same capacity. As with any drive mechanism, make sure that your spares reflect the correct type of interface for the computers they will be installed in.

Input Devices

Keyboards and mice are the commonly used input devices today. These products are subject to normal mechanical wear and will fail after a prolonged period of use. The "Pepsi Syndrome" has also doomed many keyboards. As many IT specialists have witnessed, users spill all types of fluid at their desks.

I prefer to have several different types of keyboards and mice in stock at all times. This mix ensures that I can always match the types of systems I support and that I can accommodate users who have developed preferences for particular types of products. Some would be lost without their ergonomic keyboards, while others love trackballs and disdain all mice.

MATCHING INTERFACES   Keyboards can have different types of connectors depending on the system design. Most Intel-based computers use either a PS/2 or an older and larger AT-style plug. Adapters permit the use of either style port with the same keyboard.

Mice typically use a PS/2 or serial interface. As with keyboards, adapters permit the use of a single mouse with a variety of systems. However, Macintosh and Sun systems use keyboard and mouse connections that are unique to their architecture. Make sure that your spare parts inventory reflects the mix of systems you are supporting.

Monitors

Multiscan monitors can work with virtually every type of computer in use today. While the 15-pin, D-shaped jack is the most popular, there are video cards and monitor combinations that use BNC cables with a hydra-like end. I usually purchase a few extra 17- or 19-inch CRTs for use as spares. These extra monitors are useful when I want to use a second monitor for a computer running Windows 98. They can also be a blessing for laptop users who otherwise would be stuck squinting at a tiny display.

USING ADAPTERS   If your supported systems are of various designs, make sure you have the correct adapters to hook monitors up to them. With Macintosh monitor adapters, you may have to fiddle with lots of jumpers or wheels to select the proper resolution. Be careful not to specify a resolution that is beyond the capability of your display. Problems can range from distorted images to a complete loss of screen display—or even smoke coming out of the back of the monitor!

Power Supplies

There are so many different types of system case designs that finding a universal replacement power supply is almost impossible. The ATX form factor, which is popular and used with many systems, does allow use of a standard connector and power supply. However, servers and telecommunications equipment have proprietary designs that require unique replacements from their manufacturers. I've stressed the importance of having redundant or hot-swappable power supplies available for servers and hubs, and you also need to make sure that you can get any critical component replaced quickly.

Network Cards

Ethernet cards form the bulk of all installed networking hardware. Quality PCI interface cards can be purchased for less than $50. Since the computers I support are a mix of Macintosh and WinTel, I look for cards that are compatible with either platform. For example, lately I've been purchasing the Asante 10/100 Ethernet card for all the operating systems I support, with favorable results.

Many more machines are being equipped with network cards already installed or integrated into the motherboard. While you need spare NICs for the built-in products, see if your vendor can supply a corporate standard to minimize your spare parts and driver storage needs.

Motherboards

Unless the IT department is building its own machines, most service departments do not stock extra motherboards. They can be rather expensive, especially the ones from major brand-name system vendors. Generic ATX-style motherboards and system cases can allow easy swapping of parts between various brands. However, there are many space-saving designs that utilize proprietary form factors, and these are impossible to replace without a factory-designed part.

Processors

In my 15 years in the IT industry, I cannot recall a single instance of a computer breaking due to a CPU error. Credit Intel and others for making reliable products. You still may wish to purchase some extra processors to use for upgrades or for building a system from parts.

Many motherboards can accept processors at a wide range of speeds. An Intel Pentium II can run from a low of 233Mhz to well over 500Mhz. Because a new computer can be an expensive luxury, remember that the only upgrade some slower machines may need is a speedier processor.

TIP: When you replace a CPU, try to migrate the spare part to other systems. This is a great way to stretch your budget dollars and benefit multiple users. For example, I've installed second processors into computers that only had a single chip.

Telephones

An inexpensive analog telephone handset is a great tool. A modem that refuses to work may simply be hooked up to the wrong jack, or the line might be bad. Plugging in and seeing if you hear a dial tone is the fastest way to find out whether a port is active. If there's a dial tone, you can then dial a number with the handset and listen to see if there is an answer. With experience, you should be able to distinguish between fax and modem tones.

Memory

Memory products are also exceedingly reliable. In the old days of 64K and 256K RAM chips, IT specialists learned how to install nine spider-like chips into an expansion card to add memory. SIMM and DIMM sockets make upgrades simpler, faster, and more dependable.

The reason for stocking extra memory is more to provide upgrades rather than to replace blown components. I stock upgrade kits of various sizes and ratings to support the variety of systems at my company. In some instances, new software installations have called for additional memory to ensure adequate performance. For example, sometimes users take on new responsibilities that their computers were not originally designed to handle.

Miscellaneous Parts

Anyone who has worked in the computer service field for any length of time has various boxes filled with an assortment of screws, cables, card-slot fillers, and dozens of other items. My wife has forced me to use a combination of sturdy shoeboxes and Rubbermaid containers in a vain attempt to keep my things tidy.

Woe be the hurried IT specialist who needs to retrieve the correct part from a large carton overflowing with all types of stuff. Organizing your parts supply enables you to make repairs more quickly and enjoy a more tidy work area.

ORGANIZING YOUR EXTRAS   The most logical approach is to divide all your parts into categories first. For example, I store the following items in large, translucent legal file cases. One box stores all of my AC power cables, another contains my drive ribbon cables. Still another case stores all of the different types of drive brackets and rail-mounting kits that I have accumulated over the years.

Depending on the complexity of your network and the number of systems your department supports, you may need to further subdivide the categories to simplify locating specific items. You may want to store your SCSI ribbon cables separately from your IDE drive cables, for example. Hex screws for a Compaq system could be stored apart from screws used to mount servers on communication racks.

My translucent boxes are labeled on all sides with a large hand-lettered card that indicates the contents. Fancy label makers can be great for smaller storage units. Everything from baby-food jars to milk crates can be used to store parts in your service areas.

A visit to any hardware store or home goods store can reveal hundreds of good storage choices. Most companies have a facilities department that holds office-supply and maintenance-supply catalogs, which offer even more choices. Color-coded and locking storage bins can be used if security is a major concern.

TIP: If you plan to keep any part in its generic brown cardboard box, label the carton. Clearly indicate exactly what the part is. A label that simply gives the manufacturer's product code, for example 32218a-343-387, is not nearly as informative as a label that states "6.2 GB EIDE hard drive." I suggest that you also list the date and purchase order number in case the product proves to be defective when it is first installed.

Hot Spares

When a machine breaks on your network, does the user need to wait for a repair or can you simply replace the damaged system, allowing them to return to work quickly? In many environments, it is a wise service investment to have complete computer systems ready to go at a moment's notice.

Spare Sales CPUs   Spare Engineering CPUs

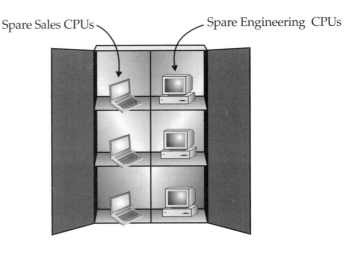

Laptop computers are especially fragile and prone to break more frequently than desktops. Rough handling and lightweight construction have doomed many an LCD screen, expansion-door latch, and battery contact. Every company that relies on portable computing devices must have an adequate standby stable of products to satisfy users' needs.

Install a Corporate Suite of Applications

Your hot spares' installed applications should mirror the ones used by the majority of your users. Most of a company's employees typically use the same general types of programs. A computer with an operating system, word processor, email client, and Web browser is enough to satisfy most users. Incremental workstation backups may even allow complete restoration of the broken system desktop environment on the replacements.

Use Older Systems

Not every company can afford to have identical, state-of-the-art systems sitting idle in a closet waiting for another system to fail. This may be a waste of resources. While a user may miss their 500Mhz Pentium III screamer, they can still remain productive with a three-year-old 200Mhz Pentium Pro.

On-Site Repairs

Many vendors sell or include service contracts for a given period, typically one to three years. Some of these contracts guarantee that any covered system will be repaired or replaced within 24 hours of the request. Look closely at your contracts to see what coverage you have.

While the $99 that Compaq currently advertises for its three-year, next-day service coverage is indeed a bargain, don't rely on a deal such as this as your only service option. A replacement part will not restore the user settings or data files. Critical servers that must wait over an extended weekend or even overnight for parts would not be adequately serviced by a 24-hour response.

WARNING: Not every repair can be addressed in one service call. The wrong part may be shipped, the new part might be broken, or the suspected component may not be faulty after all. I've seen service calls stretch into several days as the technician shuttled back and forth to my location, each day awaiting another package from the manufacturer.

Crash Carts

A great way to speed service is to bring the service department directly to the user in distress. By outfitting a teacart-sized rolling repair facility, you can build the greatest tech support device around. Instead of unplugging and dragging a computer from a desktop, a technician can bring all the tools they need to render assistance wherever the problem originated.

Equip Carts with a Workstation

On every cart, make sure that there is a fully functional system. Having a system that is known to be working lets you test whether a network error is limited to the problem computer or is due to a cabling fault in the wiring closet. The working keyboard, mouse, and monitor can all be used to test suspected bad components at the workstation.

Load Antiviral and Repair Utilities

The workstation on the cart should be preloaded with a variety of antiviral and hard-disk utilities. These can be used to generate diagnostic floppy boot disks from image files. This can also be a great way to verify that the workstation has the latest virus signature updates; if not, you can install them.

Communications Cables

Prepare the cart with some replacement communications cable. Extra Ethernet or Token-Ring cables can be used to remedy broken station wires. I recommend a parallel-printer cable to check the status of printers. Since most printers are connected only to a network, it can sometimes be difficult to diagnose problems with them.

Some printers and other network devices may need a serial interface to communicate. Equip your carts with telephone lines to handle modem-related calls. Lap-Link or other serial null-modem cable can be a great way to transfer files too large for a floppy to hold.

Spare Parts

Dispatch your crash carts with a selection of replacement parts. Network cards, hard drives, memory chips, and other universal pieces can be useful. Remember, fast replacements mean greater productivity and user satisfaction. An extra keyboard and mouse may also be appropriate.

Special-Purpose Carts

You may want to construct additional carts for specific purposes. Your company may have a mixture of Macintosh, Sun, and Intel systems, which all use different classes of components. If a technician is assigned to manage all of your printers, equip his or her cart with replacement toner and a vacuum to care for them correctly.

Cleaning Equipment

Keeping your computers and printers in top condition requires the use of cleaning products. These can be simple products like paper towels and window cleaner or more expensive tools such as vacuum cleaners designed to handle spills of fine printer toner. Remember that excessive dust and dirt buildup can block ventilation holes and raise the heat in a computer to a damaging level. Dirt can also cause floppy and CD drives to misread data if heads get clogged with debris.

General Supplies

Lint-free cloths and a mild window-cleaning solution are the basic components of any maintenance worker's arsenal. They can be used to eliminate streaks on monitors or smudges anywhere on a computer. Be especially cautious when cleaning laptop screens. The delicate nature of LCD panels may dictate the use of special products to avoid scratches and breakage. Check the system's manual for precise details.

Vacuum Cleaners

One of the noisiest and most effective tools I use is a powerful DataVac vacuum cleaner. It is the best method available for removing all the crud that can mess up smooth keyboard operations. Food particles, scraps of paper, paper clips, staples, and other objects can easily fall into the keyboard and foul up normal usage.

I always turn keyboards over and bang hard on their bases to dislodge as much dirt as possible before running the vacuum cleaner over the keys. Some cleaners have a hose that can blow a powerful air stream, a great way to drive out any debris.

Vacuums can also prove valuable for printer cleaning. Loose toner is often spilled when changing a printer cartridge and paper dust accumulates with normal use; both can affect print quality and cause jamming. Make sure that your vacuum has the dust filtration necessary to handle fine toner dust.

Large shop-style vacuums can be useful for cleaning up the dirt after a cable installation job has been done. I've also used them to get rid of water that accumulated under my computer room floor after a water-cooled AC unit developed a leak.

Mops and Brooms

I was always taught to keep the floor of my server room clean and dust-free. At one job, I was responsible for sweeping and damp-mopping the server room every other month. The elimination of dust prevents some of the clogging that can result when system fans suck in airborne particles.

I've since learned that some IT administrators cringe at the idea of having a moisture-laden mop dragged across their computer-room floors. The chance that water will seep into the floor and cause corrosion of the support structure should not be overlooked. Today I use disposable mop covers that attract dust and dirt yet don't introduce any moisture to my computer room. These are available in most supermarkets.

Alcohol and Coffee Filters

Sometimes there are low-tech solutions to high-tech problems. Using coffee filters and rubbing alcohol is a trick I learned from a Tektronix printer technician. Printer jams had been happening on an increasing basis. Paper dust, wax from the printer ink, and simple usage had caused the printer feed rollers to slip. Using a coffee filter and some alcohol, the technician got my printer to work correctly.

The alcohol works as a solvent to loosen the dirt and accumulated grime on the rollers. A coffee filter has a fairly rough surface and does a great job of scouring the rollers. Filters are also fairly tough and won't come apart as easily as a paper towel would.

Alcohol prep pads, normally used by nurses when drawing blood or giving an injection, are the premade equivalent of the coffee filter trick. These pads are sold in boxes of 100 or more at most drug stores. The packets are compact enough to fit in your pocket, and their size makes them terrific for cleaning mouse balls and other small items.

WARNING: Some manufacturers advise strongly against the use of alcohol for any cleaning chores. Electronic stores and stereo repair shops sometimes sell products specially designed for cleaning rubber rollers and belts. These won't attack delicate rubber and will restore the required grip to ensure proper functioning.

CHAPTER 12

Project Management

Beyond providing users with service and support, the IT specialist must often manage projects. Since technology is pervasive in all operations of a company, you need to be well versed in all the business functions of every department. With this knowledge and your command of computing systems, you can design and build stable solutions for your company's particular needs.

I like to define project management as the sum total of activities and functions necessary to address specific challenges in the workplace. Whether you are tackling a large problem or a small one, the approach and techniques are the same. Projects may be generated by the user community or initiated by the IT department itself.

You must always examine the situation requiring an application of computing technology. Simply throwing megahertz and software at a project will not guarantee success. The first step must be a complete and thorough dissection of the business need.

Your second step is to consider possible solutions. There are usually multiple ways to construct computing systems to service user needs. The various methods have to be judged on the basis of their cost, extensibility, and proper fit with the other demands at your firm. Of course, any proposal you design must be created with the feedback and support of those it affects.

Finally, you must manage the team effort needed to get the chosen solution operational within the company. This requires careful juggling of various peoples' talents and sometimes demands a reliance on outsourced expertise. Throughout any project, there also has to be constant communication between the IT department and those it supports.

This chapter draws on the techniques of internal consulting and company knowledge that have been discussed in previous chapters. The best IT projects are produced by people who have an intimate and thorough knowledge of both the computer use and business culture at their firms. Your mastery of technology will only be appreciated and appropriate when it is balanced by an equal command of the market dynamics at your firm.

DEFINING A NEW PROJECT

IT departments usually take on projects in response to two forces. The first are requests from the community of users that IT supports. This includes senior executives and employees at every level of an organization. It is often those at the bottom of the organizational pyramid who point out the most prominent stumbling blocks to efficiency.

The second source of projects is ideas that are generated within the department. IT specialists' constant exposure to training, news sources, trade shows, and peer group exchanges should fuel their desire to use the best and newest products to make their users' jobs easier. Certainly some of the projects that are suggested are focused toward making the IT specialist's life more productive.

Whatever it is that prompts a new project, there are a variety of factors that should justify its fulfillment. Technology can be difficult to manage and expensive to obtain. Be certain that whatever drives your desires for a new system satisfies the following criteria.

Saving Money

The primary reason that computers are so prevalent in corporations is rather simple: using them can save the company money. Making workers more efficient is the key reason funds are used for purchasing computer goods and services. Many of the projects you undertake will be designed to save money.

Productivity

Mainframe computers with punch-card data entry and batch job processing were ferociously expensive, but their introduction during the 1950s and 1960s fueled the growth of IBM and dozens of other companies. Tedious and repetitive tasks that used to take hundreds of hours to complete could be handled in a matter of minutes. Companies gladly paid to reap the rewards of higher worker productivity and increased profits.

The later technology revolution was spawned by the introduction of personal computers such as the Apple II and IBM PC. It can be argued that the purchase of IBM Personnel Computers in the late 1970s to run Lotus 1-2-3 was nearly equal in significance to the invention of electric light. Businesses could not place the power and flexibility of significant computing resources on a single person's desk and justify the expenditure.

Around that time, companies like Wang introduced office automation systems that permitted entire offices to collaborate on shared work. Networking with products like 3Com 3+ Share and Novell NetWare transformed stand-alone PCs into devices that could share resources such as printers and databases. The productive capabilities inherent in LAN technologies have spurred an ongoing revolution in the workplace, and new products that leverage LANs are frequently introduced.

Collaborating on work projects and sharing expensive peripherals is a great way to save time and money. Electronic distribution of information, such as email among company departments, is a faster and more efficient mode of communication than any previous method available. Moreover, the new instant messaging technology on the scene, such as AOL's Instant Messenger, speeds up communication even more.

Interactive Web sites permit an almost instantaneous relationship with customers. The current changes in commerce are chiefly driven by the abundant increases in computer power and connections to the Internet.

Simply put, technology has the capability to alter the way companies operate. The flexibility and capacity provided by computing systems permits gains in efficiency that can lead to higher profits. The solutions you design are often only limited by your imagination.

Technology Is the Only Way

Computers are wonderful tools capable of an extraordinary amount of number-crunching. Many activities would be impossible to do without them. Online auction houses such as eBay and electronic brokerage houses like E*TRADE are only a few years old yet have hosted many millions of dollars in transactions while experiencing explosive growth. The need to manipulate vast quantities of data makes financial calculations, weather forecasting, digital imaging, and thousands of other jobs dependent on computers.

Your firm will face business challenges that can only be addressed by the introduction of new or updated technology. A prime example is the rush to build a presence on the Web to support electronic commerce. The majority of recent technology investments can be attributed to the development and introduction of corporate Web sites.

The databases and search engines that form the back end of these systems are only part of the larger picture. It is just as important to explore the possibilities of partnering with other firms and their systems. An example of this might be a business-to-business e-commerce application or an extranet that reduces processing time between companies that are business partners. Some of your projects will undoubtedly be driven by initiatives taken on with your business partners.

IT REALLY HAPPENED: *PC Week* is printed by Brown Printing. Transmitting our data to them was an expensive and tedious process. By adopting the Wam!Net service proposed by their production team, we were able to reduce the time required to send data, cutting our transmission costs. Their suggestion triggered *PC Week* to purchase additional hardware and services to meet their goals.

User-Generated Tasks

As discussed in Chapter 6, IT specialists can function as consultants to their own companies. You must always be open to the demands of the users at your firm and create solutions to their problems. New opportunities for IT solutions can be found both by actively pursuing users' input and by their bringing ideas to your attention.

I doubt that any IT department hungers for projects to keep them busy. A proactive and productive history of achievements will garner many requests for additional work. A large percentage of all undertakings in IT are generated in response to user needs.

Assigning priorities to projects must be done carefully, since most IT specialists juggle many different tasks at the same time. Your highest priority should always be assigned to any projects that would put the company in jeopardy if not completed quickly. I tend to place all my projects in three general categories.

The first are those that must be done with minimal delay. These are time-sensitive issues that directly affect how a business operates. The second group is projects that are highly desired; while these are important, a slight delay in their implementation will not negatively impact current business operations. Finally, there are those items that would be nice to have but that don't directly influence the company's performance. A convenience feature that a user desires, such as an installation of browser enhancements, is an example of this type of work.

Observe Your Users

IT specialists must always observe and listen to their users. Even when they don't directly complain, there can be obvious signs that new solutions are needed. Once you identify a potential project, ask the users if this situation would be critical if addressed. Only the users can help you quantify how vexing a problem really is.

Listen to Department Managers

People who depend on getting information from their staff members often must make certain that the same information is passed along to others. Their inability to get data from employees in a timely and coherent manner can spur many projects. The need for Sales, Marketing, Shipping and other departments to collaborate on data creates many tasks for IT.

Company Executives

At most corporations, those in upper management direct the implementation of many projects. New business ventures, acquisitions, and mergers often require action on the part of the IT department. Since the top executives may be the only ones aware that this type of event is imminent, it is vital to make them aware of the need to keep IT informed.

Senior executives may be the most aware of departments or systems that cost the most money. You may be called upon to address issues they raise about efficiency. This sometimes is accompanied by the decision to terminate certain activities and jobs. IT specialists are just as likely to be involved in the shutdown of a department as the creation of a new one.

WARNING: Terminations and other activities that directly affect companies' operations must be treated with utmost confidentiality. Always respect the need for privacy and act discreetly.

THEY READ BUT DON'T UNDERSTAND   One of the problems you may have to confront is a manager who reads about a "really cool new thing" some other company is doing, and who now wants you to implement it at your company. Computer magazines, such as *PC Week* and other media outlets, like to report on the ways companies are implementing technology that sound sexy and wonderfully brilliant.

I often receive email from IT specialists flustered by managers who demand the installation of something that is totally inappropriate to their environment. This is the kind of management thinking lampooned by Scott Adams in "Dilbert." You must be able to listen to what is being requested and then carefully and firmly explain what the true impact of such a move might be—in business terms. While it is important to know your systems and personal strengths when building a solution, it is also wise to be aware of the limitations that exist.

IT-Created Projects

If you are like me, you are constantly learning about new technologies from a variety of sources. I am always reading magazines, scanning Web sites, and attending trade shows and conferences. Consulting with peers in my corporation and with friends that work for other companies always generates lots of wonderful ideas.

There are many occasions in which you will want to propose changes to how a company operates based on things you've learned or discovered. For example, I once attended a training course where I learned that Microsoft's Internet Information Server (IIS) was really easy to use. Apache is the reigning leader in the Web server marketplace. Nevertheless, I felt that IIS would be easier to implement in my environment and that it would be a good fit with the other Windows-centric technologies at our site.

IT regularly considers upgrades to address bugs or performance issues. New systems are being budgeted for well in advance of their purchase. Manufacturers are always bombarding my mailbox with offers for new services and products. I doubt that any competent IT specialist is at a loss for ideas to improve their systems.

The Open-Source Revolution

Many companies have devoted a great amount of capital to acquire and support networks supported by commercial software. Novell NetWare, Microsoft Windows NT, Solaris, and a myriad of other flavors of UNIX are capable (albeit expensive) products to run a business on. The past few years have seen a groundswell of interest in a cheaper and different way of running computers. Many IT professionals have been using or evaluating Linux and other open-source products as viable alternatives to traditional NOS and network applications.

Legions of IT professionals have embraced the concept of open-source, adopting the Linux platform and other open-source software as a part of their infrastructure. In my opinion, not every company will completely replace existing systems and applications with open-source equivalents. Rather, companies are using Linux and other open-source software when a less bloated solution that reduces expenses is warranted.

Project Size

Projects don't necessarily require a major expenditure or commitment of personnel. It is important to execute the same level of care and attention to every project regardless of size. The variety of projects that you face may require handling thousands of computers spread out across the globe.

Challenges with Large Projects

The larger a project grows, the more difficult overall management becomes. Often the greatest difficulty is keeping all of the participants informed of task assignments, project changes, and expected completion dates. Using electronic communications can provide the necessary edge to keep everyone who is involved with colossal systems integration efforts on the same page.

When a project is widely dispersed, it becomes critical that all IT staffers be kept aware of company standards and operations. Avoid the temptation to micromanage every aspect of system configuration. Innovation at the local level is still important. I suggest a top-down method of management. Stress broad themes and objectives at the uppermost levels and permit exact implementation decisions to be made at the divisional level.

Keeping the Focus Clear

Make sure that anything you plan to accomplish is clearly defined. You can never achieve goals if they continue to change and evolve. Every project must have a clear set of objectives. It is critical that all involved with the work agree on the exact parameters of the undertaking.

Be sure to write down early in the process what problem the project is intended to address. Make certain that there is a specific and measurable result that your work will achieve. There can be ancillary benefits to many undertakings that should also be given their appropriate weight. All of the people involved in the project should sign off on the project parameters and expectations. The surest way to delay project implementation and increase costs is to constantly respond to changes that are imposed as the work proceeds. Meeting any target is difficult if its criteria are protean rather than fixed.

Setting Reasonable Goals

The greatest danger to successful project creation and management is being overly ambitious. You must know the limitations of department performance and the ability of technology to service your computing needs. Aim high and show ambition, but don't promise more than you are capable of delivering.

Inadequate Time Allocation

Not finishing projects in a timely manner is a sure way to earn the scorn of your users. When the IT department announces that certain services will be available by a specific time, people expect that those commitments will be met. If your promised improvements are consistently late, it undermines any faith the user community has in your work.

GETTING ESTIMATES FOR COMPLETION   It is important to determine the amount of time required for each step in your project. Sometimes you can gauge your estimates by drawing on prior experiences. For example, if I know that a particular workstation upgrade requires 30 minutes to install on a test system, I will allocate double that amount of time for upgrading an actual user's machine. The extra time is to account for any unique configuration problems I encounter and to allow some time to demonstrate the new features.

Checking with newsgroups and similar resources may yield information from others who have tackled similar challenges. Like gas mileage, your results will vary. When working with a consultant or outside companies, try to ascertain the additional amount of time needed for these resources. Remember that they will increase the scope of your project and the time it will require to complete. You can sometimes get this information from white papers or from testimonials of customers who have done a similar project. The need for testing and pilot projects to determine implementation schedules is often critical. These will be discussed later in this chapter.

Inadequate Personnel

When you are tackling a large project, you must make sure that your personnel resources are adequate to meet the challenge. Even when there are automated facilities to update drivers and install applications, IT staff may still need to devote individual attention to each system to verify operations and respond to the inevitable errors that occur. For example, if your upgrade of 100 systems has problems, you don't want to be responsible for a loss of productivity when subsequent repairs take a long time due to lack of staff. Even when you rely on automated products to roll out an installation, there may be unexpected results that require a service call.

IT REALLY HAPPENED: My wife's NT workstation was rendered unusable following an upgrade done with Novell ZENworks at her company. Insufficient cache space for her desktop environment destroyed all of the system shortcuts and desktop appearance settings.

Another serious point of failure is a lack of relevant technical expertise on the part of some of your IT professionals. IT departments usually comprise people with a wide range of backgrounds and experience. If your project involves modifications to application programs, staffers with a concentration in network router management may be ill-equipped to assist.

HIRING TEMPORARY HELP   Many staffing companies can provide personnel on an hourly or daily basis to meet transient or seasonal demands. If your company is planning a project that requires a great deal of added help, then budget and plan for it. Contract for the help well in advance so that the project can proceed on schedule and you are guaranteed adequate resources.

UTILIZING EXPERT CONSULTANTS   Consulting firms or individuals can be contracted to meet specific project demands. This allows you to hire people with the expertise you need to cover the important planning and implementation phases of a new solution. A company that is contemplating a critical change in infrastructure can often benefit from the help of seasoned specialists.

For example, changing or upgrading the network operating system on servers is one of the more complex tasks that can face an IT specialist. You should attempt any major work of this magnitude in a test environment first. It's much safer to get your feet wet when live data is not at risk, and a trial run allows you to approach the actual task with the confidence gained from experience. Learning how to perform this operation while doing it for the first time on active servers can be fraught with danger, and you may be forced to address problems as they arise.

IT REALLY HAPPENED: I purchased a new 3Com NetBuilder router to segment a busy workgroup from the rest of my network and provide a dedicated ISDN link to the Internet. I hired a 3Com-trained engineer and gave him my specifications on how to complete the installation. His familiarity with the process and ability to manipulate the equipment was much more advanced than my own. He was able to configure all the protocols and routing schemes in less than 45 minutes.

Manage Expectations

A wide range of factors determine computer and network performance. If users expect their systems to operate ten times faster when the LAN is upgraded from 10 to 100 Mbps operation speed, then you did not properly describe exactly what the expected yield of the change would be. If user expectations are unrealistic, your performance will be unfairly judged.

Place a good deal of your attention on making sure that everyone affected by a project is aware of the expected gains to be seen from it. While increased speed is a common theme, there are other equally important goals to strive for. New drivers and network clients can often boost stability. Changes to email policies may be made to increase security.

Set Timetables and Control Costs

Every stage of a project should have distinct time specifications defined for it. Since some tasks may depend on other work being completed before they can be performed, it is critical that timetables be shared and kept current.

IT Project Plan

			Done	Late
Part 1	Due	March 14	☐	☑
Part 2	Due	March 21	☐	☐
Part 3	Due	April 15	☐	☐
Final	Due	May 1	☐	☐

For example, an upgrade to a desktop operating system may require installation of additional memory. If these tasks are undertaken separately by different individuals, the person doing the OS upgrade must be given proper notification after the hardware support specialist is done.

IT specialists must make sure that budget projections are kept under control. Payment for overtime work and other purchases early on cannot be allowed to exhaust all funds before the entire project is completed. Setting monetary goals for each segment of a plan will help you avoid running out of money prematurely.

Limit the Number of Project Planners

I am a firm believer in the following rules for successful project design. While the number of people that agree to support a plan should be as large as possible, the number of those directly influencing how the plan is constructed needs to be as small as possible. The old saying "A camel is simply a horse designed by committee" is very true when it comes to IT projects.

Company and department managers should certainly be involved in defining the goals that a plan should achieve. The actual tactical decisions must be left up to those most qualified to make them. Not only are IT specialists most capable of designing computing systems, they are also responsible for the installation and support of them.

Technical Evaluation Staff

The bread and butter for IT is technical expertise. We are the ones who must gauge the feasibility of project goals and make a judgment about resources. Finally, someone must be able to actually implement the plan.

Every project should be subjected to the review of IT department managers. There can be some division of authority, such as specialists in desktop issues approving related matters while others oversee telecommunications issues.

IT PROJECT SPECIALISTS   Some companies actually designate a special position within the IT department just to oversee projects. This person stays aware of staff and equipment resources and the relative progress of all current tasks. They have the most current knowledge of deadlines and act as a clearinghouse for communications.

Upgrading vs. Starting Anew

For many projects, the best practice is to build a completely new system. This allows you to build a solution that is free of any influences from existing products. The surest way to defeat server stability is to start loading new software and services on an existing system. While expensive, you can get divorced from any bad platforms. This gives you an opportunity to explore new products that may be faster or less expensive to operate.

On the other hand, using existing solutions by extending their capabilities may be the most cost-effective path to follow. Familiarity with hardware and software may make it easy to install the items necessary for the new tasks. For example, if you are already using a Linux server as a Web server, you can easily add proxy services to the same box.

THE PROJECT PLAN

Once you have decided on a particular course of action for your projects, you need to draw up a complete plan. This should include all of the requirements to get the project implemented. You need to account for all the hardware and software purchases that will be necessary.

Add to the list of products that need to be purchased all of the activities that IT staff will be doing. You need to be certain that both the number of people assigned to the project and their talents are adequate. There must also be provisions for capturing feedback from users. New systems always require some degree of tweaking to maximize their effectiveness.

Any changes to a project should be carefully accounted for and the information disseminated in a timely fashion. Schedule revisions may cause other plans to be postponed. Delays can be costly, so try to anticipate them as early as possible. Periodic meetings with those involved or simple electronic discussion forums can be great tools to keep everyone on the same page and aware of any modifications.

You may need to back out gracefully of any project that fails to deliver on its expectations. There must be benchmarks that can be used to gauge system performance and user satisfaction with the new procedures or equipment. A careful eye must be trained on the expenses involved to make sure that you don't exceed the cost constraints for the project.

Getting Everyone to Sign on to the Plan

Acceptance of a project by all factions involved is the best way to ensure accomplishment of goals. Criteria for performance, cost, and usability should be described in detail and agreed upon. While it may be possible to force acceptance upon people, it is preferable to share the responsibility for creating a sound project.

Clearly Define Roles

Every person and department should have a clearly defined purpose. Some people may be involved in testing. Others might be responsible for actually installing or monitoring systems. If you recognize the value of everyone's contribution, there will be a greater acceptance of responsibility by the various individuals involved in the project.

If people feel that their feedback and experiences are valued, they will make a more sincere effort to complete a difficult task. The early stages of any project are usually fraught with problems. Getting through the first part takes a good deal of effort, so try to encourage participation early on. This will make later work run more smoothly.

Keeping Users Informed

Nothing is worse than changing someone's routines or equipment without advising him or her about the purpose behind the change and the status of the job. The acceptance and success of a project will be much greater if the users impacted by it are kept informed.

Tell those impacted why a new project is being launched. Point out the benefits not just for the company but for all involved. IT must cultivate a reputation of caring for the user community and striving to improve the quality of the systems. If you are determined to make systems faster, easier to use, and more stable, let users know your intent.

Describe in non-technical terms the methods and products being used. While most users never enter a server room, they can at least appreciate knowing that new file servers are being installed. For example, while you may be adding a new router to boost WAN access speed and redundancy, most users will ignore the details of router performance or design. Tell them that new and better things are on the way.

WARNING: Users often don't care much to hear about megabytes and megahertz. There are few measurements of computer performance that most people can comprehend. It is better to stress the benefits in general terms, providing more details only if requested.

Providing Background Information

It may be helpful to provide interested parties with historical information on the systems. By giving a context for the changes taking place, you can gain support from both users and decision makers. For example, you may be replacing hubs that are a number of years old and don't provide management capabilities. Tell users what the new equipment will do and how you intend to accomplish your goals.

Document Goals for the New System

When creating software, developers create a master document usually called a "functional specification." This is the complete outline of what the new product will do. Every keystroke, function, screen, and other program operation is fully documented. Quality assurance programmers then make sure that the new program actually behaves as the design dictates. IT projects should be constructed to meet the same level of scrutiny.

Projects cannot be managed correctly if there is an inconsistent or vague goal for them to meet. Make sure to quantify the exact behavior expected of new or modified systems. Your testing should reveal how well the functional specifications are being met. If the results fail to meet these specifications, you may need to begin recreating and fine-tuning the solutions you are building.

For example, you may want to have every user utilize the same virus scanner engines and signature files. A verification of a project to automatically update anti-viral programs with push technologies and network management tools should reveal whether the update has worked correctly throughout the system. Variations in desktop computer hardware and installed software can cause differences in system behavior.

WARNING: Too often IT specialists try to fix things on the fly and don't record the nuances of the repairs they make. This often causes delays, as only a few people are aware of the problem and its remedy. During the testing and introduction of updated systems, make sure that all the relevant information is gathered and shared.

Complex projects can generate lengthy specifications that need to be approved by many people. Since technical issues and jargon can be confusing, you should keep the language clear and simple. Some issues call for multiple plans—one for the users of the system and another for the network administrators, for example.

Performance and Contracts

Creating a functional specification is a great way to get assurances of quality service from your suppliers. This step is especially important when you deal with consultants and system integrators. If there are specific, measurable factors that have been agreed to, you have a terrific way to prove whether the desired performance has been met.

See if a certain level of savings has been achieved. Check complaint logs to verify that new systems have reduced troubleshooting requests. Learn whether users are satisfied.

IT REALLY HAPPENED: The best user complaint I ever heard went as follows: "I really like this new system. Now I can accomplish in eight keystrokes what I used to perform in only one!" Sarcasm aside, it was a very valid comment and helped cement a decision to abandon the product.

Holding Meetings

One of the most despised yet important activities associated with all projects are meetings. Meetings with vendors, meetings with users, meetings with IT staff. Meetings to schedule other meetings! While they can be tiresome, these meetings are the best forum to gather information to formulate project goals and for periodic feedback.

Time-stressed IT specialists can ill afford to have non-productive meetings. Always make sure that you have a specific agenda before you meet. If you have questions, write them down and distribute them. Do the same with any answers you were asked to prepare. Making sure that there is a clear focus and a guideline to the proceedings will make everything go faster.

Follow Up

If a decision was made at a meeting, write it down and obtain agreement from all required parties. Information on project changes must be disseminated to all those involved, and email is often the best way to do so. You may want to record meeting minutes and distribute them as well. Electronic discussion groups may be perfect for this purpose at your firm.

Testing, Testing, Testing!

You must take every measure to be sure the new stuff works as desired. Regimented and exhaustive testing of every aspect of your project must demonstrate that it functions correctly. The functional specifications of systems need to meet actual experience in the field.

Tests should satisfy everyone involved in the project. Customers, partners, users, vendors, and every facet of your organization should be happy with the results before you can move to adoption of the product.

Be ready to refine your procedures based on your testing results. There are often circumstances that require a modification to your workflow or file types to be compatible with new technology. Record your findings and be sure to share them.

Constant Tuning

Even when a project is going well, there should be ongoing efforts to improve performance or ease of use. Testing is not a single act, but rather a continuous process to learn more about your computer use and capabilities. The best decisions on how to refine your systems come from listening to your test results.

Leaving Yourself a Way Out

One of the lessons I will never forget from Driver's Ed is the idea of "leaving yourself an out." This means making sure that your car has the ability to change lanes or adjust speed quickly if a problem arises. With technology, it means creating a safety net in the event that your new product fails.

Maintain Old Systems in Case New Ones Fail

Whenever possible, maintain existing solutions during new product rollouts. This can be as simple a process as storing the old hard drives from computers that have had larger drives installed. You can always quickly replace the previous component if the new drive is defective or your upgrade process missed some critical files.

IT REALLY HAPPENED: An upgrade of a NetWare 3.11 server to NetWare 4.11 on a new system seemed to work well. While all the data and user information transferred over properly, some of the print servers refused to link to the queues on the new server. The affected printers' network card firmware could not recognize NDS-enabled NetWare. I had to restore the old server until a firmware upgrade could be installed.

Plan a Gradual Rollout

I prefer to introduce new systems or software gradually. For example, I would never advocate upgrading every computer in a department to Linux or Windows 98 without testing a few systems first. Some problems take time to reveal themselves, and you want select users who have some experience trying new things before placing everyone into the same position.

Pull the Plug on the Old

It can be a day of utter jubilation or profound sadness when a system is taken offline. Something that has provided reliable service for many years may be fondly remembered and missed.

Most companies earmark a specific date to terminate a particular system or service. However, wait a long time before actually shutting something down. This permits the greatest opportunity to recover in case something goes wrong.

MOTHBALLING If you have both the space and the desire, you can place old systems in permanent storage. Once every year, perform an inventory and gradually discard the obsolete products. Just keeping the stuff around can be expensive, but it can sometimes provide a nice safety blanket.

Celebrate

Follow up a success with a party or other type of recognition. A reward to project participants for all their hard work will probably be much deserved and appreciated. Ice cream or a cappuccino cart for a morning can relieve lots of stress and provide a fun way to share in the accomplishment. Lots of firms offer sports days, boat cruises, and the ubiquitous T-shirt as standard fair.

WHEN TO KILL A PROJECT

It is inevitable that some projects must be aborted before completion. There can be numerous reasons for this to occur. The challenge for IT professionals is to accept that all their hard work must sometimes be abandoned.

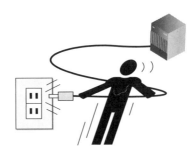

Not everything that vendors promise about their products is true, and not every solution will work well in a particular environment. For example, while the performance specifications for your new server engine may sound wonderful and prompt a change, subsequent developer work with the database may create a more telling statistic.

Excessive Costs

Project costs can sometimes outstrip any savings they were designed to create. Some software products may contain such bloated code that requirements for adequate performance may raise the adoption costs to an unacceptable level. While the cost for the software can be fairly modest, you may also need to upgrade network speed, computer memory, and other components.

The ancillary costs can be quite large and they often are overlooked in the project budget. Don't forget that users may need to be trained to use new solutions. There is often a drop-off in productivity while users become accustomed to added features or changes in procedures. Your company's clients and suppliers may also be forced to adapt to changes with your systems.

Keep Partners Informed

It is vital throughout any project to communicate with your vendors and other partners. If your corporation's standard word processor has changed, make sure that others who must read those files can do so. I've had numerous experiences with Marketing department heads who were frantic because their printer lacked the necessary font to prepare a new ad campaign. Some preparation and testing of systems can save lots of headaches later on.

It Just Doesn't Work

There are simply times when new technology proves unreliable. If a sincere and concerted effort to make something work fails, then you must make plans to abandon the project. One of the biggest problems with new systems is the difficulty in testing them in an environment that truly mimics the actual network they will run on.

Capacity issues are notorious for causing system failures. While a 384K DSL line may be fine for an office of 20 users who just use it to send email and browse the Web, it may prove inadequate when asked to also allow VPN hosting and FTP serving. In this type of situation, you must weigh the cost of extra bandwidth capacity against the benefits of the proposed system.

The Curse of Power Users' Systems

In many firms, the people developing and testing new products are blessed with the best equipment available. Faster processors, more memory, a higher speed network, and other factors may yield adequate performance on the best systems. But for the average user at the same firm, the circumstances are very different. Computers that are several years old with less fancy features can prove too slow to execute tasks satisfactorily.

Make every effort to test applications on computers typical of what the average user possesses. Also, get feedback from some of the users who will actually use the systems you are configuring. Test documents provided by software manufacturers are usually small and efficient to handle, but your test files should represent the size and complexity of the company norm.

Current Technology Is Inadequate

While computers and related products are constantly improving, some projects are simply too ambitious for current technology. Databases that are too big to efficiently search are one example. Reliability is another important feature that is often shown to be lacking.

Remember that your costs are usually highest when you are trying to initiate the very latest technology. Placing yourself in the position of an early adopter exposes you to other problems. For example, promising technology that seems poised to become the next standard may instead be made obsolete. A good example of this is all the network cards and hubs built around using Category 3 cable to achieve 100 Mbps operation. The standard eventually settled on Category 5 cabling, effectively ending the development of competing solutions.

Risks Bring Rewards

If you want your IT department to truly make a difference, you have to be willing to take risks. For example, companies that moved quickly to embrace the Web have enjoyed a strategic advantage over competitors who were slower to respond. The challenge is predicting when or what the next great thing will be.

You have to be willing to assume that a certain number of your projects are going to fail if your ambitions are substantial. Companies know that not every idea proves viable in the marketplace. While I hope that readers of this book will never see an Edsel label on their networks, it can happen!

WHY FAILURE IS GOOD   One of my brothers used to tell me to bang my head against a wall, since it feels wonderful when you stop. Admitting defeat can be difficult, but sometimes it's the best thing to do. You immediately cease unproductive and frustrating work. You can also return to the process with a newfound understanding of the true dynamics of a problem. This will leave you well situated if you decide to revisit the issue later or even if you are faced with a similar challenge in the future.

When More Important Problems Arise

There will be innumerable occasions when you will have to cease work on a particular project as a more pressing issue diverts your attention. These can be serious problems such as a crashed server or a change in a business plan. IT specialists must always be prepared to temporarily shelve or completely abandon their plans.

The Y2K Effect

I doubt that any other issue has affected existing projects more than Y2K remediation efforts. In the late 1990s, budgets were raided and work on other tasks completely frozen until companies could assess and correct the impact of the millennium bug. Scores of consultant firms, developers, application vendors, firmware manufacturers, and others made wads of money trying to allay fears of systems crashing on January 1, 2000.

While Y2K was a well-known and widespread situation, there will be other factors that cause your current work to be mothballed or abandoned. The rush to bring businesses to the Internet has seen huge spending on Web efforts, often to the detriment of other projects. Most companies at some point experience a change in the marketplace or in the internal organization that causes priorities to shift. IT must accept that it is often market forces and not necessarily their own actions that lead to the demise of a cherished project.

Bug Discovery

Sometimes, uncovering a security breech or an unexpected program operation causes IT to immediately respond to fix the situation. There have been myriad stories of flaws with the Windows operating system that revealed information about computers to intruders. In one case, a security glitch in the free HotMail system caused the administrators to down the entire system until a remedy could be implemented.

When your resources are limited, emergencies usually take precedence over other issues. A crashed system will need to be repaired before you can return to other outstanding projects. Be sure that you keep track of time lost and get things moving again as soon as the other situation is resolved.

Cutting Your Losses

Sometimes you must delay a potential solution and attempt it again later. While the problems that first prompted the project still exist, new ones with greater urgency may have gained greater importance. A sudden change in business fortunes or drastic shifts in corporate structures caused by sales or acquisitions are two obvious examples in which IT priorities change rapidly.

Unfortunately, you may experience fallout from a failed project. The loss of time and money can be especially irksome to many. Try to temper this frustration by reminding everyone that a certain percentage of all projects will fail despite the honest and concerted efforts of those working on them. External factors that are outside the control of the IT department can lie at the root of these failures.

Of course, the entire scope of your work should be used to judge you and your department, not just one facet of it. Make every effort to learn from mistakes and not repeat them. I would not have obtained my experience and abilities if I had not seen some failures in my past. Remembering these blunders gives me a more critical and focused approach to new challenges, since I can readily reject some of the possible approaches.

PROJECT MANAGEMENT TOOLS

You can use a mix of high- and low-tech methods to enhance your ability to manage projects. There needs to be a clear way to gauge progress and update people on its status. Be careful when collaborating on tasks or switching responsibilities around to avoid dropping the ball.

Many project managers have learned to construct different kinds of charts to graph task progress and interdependencies. These charts can be created with project management software or drawn by hand. Some of the more popular styles are shown in the following section.

Gantt Charts

A Gantt chart is a horizontal graph that shows the relationship of certain tasks to completion dates. It provides a visual guide to how well projects are progressing against the timetable they were designed to follow, as shown in Figure 12-1. Gantt charts can be generated manually or by using one of the many software packages available.

PERT Charts

Like a Gantt chart, a PERT chart shows the relationship of tasks to timelines. It takes the further step of showing the connection between one task and another. This extra information can provide valuable clues to the dependence of certain jobs on others. Figure 12-2 shows a sample PERT chart.

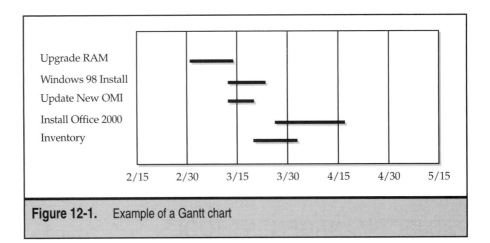

Figure 12-1. Example of a Gantt chart

You can design your own PERT charts with pen and ink. If you use Microsoft Project and like the visual impact of this chart style, you can order the PERT Chart Expert add-in from Critical Tools of Austin, Texas. A demonstration version can be downloaded at www.criticaltools.com.

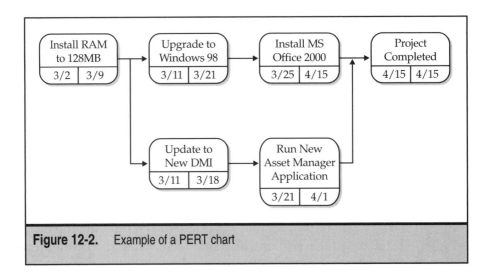

Figure 12-2. Example of a PERT chart

Flowcharts

The classic computer programmer's flowchart might be appropriate to use for your planning. The mix of circles, rectangles, squares, and other symbols can be great to diagram how systems behave, where input is received, and where output is sent.

Project Management Software

There are several good software programs geared toward managing projects. These tools provide a framework for project managers to control timetables as well as financial and personnel resources. Busy IT departments often juggle multiple projects simultaneously. Applications that help manage all the resources required for successful completion of your work can be invaluable.

Good products allow those involved in the project to get updates on work status easily. By using email and intranet servers, schedules can be disseminated quickly. Ideally, the software should support IT specialists' ability to share tasks or swap jobs. There are several good products suitable for Windows server networks. Large-enterprise users often turn to more complex systems that are hosted on UNIX, Solaris, and AS/400 platforms.

Microsoft Project

Anyone familiar with the Microsoft Office suite of applications will feel right at home with Microsoft Project. Because it allows data to be shared among all the various Microsoft Office components, it permits easy use throughout any organization that uses that software suite. Its workgroup features promise easy collaboration between everyone actively working on a particular project. You can find additional information on Microsoft's Web site at www.microsoft.com.

Milestones, Etc.

A relatively inexpensive program, the Milestones, Etc. Windows application from KIDASA is a quick and easy project management tool. You can download a demonstration copy at www.kidasa.com. The product has a wide variety of charting tools that can be used to create many different types of graphs.

Lotus Domino and Notes

Lotus, the world's leading groupware vendor, provides strong features in its Domino server and Notes client software that make them a natural fit for project management. Built-in email and discussion databases make it easy to share information. Its powerful customization capabilities are hard to match with any other product.

Having worked with Domino and Notes for many years, I am both in awe and in fear of its powerful customization capabilities. Adapting an existing Domino and Notes infrastructure to handle your projects can be a wise move, but I would hesitate to adopt Notes strictly for its scheduling capabilities. Domino and Notes are available for many different platforms, including Solaris and Linux. For more information, visit the Lotus site at www.lotus.com.

OPX2

A serious enterprise-ready product from Planisware, OPX2 can be hosted on Windows NT and a variety of UNIX platforms from Sun, HP, and others. It is designed for intranet distribution of information and can handle highly complex and distributed projects. You can discover more details on their Web site at www.planisware.com.

AMS REALTIME Product Suite

Companies seeking an Oracle-based solution should investigate Advanced Management Solutions. They offer hardware and software solutions plus a range of consulting and training services for what can be a complex and costly product. Point your browser at www.amsrealtime.com to learn more.

Low-Tech Tools

Yellow legal pads and pens are the tried-and-true methods for managing any type of project. Simply write things down, assign tasks, and meet weekly to track progress. While this low-tech system can work in smaller settings, it will be inefficient when you are dealing with hundreds of people.

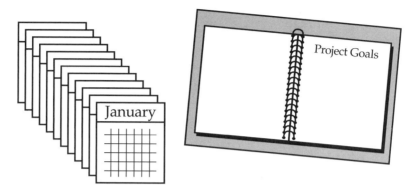

While computing technology is invaluable, it still should be augmented with some of the older methods for organizing and disseminating information. A trip to an office supply store and less than $100 could furnish you with most of the things you need. Small companies without generous budgets may wish to opt for the inexpensive route exclusively.

Wall Calendars

One of the cheapest and best ways to manage your projects is with a large wall calendar. A four-foot-high calendar will be hard to miss when tacked up to your office wall. You can tell at a single glance where multiple projects stand and if there are any looming deadlines.

Using colorful markers, you can develop a coding system to mark progress. Placing the calendar in a prominent place allows everyone in the firm to quickly scan work status. Checkmarks or a particular color can be used to indicate when a task has been completed. Other colors can indicate that a project has been delayed.

Logbooks

The individual assigned to manage a project can use a simple logbook to track progress. During periodic meetings, everyone involved can report their task status and the information can be updated in the log. This approach is appropriate for anyone who is doing the job of project management single-handedly.

Planners

My wife would be lost without her beloved Franklin Planner. I have always been more of a DayRunner fan. Whatever brand you use, daily planners can be an invaluable addition to your project planning toolkit. Find one with special pages devoted to task management and multiple types of calendar pages and you have a terrific way to record your progress and prompt yourself when deadlines loom.

COMPANION SOFTWARE   There are products available that merge the information in your paper planners with project management software applications. Some simply allow you to print pages from the calendars you generate in your time management programs. Others allow tight integration with PDAs (personal digital assistants) such as the PalmPilot.

LEARNING MORE ABOUT PROJECT MANAGEMENT

As I discussed in Chapter 8, there are many avenues for learning about topics that concern the IT specialist. There is no shortage of opportunities for gaining skills in project management. Traditional business schools are perhaps the best-known and most well-rounded choices for those with a deeper interest in this field.

However, busy IT people can't always afford the time it takes to pursue an MBA or MIS degree. Fortunately, there are several other options to consider. You can always audit a class and not seek academic credit for attendance. Community colleges and extension schools frequently permit non-matriculating students to take single classes if slots are available.

Seminars

An intensive class that lasts only a day or so can provide a great introduction to the guiding principles and techniques for project managers. For example, SkillPath Seminars produces a two-day course entitled "Fundamentals of Successful Project Management." You can find a schedule for their classes at www.skillpath.net.

For a few hundred dollars, you can gain a broad overview of the best practices for project design and control. Like most companies in the training seminar business, SkillPath offers classes on a rotating basis around the country. These courses are not designed specifically for IT workers, but the concepts can be applied to any industry.

Web Resources

The Project Management Institute (www.pmi.org) is a great place to start learning online. The organization has publications and seminars that explore the many intricacies of running successful projects. There is also an active network of member chapters to foster networking among professionals in the field.

The institute maintains an active interest in training and certification. One can become a Project Management Professional, or PMP. There is a need in some organizations for there to be an overall director of IT projects. It makes sense that someone charged with overseeing a myriad of technical projects should be astute not only in technology but also in the management of people and processes.

CHAPTER 13

Things I've Learned Along the Way

My life as an IT specialist has taught me one very important lesson. There is simply no end to the number and variety of subjects that you must learn. Certainly many of these involve technology, but there are also a fair number that are not computer-related. I believe what makes this book unique is the attention given to all the important elements that you will need to master.

No matter how many training seminars or trade shows I attend, there is always a lack of coverage on facilities management. Computing systems do not operate in a vacuum. All of the furniture, environmental controls, and ergonomic concerns that IT needs to deal with will be covered in the first part of this chapter. While I have always depended on the efforts of exceptional building managers everywhere I've worked, there is much to be gained by becoming familiar with their terminology.

It's also important to give attention to the human beings in your workplace. There is much more to it than simply anticipating and providing for the needs of your users. Learning the fundamentals of ergonomics so users can work in comfort and avoid injury is also vital. In addition, the attitude you exude and the connections you establish within your company and with your suppliers is a key to success. The second section of this chapter will present you with the winning strategies important to building positive and professional relationships with your boss, staff, and users.

Finally, I would not have thrived (or even survived) as an IT specialist if I hadn't developed certain personality traits. Resisting the temptation to toss computers out the window when something goes wrong is only the first part of a good attitude. While patience and persistence are important, often the best characteristic is a sense of humor. I can't promise you'll become the Henny Youngman of the computer world, but I will let you in on a few good ideas to add some levity to your day. While jokes can't make your systems run faster, they can sometimes be the best antidote after listening to a frustrated user's tirade.

BUILDING MANAGEMENT

All of your computer systems require electrical power to run. They also need to be placed atop office furniture so users have comfortable access to their keyboards and monitors. The design of user offices, cubicles, and your computer room are all influenced by the efforts of the Facilities department at your company. Making sure that the concerns particular to IT specialists are addressed is an important aspect of your job.

In some companies, there are several people with overlapping responsibilities for handling facility issues. For example, separate department managers may control telephone and computer infrastructures. Not only have these technologies converged of late, but there have always been critical areas in which they interact. Many corporate network server rooms also house PBX equipment.

Data cabling systems and telephone wiring are often strung at the same time by the same technicians. Make sure that modifications to one system don't disturb the other. The high cost of cabling installation makes it critical to carefully plan any work that will be done together. You never want to have data cabling installed one week and voice wiring the next if it can be avoided. Doing both in one operation will save you money and prevent multiple disruptions caused by having a bunch of cable technicians crawling through your ceiling and server rooms.

Electrical Systems

None of your computers will run without the correct type of electrical current. While most desktop systems, printers, monitors, and similar equipment can run with the voltage and amperage that are standard in most typical outlets, there are always exceptions to this rule.

Large systems that run on 220 voltage need a different plug design than the ubiquitous three-prong style found on most office walls. Higher voltage requirements demand special circuits. This may require your electrical utility suppliers to install heavy-gauge electrical cable, beefy circuit breakers, and upgraded transformers. Not only do mainframes and mini-computers need heavy-duty power lines, products such as high-volume printers often require them too.

Request Custom Circuits

Whenever your plans call for installing equipment that you are not familiar with, you should take the precaution of determining the exact circuit type required. The best place to determine the need is directly from the product manufacturer.

Not every piece of equipment can simply plug into any available outlet. Some items require that electrical power be attached with hard-wired hookups. Others will need to use a specific plug type with receptacles that look familiar but have a different geometry. (The plug blades are constructed with these special orientations to prevent use in a circuit that has the incorrect voltages.) Figure 13-1 shows the outlet types that are often required for computing equipment.

International Requirements

Voltages and plug types vary around the world. Even if computer power supplies can handle various standards, they need to be outfitted with the correct cord for the location they are being used in. Make sure that any systems being shipped to an overseas office are provided with the proper cords for the local utilities. This detail is especially important for portable computer equipment.

The best source for obtaining the correct cord is the manufacturer of your equipment. Many owners' manuals list international usage

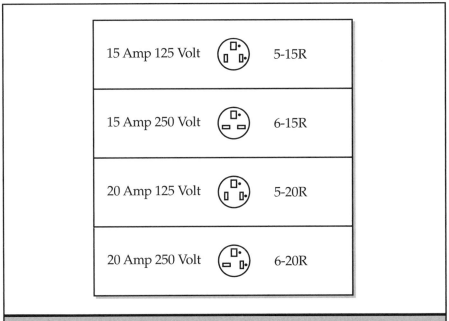

Figure 13-1.   Typical electrical outlets

instructions. The internationalization of computer manufacturing has seen universal power supplies appear on more equipment. These power supplies can automatically detect and adjust to the locally supplied power. Some computer equipment will need external power adapters to convert local current to the 115-volt United States standard.

Beware of the small adapters sold at places like Radio Shack and travel stores. Make certain that they are rated to handle the power requirements of your systems. Most are designed for travelers who have only small personal-care appliances to run. These are much less sensitive to voltage abnormalities or low current than a high-tech machine. Computers are dependent on a steady power feed to work correctly. Using the wrong plug or ignoring the voltage requirements can be hazardous to your equipment—and your health!

IT REALLY HAPPENED: I was working at a computer store when a customer came in with a broken monitor. The acrid smell told me that something electrical had burned out. She reported that everything worked fine in France but it began to smoke as soon as she tried to use the monitor in New York.

Beware of Overloads

The surest way to cripple your IT infrastructure is by overloading the electrical circuits. Massive spider webs of power strips are not only hazardous but can allow you to exceed the capacity of the circuit. Tripping a circuit breaker or burning out a fuse will render your systems inoperable and can result in data loss.

Keep your computer systems on isolated circuits whenever possible. This can be accomplished by installing dedicated power outlets that are designated solely for systems use. If your electrical system is well documented, you can label the exact sockets that are designated for computer connections.

Try to avoid plugging high-amp loads like coffee makers into the same circuits as your computers. If your users report that their monitors occasionally flicker and dim whenever someone else turns their system on, you probably have too many computers on the same line. You may want to do periodic reviews of the power cable use in your users' work areas to make sure that no risks are present.

IT REALLY HAPPENED: Frantic calls from a bunch of my users indicated that the file servers were unavailable. It turned out that a cleaning crew in the computer room had been using a massive vacuum to clean the floor and overloaded the power supply, tripping the circuit breaker.

UPS

A *UPS*, or uninterruptible power supply, is a staple of virtually every network. Designed to keep computers running despite a loss of power, a UPS can be purchased in a wide variety of sizes. Brick-sized ones can be used to support a single computer, while the massive needs of a mainframe or entire computer room can be supported by refrigerator-sized systems.

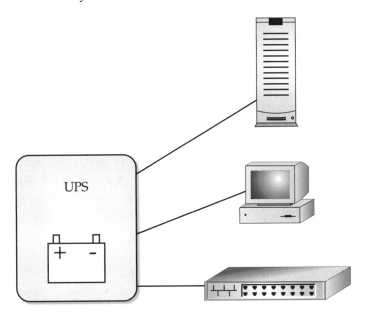

Threats to Power

A UPS can do more than just provide power in the event of a complete blackout. Transformers and other electronics permit the steady supply of current if an under-voltage or brownout occurs. Spikes and surges can occur due to lightning strikes or other electrical troubles. Power conditioning equipment can avert any aberrations in your power stream, but only a UPS provides protection against actual loss of electricity.

Sizing a UPS

Decide on your UPS purchase carefully so that the electrical load does not exceed the designed capacity. You need to account for not only the total load, but also the desired runtime of the batteries. This is a measure of the current supply and duration, respectively.

Determining your computer load is done with a simple mathematical equation. You multiply the voltage by the amperes. The result is in volt amps, or VA. It is sometimes expressed in Kilovolt amps, or kVA. Thus 1000 VA is equal to 1.00 kVA. For example, if your server was rated at 2.0A (amps) and ran on 120V (volt) circuits, its VA rating would be 240 VA. To protect ten of these servers, you would need a UPS rated at 2.40 kVA.

Some UPS vendors have precise guidelines for sizing equipment. They have documented the exact VA ratings for specific vendors' brands and models. Whatever method you use, make sure that you account for all the equipment you want to protect. You should also be sure to provide some excess capacity to handle system growth.

UPS Vendors

There are several well-known quality vendors of UPS equipment. Best Power manufactures a wide range of systems designed to protect everything from single computers up to the largest mainframes and data centers. You can find them on the Web at www.bestpower.com.

American Power Conversion's site (www.apcc.com) provides an excellent tool to help you select the proper UPS for your company. Liebert, discussed in the next section, is well known for their air conditioning units and also makes a line of products designed to manage the power needs of large computer rooms.

TIP: You may want to purchase a small UPS for critical workstations as well as for your computer room. Losing a workstation due to a power problem can often be just as catastrophic as the failure of a server.

HVAC

People use air conditioners, heaters, fans, and dehumidifiers to help them feel comfortable in different weather conditions. Computers prefer a mild temperature as well. Making your computers run efficiently and without error may necessitate the purchase of environmental control equipment. Heating, ventilation, and air conditioning systems are often referred to generically as HVAC.

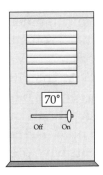

While most companies provide their offices with air conditioning and heating to keep employees happy, the needs of computer systems are a bit more complex. Computer rooms house mission-critical components, including the dedicated and expensive systems that are needed to meet the demands of a 7 x 24 environment. Another key difference is that when people breathe, they generate humidity as well as heat. Computers just generate heat.

The market leader and most well-known manufacturer of computing room cooling systems is Liebert. Point your browser at www.liebert.com to find out more about their products. Not only do they manufacture cooling equipment, but they also offer a variety of power conditioning and standby products.

Computer Rooms

Most companies that use many computers have dedicated facilities to house them. Computer rooms are equipped with all the necessary communications and electrical cable to run dozens of servers, hubs, and routers. One major byproduct of all the whirring drives and humming power supplies is lots of heat.

This excessive heat can be the root of data errors and system failures. To bring the temperature to a steady and consistent level, you need specially designed cooling units. Designed to provide a constant temperature, they are often used to control humidity as well. Humidity that is too low can be conducive to a buildup of static electric charges. Excessive humidity can lead to condensation, which corrodes network room floors and wiring.

FILTRATION   For some sensitive areas of technology centers, there are major concerns about dust. Manufacturers of delicate electronic equipment include air filtration as part of their overall environmental control. Dust that is drawn in by computer fans can degrade cooling efficiency and harm delicate disk drives. Clean rooms that demand workers to don surgical uniforms before entering are a prime example of how great this concern can be.

TONNAGE   Climate control systems are rated in tonnage. This figure indicates the heating and cooling capacity of the unit. One ton of heating capacity is the amount of energy required for melting one ton of ice per hour. This ton of energy equates to 12,000 of the somewhat more familiar BTU.

SIZING UNITS   There are some general rules to follow when determining the necessary capacity of the HVAC unit for your computer room. Liebert offers some rules of thumb for sizing your HVAC systems. They state that for a server room, you should expect to have at least one ton of cooling for every 250 square feet. When your server racks get densely packed with computers and other equipment, they recommend one ton for every 100 to 150 square feet.

Other factors can have an effect on the load as well. Depending on the number and type of lighting fixtures and windows, wall thickness, and other equipment in the room, there may be an increased thermal load. If your computer room is on a top floor, the load will be increased by the sunlight beating down on the roof. If people work in the area of the computer room, that will also contribute to the overall heat level.

Skilled HVAC professionals weigh these and other factors to determine the size of unit you need for your location. The square footage of the area will be considered, as well as the amount and type of equipment being used. Guidebooks reveal the heat output of every monitor, server, and peripheral in use.

WARNING: A unit that is oversized for your heat load will reduce the temperature quickly and then shut down. However, humidity takes longer to remove. An oversized unit can result in a cold and clammy computer room.

NOISE AND BREEZES The cooling systems designed for computers move a great deal more air than the ones designed for human habitation. Air conditioning has to be directed everywhere so that none of the computer racks create stagnant hot spots. Large compressors and fans can make a great deal of noise, so don't expect your computer room to be a quiet place.

IT REALLY HAPPENED: There have been occasions when my computer room HVAC units failed. All of the working equipment quickly sent the heat soaring. By opening the doors and using a bunch of large fans, I was able to control the temperature enough to prevent a meltdown. The amount of heat that computer equipment can quickly generate is astounding.

Fire Protection

All the electrical equipment in your computer room can be a potential fire hazard. While roaring flames have never greeted me at work, I have seen several monitors go up in a puff of acrid smoke. Detection and suppression equipment is not only a wise investment, but often required by local building codes and insurance companies.

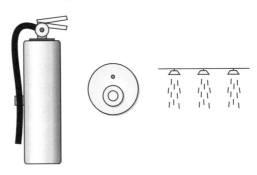

Since a computer room is noisy and not always occupied by people, the alarm must be sounded outside its walls. Through a combination of external lights, claxons, and monitoring services, IT specialists can be alerted to trouble in the computer room. Automated systems can send warnings directly to a beeper or telephone.

Smoke Detectors

First you need a sensor to check for smoke. The old adage "Where there's smoke, there's fire" is almost certainly true. As I mentioned earlier, I've seen power supplies and monitors die in a puff of smoke. Drive motor bearings have been known to wear out and burn, too. In general, I think that the biggest fire threats at most companies are from sources outside the computer rooms.

Thankfully, I have never personally had a computer room devastated by fire, but I do remember a telephone switching room in New York suffering a complete meltdown. In parts of Brooklyn and Queens, phone service was lost for several days. Most companies would not want to share such stories with others, since it obviously degrades customer confidence.

Heat Detectors

Excessive heat can be the result of a fire or an HVAC system failure. Whatever the cause, it can destroy your computers, so your computer center should also be equipped with a high-temperature alarm. Normally these are set to several degrees higher than the temperature on the HVAC thermostat. In the computer rooms that I maintain, I usually set the thermostat to 70 degrees Fahrenheit and the heat sensor to 80 degrees.

Inert Gas

Halon gas is a common and effective fire-fighting tool, but it is gradually being phased out because of environmental concerns. Contained in a big tank, it is released into the computer room when a fire is detected, essentially drowning the fire by forcing the oxygen from the atmosphere. This method is only effective in a space that is somewhat sealed off from other areas.

Since Halon gas works by depleting oxygen levels, using it or any other inert gas will certainly affect your ability to breathe. Computer facilities that are outfitted with this type of equipment normally have warning buzzers and lights that alert building occupants of an impending discharge of gas, allowing people to evacuate. A manual abort switch can be used to prevent activation of a gas release.

Another fire-fighting system is to keep carbon dioxide gas in a liquid form and then release it into the burning area when needed. It has the advantage of speed and normally leaves no residue behind. This is the type of gas best suited for electrical fires. Because it is not conductive, it poses fewer risks than using water.

Fire Extinguishers

Small hand-held fire-fighting equipment can be effective when dealing with very small fires. Strategically placed in your computer room and around the office, they are your first lines of defense. Be sure that your extinguishers are inspected periodically and are rated to handle electrical fires.

Sprinklers

One of the biggest problems with using sprinklers is that the water will damage computers. They are generally used only as a last resort when other methods to knock down a fire fail. Sprinklers always have water in the pipes and ready to flow, and a special metal is used to stem the onrush of water. The metal blocks are released when a fire's heat brings the temperature to a given melting point. There are different melting points that you can use, and the set point for your computer room should be higher than that for an area occupied by people.

National Fire Protection Association

The National Fire Protection Association's Web site (www.nfpa.org) is a great place to get information on various codes and other policies to guard your equipment against fires. Their publications outline the minimum standards to use when designing suppression and detection devices.

Many manufacturers and installers of fire-protection equipment also have Web sites that you can scan for information. The installers often concentrate on regional information, since they are not nationwide operations. With a search engine, you can find dozens of sites to check out for local coverage.

LOCAL BUILDING CODES   Every municipality can have unique requirements for commercial construction and alarm systems. Some communities place the responsibility in the hands of the fire department, which periodically conducts inspections of your equipment. Insurance companies can also require you to carry specific items before they will cover you.

Furnishings

The various offices and cubicles in your company are probably outfitted with a variety of furniture. Large desktop computers, big-screen monitors, keyboards, and mice all require a certain amount of real estate on desks. The power and network cabling all need a way to reach their respective ports and computers. If the office furniture lacks cable management features, you will end up with bundles of cables draped over the floor and caught in chair wheels.

IT REALLY HAPPENED: A new workgroup was outfitted with beautiful and expensive wooden furniture. While lovely to look at, the desks were ill-equipped to handle computer needs. There were no passage holes for network or power cables. This created a mess on the desktop and rendered access to the network jacks behind them a tremendous challenge requiring heavy lifting. My threats of wielding a drill to create access holes, combined with negative comments from users, eventually motivated the company to buy specialized computer furniture.

Ergonomics

Computer users must be comfortable in order to work efficiently and avoid injury on the job. Repetitive stress injury, or RSI, is more likely to occur when users' equipment is not configured properly. The strain placed on the body by poor posture and inferior input devices is a very real problem in today's corporations.

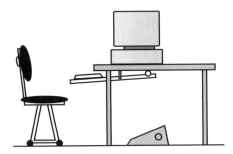

It's critical to provide users with quality products that can be manipulated comfortably. Cheap keyboards may have keys cramped together and low-quality mice can have an awkward feel. The height and position of the monitor can create neck strain if not set up in a correct ergonomic alignment, and improperly placed keyboards and mice can cause wrist problems.

LISTENING TO YOUR USERS   I have always been very conscious of users' desires for comfortable input devices. Since the cost of alternatives such as trackballs is modest, I purchase a few and allow users to try them to see which they prefer. A company that ignores its users' needs puts workers at risk of RSI, which can require physical therapy or surgery and result in a loss of productivity.

MAKING YOUR WORK AREAS ERGONOMIC   Give your users tips on workstation ergonomics to help them prevent injuries. I suggest making the following information available to all your users in a variety of formats. Some companies also run seminars or survey individual users' work habits to spot problems and present solutions.

Arms should be kept parallel to the keyboard. The keyboard should be slightly lower than the arms. Wrist rests can help prevent fatigue. The best computer desks have an articulated keyboard holder that allows a wide range of positions for various users.

Place your monitor directly in front of your eyes. You shouldn't have to constantly move your head up and down to scan your screen. A document holder placed to the side of the monitor works well for people editing or reading papers.

My optometrist always reminds me to look away from my computer monitor every 15 minutes. It takes more energy to focus your eyes on a nearby screen than it does to look at a faraway object. Your eyes actually relax when you look at something in the distance.

Some simple stretching exercises done at the desk or while standing can help relieve tension. Get up and walk around throughout the day. Periodic breaks away from the computer are good for your body and help make your workday more pleasant.

WORKING WITH OCCUPATIONAL THERAPISTS Rehabilitation specialists are a great source of information for both the treatment and prevention of RSI and similar maladies. You may want to have an ergonomic specialist audit the setup of your workstations. Educating users in how to use their equipment properly and teaching them simple exercises can prevent the majority of injuries from occurring.

To learn more about this subject, go to www.aota.org, the official site of the American Occupational Therapy Association. This site contains common-sense tips for creating a non-irritating work area and helps you locate practitioners. You can also contact any rehabilitation hospital in your area; they most likely have many occupational therapists on their staff.

Space Allocation

Many of the companies I have worked at made sure that I was part of any meetings that concerned construction of new work areas or reuse of existing areas. IT specialists should have input into how offices are designed. Electrical power and network access ports should be installed near where the desks will be located. Laying wires across the floor is unsightly and creates a tripping hazard.

Cube Layout

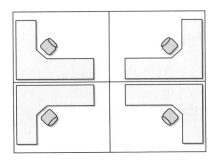

Many workers spend their workday in a cubicle. These modular units typically have all the power, lighting, and communications wiring built into their structure. Be sure that any cube furniture you purchase is computer-friendly. There must be sufficient space in the cube furniture structure to run the density of cabling your users need.

The physical layout of the cubes can influence how and where your network cabling is installed. The high cost of copper cable provides a compelling reason to limit unnecessary cable length.

STORAGE AREAS

I sometimes think that I have enough boxes to build a small city. File servers and monitors ship in boxes large enough to hide a family car under. You should make sure that your IT department is allocated a certain amount of storage space to keep both empty boxes and ones holding systems that are yet to be deployed.

When a damaged product needs to be sent in for service, it's best to ship it in the original container. I always try to keep a wide variety of boxes and packing materials available to ship defective units. Smaller boxes that are used to package hard drives or similar items should be retained, too.

HUMAN RELATIONSHIPS

Throughout this book, I have stressed the importance of understanding your computer users. This knowledge is almost always more critical than your technical ability. Computers are incapable of independent thought and actions. Only people can select the correct commands to get technology to perform a useful function. Getting users to use their systems to the fullest is the ultimate aim of an IT professional.

Unfortunately, people in IT often acquire an aura of superiority. Ignoring the humans sitting in front of the keyboard is a mistake. Always make every effort to respect the people you support and treat them with dignity. Doing so is the best way to have them reciprocate and show respect for your efforts.

You Don't Know Everything

With every new thing I learn, I discover that there are more things to know. Every operating system I use has its own unique characteristics and foibles. All hardware items have different capabilities. New technologies often present new protocols to integrate with existing networks.

When you learn about TCP/IP, you are introduced to the world of routers and DNS servers. Using routers may require you to master NAT (network address translation) techniques, and so on. Simply put, every new skill should open your mind to other tools that you can use. To me, this cycle of continuous advancement in abilities is one of the most appealing features of an IT career.

If you accept this premise, then you must believe that there are things you simply don't know. You must be willing to share this fact with your users when you are confronted with a problem. Sometimes you must crack open a manual or scan a newsgroup to get the answers you need.

While your users may be surprised to hear you admit your limitations, this can prevent what is often an unrealistic expectation of your work. Technology is too complex and diverse to be completely mastered by any one person. As I've stressed before, you must always put yourself in a position to learn what is required for any task that presents itself.

You Will Be Wrong Sometimes

Every IT specialist makes stupid mistakes. We all have performed operations that in hindsight were totally incorrect. Some of these errors can be blamed on fatigue, others can be traced to poor documentation or bad technical support.

Regardless of the cause, it's important to learn how to recover from your mistakes. The first thing to do is make sure the same mistake isn't repeated. Record your errors and don't be afraid to share them with other IT staff members. Learning from each other is a great way to make sure that no one else creates the same problem.

IT work is constantly evolving, and new demands will be placed on you frequently. You have to move on when a mistake occurs and not let prior failures cloud your ability to accept new challenges. Unlike doctors, IT specialists' mistakes don't typically result in loss of life. Of course you must be cautious and precise, but the quality of your work should be judged by many factors, not just a mistake every now and again.

IT REALLY HAPPENED: I was attempting to install more memory in an all-in-one Macintosh computer. As I took the wiring harness off the back of the video monitor, I heard a faint crack and then a hiss, as the vacuum in the tube was lost. My clumsy fingers and bad technique had wrecked a brand-new CRT.

Computer Cartoons

Stroll through any large company today and you will undoubtedly see people's work areas adorned with "Dilbert" clippings. The cartoon's creator, Scott Adams, pokes fun at the folly and foibles of the workplace and reportedly gets many of his ideas from his readers. The fact that so many of his comic strips deal with computers only strengthens the impression that computers have become an integral part of business.

Popular comic strips such as Bill Amend's "Fox Trot," Brian Bassett's "Adam," Garry Trudeau's "Doonesbury," and others frequently feature computer-centric themes as well. Jeff MacNelly's strip "Shoe" features a recurring character called the Computer Whiz whose repair methods are always shrouded in mystery. Of course, Rich Tennant's "The 5th Wave" is devoted to poking fun at the computer too. My friend Paul Connolly pens the "Spencer F. Katt" strip in *PC Week* and always targets the computer industry.

I have adorned my office with a few of my favorite strips. Some help to remind me not to take computers or myself too seriously. Others allow visitors to get an indication of what subjects I find most amusing. It never hurts to have humor to help remember the difference between UNIX and eunuchs.

Beating Stress with Humor

Stress is a very real problem in many companies. People can get frazzled with looming deadlines and troublesome computers. Sometimes dealing with problems can be made easier by adding a little levity to the situation.

WARNING: Know your audience. To some, making a joke can be interpreted as not caring about a problem. Don't fire off a quick one-liner until you size up the situation and the mood of the user.

"Turn and Cough"

These three little words have been used by many comics to evoke the sense of loss of control and embarrassment that can occur during a medical examination. Using the same phrase with a troublesome computer is a killer line that I like to use. I place my hand directly under the monitor and command the computer to cough. It has always gotten a laugh from my users and helps break the tension.

Funny Web Sites

The Internet abounds with humor sites, and several highlight computer humor in particular. My favorite is HelpDesk Funnies at www.helpdeskfunnies.com. I can't claim credit for any of the submissions, but I certainly have some good candidates based on my experience.

The site features a collection of hilarious true stories submitted by computer support technicians. Some are of the "Which is the 'any key'?" variety, but most point out the frustration of supporting the totally clueless. I especially like the .wav files of tech support calls. Anyone who has ever done technical support will immediately identify with the types of incidents related here.

Relax and Have Fun

I would not enjoy my work as an IT specialist if I were always crushed by deadlines and irate users and did not have a release. Don't let your job become so all-consuming that you don't have a chance to enjoy the people you work with. I have formed many lasting relationships with my coworkers despite my penchant to tell bad puns. This is not the most technical tip I have given in this book, but it is the one that I use most often.

Index

 A

 B

C

D

E

I

Q

R

S

T

▼ U

uiarchive.cso.uiuc.edu, 347
Unicenter TNG (CAI), 387
Unified directory modes, 101
Universal Serial Bus (USB), 285
Universities. *See* Colleges/universities
Unstable system, 162-167
Updates, user downloads of, 73
Upgrades, 284-285
    alerting others to, 199
    not for the sake of upgrades, 285
    picking carefully, 196
    planning for, 63-64
    planning for system outages for, 137
    vs. starting anew, 423-424
UPS (uninterruptible power supply), 49, 299, 448-449
Usenet newsgroups, technical support from, 348-350
User access rights, 383
User accounts, 5-8, 103, 368-369
User errors, 380-383
User forums, hosting, 198
User groups, 256-257
    creating, 84-86
    informal, 85
User guides to applications, 102
User home directories, 158
User profiles, 103
User rights, 6-7, 86-92
User roles, special, 83
User schedules, having concern for, 137-138
User skill levels, learning, 143
User support systems. *See* Help desk
User templates, 103
User training. *See* Training
User work habits, learning, 143
User-generated tasks, 413-416
Usernames, 7, 384
Users, 65-92. *See also* Training
    answering their questions, 14-15
    asking for their problems, 139-140
    the Click-a-Holic, 68-71
    the Click-a-Phobe, 71-72
    commitment to skill-building, 229
    the Daredevil, 73-75
    the Demander, 75-77
    dissatisfied and angry, 145-147
    documentation for, 107-109
    inadequately trained, 197
    instructional information for, 94
    keeping informed of projects, 425-426
    limiting scope of control they have, 163
    listening to complaints of, 89
    listening to ergonomics comments, 456
    listening to suggestions from, 89
    may feel slighted, 86
    motivating, 27
    network demands of, 30-31
    new hires, 6, 8, 95-99, 104-107
    observing and listening to, 414-415
    with obsolete or inadequate equipment, 86

    power user, 77-80
    relationships between, 83-86
    respecting deadlines of, 90-91
    satisfied, 174
    testing new products, 83
    treating with respect, 88-89
    types of, 67-83
    want faster system or larger display, 85
User's Bill of Rights, 86-92

▼ V

Vacuum cleaners, 406-407
Vendor certification, 244-248
Vendor contact information, 336
Vendor documentation, 260, 262, 352-353
Vendor expositions, 273
Vendor prominence, trend of, 300
Vendor quotes, 314-315
Vendor seminars, 128
Vendor support contracts, 117
Vendor telephone support. *See* Telephone support (vendor)
Vendor Web sites, 328, 344-345
Vendor-approved certifications, 239
Vendors. *See also* Purchasing (IT)
    close relationship with, 328
    commitment to future business, 316
    communicating with, 183
    competition to, 264
    direct sales, 301-302
    email subscriptions to, 262
    letter template for, 328-329
    meeting support staff, 328
    negotiating price with, 312-317
    rating, 310-311
    security updates from, 374
    systems engineers support staff, 343
    tech support from, 321-356
    at trade shows, 328
    types of, 299-317
    of UPSs, 449
    vertical marketers, 302-304
Version numbers (software), 385-386
Vertical market software systems, 103-104
Vertical marketers, 302-304
Video card interfaces, 310
Videotapes
    instructional, 127
    surveillance, 364
Virtual memory managers (VMM), 325
Virtual Private Network (VPN), 137, 290
Virus attacks, 19-20, 371-380
Virus bugs, 372
Virus protection, 19-20, 374-376
Virus-scanning programs, 374-376
Vise grips, 391
Voltage requirements, 445-446
Volume purchases, 315